Exeter's Railways

Half title: The distinctive 70-year-old Exeter Middle signal box casts a shadow over the tracks at 16.15 on Saturday 20 October 1984 as No 47103 approaches Exeter St David's station with 1V31, the 10.30 York to Penzance relief train. The box and its semaphore signals will be redundant within six months; it was built with a narrow brick base and an overhanging cabin due to its position in limited space between two tracks. *DHM*

Title page: In September 1993 steam climbed the bank from St David's station for the first time in almost 27 years when 'West Country' 4-6-2 No 34027 *Taw Valley* worked two railtours from the city. The second of these trains on the 19th was 'The Sarum Limited', the 08.15 from Bristol Temple Meads to Salisbury, which was hauled by No 47578 to St David's station where the 'Pacific' took over. The train then ascended the incline using the down line with the '47' providing banking assistance; the railtour is regaining the up line by using a crossover that was installed in October 1984 as part of the Exeter MAS resignalling scheme. *DHM*

Above: On Sunday 17 June 1984 No 50042 *Triumph* is seen from Longbrook Street as it powers up the 1 in 100 grade from Exeter Central station with the 09.45 Exeter St David's to Waterloo service; the lines on the right lead to the goods yard. *DHM*

Exeter's Railways

David Mitchell

SLP

A Silver Link Book

© David Mitchell 2022

All rights reserved. No part of this publication may be reproduced, stored in a retrieval system or transmitted, in any form or by any means, electronic, mechanical, photocopying, recording or otherwise, without prior permission in writing from Silver Link Books, Mortons Media Group Ltd.

First published in 2022

British Library Cataloguing in Publication Data
A catalogue record for this book is available from the British Library.

ISBN 978 1 85794 474 7

Silver Link Books
Mortons Media Group Limited
Media Centre
Morton Way
Horncastle
LN9 6JR
Tel/Fax: 01507 529535

email: sohara@mortons.co.uk
Website: www.nostalgiacollection.com

Printed and bound in the Czech Republic

Select bibliography

Research for this title included consulting many books, magazines and other material, and the following were particularly useful:
Beck, Keith and Copsey, John *The Great Western in South Devon* (Wild Swan, 1990)
Bradley, D. L. *L&SWR Locomotives; The Early Years and Beattie Classes* (Wild Swan, 1989)
    L&SWR Locomotives: The Adams Classes (Wild Swan, 1985)
    L&SWR Locomotives: The Drummond Classes (Wild Swan, 1986)
    L&SWR Locomotives: The Urie Classes (Wild Swan, 1987)
Cooke, R. A. *Atlas of the GWR* (Wild Swan, 1988)
    Track Layout Diagrams of the GWR, Section 14 South Devon (R. A. Cooke, 1976)
    Section 15 North Devon (R. A. Cooke, 1986)
Garnsworthy, Paul (ed) *Brunel's Atmospheric Railway* (Broad Gauge Society, 2013)
Gray, Peter W. *Rail Trails: South West* (Silver Link, 1992)
Gregory, R. H. *The South Devon Railway* (Oakwood Press, 1982)
Hawkins, Chris and Reeve, George *L&SWR Engine Sheds* (Irwell Press, 1990)
Heaton, John *Devon Railways: The Area Manager's Diary Volumes 1-4 1986-1990* (Amazon 2017-2020)
Kay, Peter *The Teign Valley Railway* (Wild Swan, 1996)
    The First St Thomas (British Railway Journal No 45, 1993)
    The City Basin Branch in Broad Gauge Days (British Railway Journal No 49, 1993)
Lyons, E. *An Historical Survey of Great Western Engine Sheds 1947* (OPC, 1972)
Maggs, Colin G. *Rail Centres: Exeter* (Ian Allan, 1985)
    The Exeter & Exmouth Railway (Oakwood Press, 1997)
Mitchell, David *British Railways Past & Present No 8: Devon* (Past & Present, 1991)
    British Railways Past & Present No 52: East Devon (Past & Present, 2005)
    British Railways Past & Present No 53: North and West Devon (Past & Present, 2005)
    British Railways Past & Present No 68: South Devon (Past & Present, 2014)
    Devon & Cornwall Railfreight (Silver Link, 2019)
Nicholas, John and Reeve, George *Main Line to the West Part 3: Yeovil to Exeter* (Irwell 2009)
    The North Devon Line (Irwell Press, 2010)
    The Okehampton Line (Irwell Press, 2011)
Owen, John *The Exe Valley Railway* (Kingfisher, 1985)
Pryer, G. A. *Track Layout Diagrams of the SR, Section 5 Salisbury-Exeter* (R. A. Cooke, 1982)
RCTS *Locomotives of the GWR* – various volumes (RCTS)
    Locomotives of the Southern Railway Vols 1 & 2 (RCTS)
    BR Standard Steam Locomotives – various volumes (RCTS)
Thomas, David St John and Rocksborough Smith, Simon *Summer Saturdays in the West* (David & Charles, 1973)
Vaughan, Adrian *Exeter West* (Exeter West Group, 1984)
    The West of England Resignalling (Ian Allan, 1987)
Woodley, Richard *The Day of the Holiday Express* (Ian Allan, 1996)

Various issues of *The Railway Magazine*, *Trains Illustrated/Modern Railways*, *The Railway Observer* (Journal of the RCTS), *Great Western Journal* and *The Locomotive News and Railway Contractor*

Contents

Introduction		7
1	The broad gauge companies and beyond	10
	The Bristol & Exeter Railway	10
	The South Devon Railway	12
	The Great Western Railway	14
2	The rivals	25
	The Exeter & Crediton Railway	25
	The London & South Western Railway	25
	The Southern Railway	29
3	The Exmouth branch	33
4	The Exe and Teign Valley lines	44
	The Exe Valley line	44
	The Teign Valley line	46
5	Signalling and signal boxes	50
	The 'Western' route	50
	The LSWR/SR route	59
	Exeter MAS	64
6	The bank	69
7	The GWR engine shed and locomotives	77
8	The Southern engine sheds, locomotives and other works	88
	Exmouth Junction Carriage & Wagon Repair Works	104
	Exmouth Junction Concrete Works	105
9	Off the beaten track	106
10	Passenger services on 'Western' lines	116
11	Passenger services on 'Southern' lines	133
12	Goods traffic in steam days	146
	Great Western Railway	146
	LSWR and SR	157
13	Railfreight in the modern era	166
14	Water, water everywhere	180
15	Men at work … and at play	187
16	Closely observed trains	194
17	A chronology of some events since nationalisation	203
Index		223

In the 1950s the 4.25pm Plymouth Millbay to Paddington perishables train was one of three such up workings over Devon's main line. In the summer of 1955 it is passing Aller Junction hauled by two 4-6-0s; No 6807 *Birchwood Grange* has piloted No 1005 *County of Devon* over the banks from Plymouth but will soon be removed on arrival at Newton Abbot. The first wagon is a milk tank and behind it are three empty 'Cordon' gas tanks returning to Exeter St David's, where they will be recharged at the railway's Gas Works; the gas was used for cooking in restaurant cars. *C. H. S. Owen*

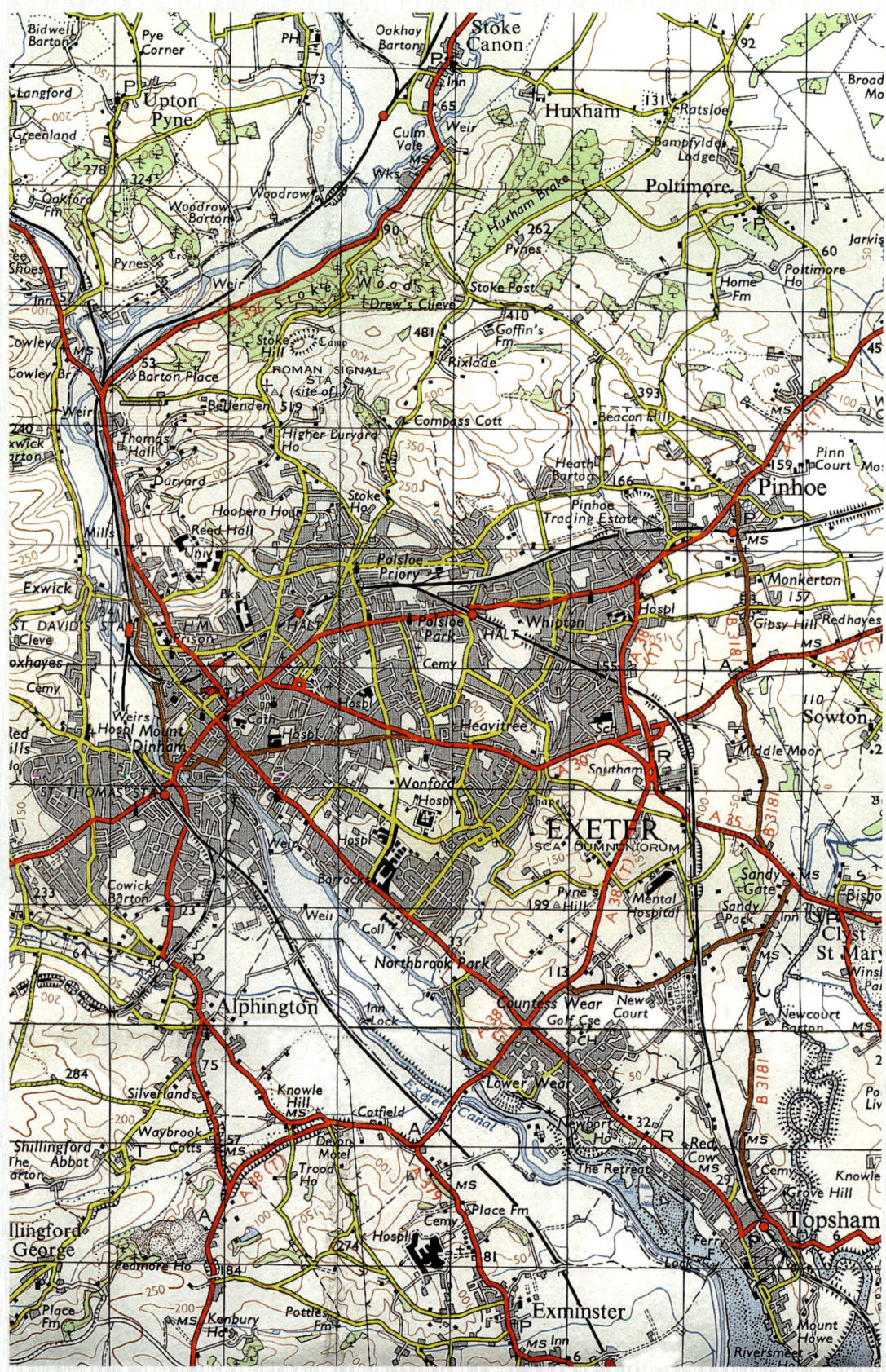

An extract from the 1960 Ordnance Survey map for the Exeter area; as this edition only had certain revisions to the 1957-58 edition the map still includes the Teign Valley line lower left which had closed in 1958. *Crown Copyright*

Introduction

Although Exeter is known as a Roman town, prior to their arrival there was an Iron Age ridgeway that is followed by today's High Street, with a settlement occupied by the Dumnonii, a Celtic tribe. It was located above the head of the navigable waters of what became known as the River Exe, a name that derives from an ancient British word Eisca, meaning 'a river abounding in fish'. The river became Isca in the Roman period and the tribal settlement grew into Isca Dumnoniorum, the most important Roman town in the South West where a number of roads converged. After the Roman withdrawal little is known for several hundred years until the town was occupied by the Saxons.

In this very brief history it should be mentioned that Exeter was later both plundered by the Danes and besieged during the Norman invasion, but thereafter grew in importance; the Normans built a castle on a volcanic hill later named Rougemont, and also developed a great cathedral from the 12th century at a time when Exeter was a rich trading city

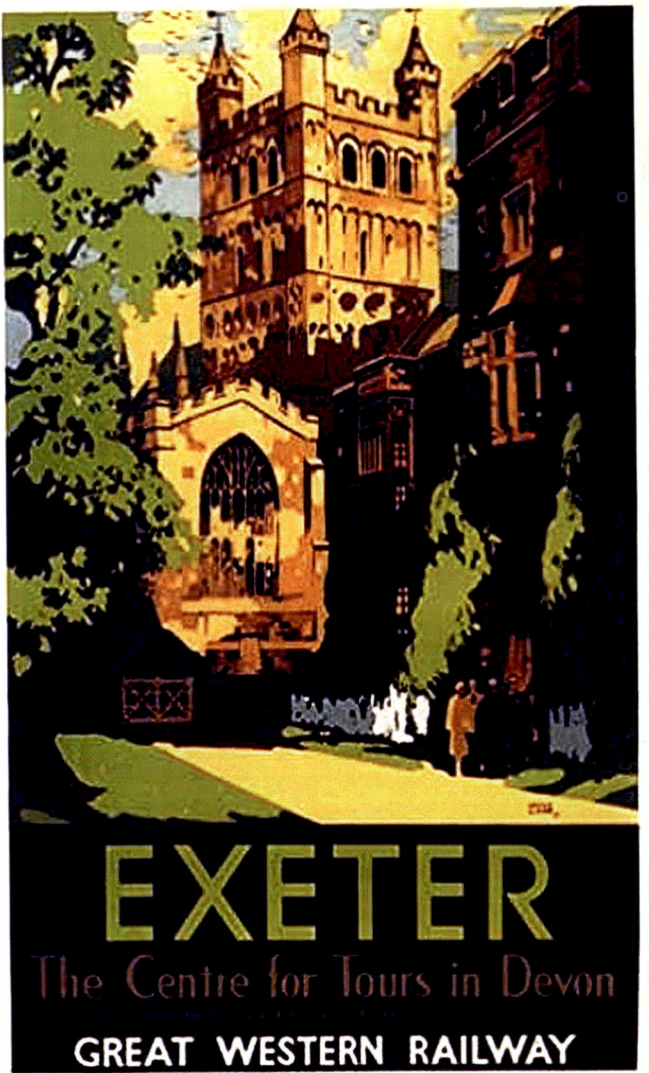

These two GWR publicity posters from the 1930s include images of Exeter's most historic buildings, the medieval Guildhall on the High Street and the Cathedral.

considered by many to be the fourth city in England in terms of wealth and reputation after London, York and Winchester. Although the Exe was only navigable by ships as far as Topsham, smaller craft and barges were able to reach the city on the tide.

Beneath the city walls reclaimed land by the river was controlled by the Courtenays, who were the Earls of Devon, and they interfered with the navigation of the river by building two weirs that prevented craft from reaching the city, forcing ships to use the quay at Topsham, which was controlled by them. This situation lasted for some 200 years until the Courtenays' downfall at the hands of King Henry VIII; attempts to clear the heavily silted-up river were unsuccessful and led to the construction of a 1¾-mile-

Exeter St David's role as a railway crossroads is illustrated on 18 July 1963 as 'Hymek' No D7072 and 'Warship' No D820 *Grenville* arrive in Platform 5 with a train for Paddington; they are passing 'N' Class 2-6-0 No 31836, which may be on an Okehampton service. *G. V. Lendon*

long canal; this was badly needed due to the growth in the woollen trade, which had become Exeter's chief industry. The canal opened in 1566 and featured three pairs of lock gates that are thought to have been the first known form of pound lock in Britain; it was large enough to handle the lighters that transferred goods to and from ships anchored in the Exe estuary. The canal was extended in 1676, and later work started on widening and deepening it to accommodate sea-going ships; the rebuilt canal was opened in 1701 and was a huge success, greatly aiding Exeter's prosperity.

By the 19th century Exeter's role as an important industrial and commercial city with a considerable overseas trade had changed, mainly due to blockades during the Napoleonic Wars, which had largely killed this trade. Although the once-flourishing woollen industry had diminished, it was still a wealthy place, not only from the proceeds of other traditional activities such as banking, brewing and tanning, but also from an influx of well-to-do families and retired people who were attracted by its climate and amenities. Although the population grew steadily the city was soon dwarfed in size by other rapidly expanding places during the Industrial Revolution, but with a fairly affluent population and a position at the centre of Devon's commercial activity it continued to thrive.

This was helped by the coming of the railway, and the city's importance was maintained when it became an important railway crossroads in the same way that it had been a focal point for the ancient road network. The railway was also a major employer in Exeter and, although what became the Great Western Railway's main line to the South West was the first to be built, and has always been the busiest and most important route, developments by the London & South Western Railway and the Southern Railway meant that these companies employed more people in the city, and even today old affinities mean that many locals still consider Exeter to be a 'Southern' town.

Exeter continues to be the most important railway centre in the South West and St David's and Central stations are the two busiest west of Bristol. Passenger numbers have boomed in recent years and in just the last year new developments have included the opening of an enlarged train maintenance depot and the reopening of the branch line to Okehampton; as this is being written work is well under way on a new station at Marsh Barton.

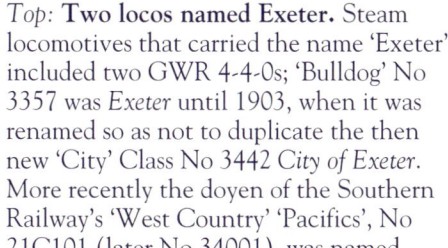

Top: **Two locos named Exeter.** Steam locomotives that carried the name 'Exeter' included two GWR 4-4-0s; 'Bulldog' No 3357 was *Exeter* until 1903, when it was renamed so as not to duplicate the then new 'City' Class No 3442 *City of Exeter*. More recently the doyen of the Southern Railway's 'West Country' 'Pacifics', No 21C101 (later No 34001), was named *Exeter* by the City's mayor in a ceremony at Central station on 9 July 1945, with top SR officials present including the company's Chairman and Chief Mechanical Engineer, O. V. S. Bulleid. The engine was allocated to Exmouth Junction shed from new and remained there for more than 12 years; in about 1954 it is seen approaching Pynes Road, half a mile from Cowley Bridge Junction, with the 3.00pm Ilfracombe to Exeter Central train, which has through coaches for Waterloo. *Exeter* was rebuilt in 1957 and thereafter was based at five different sheds and was seen less frequently in its 'home' city, although it was one of the last steam engines to reach Exeter on a service train when it worked the 13.00 from Waterloo on 10 September 1965. *John Stredwick*

Above left: One of *Exeter*'s nameplates after the engine had been rebuilt.

Above: When it was decided to name the Class 50 fleet after warships, No 50044 was given the name *Exeter* in a ceremony at St David's on 27 April 1978. Five Royal Navy ships have been named HMS *Exeter*; probably the most famous being the fourth, a heavy cruiser that fought in the 'Battle of the River Plate' in 1939. At the time of the naming, the fifth ship, a Type 42 destroyer, was under construction. On Sunday 24 March 1985 No 50044 is seen from the Queen Street road bridge as it nears the summit of the 1 in 37 climb to Central station with the 09.45 St David's to Waterloo service. This engine was preserved after it was withdrawn in 1991 and has since operated on the main line. *C. M. Parsons*

1. The broad gauge companies and beyond

The Bristol & Exeter Railway

Bristol was the second most important port in the country in the early 19th century, and to help maintain its status Bristol interests were prominent in founding a company in 1833 to build the Great Western Railway from London. Isambard Kingdom Brunel was appointed as chief engineer and he chose a broad gauge of 7ft 0¼in rather than the 'narrow' gauge of 4ft 8½in that was adopted by most other railways at the time. He believed that this would allow smoother running at high speeds, but although there were good reasons for adopting the wider gauge it would mean that the GWR would be out of step with the rest of the country and this would eventually result in connectivity issues. The GWR opened in stages between 1838 and 1841.

The GWR was typical of many early railways as the prime movers behind its construction were located at the opposite end of the line from a larger and more important place. However, its parliamentary birth encouraged a separate group of Bristol merchants to build a railway that would connect with the GWR and run westwards to Exeter. Brunel was engaged as the engineer and a Bill to construct the Bristol & Exeter Railway became an Act of Parliament on 19 May 1836; only two of the B&E's 16 directors came from Exeter.

As the railway was to connect with the GWR the broad gauge was chosen, but there were then delays in construction due to a shortage of finance, mainly because about a quarter of the original shareholders were speculators who failed to fulfil their obligations. Eventually the first section to Bridgwater was opened in June 1841, and by May 1843 services were running to Beam Bridge (west of Wellington); this was a temporary terminus where the main turnpike road to Exeter was diverted to pass under the railway. Construction work thus far had been straightforward, but the line was now faced by the Blackdown Hills, and what had been a gradual ascent from Taunton became a mile-long climb at up to 1 in 81 towards the most important engineering feature of the line, the 1,088-yard-long Whiteball Tunnel. The border between Somerset and Devon is in the tunnel and just beyond its western mouth the line's summit is attained at almost 400 feet above sea level. Beyond here the railway descends for more than 2 miles before entering the valley of the River Culm, then descends gently towards Exeter by following this watercourse. The works at Whiteball delayed construction, but the line finally opened to Exeter on 1 May 1844 and the temporary terminus at Beam Bridge was closed.

It was originally planned that the B&E would terminate at Exeter's canal basin, but in the event it ended in river meadows adjacent to Red Cow village in the parish of St David's, the name later adopted for the station. The city council was not in favour of the railway, probably due to the threat that it posed to the municipally owned Ship Canal, and refused permission for it to enter Exeter; this would in any event have been difficult as the city was located on the hillside high above the terminus. Brunel had already designed a number of one-sided stations on both the GWR and the B&E that had separate up and down stations on whichever side of the line that the town stood; this avoided the need for passengers and their luggage to cross the running lines, and the Exeter terminus was constructed accordingly with both stations on the 'down' side. Rather unusually the total cost of the new railway did not exceed the budgeted amount of £2 million.

An artist's impression of the 'one-sided' station provided at Exeter for the opening of the Bristol & Exeter Railway in 1844.

The B&E leased access to the GWR station at Bristol Temple Meads and the new railway was also leased to the GWR for five years after completion to save the cost of acquiring locomotives and rolling stock. The GWR now had a 194-mile line from Paddington to Exeter, and just a week after the B&E opened the completion of the Bristol & Gloucester Railway meant that Exeter now had rail connections with towns as far away as Newcastle-upon-Tyne. The B&E opened its own station in Bristol in 1845 and when the GWR lease ended in 1849 the B&E board opted to work their railway and obtain their own engines and carriages.

When the independent broad gauge Exeter & Crediton Railway (E&CR) opened in 1851 it also used the B&E terminus. Prior to the London & South Western Railway (LSWR) reaching Exeter in 1860 it entered into negotiations with the B&E with a view to extending its line from its Queen Street terminus to St David's and to obtain 'running powers' over the B&E to connect with the E&CR. The one-sided B&E station was not popular with either staff or passengers and was not suited to handling the additional LSWR traffic, so reconstruction started in 1862. When the new station was completed in July 1864 it had an attractive 420-foot-long stone frontage and four platforms that were

The broad gauge companies and beyond

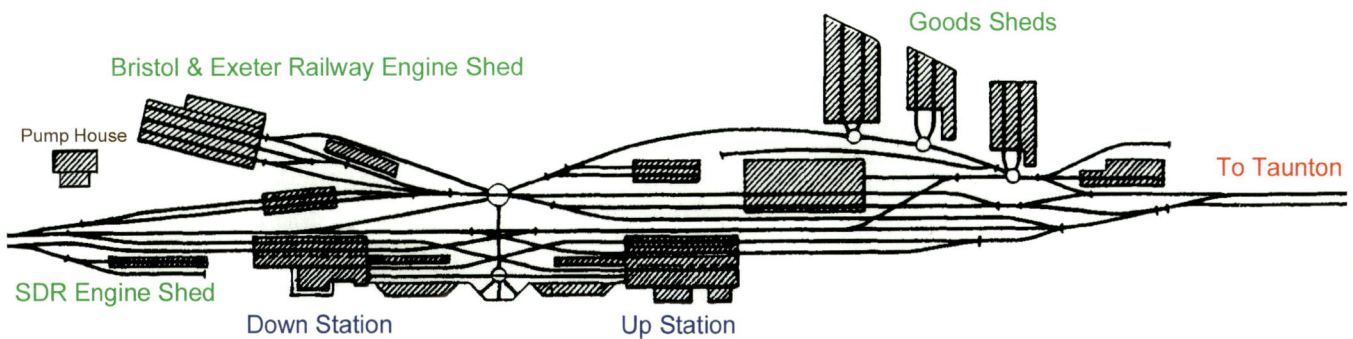

A plan of the joint Bristol & Exeter/South Devon Railway station at Exeter in about 1860 before it was rebuilt for the first time.

covered by an overall single-span partly-glazed roof, 132 feet wide and 363 feet long. The main offices were on the east side of the station, including separate booking offices for the B&E and LSWR; looking from the east there was a 640-foot-long down platform for B&E trains, then a 510-foot-long island platform used mainly by the LSWR, although that company was not pleased at the GWR's insistence that all its trains should stop at St David's, a measure that would continue until after nationalisation.

Continuing westwards there was just a single road between the LSWR platform and a further 750-foot-long island platform, the western face of which was for up B&E services. A fifth or 'spare' line, sometimes described as a storage road, ran alongside this line and inside the outer wall of the train shed. A footbridge of ornamental ironwork crossed the station at about its centre and provided access to all the platforms. In the wall on the up side of the train shed there was a double row of windows that, together with the glass roof and ends, made the interior of the shed quite bright; at night a triple row of gas lamps provided illumination. A third rail was added where necessary through the station and as far as Cowley Bridge Junction to accommodate the 'narrow gauge' LSWR trains; mixed gauge was also provided on the E&CR, and the LSWR took over its operation from the B&E on 1 February 1862. The LSWR's use of St David's introduced a distinctive operating feature at the station: due to their different approaches, B&E and LSWR trains bound for the same destination travelled in opposite directions.

The South Devon Railway (SDR) 'Atmospheric' engine house (see below) survived this rebuilding and, in addition to holding the depot water tank, it was later used for the manufacture of compressed oil gas that was initially used for carriage lighting and subsequently for cooking in restaurant cars; vehicles were supplied via underground pipes while trains stood in the station. Each main track was served by a series of hose connections that would be within reach of a restaurant car's gas cylinders; gassing and watering at St David's was completed in about 5 minutes. Exeter was the furthest point west that the gas was manufactured and met gas requirements from Bridgwater down; when it was needed at other locations it was carried there in distinctive 'Cordon' travelling gas tank wagons. Gas production ceased in 1962.

As the railway system in the West developed the broad

Bristol & Exeter Railway No 40 was one of eight 4-2-4 coke-burning well- and back-tank engines built in 1853-54 for express service. They had enormous flangeless 9-foot-diameter driving wheels and were the fastest engines of their time; one was credited with achieving a speed of 81.8mph while descending Wellington bank. Four were rebuilt by the GWR, when they were fitted with 8ft 10in driving wheels; work on No 40 was completed in June 1873, so this photo must date from the following 2½ years, as the engine was renumbered 2002 in January 1876.

gauge companies acquired narrow gauge lines, where they had to provide mixed gauge track, and they also had an increasing workload in transhipping goods between their wagons and those of other railways using what had effectively become the 'standard gauge'. This could mean losing business; the completion of the Somerset & Dorset Railway's Bath extension in 1874 meant that a standard gauge wagon from the Midlands could now reach Exeter via the S&D and LSWR. The B&E's use of two gauges also meant that it needed a larger wagon fleet than would normally be necessary. Thirteen and a half miles of the main line had already been converted to mixed gauge when in 1875 the B&E Board decided to add a third rail to the remaining 62 miles of track between Bristol and Exeter. This was completed between Taunton and Cowley Bridge in November that year, but as mixed track still had to be added to the station goods yards, a regular standard gauge goods train from Taunton to Exeter was not established until March 1876. A daily passenger train between Taunton and Exeter started using the narrower rails in July 1877.

Previously Bristol had been the transfer point for goods between the two gauges, but now that the standard gauge had reached Exeter it became the main place for this activity and a goods transhipment shed was provided; within it narrow and broad gauge trains occupied opposite sides of a platform across which goods could be transferred. As the number of standard gauge passenger trains increased there was also a considerable transfer of passengers who were heading further west on broad gauge services, and vice versa. This meant that the whole contents of a train, whether it be passengers, luggage or mail, would be disgorged on to the platform at St David's and reloaded on to another train; at a time when such trains could also include a horse box this transfer could also include horses.

By 1875 the B&E owned or leased a number of branch lines and subsidiary routes and was a financial success; during its 30 years of independence it paid an average dividend of 4½%. However, due to the costs involved in adding the third rail, the directors decide that it would be beneficial to amalgamate with a company with greater financial resources, and talks were successfully concluded with the GWR; the B&E passed into GWR control in January 1876 and was fully amalgamated from 1 August of that year.

The South Devon Railway

After the B&E was authorised, Plymouth interests proposed building a railway from there to Exeter, and Brunel was engaged to survey a route. He planned a coastal route from Exeter to the River Teign, where it would cross the estuary before heading for Torquay, Dartmouth and Kingsbridge; this would have involved extensive engineering work, not least in bridging the Teign and Dart estuaries, and the project was abandoned when the necessary finance could not be raised. There were subsequent proposals for other routes, but Devon's difficult topography meant that each had its drawbacks. When the B&E was nearing completion, that company, the GWR and a new ally, the Bristol & Gloucester Railway, all became interested in a Plymouth line and agreed to provide about a third of the capital to build a railway over a revised route that would take Brunel's proposed line inland from Teignmouth to Newton Abbot and onwards via Totnes.

Although this route has since been criticised, at the time it was selected to ensure the financial success of the railway by serving as much of the population as possible, and it achieved this by either passing through or being within relatively easy reach of most of Devon's larger towns and villages in what was otherwise a sparsely populated county. There was not, however, a great deal of enthusiasm for this project from vested interests in Exeter, who would lose most of the business associated with the existing stage coach operations.

The South Devon Railway Bill passed through Parliament in 1844, where it was promoted as a traditional double-track locomotive-worked line; however, subsequently the Board received a proposal from the patentees of the 'Atmospheric Railway', a system whereby a train was drawn along by a partial vacuum in a slotted pipe between the tracks, using a

After the atmospheric debacle the SDR turned to the GWR for locos, but as the main lines of both that company and the B&E were mainly level it had nothing suitable for the gradients west of Newton Abbot, and a 4-4-0ST was specially designed for the route. The SDR had no tender engines throughout its existence and engines of this type handled services west of Exeter until the end of the broad gauge. *Hawk* was one of a batch of an improved design supplied in 1859 and is seen at the 'old' St David's before working a westbound train.

piston fixed beneath the vehicles, and this idea was referred to Brunel for his consideration. Due to several factors, including the inadequacies of existing steam locos and a successful, albeit limited, use of the atmospheric system elsewhere, Brunel conclusively came down in its favour. He believed that it would improve performance over the hilly country between Newton Abbot and Plymouth, where a better alternative to spreading the gradients evenly would be to construct steeper gradients at four places, two in each direction, where larger pipes and additional pumping engines would be provided to lift the trains up the inclines. The board accepted Brunel's advice and work commenced in 1844.

Difficulties in building along the Exe estuary and the coastal section at Dawlish meant that the line did not open for passengers over the 15 miles from Exeter to Teignmouth until 30 May 1846, and delays in building and equipping the engine houses meant that initially services were operated by locomotives hired from the GWR. Passenger services were extended to Newton Abbot in December 1846 and a daily goods train between Exeter and Newton started on 1 May 1847. The line was opened as far as a temporary station on the outskirts of Plymouth in May 1848.

Engine houses were built at intervals of about 3 miles and test atmospheric passenger trains started on 16 August 1847; four public passenger services between Exeter and Teignmouth using the system began in the following month, and by February 1848 all trains between Exeter and Newton Abbot were worked this way. Initially the system was well received, with the service noted for its speed and smoothness, and the majority of trains arrived on time or even early. However, serious technical problems then became apparent and eventually, rather than continuing to throw good money after bad, the directors decided to abandon the system, and locomotive operation between Exeter and Newton resumed

The broad gauge companies and beyond

on 10 September 1848. In addition to losing a large amount of money by adopting what locals referred to as the 'Atmospheric Caper', the SDR was also left a legacy of two major handicaps, the first being that most of its main line was built as single track; as the continuous cast-iron pipes were expensive precision items, it had been decided to save the cost of having the two sets of pipes that would be needed if double track was laid. Secondly the steep gradients and curves beyond Newton Abbot have hindered the provision of a fast service ever since.

The SDR shared the B&E station in Exeter, its line crossing the River Exe on a 75-yard-long eight-span trussed-timber bridge. Heading south, the track then gradually rose at 1 in 640 on an embankment to cross the turnpike road to Okehampton on a stone bridge and after another stretch of embankment it ran on to a 62-arch 501-yard-long stone viaduct through the parish of St Thomas, which passed over two further major roads; the three roads converged at a bridge over the Exe, providing the western access to Exeter. The viaduct was constructed to avoid road traffic having to cross the atmospheric railway pipe that ran between the rails, and this is a fortunate legacy of the atmospheric debacle as, apart from some occupation crossings, there are no level crossings

The St Thomas station ground-level 1861 building is viewed from Cowick Street at around the turn of the century; steps under the canopy on the right lead to the north end of the down platform. *GWR*

between Exeter and Plymouth; this particularly applies to Exeter, as today these roads are extremely busy and often congested.

Just over half a mile from St David's the SDR built St Thomas

This view of St Thomas station from the up platform looking towards St David's in 1904 shows the station in its prime; a small signal cabin can be glimpsed at the far end of the down platform just inside the train shed. Although the station was referred to as Exeter St Thomas in the public timetable from the 19th century and the parish had become a part of Exeter in 1899, the station nameboards such as the one just visible on the extreme left still merely read 'St Thomas'.

station on this viaduct next to the second of the roads. The station opened with the line at a time when the only built-up areas in the locality were for short distances along the three roads; however, all trains stopped there as the SDR regarded it as being its main station for local traffic to Exeter, as its location near the Exe bridge meant it was closer to the city centre than St David's. It also benefitted the SDR financially as the rental for using St David's was based on the number of its passengers using it. However, only minimal facilities were initially provided on the 175-foot-long platform, which was constructed on a widened section of the viaduct on the down side of the single line; a booking office was built into the viaduct at the foot of steps that provided access to the platform. Despite its exposed position, no cover was provided on either the platform or steps. The station was nonetheless an immediate success, with many passengers choosing to alight there rather than at St David's, and large numbers of Exonians used it for trips to the coast. Improvements were soon needed, and by early 1847 the platform had been extended at its south end to about 260 feet, and was partly covered by a timber train shed; additional booking and staff accommodation was also provided at ground level and later the flight of steps was covered.

The atmospheric fiasco had left the SDR in an impecunious state, and it only narrowly avoided bankruptcy, but as finances improved work started on doubling the line. By 1855 the section between Newton and Totnes had been doubled over Dainton summit, but further work could not be afforded until 1860, when the stretch between Exminster and Starcross was completed; this was followed in the following year by the section between Exminster and the south end of St Thomas station in June, then through the station to St David's in September. At St Thomas the viaduct and embankments were widened on the up side to accommodate the second track, and at St David's an iron girder bridge for the up line was erected alongside the existing timber bridge over the Exe. As a second platform was needed at St Thomas the station was rebuilt and a partly staggered 420-foot-long up platform was provided. The down platform was further extended at its south end to a total length of 400 feet and a new train shed was constructed to cover about half the length of both platforms; a new elegant station building was also provided at ground level.

By 1875 the SDR was a moderately prosperous company, but its important Plymouth traffic was being threatened by the arrival there of the LSWR. Having seen how the threat from the encroaching standard gauge companies had pressurised the GWR into making a takeover bid for the B&E at an enhanced price, the SDR directors felt that it was an opportune time to open negotiations with that company. An agreement was reached for the SDR to be worked by the GWR from 1 February 1876, and the two companies merged in 1878; the SDR never did manage to double all of its main line, and 14½ miles were still single at the end of its existence.

The Great Western Railway

The three 'Associated Companies' (GWR, B&E and SDR) had already acquired the West Cornwall Railway in 1866, and they were also lessees of the Cornwall Railway from Plymouth to Falmouth. After the amalgamations the GWR effectively controlled the latter company and it passed fully into Great Western ownership in 1889, which meant that the GWR now owned the line from Paddington to Penzance. With expansion elsewhere it now had the largest network in the country, but was not particularly profitable and was committed to spending a great deal of capital to improve its system, not least on the B&E main line, where the poor state of the track had been blamed for two accidents.

The nature of the GWR system had changed by then, particularly in the east where by 1877 broad gauge operations from London to Bristol were becoming rarer with just two regular goods trains using the wider rails to carry through traffic from the West. Of the 51 daily passenger train departures from Paddington only 12 still used the broad gauge; three were local trains with the remainder through trains to Bristol, some of which continued to Exeter and beyond. The Bristol to Exeter line was, however, still largely a broad gauge operation with only four passenger and four goods trains running daily on the narrow rails, but this was changing and by the mid-1880s broad gauge traffic east of Exeter was confined almost exclusively to trains that continued through the city to the west, and there were just six regular broad gauge passenger and two goods trains running from and to London. West of Exeter the wider gauge was still supreme, however, with only odd branches using the standard gauge for reasons of history.

Abolition of the 'seven-foot' seemed inevitable and the matter rose in importance in 1890 when work started on quadrupling the line between Taplow and Didcot; as a consequence it was decided to abandon the wider gauge and convert the remaining 171 miles of broad gauge west of Exeter; as 42 miles of this was double track, 213 miles of track were altered over one weekend in May 1892. The third rail on a further 253 miles of mixed gauge line was left to be lifted at leisure, but had mostly disappeared by the end of that year.

Connections between St David's station and the city had been improved in 1882 when a horse-drawn 3ft 6in-gauge tramway was opened; the main route ran from the station and close to the LSWR's Queen Street station, but the operators failed to obtain permission to have rails laid along Queen Street itself, as well as High Street, and this contributed to it soon having financial problems. It was dissolved in 1889, but was then taken over by another company; however, it too experienced financial problems and the route up the steep hill from St David's was abandoned in 1893. Eventually the city council decided to take over the operation and construct a more extensive tramway using electric power; this opened in April 1905 and the route from St David's now ran along Queen Street. By September 1906 a new route crossed a new steel road bridge over the Exe, with branches then running along Alphington Road and Cowick Street, the latter running beneath the railway at St Thomas station.

Rail traffic was increasing around the turn of the century and the LSWR often suffered delays over the shared tracks

The broad gauge companies and beyond

At the north end of St David's station in about 1911 the 1864 train shed is still intact, but there is evidence of rebuilding work on the up side on the right. This photo also shows that just a single road ran between Platforms 3 and 4 at that time. *GWR*

northwards between St David's and Cowley Bridge Junction, where the two routes parted company, particularly as the GWR would give its own trains priority. In 1905 the LSWR planned an avoiding line that would have passed over the GWR at the south end of St David's, then follow the River Exe before rejoining its existing line west of Cowley Bridge. However, publication of the necessary Bill aroused opposition from the GWR on the basis that this would breach the existing agreements between the two companies, and these objections were upheld when the matter was referred to arbitration.

Nevertheless improvements were needed at St David's, and in 1909 the down GWR platform was extended at its east end to a length of 1,007 feet and a new bay platform (No 2) was provided adjacent to this extension, primarily for Exe Valley branch trains. Between 1911 and 1914 the station was substantially rebuilt at an estimated cost of £33,325. The works provided for enlargement on the up side of the station, where a new platform was constructed outside of the west wall of the train shed; this platform was then widened inside the wall to form a new island platform (Nos 5 and 6) for the up main and relief GWR lines. Subsequently the two existing island platforms were converted into a single structure (Nos 3 and 4), which was mainly used by LSWR services, and that company even provided its own ticket collectors at the foot of the stairs from the station footbridge; additional capacity was also provided by now having two running lines between Platforms 4 and 5. The GWR would also use Platform 3 if No 1 was already occupied, or if it was necessary to reverse the running order of two down GWR trains by allowing one to overtake the other. As the rebuilding created extra space between Platforms 1 and 3 a down through road was also provided.

The train shed was then demolished and awnings were erected over each platform. Despite the removal of the old station roof it was possible to retain the handsome limestone 1862 frontage wall that had provided support for the roof. The existing footbridge was extended and a new luggage bridge was provided, which was accessed via electrically operated lifts of 30cwt capacity housed in masonry towers. There were also extensive alterations to the permanent way at both ends of the station, and all the signal boxes were replaced. It appears that by the time this work had been completed it had already been decided to improve the facilities further and additional expenditure of £7,905 was authorised to extend the two island platforms at their north ends to 1,100 feet (up) and 900 feet (middle). To create the necessary space alterations had to be made to the goods shed and yard; delayed by the First World War this further work was not completed until 1920.

The railway spurred development in St Thomas, and streets of terraced houses now filled the land between the three original roads; the parish became part of the Exeter municipal area in 1899. The station was closed for part of the First World War to release staff for other duties, but thereafter became increasingly busy as the area continued to develop. In 1929 the up platform was extended by about 220 feet at its south end; this extension was quite narrow and built to a higher level than the existing platform. The GWR's 1947

Exeter's Railways

The broad gauge companies and beyond

Top left: A view from the old atmospheric engine house in about 1913 depicts St David's during reconstruction. The south end of the station appears to be largely complete, although a bracket signal is standing where the through road has to be completed; more work is outstanding at the north end, and the last section of the train shed has still to be removed. A 'Saint' Class 4-6-0 is waiting to leave from the down GWR platform; a distinctive glazed screen is being installed over the buildings on this platform to enclose the area between the new platform awning and the top of what was previously the outer wall of the train shed. *GWR*

Left: In a similar view on 23 September 1962 'Warship' No D824 *Highflyer* is leaving Platform 1 with the 2.20pm St David's to Kingswear service. *R. C. Riley*

Sectional Appendix stated that 'Owing to the difference in height in platform levels, Drivers of up Auto Trains must bring their trains to a stand at the platform west of the station roof except during inclement weather.' By 1930 the down platform had been given its third extension, but on this occasion 220 feet was added at the north end to give a total length of 620 feet.

At this time road traffic in Exeter was increasing and the narrow streets in the city centre were becoming congested, with High Street a major bottleneck. It was felt that the slow speed of the tram cars and the 'bunching' caused by much of the tram system being single-track was contributing to the problems; and as there was also a backlog of track renewals and other repairs, it was decided to abandon the system in 1931.

Above: In a scene from before the First World War St David's ornate frontage can be viewed as tram car No 4 waits to leave. The tram system used 37 vehicles, the first 20 of which were supplied by Dick, Kerr & Co of Preston in 1905-06 and could seat 20 in the lower saloon and 22 on the top deck. The only other vehicles in view are horse-drawn, including a GWR parcels van parked next to the Parcels Office.

By the 1930s St David's was largely in a form that would be recognised today, but if it were not for 'outside events' the story could have been very different. As part of a Government-sponsored scheme in 1935 for the relief of unemployment, and to help the railways and industry, the well-known proposal to build a double-track line inland between Exminster and the Teign estuary was initiated. It was felt that traffic levels at that time justified quadrupling the line, but with no room for the additional rails along the sea wall an alternative route was thought appropriate; although some preparations were made, the scheme was at first deferred and eventually scuppered with the advent of war. Another scheme at the time involved rebuilding the line from Central station on a 1 in 100 gradient. At St David's the SR tracks would have crossed the GWR on a bridge at the south end of the station before entering a new dedicated 850-foot-long island platform on the west side of St David's, which would have been about 20 feet above the existing platforms and the track thereon to Cowley Bridge would have been quadrupled. It was also planned to extend the existing platforms yet again, and as the new SR platform would mean using much of the goods yard, freight facilities would move to a new yard beyond the north end of the station. Some work, including

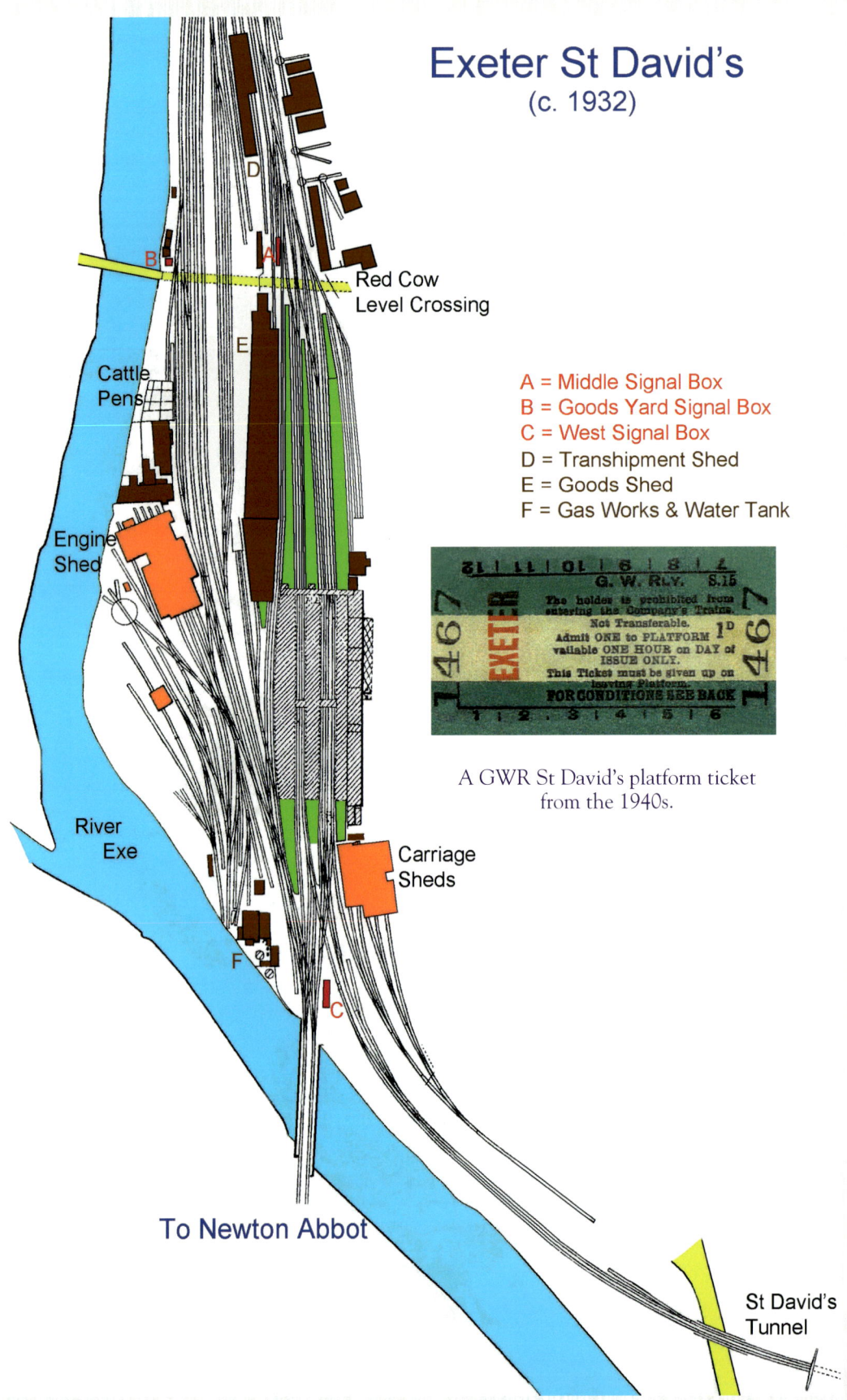

A plan of Exeter St David's in about 1932.

The broad gauge companies and beyond

The changing scene at the south end of St David's station. Semaphore signals abound on a wet 25 November 1975 as two trains illustrate the different directions to London; No D1068 *Western Reliance* is entering Platform 5 with the 13.55 Paignton to Paddington train as 'Crompton' No 33003 cautiously descends past West box as it arrives with the 11.00 departure from Waterloo.

The second view shows two directions from Paignton on a lovely 14 June 2003. South West Trains Nos 159010 and 159018 (left) are leaving as the 14.55 Paignton to Waterloo train, while Virgin Trains 'Voyagers' Nos 221108 and 220002 approach forming the 15.12 Paignton to Manchester Piccadilly service. *Both DHM*

Viewed from the narrow 1929 extension to the up platform at St Thomas station, Newton Abbot's 2-6-2T No 5536 is leaving with the 4.35pm St David's to Heathfield Teign Valley service on 8 February 1957; the glazing in the roof was removed during that decade and this platform extension was dismantled in 1966. *Peter W. Gray*

The third and final extension to the down platform at St Thomas is the vantage point from which to observe 'Warship' No 858 *Valorous* on 4 July 1970 as it passes beneath the SDR train shed with the 16.15 Plymouth to Cardiff General train; demolition of the shed commenced within days. The BR-style 'Exeter (St Thomas)' nameboard was erected in about 1955; until then the previous GWR boards still merely said 'St Thomas'. *DHM*

The broad gauge companies and beyond

The boarded-up station buildings contribute to a sorry-looking St Thomas station during the evening on 20 May 1975 as No D1068 *Western Reliance* runs through light engine over the up line. *DHM*

St Thomas is both tidier and busier today. 'Pacers' Nos 143621 and 143617 are calling as the 15.24 Exmouth to Paignton service on 6 March 2015. The shortened wall on the left once formed part of the train shed and the vacant area in front of it was where the final extension to the down platform was located before it was dismantled in the 1990s. *DHM*

channelling the River Exe away from the station to create additional room, was undertaken, but this scheme was also then halted.

However, in 1938 a contract was awarded for the complete remodelling of the buildings on the down side at St David's, which involved widening them on the station approach side by 11 feet for a distance of 170 feet, and erecting a canopy covering for motor vehicles that ran for 350 feet along the front of the building; the architectural features of the station were retained and the new work was faced with stone to match the existing structure. The first stage provided a wider station entrance, a larger booking hall and office, an enquiry office and spacious refreshment and dining rooms. A second stage provided a new parcels office, cloakrooms, telephone exchange and station offices, with all work completed in 1939-40. Loudspeakers were provided at the station in 1941, and it was converted from gas to electric lighting in 1946.

The 501-yard-long St Thomas Viaduct is an impressive structure that is not usually easy to appreciate as for much of its length it is hemmed in by buildings on both sides. Just beyond its north end the line is carried on a long embankment where, on 17 July 1984, No 50022 *Anson* is about to cross Okehampton Street with the 10.24 Penzance to Liverpool Lime Street service. *DHM*

Work on redeveloping land to the east of St Thomas station in 1984 temporarily opened up a view of the station building and a section of the 62-arch stone viaduct; a DMU is departing as a down service on 29 July. *DHM*

The broad gauge companies and beyond

No 47252 is approaching the up platform at St Thomas station with the 19.30 Newton Abbot to Stirling Motorail service on 20 May 1975; the 1960 warehouse in Alphington Road Goods Yard can be glimpsed in the distance. *DHM*

At the south end of the St Thomas Viaduct the railway crosses Alphington Road before continuing south on an embankment past the site of Alphington Road Goods Yard; power car No 43134 is passing over the road at the head of the 15.00 Paignton to York HST service on 26 July 1986. *DHM*

This aerial view of Exeter St David's station from the south on 14 June 2021 includes a 'Castle' HST set standing in Platform 6; the green-roofed power signal box is in the centre, with the newly enhanced TMD to the left of the station. Further left are the River Exe and the Exwick Spillway flood channel. *Sadie B., Wikimedia Creative Commons (CC BY-SA 4.0)*

At the time of writing a new £16 million station is being constructed on the edge of the Marsh Barton Trading Estate, almost a mile south of St Thomas station. The worksite is pictured from Clapperbrook Lane bridge on 25 September 2021 as 'Turbo' No 165135 passes forming the 14.57 Exmouth to Paignton service; it will be these services that will stop here in the future. The building on the right is an 'energy-from-waste' plant. The station is scheduled to open in the winter of 2022. *DHM*

2. The rivals

The Exeter & Crediton Railway

The Exeter & Crediton Railway (E&CR) was formed in 1844 to build a 5¾-mile broad gauge railway from a junction with the B&E at Cowley Bridge to the ancient town of Crediton; an Act was obtained in the following year with powers to lease the line to the B&E. Another local company, the North Devon Railway (NDR), then proposed extending the broad gauge from Crediton to Barnstaple. Previously the Taw Vale Railway (TVR) had obtained powers to open a line from a dock at Fremington to Barnstaple, but did nothing to build it. Seeing an opportunity, the TVR attempted to sell its undertaking to the NDR, but when this was unsuccessful the company formed an alliance with several 'narrow gauge' railways that were being proposed in association with the London & South Western Railway (LSWR). With their help the TVR developed plans for the Taw Vale Extension Railway (TVER), a narrow gauge line from Crediton to Barnstaple that rivalled the NDR proposal.

Despite local support, the NDR Bill failed to get parliamentary approval and the TVER then made the pretence of abandoning the alliance and came to an agreement to lease its railway to the B&E instead. This helped the TVER obtain its Act, but when the agreement was put to its shareholders the directors recommended its rejection! Instead agreement was reached to lease the line to the LSWR; the latter lent money to the TVER for it to buy shares in the E&CR, and when a meeting of that company was arranged for the purpose of sealing the lease with the B&E it was also rejected. Soon afterwards this new majority shareholding agreed to lease the E&CR to the TVER and the shareholders also obtained an injunction forbidding the directors of the E&CR from opening it using the broad gauge, as at that time a line that had been opened to passengers could not change its gauge without a fresh Act of Parliament.

By then in early 1847 the E&CR was actually nearing completion as a double-track broad gauge railway, although it did not yet have a connection with the B&E at Cowley Bridge and a temporary wooden station was being constructed close to the junction. When the TVER had been authorised the track gauge was not specified, but it had to be approved by the Board of Trade. The TVER applied to the commissioners for its line be constructed as narrow gauge, and in anticipation of a favourable response built the railway from Fremington to Barnstaple accordingly, then also 'narrowed' the broad gauge track between Exeter and Crediton. However, the commissioners considered that the LSWR's actions had been illegal and confirmed that the gauge over the TVER, and by implication the E&CR, should be broad to connect with the B&E, from which most traffic was expected to either arrive or depart. This decision foiled the LSWR's plans, all construction work on the TVER was stopped, and nothing was done to open the E&CR.

Eventually the LSWR agreed at its own expense to implement the commissioners' decision by altering one of the two narrow gauge tracks between Cowley Bridge and Crediton to broad gauge and installing a junction at Cowley Bridge; the temporary station there was dismantled, having seen no use The line was leased to the B&E as a single broad gauge line with an unused narrow gauge line running next to it, and services finally commenced on 12 May 1851, more than four years after the line had originally been completed.

The TVER renamed itself as a new North Devon Railway Company (NDR) and constructed a single-track broad gauge line from Crediton to Barnstaple; it opened on 1 August 1854 and, although through trains operated from Exeter to Barnstaple, engines were changed at Crediton.

The London & South Western Railway

The LSWR was originally the London & Southampton Railway, but had ambitions to invade the broad gauge territory in the West, hence its involvement in the machinations related above, even though by 1847 it had only reached Salisbury, almost 90 miles from Exeter. A reaction to the 'Railway Mania' now set in, making it increasingly difficult to raise finance for new projects, and there was also indecision in choosing a route westwards. In 1853 the LSWR defeated attempts from a rival company to build a line, and pledged to build a railway from Dorchester to Exeter that followed a coastal route; however, this was thwarted when the independent Salisbury & Yeovil Railway obtained an Act to build a line between those places.

In 1855 the LSWR went to Parliament with a Bill for powers unconnected with a railway to Exeter, but when it was passed Parliament inserted a clause insisting that it honour its pledge to build an Exeter line by extending from either Yeovil or Dorchester under the penalty of stopping dividend payments if neither proceeded. The company therefore had no option but to prepare estimates for both routes, and the former was selected as it was shorter and less heavily graded; construction started in 1856. The Salisbury & Yeovil Railway was leased to the LSWR and opened to Yeovil Junction in June 1860, and the extension to Exeter opened soon afterwards on 19 July.

This 49-mile extension was single track with a number of passing places, but with 10 miles of double track between Axminster and Honiton. However, looking to the future the bridges and some of the earthworks were built to accommodate a second track as traffic increased. Doubling work started in 1861 and the section from Broad Clyst to Exeter was completed by April 1864; the line from Salisbury to Exeter was completely double by July 1870. The undulating route was built parallel to the coast and against the grain of the valleys, but on entering Devon it followed the Axe valley for about 12 miles before turning inland and climbing at 1 in 100 over a headland to reach Seaton Junction. After a brief respite there the line then climbed for about 5 miles to the 1,353-yard-long Honiton Tunnel, mostly at a gradient of 1 in 80; thereafter there was a gradual descent towards Exeter, but with three short rising sections.

Approaching Exeter the line passed through the village of Pinhoe, then ran to the north of Whipton village through an agricultural area known for fruit growing and other market gardening. Subsequently this area was swallowed up by Exeter as the city expanded and became mainly a residential area but with some industrial activity; land in Whipton parish would eventually be acquired by the LSWR for developments at Exmouth Junction that would become the main business in the area, with hundreds employed, most of whom lived locally. However, the first passengers would have enjoyed a rural view and it was not until their train had emerged from the 263-yard-long Blackboy Tunnel that it reached the city; after a further half mile or so the line terminated close to the city centre at Queen Street station, 171 miles from Waterloo station. The terminus was built in the Longbrook Valley in the shadows of Rougemont Castle on land once partly occupied by the castle moat. Although much more convenient than the B&E station, Queen Street was less grand and at first only had one main platform and a bay that was used for Exmouth branch trains from 1861; it was spanned by a train shed that had a partly glazed overall roof on an iron framework supported on cast-iron pillars.

Relations with the B&E must have improved by this time as an Act of Parliament in July 1860 authorised an extension of the LSWR's line down the hill from Queen Street to St David's station. The LSWR took over the lease of the Exeter & Crediton Railway and converted the track to mixed gauge; a narrow gauge train service from Queen Street to Crediton started in February 1862. Having previously been broad, then narrow (neither of which actually saw public use), then broad again, the E&CR now remained mixed gauge for 30 years as the B&E had the right under the 1860 Act to run broad gauge goods trains to Crediton; after the wider gauge was abandoned, the GWR continued to operate goods trains to Crediton until 1903. In July 1862 the LSWR took over the NDR from Crediton to Barnstaple and, after dualling the gauge, the Crediton service was extended to north Devon in 1863. However, to save having to tranship goods the LSWR continued to also run a regular broad gauge goods train between Crediton and Bideford until May 1877, when the completion of mixed gauge from Bristol to Exeter made this unnecessary. Apart from having had a remarkably chequered history for such a short stretch of railway, the E&CR was notable in that it formed a root from which the LSWR developed its network of lines west of Exeter including to Plymouth. Narrow gauge rails also reached several coastal destinations in north Devon and north Cornwall, enabling the company to benefit from the growing demand for seaside holidays.

Initially up trains from the west ran through Queen Street, then had to back down to the only platform, but an up platform was added in

In this vintage view of Pinhoe station looking west from the level crossing, the timber footbridge provided in 1893 can be seen, and the original crossing keeper's cottage on the right is still in its single-storey state; as a second storey was added in about 1897, the photo must date from between these two events.

In a similar viewpoint at Pinhoe on 18 August 1964, No 34080 74 *Squadron* is stopping with the 8.48am Ilfracombe to Salisbury train; the now two-storey cottage is the station master's house and the footbridge is a replacement from the Exmouth Junction concrete works.
R. A. Lumber

1862 to handle increasing traffic; however, it lacked any facilities or a connecting footbridge and passengers had to use a foot crossing between the platforms to reach the main station building. By 1867 there were timber and corrugated-iron waiting and refreshment rooms on both platforms. On the eastern approach to the station there was a ticket platform next to an engine shed where tickets were collected or inspected for passengers arriving on down trains; it was unpopular as this delayed a train's arrival, but enabled staff to collect tickets before passengers were able to leave the station. In 1874 a bay platform was added behind the up platform and a footbridge was finally erected around the same time.

When Pinhoe station was reopened on 16 May 1983 the morning proved to be very wet and the rain was falling as No 50007 *Hercules* arrived with the 06.50 Waterloo to Exeter St David's service; this marked the official opening, although two earlier trains had already called by then. A reception was then held in a marquee erected in an adjacent playing field. *DHM*

A station was not provided at Pinhoe when the line opened despite it passing through the village, although the LSWR did employ a level crossing keeper who lived in a cottage next to a road crossing. Pinhoe was on the route of the old Bath to Exeter road (later the A38) and was an archetypal Devon village with thatched buildings. A station was finally opened on 30 October 1871 immediately west of the level crossing, which was also used by passengers until a timber lattice footbridge was installed in 1893; this was replaced in 1923 by one manufactured at the Exmouth Junction Concrete Works. The crossing keeper's cottage became the station master's house and a second storey was added in about 1897.

On 26 January 1906 the LSWR inaugurated a steam railmotor service from Exeter to Honiton, and three halts with 120-foot-long wooden platforms were provided in or near the city, partly

Above: Mount Pleasant Road Halt is in the foreground of this 1927 view, with the Exmouth Junction marshalling yard and concrete works behind; the two steep paths running down from the road to the shelterless 120-foot-long wooden platforms can be noted.

Above: On Sunday 10 June 1984 No 50046 *Ajax* is about to enter Blackboy Tunnel as it descends past the site of Mount Pleasant Road Halt with the 08.30 Basingstoke to Paignton train; an indentation in the embankment marks the route of the path that ran to the down platform, while the yard is now a coal concentration depot. *DHM*

Left: In recent years the embankments have become heavily overgrown and the yard has resembled a small forest, although it was partly cleared early in 2022 prior to the site being redeveloped. On 14 June 2018 'Pacer' No 143618 is waiting to cross over to the Exmouth branch forming the 13.08 service from Paignton after being held for the 11.03 Paddington to Penzance HST, which was being diverted while a new culvert was being constructed at Cowley Bridge Junction. *DHM*

Although SR 'Lord Nelson' Class engines reached Exeter over the years, they were mainly used on other routes, but on 2 September 1962 No 30861 *Lord Anson* hauled the 'South Western Limited' railtour from Waterloo to Sidmouth Junction to commemorate the passing of the class; the tour was then taken along both Exmouth branches by 'M7s' Nos 30024 and 30025. The 4-6-0 hauled the returning charter between Exeter Central and Salisbury and is seen passing St James Park Halt; it was withdrawn just over a month later. *R. A. Lumber*

to rival the new electric tram system; these basic structures cost about £200 each and were illuminated by oil lamps. Working down the line, Whipton Bridge Halt was the first, although it did not actually open until March 1906. It was located north of Whipton village, immediately to the east of Summer Lane and almost 2 miles from Queen Street. By 1923 the halt required repairs, which were not authorised, and it was closed from 1 January; apparently traffic had largely evaporated as the main road passing through the village had a regular bus service.

The other two halts were ready for the start of the railmotor service. Mount Pleasant Road Halt was at the east end of Blackboy Tunnel just under a mile from Queen Street and was named after a road that passed over the tunnel. In addition to the Honiton trains this stop was also served by a railmotor service to Topsham on the Exmouth branch, which was introduced in 1908. It appears that the halt was quite busy at first, but the service declined when the railmotors were withdrawn in 1917 and it was also susceptible to competition from buses and trams that ran quite close by; it was decided

The very short up platform at St James Park can be noted as No 33032 passes with the 13.00 Waterloo to Exeter St David's train on Tuesday 29 April 1980, a few days before Class 50 locos took over this service. The old Exeter City FC grandstand (which was replaced in 2018) is prominent top right, and although fans use the station to attend matches, the short platforms have precluded its use for 'Footex' excursions. However, there have been occasional interesting workings, not least on 23 October 1954 when the Southampton FC team was due to change to a train at Salisbury hauled by No 10203; unfortunately the diesel suffered a blown fuse and the train had to be towed into Salisbury where the fault was repaired. It was 48 minutes late leaving, but a special stop was arranged for the team here, although the 3.00pm kick-off had to be delayed by 15 minutes. Another visitor to the halt on 12 May 1956 was 0-6-0PT N0 9765 hauling four non-corridors forming the 1.35pm Dulverton to Exeter train in connection with the Devon Cup Final. *DHM*

The Rivals

From October 2020 work started to extend the down platform at St James Park by 10 metres, and the up one by 49 metres, to handle four-car trains; previously the doors were only opened on two coaches when a train called. The existing platforms were also resurfaced and new energy-efficient lighting installed. On 29 July 2021 No 159019 is approaching as the 10.25 Exeter St David's to Waterloo service. *DHM*

not to rebuild it after one of the platforms was demolished by a derailed coal train, and it closed from 2 January 1928.

The third halt was named Lion's Holt and was located in a cutting to the west of Blackboy Tunnel, less than half a mile from Queen Street. It was next to Exeter City FC's ground, but in 1906 the club was still amateur and the ground was probably little more than a field; it was only in 1908, after it joined the professional Southern League, that work started to develop the site as a stadium. Gas lighting was installed at this halt and at Mount Pleasant Road in 1911. Lion's Holt Halt was evidently more successful than the others, presumably in part helped by its proximity to the stadium, and in about 1927 the platforms were rebuilt in concrete and a shelter was erected on the up side. The down platform was also extended to 240 feet although the up one was not to be lengthened until 2020! The station was renamed St James Park Halt after the stadium on 7 October 1946; since the withdrawal of local services on the main line, only Exmouth branch trains now stop there.

The Southern Railway

Queen Street was a gloomy station beneath its overall roof, and by the turn of the century it was showing its age and was ill-suited to its status as the LSWR's most important centre in the West; it was a major hub where all through trains changed locos and trains could be split or have carriages added or removed. Apparently the company's directors had no great wish to modernise it as the existing structure was considered to be a 'shed' and had a lower rateable value! Nothing of any substance would be done until after the 1923 'Grouping' when the Southern Railway commenced a staged programme of reconstruction with help from Government money made available during the Depression.

In 1925 work started on revising the track layout and signalling, with two new signal boxes erected; space was created by the opening of a marshalling yard at Exmouth Junction, which removed much of the goods activity. The main up platform was increased in length by about 510 feet to

Exeter Queen Street and Exeter Central platform tickets.

Exeter Queen Street station was considered to be a dark and gloomy place beneath its overall roof, something that is certainly suggested in this scene looking east from the down side of the station.

a remarkable 1,210 feet, and the platform road was connected to the up through road by a scissors crossover about halfway along its length enabling the easy unification of the portions of trains arriving from the West. The bay platform on the up side was lengthened by 300 feet and was mainly used by Exmouth trains, although up main-line stopping services could also start from there; the down platform was now 950 feet long and both platforms were partly covered by awnings.

In 1930 a three-road carriage shed was erected on the site of the old engine shed, and in the following year further carriage sidings were provided at the west end of the station in place of some goods sidings. During 1932 the old wooden platform buildings and train shed were removed, although some of the buildings had already burned down in a 1927 fire. The newly named Exeter Central was opened by the city's mayor on 1 July 1933; at the front of the station on Queen Street an impressive brick and concrete three-

This view of Queen Street station looking west from New North Road in the Edwardian period includes a glimpse of the original 'B' signal box on the extreme left and the goods yard on the right. The two nearest engines are both 4-4-0s, 'T9' No 727 and 'T3' No 576, and are probably waiting to take over up trains. Originally there were four through roads, but 'C' signal box was built at the far end of the station in about 1880, blocking one of the two down through lines.

The Rivals

Looking in the opposite direction from New North Road, Howell Road bridge is in the background, the goods marshalling sidings are on the left of the two running lines, and the carriage sidings on the right are on the site of the engine shed. Nearer right it appears that coach set No 208 may be waiting to be propelled into the station, perhaps to form a service to Exmouth.

storey main building was erected, flanked by two-storey wings forming a crescent shape. The building was partly occupied by the SR's Divisional offices where the company's territory west of Salisbury was supervised. The middle section of the building provided the main entrance and had a spacious booking hall that led directly to a footbridge linking the two platforms; this bridge was divided into two halves, one side for passengers and the other a corridor for luggage that had lifts at each end. Blocks of single-storey brick buildings were constructed on each platform to house refreshment and waiting rooms, and bookstalls. Previously a footbridge had been located at the centre of the station, but this was replaced by a second footbridge at the eastern end that also served as a second entrance. Both footbridges and many other smaller items came from the company's concrete works at Exmouth Junction.

After some isolated events early in the Second World War, including a bomb that fell on the line between St David's and St Thomas stations in May 1941, Exeter was heavily bombed in April and May 1942 as part of the so-called retaliatory 'Baedeker Blitz', where targets were chosen for their cultural and historical importance rather than any strategic value. Much of the city centre was destroyed during a raid on 4 May, with 161 fatalities. At Central station the goods yard and buildings including one of the signal boxes were damaged; the running lines were destroyed at the east

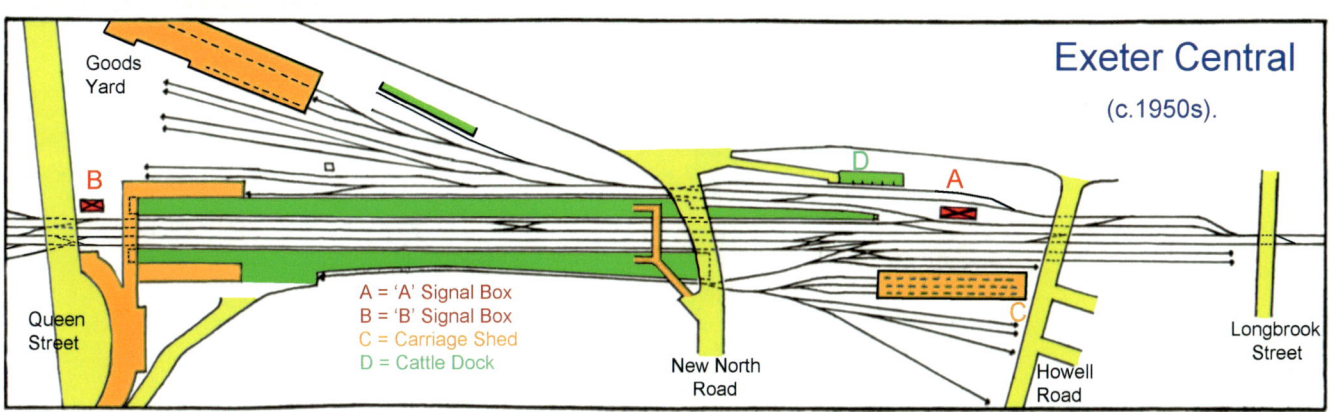

A plan of Exeter Central station in the 1950s.

Right: Exeter Central is seen in its prime from the main footbridge at the west end of the station at 2.25pm on Saturday 28 June 1958. 'E1/R' 0-6-2T No 32697 is standing on the up through road on pilot duty while 4-6-2s Nos 34031 *Torrington* and 34024 *Tamar Valley* appear to be propelling stock through Platform 2 towards the carriage sidings west of the station; they will wait there before taking forward two sections of the down 'Atlantic Coast Express' that is due shortly. A Fyffes banana depot can be seen in the goods yard, while Exeter Prison is prominent in the top left of the photo. *Peter W. Gray*

end of the layout, with damage also to a bridge. At Exmouth Junction sidings and buildings, including the concrete works, were also damaged.

Pinhoe's population was only 952 in 1901, but had risen to about 5,000 by the end of the 20th century. During this period urbanisation crept ever closer and the road towards Exeter was eventually lined by housing, retail units and trading estates. Most passengers used the station to travel into Exeter, but this business was largely lost to road and the station was listed for closure in Dr Beeching's 'Reshaping' report. This was implemented on 7 March 1966, about three weeks before Pinhoe was absorbed into Exeter, and the platform buildings and footbridge were demolished. However, in 1981 Tony Speller, the MP for North Devon, introduced an Act in Parliament that permitted a station to be reopened on an experimental basis without it then having to go through an elaborate closure procedure in the event of the trial failing. Pinhoe was now an expanding suburb of Exeter and its station was the first to be reopened under the 'Speller Act', with Mr Speller performing the official opening on 16 May 1983. Initially the station had just three services into Exeter in the morning and three back in the afternoon and early evening, but all trains now stop there.

Above: Central's up-side platforms are both occupied on 20 June 1958 with 'Merchant Navy' No 35024 *East Asiatic Company* having just backed on to the front portion of the 5.52pm departure to Waterloo in Platform 3, while 'M7' 0-4-4T No 30670 is waiting to leave from Bay Platform 4 with the 5.35pm stopper to Honiton. *Peter W. Gray*

Right: The up middle road at Central was removed in 1971. 'Crompton' No 33039 is leaving Platform 3 with the 12.20 St David's to Waterloo train on 28 July 1984 while passengers disembark from the 09.10 from Waterloo, which has arrived in Platform 2 behind No 50025 *Invincible*, and Class 118 DMU set No P460 is in Bay Platform 1 forming the 12.35 departure for Exmouth. The brutalist piece of architecture dominating the background is the BT Telephone Switching Centre. The down through road was removed three months later under the Exeter MAS scheme. *DHM*

3. The Exmouth branch

Still in 'Southern' livery but carrying its BR number, 'M7' 0-4-4-T No 30124 is slowing to a stop at St James Park in about 1950 with an Exmouth train of five assorted ex-LSWR coaches; there appears to be a reasonable number of passengers waiting on a sunny summer's day. *R. A. Lumber*

During the Napoleonic wars Exmouth was frequented by fashionable people while access to the continent was closed; they were particularly attracted by its mild winter climate, and the town is considered to be Devon's oldest holiday resort. Its use as a port was, however, limited for many years by shallow water on the approach to its quay, whereas a few miles up the Exe estuary Topsham offered a sheltered harbour to coastal shipping and became the port for Exeter in Roman times, remaining as such for some of the city's trade after its canal was built.

There were various schemes to build a railway to Exmouth during the 'Railway Mania', including one proposed by the South Devon Railway in 1845 that would have seen trains running over SDR metals from Exeter to just north of Exminster, where a branch would have diverged and crossed the canal and River Exe on a viaduct to Topsham, then on to Exmouth. This scheme was revived by the Exeter & Exmouth Railway in 1855, but later that company threw in its lot with the LSWR, which agreed to build a branch from its new main line to Topsham and continue from there over the E&E's proposed route. This 9½-mile branch opened on 1 May 1861 with intermediate stations at Topsham, Woodbury Road (renamed Exton in 1958) and Lympstone. Its opening brought relief to Exmouth as the town had suffered decline as a resort after the SDR had opened on the opposite side of the estuary and made Dawlish and Teignmouth more accessible. The LSWR worked the whole branch from the start and absorbed the E&E on 1 January 1866.

At Topsham a steeply graded branch was opened on 23 September 1861 from sidings at the station to the quay, where spoil excavated during construction of the Exmouth line was used for a new wharf. The short 32-chain-long branch was worked as a siding on the 'only one engine in steam' basis, and trains were propelled down the line and hauled on the return journey; all movements had to be carried out in daylight hours and due to the gradient the trains were restricted to eight loaded wagons and a brake van. Historically the port had played an important role in Exeter's wool trade, but by this time it mainly handled imports of coal, timber and building materials. A more unusual cargo was guano (concentrated bird droppings) from South America, which was taken by rail for less than a mile to the private siding of Odam's

Ivatt Class 2 2-6-2T No 41307 is about to enter Blackboy Tunnel with an Exmouth train in June 1955. Although of an LMS design, this was one of 30 locos allocated to the SR from new; when this photograph was taken it had just been transferred to Exmouth Junction from Three Bridges shed in Sussex, but had yet to have a '72A' shed plate affixed to its smokebox door. *John Stredwick*

fertiliser and chemical works on the south bank of the River Clyst. Trains were hauled to the siding, which had a trailing connection with the running line; however, as there was no run-round facility the returning empties were propelled back to Topsham.

New docks were opened at Exmouth in 1866, making it the largest harbour on the east Devon coast; it could handle vessels of up to 700 tons and it was no longer necessary for ships to anchor in the bay and transfer their cargo to lighters. A quarter-mile-long siding was laid from Exmouth's goods yard to the quayside; run-round facilities were never provided at the docks and trains had to be propelled there. Most cargoes here were also inbound, particularly coal, timber, grain and fertiliser, and locally caught fish was dispatched by train.

Although not directly relevant to this book, Exmouth was later served by a second railway, when a branch from the LSWR main line at Sidmouth Junction to Sidmouth was opened in 1874, and a branch from Tipton St Johns, an intermediate station on the Sidmouth line, was opened to Budleigh Salterton in 1897. An extension of this line to Exmouth was completed by the LSWR in 1903 and this link meant that through coaches detached at Sidmouth Junction could run from Waterloo to Exmouth, and later through holiday trains operated to the town from various places.

The opening service over the Exeter to Exmouth branch comprised five trains each way daily, including unusually Sundays, but a summer service of seven weekday and six Sunday trains was provided just two months later, the journey from Queen Street to Exmouth taking about 30 minutes. Thereafter train frequency continued to increase to meet a growing demand, and an article published in the Edwardian era commented that Exmouth's population had grown to about 12,000 and the port had 'almost become a residential suburb of Exeter'. In 1906 the LSWR obtained powers to double the branch and an additional track was laid on the east side of the line for the 4 miles from Exmouth Junction to Topsham, although no work was ever undertaken on doubling south of there. Wooden halts were opened on the newly doubled section at Polsloe Bridge near Exmouth Junction and at Clyst St Mary & Digby; the latter was built on the north side of a bridge over the Exeter to Sidmouth road, its name referring respectively to a village a mile away, and to land on which the Exeter City Asylum had been built. A siding had been installed in 1884 for materials used to build the asylum, and was retained until 1957 to receive

The Exmouth branch

Salisbury shed's 'West Country' 4-6-2 No 34026 *Yes Tor* is a rare visitor to the branch as it works a van train from Exmouth on Sunday 30 June 1963; it has just passed under the Exeter bypass and is descending from the line's summit at Hill Barton towards Polsloe Bridge. This is thought to be a 'Pigeon Special' from Brookwood in Surrey, conveying baskets of racing pigeons, and is now returning after the birds have been released. *R. A. Lumber*

After the branch was dieselised in September 1963, two peak passenger trains continued to be booked for steam haulage until January 1965: the 8.20am fast train from Exmouth to Exeter Central and the 5.49pm Central to Exmouth 'all stations' service. The latter is in the hands of BR Standard Class 4 2-6-4T No 80039 on 19 April 1964 as it steams over the double-track section of the branch; it has just passed beneath the Apple Lane overbridge and is near the site of the lifted Digby siding. *D. J. Frost*

coal for the hospital's boilers. The double track and halts came into use on 1 June 1908 when a new Queen Street to Topsham railmotor service also started; nine such trains operated daily in addition to the 18 conventional weekday trains to Exmouth.

The original terminus was a modest affair comprising an island platform, two run-round loops and a goods yard; on the east side of the station there was a turntable and small engine shed, a sub-shed of Exmouth Junction depot. The station was rebuilt in 1924 to handle the growing traffic and a second island platform was added to the west; among other improvements an impressive terminus building and a 70-lever signal box were erected. The shuttle service to Topsham had ceased from 1 January 1917 and by the time that the new station opened there were 20 down and 21 up trains each weekday between Exeter and Exmouth. In the days before mass car ownership the line remained busy with passengers commuting into Exeter in ever-increasing numbers, and at peak times it was often difficult to get a seat. The branch was also well used by holidaymakers, and Exonian day-trippers would flock to the seaside on summer weekends, so much so that extra trains would be arranged at short notice to cater for the demand. By 1930 Exmouth was second only to Queen Street as the busiest SR station west of Salisbury. Polsloe Bridge Halt was well used and was rebuilt in 1927 using concrete components that had been pre-cast at the Exmouth Junction Concrete Works; however, Clyst St Mary & Digby was not as popular and was in a poor state of repair by 1948, when the decision was made to close it.

Various classes of small tank engines were used initially, and by the mid-1870s Beattie 2-4-0WTs were appearing. In the next decade Adams '0415' Class 4-4-2 'Radial Tanks' were used; this class was later famous for its long use on the Lyme Regis branch. A report on engines seen in the 1897-98 period mentioned 'O2' Class 0-4-4Ts Nos 187, 209 and 231, '0415' Nos 52, 53, 107 and 424, and a solitary 2-4-0 well tank,

No 314, as being regularly employed on Exmouth services, while a 'Neilson' 0-6-0 goods engine also had a daily evening passenger turn; another 0-6-0 type known as the 'Ilfracombe Goods' handled the freight traffic. The well tank was transferred to Wadebridge in 1898 where it became one of the legendary trio that worked the Wenfordbridge branch until 1962.

By the turn of the century the 'O2s' were dominating Exmouth services and proved to be well-suited to the work; they were also the heaviest locos allowed on the branch as a viaduct over the River Clyst south of Topsham was considered unsuitable for anything larger. However, in 1932 'M7' Class 0-4-4Ts were authorised and began to take over most of the passenger work; restrictions on the Topsham Quay branch meant that an 'O2' continued to work there until it closed in 1957, and only 'O2s' were allowed over the Odam's siding. It was also the largest type permitted to Exmouth Docks until 1957, when Ivatt Class 2 2-6-2Ts were allowed. In 1946 'West Country' 'Pacific' No 21C115 *Exmouth* was named in the town, but it had to get there via the 'other' line via Sidmouth Junction due to the viaduct restrictions.

In the summer of 1948, the first after nationalisation, 23 down trains and 24 up trains were scheduled on weekdays, with 13 each way on Sundays. In the following year a summer Saturdays through train from Exmouth to Manchester was introduced; it was formed of London Midland Region stock and routed via Exeter, where it transferred to Western Region (WR) metals at St David's; despite nationalisation, old company rivalries prevailed and BR's Southern Region (SR) timetable showed it as an Exmouth to Central working, while the WR one had it as a St David's to Manchester train! The 1958 SR timetable finally showed it running through to St David's, but it was not until after the WR had control of the branch in 1963 that the train was finally fully described. An observer in 1953 reported that the ten LMR coaches were stabled at Exmouth from Monday onwards, and on the Saturday they were used on the 8.10am train to Exeter hauled by an 'M7' tank; two coaches were detached at Central station and the remainder returned as the 8.50am to Exmouth. The Manchester service left at 9.22am and at Central the 'M7' gave way to the WR 4-6-0 engine, usually a 'Hall', and the two coaches we reattached. The service continued until the summer of 1967, but presumably a severe 'rationalisation' of facilities at Exmouth early in 1968 precluded its operation afterwards.

'Warship' No D860 *Victorious* is passing Polsloe Bridge Halt on 15 July 1967 with the 09.50 Saturdays-only Exmouth to Manchester Piccadilly service in the final summer of the train's operation. *R. A. Lumber*

Since 1968 any locomotive workings to Exmouth have had to be 'top-and-tailed'. Here 'Crompton' No 33042 is leading the Chipman's weed-killing train into Topsham on Sunday 1 May 1983, with No 47205 on the rear, which will lead on the return journey from Exmouth. *C. M. Parsons*

In July 1952 Exmouth Junction's tank engine fleet was modernised with the arrival of brand-new Ivatt Class 2 2-6-2Ts Nos 41313-15 and BR Standard Class 3 2-6-2Ts Nos 82010-13, with more of each type to follow. On 23 July No 41314 ran a series of trials between Exeter and Exmouth hauling seven coaches, the maximum permitted owing to the platform lengths at the intermediate stations. It was not found to be a noticeable improvement, but No 82011 did prove superior in similar trials, and by October it was reported that

The Exmouth branch

On Saturday 25 January 1986 Class 118 DMU set No P469 is leaving Polsloe Bridge Halt forming the 10.55 Exmouth to Barnstaple service. *DHM*

Nos 82010/11/13/17/18 were hauling most of the branch trains with occasional assistance from No 41314 and five remaining 'M7s'. Until this time the trains usually comprised elderly LSWR non-corridor carriages, but the coaching stock was also being modernised with new BR suburban vehicles appearing. On 10 August 1952 No 82013 hauled a ten-coach Royal Marines special to Exmouth, presumably in connection with a Marine base that had been established between Exton and Lympstone in 1940. An observer's report during the summer of 1953 commended the punctuality of the service and cleanliness of the stock. The trains ran about hourly and half-hourly at peak times, when they were often crowded; this was no doubt helped by a return fare between Exeter and Exmouth of 1s 8d, against 2 shillings by bus. Most of the peak workings comprised seven-coach trains hauled by the BR Standard tanks.

On weekdays in the summer of 1958 there were 30 down trains from Exeter Central, with the first leaving at 6.45am and the last at 11.10pm, but only seven were scheduled to stop at St James Park. Frequency varied during the day, but most left at about half-hourly intervals with a gap of between 45 and 61 minutes in quieter periods. There was also a lunchtime train for commuters that left Central at 1.25pm and only went as far as Topsham. Seventeen trains ran from Central on Sundays with an additional departure from Polsloe Bridge at 2.10pm that preceded the 2.15pm from Central to cater for heavy day trip traffic; in the opposite direction there were 31 up trains on weekdays and 18 on Sundays. From January 1960 an additional non-stop working was introduced from Exeter at 5.45pm that reached Exmouth in just 19 minutes; after arrival it then continued to Budleigh Salterton. After Exmouth Junction acquired its first ex-WR pannier tank in 1959 the type was trialled on the branch, and from February 1960, when one was used as a pilot at Central, part of its duties included a morning round passenger trip to Exmouth. The viaduct over the River Clyst was replaced in 1960 and all classes previously allowed to work as far as Topsham were now permitted to Exmouth, including the Bulleid 'Light Pacifics'. From May 1962 this also included BR Standard Class 4 2-6-4Ts after 12 of the class were transferred to Exmouth Junction to replace the BR Class 3 2-6-2Ts.

Following the SR's successful introduction of diesel-electric multiple units (DEMUs) on parts of its non-electrified territory under the 'Modernisation Plan', consideration was given to extending the range of these units. In a Memorandum to the Southern Area Board dated 29 October 1958 various proposals were set out including the following 'East Devon Scheme':

'Detailed study is being given to proposals for replacing the existing Exeter to Exmouth standard interval steam service and the Exeter to Tipton St John's steam trains by DEMUs. Originally the rolling stock requirements were estimated at 12 x 3-car units, but these have lately been re-estimated at 10 x 3-car units. The probable target date is in the winter of 1960 or summer of 1961. The existing steam service is however reasonable and unless the commercial prospects to be opened up are unusually attractive, the dieselisation scheme may have to be postponed for consideration in association with electrification of the main Waterloo to Exeter route.'

Further items for consideration included the form that such electrification would take, and it was thought that 'a proportion of DEMUs, or railcars, could be employed on the Seaton and Sidmouth branches'. It was proposed that a new DEMU depot would be constructed in the 'V' of the junction at Exmouth Junction on the site of the down goods yard. A year later the scheme was still alive and it was thought that, as the previous DEMU schemes had resulted in additional business, the frequency of trains could be increased to 20 minutes each way; to achieve this an island platform would be built at Exton, which would become a passing place. The possibility of absorbing the WR service from Exeter to Tiverton into the scheme was also raised. None of this was to materialise, however, and the scheme was deferred indefinitely, possibly due to BR's ever worsening financial position or perhaps due to the SR realising that it would be rid of the matter with the transfer of these lines to the WR!

When control of the Southern's territory in the West passed to the WR in 1963, the Exmouth branch's fortunes were fading; in 1959 1.5 million journeys had been made, but this had shrunk to half a million in 1962. Although many lines were suffering from road competition, this dramatic decline was surprising as the branch's stations were well-situated and journey times by rail were faster than by bus. The branch still had substantial peak-hour traffic with about 1,000 season ticket holders, but this was offset by a diminishing off-peak patronage for most of the year. However, it was still a surprise to most when it was recommended for closure in Dr Beeching's 'Reshaping' report; in 1962 its receipts were £110,000, but the costs of the operation were estimated to be £205,000, which meant a loss £95,000 (equivalent to more £2 million at 2020 values). No doubt much of this loss can be attributed to it being unmodernised and overmanned and still totally steam-operated.

This was to change under the new regime and a three-car Class 120 'Cross-Country' diesel multiple unit (DMU) made two trial trips over the branch on 12 June 1963. From 15 July 12 weekday workings each way were operated by DMUs, and

Digby & Sowton station was under construction when viewed from Apple Lane on 12 March 1995. Nos 158865 and 153327 are passing as the 13.22 Exeter St David's to Exmouth service. DHM

on the first day another Class 120 set was seen working the 12.45pm from Exeter Central, while a four-car Class 120/122 combination operated the 12.15pm departure from Exmouth; steam workings that day included No 41320 on the 12.45pm from Exmouth and No 80040 on the 1.15pm from Exeter Central. Diesel operation was fully implemented at the start of the winter timetable on 9 September, other than one daily steam turn each way, and Exmouth's sub-shed was closed from 4 November 1963. Initially the timetable remained much as before, but a few trains now worked through to St David's and certain diagrams took the DMUs further afield to Kingswear and Plymouth; subsequently, to maximise the use of both crews and trains, further through workings were diagrammed to other destinations. This was overdue, as previously anyone travelling from Exmouth to, say, Dawlish had to change trains twice in Exeter, but it would still be many years before most trains ran through between these routes. In the winter 1964 timetable some off-peak Exmouth trains were pruned to further save costs, and there were now 25 down and 27 up trains; other economies included de-staffing Polsloe Bridge, Exton and Lympstone stations in 1965.

A steam-powered weekday goods train continued to run from Exmouth Junction until May 1965, at which time the turn was dieselised using 'D63XX' Type 2 locos. After Exmouth Junction yard closed in January 1966 a thrice-weekly train operated from Riverside yard until 4 December 1967, when general freight services over the branch ended.

The Exmouth branch

In the 1980s and 1990s 'Leave specials' were organised about three times a year from Lympstone Commando station for recruits at the Marines base; at first they were locomotive-hauled but latterly HST sets were used. On 27 March 1997 Nos 43065 and 43123 are descending away from the camera at Thornpark Rise as they head towards Polsloe Bridge, which is just visible in the distance; high security meant that details of these trains were difficult to obtain, but it is understood that this one was bound for York. *DHM*

Topsham was absorbed into the city of Exeter in 1966. By the start of the winter timetable that year the weekday service comprised 19 down and 18 up trains, with 14 services running each way on Saturdays, and just five on Sundays. BR did not deny that some reasonably well-loaded services had been removed, but insisted that the line was still barely profitable and redrafting the timetable meant that the underutilisation of DMUs and crews had been eliminated; this does appear to have quelled any further thoughts of closure. The 'other' branch from Sidmouth Junction did, however, succumb on 6 March 1967, and Exmouth signal box closed on 10 March 1968 when all trackwork at the terminus was removed apart from a single line running into Platform 4; there were no run-round facilities, and since then any loco-hauled trains have had to be top-and-tailed over the branch. Staffing at Topsham ceased in May 1968 and the period of retrenchment was completed in 1973 when the line between Exmouth Junction and Topsham was singled, but with double track retained at the latter place to provide the only crossing point on the branch.

On weekdays in the May 1970 timetable there were 20 trains in each direction including an up morning 'express' service for commuters that only stopped at Topsham; at this time only six down and eight up trains stopped at St James Park. During the summer there were 25 trains on Saturdays, but this reduced to 16 in the winter. Similarly peak summer Sundays saw a service of 12 trains, but there were only seven at other times, and on Sundays from December to March there was no service at all.

A relief road was planned to run through part of the largely derelict Exmouth station site, including over the land occupied by the remaining platform; this involved the demolition of the station buildings. Devon County Council funded a new terminus, set back 80 yards from the old one., which formed part of a transport interchange. The running line was slewed into a 'new' platform, a shortened section of the original Platform 2, and the new station was opened on 2 May 1976. The next day Lympstone Commando station was opened between Exton and Lympstone stations for the exclusive use of staff and recruits at the Royal Marines Commando Training Centre, the principal training base for the Marines in the UK. Other than the morning 'express' train, all the 20 weekday services were now scheduled to stop at both Lympstone Commando and St James Park. By then most of the other trains (12 down and 14 up) were running through to St David's rather than terminating at Central station, and two services in each direction ran to Barnstaple. At that time there were still no Sunday trains in the depths of winter, but in the 1978-79 timetable a service of six Sunday afternoon/evening trains was reinstated throughout the winter timetable.

Since DMU operations had started, various classes of BR's 'first generation' units had been used on the branch, including Classes 116, 117, 120, 121 and 122, but by the mid-1980s most services were worked by a fleet of 13 1960-vintage Class 118 units allocated to Plymouth Laira depot. Local

On 25 February 1998 'Sprinter' No 150219 is joining the main line at Exmouth Junction forming the 10.24 Exmouth to Barnstaple service; on the left Nos 37156 and 37711 are reversing the second portion of their stone 'dust' train into the yard. *DHM*

services were the poor relations within BR and had received little investment and had only survived by receiving financial support from the Government; however, BR was now in its 'sectorisation' period and these services came within a new Provincial Sector, with a dedicated management intent on revitalising the business. Most of its rolling stock was life-expired and, with little finance available, fleet modernisation was initially achieved by the introduction of the 'Pacer' classes on a 'needs must' basis. They were low-cost railbuses that were intended as a short-term solution with an expected lifespan of no more than 20 years; the Class 142 variant had a body based on a Leyland National bus on top of a long-wheelbase four-wheel chassis. At the end of 1985 13 of these £350,000 two-car units were allocated to Laira and were marketed locally as 'Skippers'; they were delivered in a supposed GWR-style livery, which rather than 'chocolate and cream' has been described as being 'muddy brown and spilt semi-skimmed milk'! On 15 October No 142015 was observed undertaking driver training on the Exmouth branch, and the units were then gradually introduced into service, the first recorded use of one being on 27 November. From 7 April 1986 three 'Skipper' diagrams were introduced between Exmouth and Barnstaple, and from 12 May a new Class 142-based timetable was introduced on the Exmouth branch with 28 services (previously 20) on weekdays and Saturdays, and a Sunday service of 13 trains, which included some morning trains. All bar one service each way now ran through to St David's.

Unfortunately as each vehicle rode on two axles rather than bogies their long wheelbase soon caused heavy flange wear on the tight curves of some Cornish branches and adhesion problems were encountered on the more steeply graded lines. There were also problems with their transmissions and folding doors, and they were therefore withdrawn from several Cornish lines in August 1986. Although they could have continued on the Exmouth and Barnstaple branches, it was decided to banish them to the north, where they joined the rest of the type; they departed between August and December 1987 and were replaced by 'heritage' DMUs including vehicles from Classes 101 and 108, which arrived from the Midland and Eastern Regions. Although their brief sojourn was unsuccessful, at the time of writing the 'Skippers' remain the only brand-new units to have operated Exmouth branch services, as every other type both before and since has been a 'hand-me-down' that has worked elsewhere. The Provincial Sector also acquired a new generation of DMUs of a more traditional design and eventually units from Classes 150, 153, 155 and 158 were used on Exmouth services, the transformation being completed in 1992.

On 23 May 1995 Digby & Sowton station was opened 380 yards south of the site of the old Clyst St Mary & Digby Halt; it was funded by Devon County Council and Tesco, which has a superstore nearby. Initially it mainly served the Sowton trading estate, but later the closed Digby psychiatric hospital was converted into residential use and its extensive grounds were redeveloped for housing; the station is currently the second busiest on the branch.

In the run-up to privatisation the Regional Railways network was divided into Train Operating Units, each of which was franchised out separately. The lines in the West were part of the Wales & West TOU, which was secured by Prism Rail in October 1996, but soon cutbacks were introduced after the new operator found that it had overbid for the franchise and was losing money. When it was decided to have a discrete Welsh operation in 2001, a Wessex

The Exmouth branch

The privatisation era has seen many colourful liveries on the branch, not least on those DMUs sub-leased from other TOCs. ScotRail's No 158741 worked for FGW for a while and is seen at Topsham as the 14.50 Exeter St David's to Exmouth service on 26 April 2006; it is crossing Wessex Trains-liveried No 150238 forming the 14.54 Exmouth to Paignton service. *DHM*

franchise was created to run local services in the West; the new operators were based in Exeter and worked to build community support for the railway. It was envisaged that the Waterloo to Exeter route would be incorporated into the franchise, but although some planning was done it fell by the wayside when changes at the Strategic Rail Authority (SRA) led to a desired reduction in the number of Train Operating Companies (TOCs). Then in a review of the rail industry, the SRA was itself dissolved and a unit of the Department for Transport assumed its role and created a combined Greater Western franchise by merging the First Great Western, Thames Trains and Wessex Trains operations; the contract was awarded to First Group and the Wessex operation transferred to First Great Western (FGW) on 1 April 2006.

It soon became apparent that this date was highly appropriate as, in an attempt to cut costs, the DfT had specified an unrealistically small train fleet for the new franchise's services; thereafter FGW struggled to have sufficient DMUs, and units had to be sub-leased from other TOCs. Less welcome to the travelling public was the return of the 'Pacer' when 12 Class 142 units were leased from Northern Rail and arrived at Exeter towards the end of 2007, partly to cover for the refurbishment of FGW's 'Sprinter' fleet; they had, however, all returned north by the end of 2011.

Less than a mile south of Digby & Sowton another new station named Newcourt was opened on 4 June 2015 to serve developments on land previously occupied by a Royal Naval Stores Depot. In 2006 the Exeter Chiefs rugby club relocated from its previous ground in St Thomas to a new stadium at Sandy Park, and since the 2010-11 Season the team has been playing in the Premiership, the top flight of the English RFU league system. Crowds have grown substantially, but, with no parking at the stadium, supporters mainly use public transport including the Exmouth branch; Digby & Sowton is a less than 10-minute walk from Sandy Park, and Newcourt station is about 15 minutes away. In 2015 there were 32 services each way between Exeter and Exmouth from Mondays to Saturdays, with most trains running alternately to or from either Barnstaple or Paignton; on Sundays there were 22 trains, reducing in the winter to 16 from December to May.

At that time each train usually comprised a two-car unit, either a Class 143 'Pacer' or 150/2 'Sprinter', with some assistance from some Class 150/1 DMUs and single-car Class 153 units. The increasing popularity of local services around Exeter meant that there were insufficient DMUs to cater for the demand, not least on the Exmouth branch, where passengers often had to stand at peak commuting times. However, the electrification of FGW services in the London area permitted the cascade of some DMUs to Bristol, and in turn additional Class 150/2 units were then released to work in Devon to replace the Class 150/1 and 153 units. In a major revamp of the timetable in December 2019 the service between Exmouth and Paignton was doubled in frequency and a separate service was introduced between St James Park and Barnstaple. Trains from Exmouth were scheduled for either two Class 150/2 units or a 143/150 combination; 12 months

Most of the trackwork on the branch has been renewed this century. On 20 February 2008 work was being undertaken between Polsloe Bridge and Hill Barton, and No 66176 (tailed by No 66119) is hauling 15 Autoballaster wagons as the 06.13 train from Westbury. *DHM*

Newcourt station opened on 4 June 2015 and 'Pacers' Nos 143618 and 143619 are stopping with the 12.43 Barnstaple to Exmouth service on the first day. The Exeter Chiefs' Sandy Park rugby stadium can be seen in the distance from the platform but is out of view to the right of this photo; Digby & Sowton station is slightly closer to the ground, but to help train capacity on match days services to Exmouth do not pick up passengers at Digby & Sowton immediately after a game and supporters heading in that direction are advised to use Newcourt instead. *DHM*

The Exmouth branch

later the 143s were finally withdrawn after a service of 35 years – 15 more than originally intended. One of the seven daily diagrams on the Exmouth to Paignton circuit was then scheduled for a three-car Class 166 'Turbo' DMU, and at the time of writing three of these former Thames trains are usually employed on the service.

The Exmouth line is currently the busiest branch in the South West and, prior to the Covid pandemic, had an estimated 1.7 million journeys a year; the greater Exmouth area is home to about 50,000 people, and in addition to being the busiest station on the branch Exmouth is the fifth busiest in all of Devon. As there is only one crossing point on the branch, currently trains only stop hourly at St James Park, Polsloe Bridge, Exton and Lympstone Commando stations to allow some latitude in the timetable, and the latter two stations are request stops.

Just south of Topsham the River Clyst delineates the Exeter city boundary, and on 16 July 2021 No 166216 is crossing the 114-yard-long five-span Clyst Viaduct forming the 08.15 Paignton to Exmouth service; the previous viaduct was located on the other side of this 1960 replacement. Despite having been taken out of use in 1940, the course of the 500-yard-long siding to Odam's manure and chemical works can easily be traced a short distance behind the camera. From here the Exmouth branch follows the Exe estuary, giving some fine views from the train; the estuary is of international importance for wintering waders and wildfowl, and the branch is marketed as 'The Avocet Line'. *DHM*

4. The Exe and Teign Valley lines

The Exe Valley line

Although the branch junction was actually at Stoke Canon, the terminus for services over the Exe Valley line was at Exeter St David's and trains had to hurry over the main line for 3½ miles before joining the branch. When the Bristol & Exeter Railway was built, Tiverton was an important market town that owed much of its prosperity to the wool trade. Despite this the B&E decided to bypass it by using a route along the Culm Valley, which was not only shorter but also on an almost continuous gently falling gradient, whereas a route via Tiverton would have crossed undulating countryside that would have needed expensive engineering work. A connection to Tiverton was, however, essential and a branch was planned from the outset, making it one of the very first such lines in Britain. The 4¾-mile broad gauge branch from Tiverton Junction was opened in 1848 and was converted to standard gauge in 1884 to connect with the independent Tiverton & North Devon Railway, which opened north from Tiverton to Morebath Junction on the GWR's Taunton to Barnstaple line in August of that year; there was no station at Morebath and branch trains actually terminated at Dulverton.

The branch from Tiverton Junction was fine for travellers to London or Bristol, but it was a circuitous journey for anyone wishing to reach the county town of Exeter. The Exe Valley Railway received its Act in 1874 to build a direct line, but after its powers were taken over by the B&E nothing had been done to build the line by the time the B&E was absorbed by the GWR. It was eventually opened on 1 May 1885 when the whole route from Stoke Canon to Dulverton was worked by the GWR, although the Tiverton & North Devon Railway remained a separate company until 1894. The original B&E station at Stoke Canon was east of the junction, so could not be used by branch trains, but a replacement was opened at the junction in July 1894.

In 1885 a weekday service of five trains ran each way between Exeter and Dulverton, and apart from one mixed passenger and goods working the 24¾-mile journey took 70 minutes; a sixth train operated from Exeter to Tiverton and back. The volume of freight traffic meant that a separate goods train had to be introduced, but otherwise this service remained constant until the First World War, when it was cut to four trains each way as an economy measure, although an additional service ran on Friday evenings to cater for people returning from market day in Exeter and for boarding school children going home for the weekend. When auto-trains were

On a crisp 9 December 1961 0-4-2T No 1471 is rushing over the main line towards Cowley Bridge Junction with the 11.40am Exeter St David's to Dulverton Exe Valley service. Peter W. Gray

introduced in 1923 there were six through trains each way with an additional working from Exeter to Tiverton Junction via Tiverton. It was only the start of a Devon General bus service that prompted an improvement in the timetable, and in 1926 a Sunday service was finally introduced, albeit at first just two trains each way. From July 1928 12 trains ran from Exeter each weekday, eight to Dulverton and four to Tiverton and Tiverton Junction; there were three departures to Tiverton on Sundays with an additional train from Tiverton catering for day-trippers to the coast.

As on many rural railways, goods traffic generated much of the line's revenue and a daily goods train would depart from Exeter each weekday morning with wagons off overnight freights, and would call at those branch stations with a goods yard; this did not include Stoke Canon, which was served by a main-line 'pick-up' goods train. The branch goods returned from Dulverton after lunch and a fresh crew at Tiverton would spend the afternoon shunting before working a train to Tiverton Junction. After returning light, the loco then departed from Tiverton in the early evening with the return goods to Exeter.

When the Exe Valley line opened, passenger services usually consisted of three or four short-wheelbase coaches pulled by Armstrong '517' Class 0-4-2Ts. From about 1923 auto-trailers were introduced, and from 1932 the '517s' were superseded by new '48XX' Class 0-4-2Ts. This type then monopolised the passenger service until the late 1950s, but by then there was a shortage of auto-trailers after many of the older vehicles had been withdrawn, and pannier tanks were also used, hauling conventional stock. New auto-trailers

The Exe and Teign Valley lines

were built in 1954 to help alleviate the shortage and two of these were used on the line. For a long period goods trains were usually hauled by 0-6-0STs, but from about 1929 these were replaced by pannier tanks. Occasionally 'Prairie' tanks could be seen on both passenger and goods workings; on Saturday 18 July 1953 No 5522 was recorded on the 5.55pm Exeter to Dulverton service, which consisted of two auto-trailers with about 150 passengers on board. A most unusual visitor to the line on 5 March that year was a 'West Country' 'Pacific', which made a trial run from Exeter to Barnstaple via Tiverton and Dulverton to see whether diversions could use the route should the SR line to Barnstaple be unavailable.

In the 1950s road competition seriously affected the freight business, and as early as 1954 the daily through goods working to Dulverton ceased with the train now only running as far as Tiverton. Traffic continued to dwindle and by 1962 the goods train from Exeter only ran 'as required',

The usual home for Exe Valley services at St David's station was the east end bay Platform 2, and No 1466 is about to leave from there with the 3.20pm departure to Dulverton in 1961. This engine was secured for preservation by the Great Western Society in 1964. *B. B. Williams*

Some Exe Valley services only ran as far as Bampton, and the 3.30pm departure from there is being propelled by No 1470 into Platform 2 on 30 May 1961.

mainly for grain traffic to a mill at Thorverton. The line was still fairly well used by passengers, but numbers were declining, in part due to a parallel bus service.

Closure was already proposed before the 'Beeching Report' was published in March 1963 and the final passenger services ran on 5 October of that year; there had been no real attempt to make the operation more economic, it was labour-intensive including the employment of several crossing keepers, and although there was an occasional sighting of a DMU on summer Saturdays in 1963 on through diagrams from Exmouth, the branch otherwise remained steam-only until the very last day, when the trains comprised up to six corridor coaches hauled by Type 2 diesels to cater for the expected crowds. The branch from Tiverton Junction survived for a further year, and the rails from Stoke Canon to Thorverton were retained for the grain traffic until it ceased in 1966 and this final section closed in November of that year.

The Teign Valley line

The Teign Valley line had its origins in the railway boom of the 19th century when even small towns thought that they had to have a railway connection to avoid decline. The first section of more than 6 miles, opened in October 1882, was the rump of a more grandiose scheme for a railway that would penetrate sparsely populated central Devon; it ran from Heathfield on the Moretonhampstead branch to the village of Ashton, with a goods-only extension to Teign House Siding, which was named after an inn and was near the site of the later Christow station. When the line was first proposed the valley was in a lead-mining boom and it was expected that the railway would benefit from a good amount of freight traffic; however, due to a long gestation period the boom had actually ended before the line opened, and even at the time there were doubts that it would succeed with such a limited traffic potential. Although the GWR worked the new railway there was a complication as the Teign Valley Railway was standard gauge whereas the Moretonhampstead line remained broad gauge until May 1892; thus the new line operated in isolation with its own rolling stock and an engine shed at Ashton. The first timetable had four trains each way that were timed to connect with Moretonhampstead trains at Heathfield; there was never a Sunday service.

Although it was intended to extend the line the 8 miles from Christow to Exeter, this could not be undertaken by the impecunious TVR and eventually this was built by a separate company, the Exeter Railway. The route left the river valley soon after Christow and climbed through the Haldon Hills over gradients as steep as 1 in 56, which required considerable earthworks including two tunnels. With persistent financial problems the extension took more than eight years to build and was not opened until 1 July 1903; in Exeter it joined the main line just south of St Thomas station at Exeter Railway Junction, and passenger trains then ran through to St David's. The only crossing place was at Christow.

The GWR operated the 16-mile line on behalf of the two owning companies, but there was little agreement as to the level of service provided; the promoters of the Exeter Railway had certain expectations, but had failed to enter detailed discussions with the GWR prior to opening and there was disharmony between the parties for several years. Five trains ran each way between Exeter and Heathfield until the First World War, but from 1904 to 1911 three additional Exeter to Christow trains were also introduced for 'political' purposes rather than traffic need. By the end of the war the service was down to just three trains in each direction.

It is thought that '517' Class 0-4-2Ts worked all of the passenger trains from 1882, but in 1904 the GWR drew up plans for a more frequent service using steam railmotors; this was vetoed by the Exeter company, which apparently regarded the motors as not being 'proper' trains! However, a railmotor trip was added in 1920 to fill in a long afternoon gap in the timetable, and by 1923 a second motor duty had been added, thus restoring the service to five trains.

The two companies were absorbed by the GWR in the 1923 'Grouping' and from October of that year all trains were either auto or motor operated, which reduced costs and allowed for an improved service. From 1923 until their withdrawal in 1935 the branch was regularly

During the first few decades of the 20th century Exeter shed had an allocation of steam railmotors, which were vehicles with a vertical boiler over a power bogie at one end, with the guard and passenger seating taking up the rest. At first they were used between Exeter and Teignmouth on local services, but were later mainly used on the Teign Valley line. In the late 1920s No 77 was based in Exeter and was observed on Teign Valley services.

The Exe and Teign Valley lines

operated by motors, and by 1927 there were seven daily trains over the full length of the line. A report in 1931 advised that 0-4-2T No 847, 2-6-2Ts Nos 4530 and 4577 and railmotors Nos 92 and 97 were seen on the line. In an attempt to combat bus competition three halts were also opened in that decade.

The original hopes regarding freight traffic were finally realised in the early 1900s when a number of quarries were established in the Trusham and Christow areas. These produced a stone highly suited for use as roadstone chippings, and it was dispatched by rail to markets throughout southern England; the GWR also took large amounts for railway ballast. This traffic was often routed via Heathfield, presumably due to the steep gradients at the Exeter end of the line, although in 1924 a 6.55pm stone train from Trusham to Exeter was timetabled. It is likely that this period was the only time that the line was close to being profitable, but the boom came to an end in the early 1930s when most of the quarries closed after either becoming exhausted or succumbing to competition from elsewhere.

Passenger numbers were never high and a survey compiled in the line's first year revealed that there was an average of only 16 people on each train. Chudleigh was the largest town served, but for all of the line's existence its population was probably less than 3,000; additionally its station was outside the town and the establishment of a Devon General bus service in 1919 quickly took away most of its business. Other stations were also some distance from the villages that they purported to serve and it was only at a handful of places, where no one considered it worth providing a bus service, that the already meagre passenger numbers managed to hold up. However, car ownership then affected the patronage at even those stations, and the GWR considered withdrawing the passenger service in 1930; in the event this did not happen, possibly due to the need to maintain the line to passenger standards in case it was needed for emergency diversions.

It was only after the sea had undermined the wall at Dawlish in 1916 that the GWR actively considered using the route for diversions, and a direct connection with the Moretonhampstead branch was finally provided at Heathfield; other work included replacing some timber bridges to permit heavier trains. Subsequently the line was occasionally used for diversions in the event of accidents, cliff falls or breaches in the sea wall; Plymouth and Cornish traffic was, however, usually sent by the SR route via Okehampton as it was more suitable for main-line trains. Due to restrictions over the Teign Valley route, in the 1920s any diversions were normally double-headed by two '45XX' Class 2-6-2Ts, but by 1930 'Bulldog' Class 4-4-0s had been authorised and four of these were loaned by Reading shed to Exeter in January of that year when the sea wall was damaged and the main line was closed for three weeks. Trains diverted over the Teign Valley included the down sleeper and newspaper trains and the 'Torbay Limited'; other trains, including the up and down 'Cornish Riviera Limited', ran via the SR.

During the Second World War there was concern that the coastal main line would be vulnerable to enemy action, particularly as it was the main supply route to the dockyard and naval base in Plymouth, and further works were undertaken including upgrading track and adding an emergency loop at Longdown. '43XX' Class 2-6-0s and 'Manor' 4-6-0s were also authorised subject to speed limits of 25mph and 20mph respectively. In the event as far as is known no diversions were actually needed, but after D-Day ambulance trains operated to Chudleigh station to convey wounded to an American Military Hospital.

With closure already planned, in the September 1957 timetable most Teign Valley services ran through to Newton Abbot rather than Heathfield; all trains consisted of two ordinary coaches and for the first time a Newton Abbot loco and train handled half the workings. The 4.35pm departure from St David's still only ran as far as Heathfield, though, and on Monday 10 February 1958 Exeter's 0-6-0PT No 9629 is leaving from Platform 6 with this train; Teign Valley departures normally used Platform 1, but could also use this one. *Peter W. Gray*

On the following Saturday 0-4-2T No 1451 is standing at Platform 5 at St David's, the usual one for Teign Valley arrivals, with the 12.40pm service from Newton Abbot. Although not advertised as such, this train would then continue to Bampton. Over the years there was a limited amount of through running over the two branches, but this appears to have been more a matter of operating convenience than anything, as the services were always shown separately in the timetables. *B. B. Williams*

After leaving Alphington Halt trains from Exeter had a stiff climb for more than a mile, mainly at a gradient of 1 in 58, before reaching the village of Ide, which is just outside the city boundary; after a brief respite there was then a similarly graded climb for almost 3 miles to Longdown. On 7 June 1958, the final day for passenger services, 'Prairie' tank No 5530 is leaving Ide Halt with the 12.45pm Exeter to Newton Abbot train, its normal two-coach load strengthened with the addition of three ex-LMS coaches. This station was never very busy and the position of station master was abolished in 1923 when staffing was reduced to a porter on an early turn. With daily passengers numbering about ten a day, the station was de-staffed altogether in March 1955 and the theoretical goods facilities were also withdrawn, no goods trains having actually been timetabled east of Christow since 1947. The photographer is standing on the site of the station's lifted loop siding. *B. B. Williams*

When the Teign Valley line was closed, about three-quarters of a mile of track was retained at the Exeter end for freight traffic. On 5 August 1995 power car No 43190 is seen from the site of Alphington Road goods yard as it leads the 14.01 Paignton to Paddington HST past Exeter Railway Junction. No 60036 *Sgurr Na Ciche* is waiting to follow with 6B19, the 15.00 Exeter City Basin to Cardiff Tidal Yard scrap metal train. *DHM*

The Exe and Teign Valley lines

After the railmotors were withdrawn in 1935 passenger services were usually auto-trains hauled by '48XX' Class 0-4-2Ts, although it was reported in 1939 that an Exeter '45XX' Class engine regularly worked the 4.28pm to Heathfield and 6.20pm return. In the 1950s other steam classes, including '54XX' and '57XX' pannier tanks, appeared on Teign Valley services; trains were still diagrammed for auto operation but as the latter class was not so fitted they could be used on conventional stock. In later years an auto-train made four round trips each weekday between Exeter and Heathfield (one extended to Newton Abbot), with an additional morning round trip from Exeter to Christow and an evening run to Heathfield, both scheduled for a pannier tank and one coach. There were a couple of extra trips on Saturdays.

With restrictions on private transport during the war there was an increase in both passenger and goods traffic, but by 1949 there had been a dramatic fall in patronage, probably due to the end of petrol rationing that year. There was presumably a further small decline from the 1951 summer timetable when three Saturday morning services were terminated at Alphington Halt to ease a peak congestion period over the main line to St David's station; an Exeter Corporation bus connection was provided between the two stations, but 'heavy luggage was not conveyed'! Cuts in the 1930s had left the line with daily Exeter to Trusham and Newton Abbot to Christow goods services, but the former was cut back to Christow in about 1941 and withdrawn in 1947. In 1955 the remaining Newton Abbot to Christow goods train only ran on three days each week.

When the WR was contemplating closures to reduce its losses, it was no surprise that the Teign Valley line was near the top of the list as, according to press reports in 1957, it was losing £15,000 a year. Ironically, despite talk of closure, a more sensible service was introduced in the winter 1957 timetable with five round trips, and most trains now ran through to Newton Abbot for the first time. Two train sets of two ordinary corridor coaches were used, one set based at Exeter and the other at Newton Abbot – they were scheduled to cross at Christow – and there was an additional Saturday evening train. The line's fate was, however, sealed and it was scheduled for closure from 3 March 1958; this was postponed due to opposition to the proposed replacement bus service, and the final passenger trains ran three months later on 7 June.

5. Signalling and signal boxes

The 'Western' route

At first signalling was based on a time-interval philosophy and trains were not allowed to depart until a predetermined time had passed after the departure of the previous one; permission to leave was given manually by a railway 'policeman' (thereafter signalmen were often referred to as 'Bobbies'), who would hold his arms in different positions to indicate whether a train should stop, proceed at caution or if it was clear to go.

By the time that the Bristol & Exeter Railway opened, Brunel's 'disc-and-crossbar' signals were widely used and became standard on the broad gauge lines. This type of signal comprised a tall mast with a large disc at the top to show that the road was clear. This was the default position and there was a crossbar immediately below and at right angles to the disc to show 'Danger'; the signal was changed by turning it a quarter of a circle by means of a lever at the foot of the mast. A subsidiary 'Flag Signal' or 'Fantail' could also be installed to indicate 'Caution', but these were soon shown to be impractical on the B&E after being shredded by the wind on the Somerset levels, and were replaced by an arrow-shaped wooden board on a revolving post. The signals were operated by a policeman who had a sentry-type box for shelter; all points were also manually operated.

It was not until the 1870s that signal boxes with electric block telegraph instruments for signalling communication from one box to the next were widely introduced on the GWR; they had a row of mechanically interlocked levers in what was known as a frame, and they controlled semaphore signals. Initially the method of operation meant that a line was considered clear unless advised otherwise, and although the signals would be changed to 'stop' after a train had passed, they would be put into a 'clear' position after advice had been received that the train had passed the next box. However, from 1883 a line was considered to be blocked unless the signals were off to show the 'all clear'; when expecting a train a signalman could now ask the next box ahead whether the line was clear before changing his signals. Mechanical interlocking of point and signal levers was also introduced, which meant that a signalman was unable to change a set of points for a conflicting route once he had lowered his signals.

This view of Cowley Bridge Junction in perhaps the 1880s includes the original 16-lever signal cabin and some very tall home signals; there is mixed gauge track on the main line to the right and also running to Crediton on the left. The signalman is standing at the top of the steps with a white flag, possibly to show the line is clear for a down LSWR train. At this time there was also a small LSWR signal cabin, which is hidden by the trees on the left. *GWR*

A replacement Cowley Bridge Junction signal box was opened in 1894, with a 19-lever frame that was increased to 35 levers in August 1942, shortly before a down goods loop was brought into use between Cowley Bridge and St David's. The box was extended by 7 feet at its north end to accommodate a larger frame in 1943 when another nine levers were added for the opening of Riverside Yard; the single-window-length extension can be identified on 16 July 1978, and the off-centre nameboard can also be noted, as this was kept in its original position. *DHM*

Signalling and signal boxes

Table 1: Summary of GWR signal boxes in Exeter						
Mileage (miles.chains)	Name	Box No	Opened	Closed	No of levers
192.53	Cowley Bridge Junction	1	1871	1894	16
Ditto	Ditto	2	1894	30 Mar 1985	19-44
193.40	Exeter Riverside		2 Jul 1943	5 Apr 1981	54
?	Exeter 'D'		1877	1912-13	26-52
193.45	Exeter East	1	1911-13	4 May 1942	52
193.44	Ditto	2	17 June 1942	18 Nov 1973	52
?	Exeter 'C'		1876	1912	32
?	Exeter Middle	1	1911	4 Jul 1914	94
193.62	Ditto	2	4 Jul 1914	30 Mar 1985	105
193.62	Exeter Goods Yard		Feb 1896	27 Feb 1978	5
?	Exeter 'B'		1876	1912-13	16
?	Exeter 'A'		1876	1913	36-55
194.04	Exeter West		1913	6 May 1985	118-131
194.65	St Thomas		1867?	19 Apr 1959	11-15
195.16	Exeter City Basin	2	9 Dec 1962	15 Nov 1986	27
195.19	City Basin Junction	1	1902	9 Dec 1962	33
196.59	Cotfield		Jul 1924?	29 Mar 1964	4

Table 1 lists those signal boxes that were installed on the GWR/WR route through Exeter, working down the line in journey order. The information has been gathered from several sources and these reveal some discrepancies, particularly in the 19th century, so cannot be claimed to be totally accurate. There were four boxes in the vicinity of Exeter St David's that dated from 1876-77 when the first semaphore signals were erected. Working from west to east the boxes were named Exeter 'A' to 'D', but all were replaced during 1913-14 when the station was rebuilt. 'A' box was located on the western side of the station, just to the north of the old atmospheric engine house, 'B' box was at the north end of the central island platform, and 'C' box was just south of Red Cow crossing and on the opposite side of the running lines from the later 'Middle' box. 'D' box was positioned at the east end of the layout at St David's adjacent to a ticket platform. Details of the replacement boxes are provided in the picture captions.

It is unclear when St Thomas became a block post, but it is thought that a small signal box was erected in 1867 within the train shed on the north end of the down station platform, possibly in connection with the opening of the City Basin branch; in about 1893 an 11-lever frame was installed in this cabin. The station was closed for part of the First World War to release staff for other duties and the signal box was closed from 1917 to 1921. The somewhat obscure life of St Thomas box ended on 19 April 1959 when the frame at Exeter West was renewed and its sphere of operation extended to encompass St Thomas.

The goods-only City Basin branch was about half a mile south of St Thomas, and when it opened in 1867 it had a trailing connection with the down main line at City Basin Junction. This was hand-worked with no signalling; there was no connection with the up main line, which meant that both down and up branch trains could only use the down main. When the broad gauge was abandoned in 1892 the GWR had to install interlocking at any remaining non-interlocked locations, including this junction, and a two-lever ground frame was brought into use to operate the branch points and a signal was erected for trains coming off the branch. There was still no crossover at the junction and workings from the branch had to travel over the down line to a crossover at St Thomas station. By the turn of the century this practice was becoming unsustainable and a crossover was installed at the junction in 1901, but was initially unusable as plans to convert the ground frame to a block post were not progressed. Instead in anticipation of the opening of the Exeter Railway from Christow, a timber-built 33-lever frame signal box named City Basin Junction was opened in August 1902 on the up side of the main line between the junctions for the Basin branch and the new Exeter Railway, with the box controlling both junctions. The crossover at City Basin Junction was brought into use and the Basin branch trips no longer had to work 'wrong line' to St Thomas when returning to St David's.

By December 1962 City Basin Junction box was in a poor state of repair and was replaced by a contemporary standard WR box about 50 yards or so to the north, which was given the different name Exeter City Basin. As the Teign Valley line had closed as a through route and other connections had been converted to hand points, a smaller frame from a closed box at Culham near Didcot was installed.

Between the world wars the GWR erected several small signal boxes in Devon solely to increase line capacity by shortening block sections during busy periods. One was opened at Cotfield, about halfway between the boxes at City Basin Junction and Exminster, in July 1924. This basic four-lever affair had previously been at Stratfield on the Reading to Basingstoke branch and was the final box opened by the GWR within the Exeter area; it was closed on 29 March 1964 when reduced traffic levels made these 'break section' boxes redundant.

The new Riverside Yard was provided with a signal box, the basic structure of which was second-hand, having been previously at Hatherley Junction between Gloucester and Cheltenham since 1906. There it housed a 25-lever frame, so presumably the box was enlarged to accommodate the 54-lever frame that it had in Exeter, perhaps only using parts from the original; timber boxes could easily be repurposed. 'Peak' No 129 (later No 45073) is seen from New Yard as it passes the box on 29 September 1973 with 1V62, the 07.04 Derby to Plymouth train. The box was closed on 5 April 1981 with a downturn in freight activity. *DHM*

During the 'Exeter Blitz' on 4 May 1942 two bombs caused some damage to Middle box and extensive damage to East box, and eight railwaymen were killed. The latter box was replaced by a second-hand structure from Milton, near Didcot, which was erected just to the north of its predecessor between the running lines and New Yard, and almost faced Riverside box. Another 'Peak', No 140 (46003), is passing it with 4B10, the 13.30 Bristol to Plymouth parcels train on 25 August 1973 just three months before the box was closed. *C. H. S. Owen*

Signalling and signal boxes

No 47140 is passing the old transhipment shed as it leaves St David's with the 13.36 Penzance to Paddington train on 19 April 1982; the Exeter Middle box down home gantry is on the left, one of a number of gantries in the environs of St David's that made the station an attraction for connoisseurs of mechanical signalling. *DHM*

Normally it was a requirement that the road ahead from one box to the next should be clear for at least 440 yards, but as there were only 360 yards between East and Middle boxes special rules were applied at the latter when permitting a train to approach from the west. On 28 July 1984 'Peak' No 45128 is accelerating past Middle box with 1M08, the 09.24 Paignton to Birmingham New Street summer Saturday train. The Red Cow crossing attendant can be noted to the left of the train in his orange vest; this busy crossing is much used by pedestrians and attendants are still employed today with the position partly funded by the local council. *DHM*

Above: Red Cow level crossing once passed over up to 18 tracks, with ten behind Middle box that included two goods avoiding lines and sidings in the goods yard; this half of the crossing was also known as Exwick crossing. The small five-lever Exeter Goods Yard box was positioned at the west end of the crossing in 1896 to control movements over this part of it, and is seen in July 1971. It was closed on 27 February 1978 when the avoiding lines were taken out of use. *R. A. Lumber*

Above: When work started to rebuild St David's station in 1911 a temporary Middle box was opened at the east end of the station, but as the work neared completion a permanent structure was opened in July 1914. On Saturday 3 August 1957 Newton Abbot's 4-6-0 No 5005 *Manorbier Castle* is monitored by the crossing attendant as it passes the box at 3.39pm (46 minutes late) with train No 708, the 8.17am Carmarthen to Penzance. 'E1/R' 0-6-2T No 32124 is waiting on the banking spur for its next job up to Central. The GWR introduced a scheme for the numbering of all its principal trains in 1935, and 16-inch-high figures were mounted on a 3-foot-wide frame carried on the front of the smokebox. Each train was allocated a three-digit number; the first indicated the train's starting point, while the others were its individual number. This system was particularly useful for signalmen, who could easily identify exactly which train was passing. *Peter W. Gray*

'Merchant Navy' 'Pacific' No 35017 *Belgian Marine* is signalled away from Platform 4 on 23 May 1965 after descending from Exeter Central with a Stephenson Locomotive Society railtour that had started at Birmingham Snow Hill at 8.45am. Another 4-6-2, No 34051 *Winston Churchill*, had worked the circular tour as far as Salisbury, from where the larger Bulleid 'Pacific' took over for the leg to Westbury; from there 4-6-0 No 7029 *Clun Castle* will return the special to Birmingham. The short semaphore signal on the right-hand side of the gantry was later replaced by a disc signal, as seen in the next photo. *R. A. Lumber*

During the last summer for mechanical signalling at St David's, 'Peak' No 45069 is waiting for the road from Platform 5 with the 10.20 SO Paignton to Glasgow train on 21 July 1984. New 'blanked off' colour light signals are already in place and can be glimpsed beyond the semaphores; a contributor to this title, the late Eric Youldon, is standing on the left of a small group of enthusiasts. *C. M. Parsons*

One of the gantries at St David's was positioned on Platforms 3 and 4; 4-6-0 No 5041 *Tiverton Castle* has the road into Platform 1 with a Plymouth train in October 1935 and is passing a scissors crossover which was normally only used for shunting movements. At this time the gantry had five posts that carried 13 arms, the other two visible posts relate to this crossover, the one on the left controlling a movement from the down main' (middle road) to Platform 1 and the other controlling a movement from Platform 1 to the middle road. This is one of two images in this chapter that were taken in October 1935 and are almost certainly among the oldest colour railway photographs taken in Exeter. *D. R. Barber, Colour Rail*

The scissors crossover was taken out on 5 October 1952 and the relevant signal arms were removed; however, the posts remained until the gantry was tidied up in about 1959. Two of the posts were then reduced in size and the down main signals were transferred to the former 'down main to platform 1' crossover post, as seen here on 8 June 1963. 'Castle' No 5070 *Sir Daniel Gooch* is running in with the 10.10am Paddington to Penzance non-stop train. On the left 'Battle of Britain' Class No 34072 *257 Squadron* is waiting to leave from Platform 4 with the 9.00am Waterloo to Ilfracombe service; it will be given the road by lowering a WR semaphore arm, whereas for most of its journey it will be governed by SR upper-quadrant signals. *Peter W. Gray*

'700' Class 0-6-0 No 30317, 'U' Class 2-6-0 No 31610 and 4-6-2 No 34060 *25 Squadron* are blocking three running lines as they pass under the Exeter West home signals with what might seem to be a long 11.35am Plymouth Friary to Waterloo train on 9 August 1958. However, it actually comprised just four carriages and the first two engines had been added to the train at Yeoford after arriving there on 'unbalanced' workings, a goods train from Exeter and the 10.37am Barnstaple Junction to Yeoford passenger train respectively. They are now 'hitching a ride' back to Exmouth Junction shed to save paths. The signals have been marked with the route to which they apply to assist drivers. The 'M' on the middle signal refers to the down main line for WR trains, while the signal partly obscured by the awning was also marked 'To SR' for that Region's trains using the middle road. The signal on the left beneath the gantry is marked 'M' for WR trains leaving Platform 1; for safety reasons the track on this road was set to run into a siding when not required, and trains for the SR were not able to leave from this platform. *Peter W. Gray*

Apparently originally intended to be only a temporary structure, Exeter West box was the largest in the area and was positioned in the 'V' between the SR and WR routes. It controlled the west end of St David's, the entrance to the engine shed, the goods lines and the incline to Central. Despite its size the box usually had just one signalman, with a booking lad to maintain the train register, answer phones and otherwise help in liaising with the men at the four other connecting boxes, Middle, Goods Yard, St Thomas (later City Basin Junction) and Exeter Central 'B'. An extra signalman and inspector would be drafted in on peak summer Saturdays to help maintain order on days that could become quite chaotic. On 16 April 1972 'Warship' No 821 *Greyhound* is arriving with the 07.00 Plymouth to Hayward's Heath Plymouth Railway Circle/Great Western Society 'Bluebell Railtour'. *DHM*

Signalling and signal boxes

Perhaps the most famous of the gantries at St David's was the one for the West box up inner home signals; below the home arms were the distant signals for Middle box, 495 yards away. This gantry evolved over the years as depicted in three photographs; this view, another from October 1935, has 4-6-0 No 4957 *Postlip Hall* passing with a down train. Signal renewals were undertaken at West box in 1937/38 and this gantry was replaced at a cost of £286. *D. R. Barber, Colour Rail*

The replacement gantry was another wooden structure that No D1027 *Western Lancer* is passing with 4B10, the 16.05 Bristol Temple Meads to Plymouth Parcels train on 17 June 1975. The main three signals on the gantry, reading from left to right, related to the up relief (Platform 6), up main (5) and up middle (4) roads. The up main home signal has an operational distant signal, and both arms would be 'off' for a northbound train running non-stop through the station. The two distant signals on either side are fixed and limited the speed of trains approaching their platforms over facing connections. The three very short signals beneath the main arms gave 'calling on' indications to admit an engine or train into a platform that was already occupied. The signal on the far left was for either the engine shed or the up goods avoiding line, and a further signal beyond the gantry determined which of these applied. The second signal from the left was for the carriage sidings that were enclosed between the goods lines and Platform 6; this signal was rarely seen in an 'off' position, as activity over these sidings was usually confined to shunting moves controlled by ground signals. However, for a period on summer Saturdays in the 1950s it was regularly used when a Teign Valley line service terminated at St Thomas and the empty stock continued to St David's where it ran straight into the sidings. *DHM*

On 23 November 1975 the gantry was replaced by a taller tubular metal affair that had just three main posts, and the two short ones were replaced by shunt signals on a separate adjacent post. HST power cars Nos 43035 and 43004 are passing with the 13.45 Paddington to Penzance service on 20 April 1984. *DHM*

Probably due to its location on an embankment and being largely inaccessible, the original 1902 City Basin Junction signal box appears to have been camera-shy, but the replacement 1962 Exeter City Basin box was recorded on 1 December 1984; this design had the derogatory nickname of 'Plywood Wonder'! *R. A. Lumber*

Newport Ebbw Junction-based 'Mogul' No 6370 is nearing St David's as it passes the Exeter West up main intermediate home signal with (probably) the 4.25pm Plymouth Millbay to Paddington Parcels train on 2 May 1959; in the foreground is a 'Limit of Shunt' sign. *R. A. Lumber*

This view from Exeter City Basin box on 26 July 1970 includes Nos D6338 and D6333 as they head west with the 20.10 Exeter St David's to Newton Abbot train. At the time this was the last scheduled passenger duty for the class in Devon, the train comprising the stock off the 15.08 Waterloo to Exeter train. Alphington Road goods yard is on the left. The track from the down main to the down branch was removed in January 1979, and afterwards when accessing the branch any down freight trains had to first reverse over a crossover to the up main line between the junction and St Thomas station. *DHM*

Signalling and signal boxes

Located in open country and accessed through a farm, the tiny intermediate or 'break section' Cotfield signal box was another camera-shy cabin. It was being threatened by flood water when photographed from a passing train in October 1960. *D. J. Frost*

The LSWR/SR route

When the LSWR line was opened, the 121-mile single line from Worting Junction, near Basingstoke, to Exeter was controlled by the telegraph system of single-line working under the charge of the station master at Queen Street. When the line was extended from Queen Street to St David's station, a set of block signalling instruments was trialled, but it was not until the 1870s that the LSWR began to install the absolute block system on its lines, being implemented on the Exeter route in 1875. In the Exeter area signal boxes were erected at Pinhoe and Exmouth Junction, and there were two at Queen Street: 'A' box at the eastern end of the station layout and 'B' box just beyond the east end of the station platforms. In about 1880 'C' box was provided at the west end of the station near the start of the descent to St David's; it was erected on land previously occupied by the down through road.

When work started to rebuild Queen Street station a new 35-lever 'C' box was opened in 1925 next to the west end of the up through platform. In 1927 a new 90-lever 'A' box was erected on the up side at the east end of the station; this replaced the original 'A' and 'B' boxes, and the new 'C' box was then redesignated 'B'. Also that year the frame in Exmouth Junction box was enlarged to take 49 levers due to developments there including the construction of a new engine shed. The two boxes at Queen Street were renamed from 1 July 1933 when the station became Exeter Central; to facilitate the many movements at Central all four roads through the station were signalled for running in either direction.

In the late 1950s the Southern Region started to renew some of its rather ancient signal boxes and the one at Exmouth Junction was replaced in 1959 by a new standard brick building with a flat concrete roof. Exeter Central 'B' box was closed in February 1970 when all the sidings were removed at the west end of the station, and 'A' box then controlled all of the station, but such was the rationalisation at that time that even here the number of active levers was reduced to 50.

Table 2: Summary of LSWR/SR signal boxes in Exeter					
Mileage (miles.chains)	Name	Box No	Opened	Closed	No of levers
168.39	Pinhoe	1	1875	13 Feb 1988	11-17
170.20	Exmouth Junction	1	1875	15 Nov 1959	25-49
170.21	Exmouth Junction	2	15 Nov 1959	30 Jan 1988	64
	Exmouth Junction	2	15 Feb 88		Panel
c171.07	Queen Street 'A'	1	1875	15 Jun 1927	23
c171.25	Queen Street 'B'	1	1875	15 Jun 1927	61
c171.38	Queen Street 'C'	1	c1880	13 Sep 1925	27
171.18	Queen Street 'A' (later Exeter Central 'A')	2	15 Jun 1927	6 May 1985	90
171.40	Queen Street 'C' (later Exeter Central 'B')	2	13 Sep 1925	23 Feb 1970	35

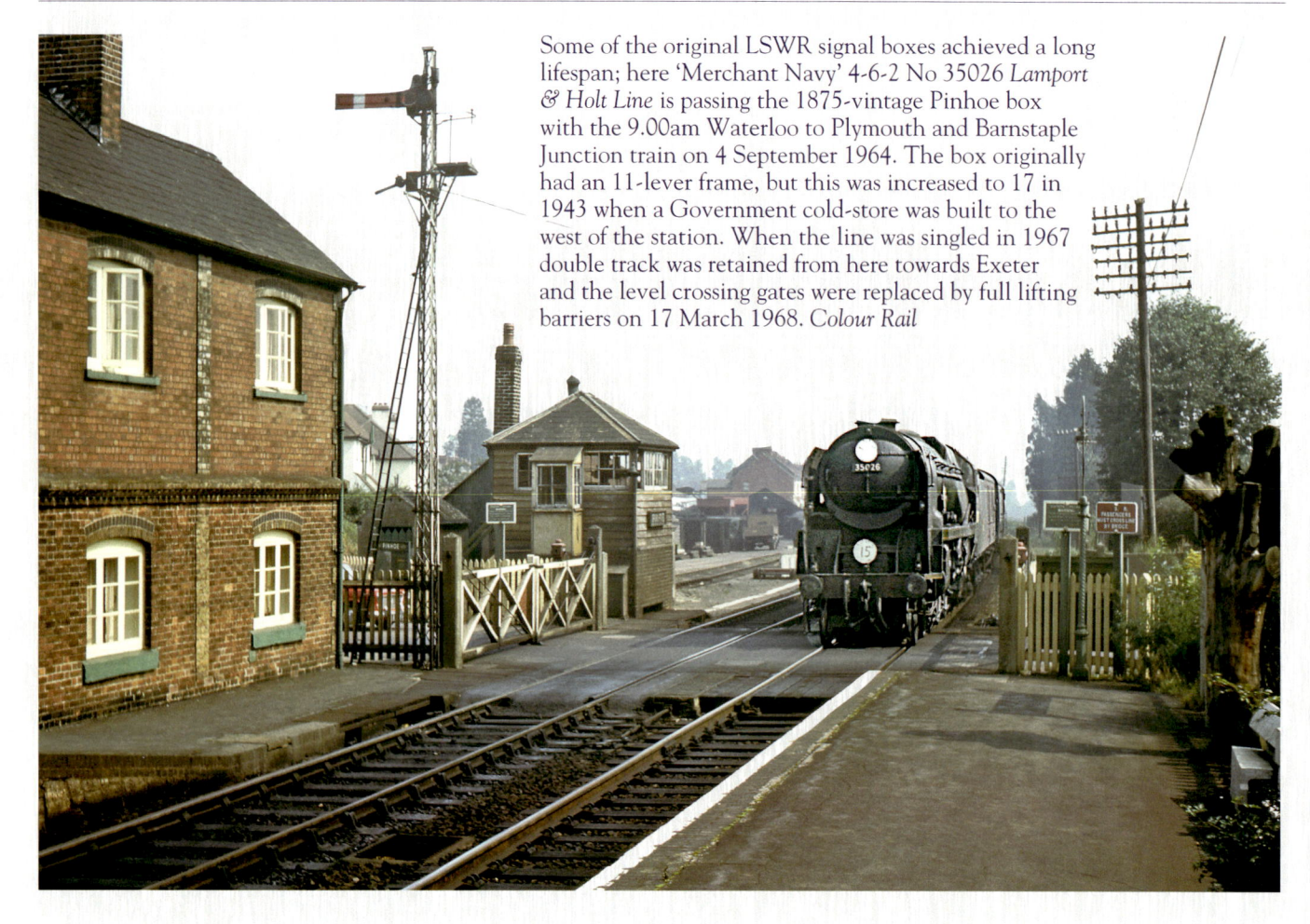

Some of the original LSWR signal boxes achieved a long lifespan; here 'Merchant Navy' 4-6-2 No 35026 *Lamport & Holt Line* is passing the 1875-vintage Pinhoe box with the 9.00am Waterloo to Plymouth and Barnstaple Junction train on 4 September 1964. The box originally had an 11-lever frame, but this was increased to 17 in 1943 when a Government cold-store was built to the west of the station. When the line was singled in 1967 double track was retained from here towards Exeter and the level crossing gates were replaced by full lifting barriers on 17 March 1968. *Colour Rail*

Below: English Electric No 50009 *Conqueror* approaches Exmouth Junction signal box with the 09.10 Waterloo to Exeter St David's service on Sunday 29 July 1984; the area of land on the right was formerly the site of the down yard. *DHM*

Signalling and signal boxes

Right: 'M7' Class 0-4-4T No 30024 is passing both signal boxes at Exmouth Junction with a train for Exmouth in 1959; the original box on the right will soon be demolished. *C. M. Parsons collection*

Below: On Saturday 14 April 1962 Ivatt 2-6-2T No 41320 is approaching Exmouth Junction with the 1.50pm SO Exeter Central to Honiton stopper. On the right 'S15' 4-6-0 No 30842 is waiting to follow from the marshalling yard with the 2.00pm goods train to Salisbury, while the yard shunter, 'Z' Class 0-8-0T No 30957, is resting between duties. The points for the Exmouth branch are in the immediate foreground. *C. H. S. Owen*

signal was provided adjacent to the Howell Road overbridge on the eastern approach to Exeter Central. By 8 October 1964 the 11.30am Brighton to Plymouth train was rostered for 'Warship' haulage, but on this occasion 'Battle of Britain' 'Pacific' No 34076 *41 Squadron* is substituting and is signalled into Platform 2 on the down main line; the other signals refer to the down through line on the left and bay Platform 1 on the right. *R. A. Lumber*

Class 50 No 50035 *Ark Royal* is passing the Exeter Central 'A' signal box as it arrives with the 09.10 Waterloo to St David's train on 10 June 1984. *DHM*

Signalling and signal boxes

Above: On Saturday 1 August 1964 4-6-2 No 34107 *Blandford Forum* is signalled out of Central's Platform 3 with a Waterloo train from Padstow and Bude; the scissors crossover is in the right foreground. An Exmouth DMU can be glimpsed in bay Platform 1, and banker No 4694 is at the far end of the up middle road. *R. A. Lumber*

Right: On 3 September 1955 BR Standard 2-6-2T No 82018 is passing Exeter Central 'B' box as it arrives with the 2.15pm train from Plymouth Friary. *J. H. Bamsey*

Below: 'Skipper' No 142019 is leaving Topsham as the 11.00 service from Exmouth to St David's on 14 September 1987. The 1875 23-lever signal box was still operative but a colour light signal is in place ready for when the branch will come under the control of Exmouth Junction box in the following January. Topsham box is Grade 2 listed and is still in situ. *DHM*

Exeter MAS

A programme to convert Western Region signalling to colour light multiple-aspect signals (MAS) started in the 1950s, but it was to be three decades before a scheme was developed to modernise the signalling in much of Devon and Somerset, with more than 20 mechanical signal boxes replaced by a new power signal box (PSB) at Exeter. The new panel was designed to connect with a companion installation at Westbury in a £35 million scheme. Westbury opened in May 1984, with its area extended in stages until the section to Somerton became operative in February 1985, the boundary between the two Signalling Centres being just to the east of Somerton Tunnel. The boundary of the Exeter panel with that at Bristol is at Fordgate, about 4 miles north of Cogload Junction. To the west the Exeter PSB controls the line until just beyond Totnes station; thereafter the route is operated from the Plymouth panel, which opened in 1960 and was extended to Totnes in 1973. Exeter is also responsible for the Torbay branch where it interfaces with a panel at Paignton, and a short section of the former SR route through Exeter Central; thereafter Exmouth Junction was retained as a fringe box.

Preliminary resignalling work took place at Exeter Central in October 1984 when the track was rationalised and the down through road taken out of use; new colour light signals were controlled from a temporary panel located in 'A' box. In November the east end of the up platform was demolished and the track was realigned. The route between Cowley Bridge and Crediton was singled over the weekend 15-16 December 1984 with the up line retained; token working was then introduced for a few months between Cowley Bridge and Crediton boxes pending the commissioning of the Exeter panel.

In February 1985 two new crossovers were installed just west of the River Exe bridges to assist bi-directional running through St David's station. Red Cow level crossing was then closed for five weeks while track at the east end of the station was remodelled. In April the down through road was removed and work started on remodelling the up side at the west end, including the loco yard. The final phase of work at St David's was completed between 27 April and 5 May, during which time the line to Central was closed. The remodelling was designed to separate trains using the main routes and largely remove previous conflicts; Waterloo, Exmouth and Barnstaple trains now use Platforms 1 and 3, and those running to/from Paddington and Bristol mainly use Platforms 4 to 6. Bi-directional running is allowed through all the platforms and also over the down line between Central and St David's.

The area controlled by the Exeter panel was extended in further phases, to Tiverton Junction (exclusive) in December 1985, Taunton West (March 1986), Fordgate and Athelney (April and May 1986), City Basin to Teignmouth (November 1986), Newton Abbot to Paignton North (May 1987), and Dainton Tunnel to Totnes in November 1987. A panel was installed in place of

Work has started on demolishing the old engine house and water tower at St David's on 28 February 1982 to clear the site for the new power box, construction of which started in July of that year. *DHM*

Semaphore signals stand sentry at St David's on 8 January 1983, but their fate is sealed with the framework for the new power box in place. *DHM*

The new signalling centre is complete on 22 April 1985, while in the foreground track is being remodelled in the loco yard. *C. M. Parsons*

Signalling and signal boxes

A DMU is running 'wrong line' as empty stock from Exmouth Junction as it approaches Exeter Central on 21 October 1984; it is passing stationary 'Peak' No 45001 on an engineering train, with No 45005 on the left. The down through road at Central had just been taken out of use and its signal arm removed from the bracket. *C. M. Parsons*

During the short period that the line to Crediton was token-operated, one is being offered to the Cowley Bridge signalman on 25 February 1985 as No 47309 passes with 7O70, the 11.30 Meldon Quarry to Salisbury ballast train. *DHM*

The trackwork on the up side at St David's is being modified on 24 March 1985, but the down main has been reconnected, thus permitting No 50005 *Collingwood* to enter the station with the 11.45 Paddington to Plymouth train. *C. M. Parsons*

the frame in Exmouth Junction box, and from 15 February 1988 it took over the work of the signal boxes at Pinhoe and Topsham.

The Exeter and Westbury panels depend on relays to operate, and as the last of their type on the WR they were already out of date when they opened and are due to be superseded in the near future. The Thames Valley Signalling Centre at Didcot was opened in 2010 and currently controls the Great Western main line from London Paddington to the Severn Tunnel; it was announced that eventually its range would expand to the west, with the Exeter PSB and the signal boxes at Crediton, Exmouth Junction and Paignton all scheduled to close in 2026.

It is, however, understood that these plans have been reconsidered and the situation is something of a moveable feast; it has been suggested that a modernised Exeter PSB will survive and take over the work of the antiquated Plymouth panel and may also absorb the Westbury area and possibly

By Saturday 6 April 1985 the Exeter West down gantry had been denuded of semaphores, but it is temporarily carrying a colour light signal that will be later re-sited on the ground. The gantry was taken down four days later. No 45070 is leaving under hand signals with the 10.30 York to Penzance relief train. *R. A. Lumber*

much of the route between Exeter and Salisbury. In the meantime, most of Cornwall is still an oasis of mechanical signalling and work is currently in hand to control the main line from Liskeard (exclusive) to Truro (inclusive) from a new workstation at Exeter that is due to be commissioned in November 2023.

Signalling and signal boxes

Work is under way to remodel the track at the west end of St David's on 21 April 1985. In the background the home signal arm for Platform 6 is being removed from the gantry. *C. M. Parsons*

Exeter West box was preserved and has been re-erected at the Crewe Heritage Centre, where it is a working museum to demonstrate the operation of large mechanical signal boxes. It was being dismantled on 7 June 1985 as No 33017 arrived with the 15.10 service from Waterloo. *C. M. Parsons*

A Class 47 is standing next to a new section of track while working an engineering train at Pinhoe on a miserable 3 January 1988. The track was being realigned here to permit high-speed running at up to 70mph over the connection between the double- and single-track sections. This signal box was also preserved and re-erected at Bere Ferrers station on the Gunnislake branch. *C. M. Parsons*

Left: South West Trains No 159018 is passing Exmouth Junction box forming the 09.00 Honiton to Exeter St David's service on 18 February 1998. On the left No 59103 is waiting in the East Sidings before working light to Riverside Yard to collect the second portion of its stone 'dust' train. The Exmouth branch is on the right; under the MAS scheme the previous double-track connection with the main line was replaced by a single 'ladder' junction in December 1987. A temporary panel was operative from February 1988, but a few months later the signal box became the first on BR to use visual display units to manage the track layout. The box now controls the main line until just west of Whimple and the Exmouth branch, and has CCTV cameras covering the level crossings at Pinhoe, Crannaford and Topsham. *DHM*

Left: Crediton is one of two passing places on the Barnstaple branch and is a fringe signal box to the Exeter Signalling Centre, with its own panel that became operational in December 1984. Once one of two cabins at Crediton that opened in 1875, the original West box is a remarkable survivor on today's railway. On 26 June 2000 the signalman is receiving the single-line token from the driver of No 37174, which is working 6Z81, the 09.45 Meldon Quarry to Exmouth Junction stone 'dust' train. *DHM*

6. The Bank

'N' 2-6-0 No 31853 is about to enter St David's Tunnel with an eight-coach train during the summer of 1964 with banking assistance from 0-6-0PT No 4692. *Colour Rail*

The LSWR's Queen Street station was located on high ground, with the B&E's St David's station some 150 feet below in the Exe valley, and to extend its route westwards the LSWR had to build a 50-chain-long connecting line that descended at 1 in 37 immediately beyond the platforms at Queen Street; the gradient is comparable with the famous Lickey and Dainton inclines. Further impediments for a train climbing the bank are that it is on a curve and there is also the 184-yard St David's Tunnel; these structures tend to be wet and provide lubrication to the surface of the rails. Although the tunnel is short, conditions for engine crews in steam days must have been quite unpleasant, particularly for those on the rear banking engines as, when working a heavy train, they would have felt the full effect of noise, smoke and heat from up to four locomotives. Thus the bank, which was opened on 3 February 1862, presented a serious difficulty while at the same time providing entertainment for the observer, who could easily witness much of the climb from the platforms of either station.

Care was also needed when working down trains, which were limited to a maximum of 20mph; in pre-MAS days a passenger train did not need a clear path to St David's but could leave Central when ready, but if the WR was not ready to accept it the train would be held at a home signal at the entrance to the tunnel. At busy times a train may have been held there for several minutes, and if it was a lengthy one the tail end would still be alongside the platform at Central and the station staff had to ensure that no one tried to board it. A down goods train needed a clear road; these were limited to 45 loaded wagons and before leaving Central the guard and driver would have to agree the number of hand brakes to be applied.

When an up train needed assistance, telephone advice had to be given to the signalman at Central's 'B' signal box from the last stopping point after Okehampton, such as when a remarshalled goods train was leaving the yard at Yeoford, to ensure that the requisite number of banking engines was available at St David's; these were held in a short siding adjacent to Middle box. The maximum loads for an unassisted locomotive are shown in Table 3; when a passenger train required help it would be banked at the rear by one or two engines, and this might also suffice for a freight train, but the heaviest of these such as the ballast trains from Meldon Quarry, and latterly the cement trains from Westbury, would

Bankers were returned to St David's either light engine or attached to the front of a down train to save a path. On 25 May 1929 two 'G6' Class 0-6-0T engines Nos E237 and E257 have been added to 'T9' No E724, which is working a train to Plymouth, and the trio are passing Exeter West signal box. A 'Cordon' gas tank can be noted on the far left. *H. C. Casserley*

Regular bankers were not used on Sundays, and tender locos could be employed between their booked duties; observations in 1946 include 4-6-2 No 21C115 *Budleigh Salterton* and 'N' Class 2-6-0 No 1833 on 31 March and 21 April respectively. A light engine returning to Exmouth Junction could also be utilised, and on a very wet Saturday 20 December 1958 'T9' Class 4-4-0 No 30702 was en route from Okehampton when it was commandeered to assist 'N' 2-6-0 No 31841 on a short goods train. Also in view is a fine example of a GWR wooden post bracket signal, which carries the starting signal for trains leaving from Platform 4 towards Newton Abbot, below which is a 'calling on' arm. On either side are 'backing' signals, which enabled shunting to be carried out in the 'wrong' direction within station limits. Beyond this bracket is a post carrying two more 'backing' arms. *Peter W. Gray*

The Bank

The loads of up passenger and fully fitted parcel, van and similar type non-passenger carrying trains should not exceed 400-tons, equivalent to 12 bogie coaches, except by special authority.

The hauling capacity of the various types of locomotives working over this section of line is:—

Class of Locomotive	Power Classification	Maximum single engine load between Exeter St. David's and Exeter Central
W.R./D. 63xx	—	130 tons
W.R. 57xx	—	140 tons*
L.M.2 (2-6-2T)	2P	140 tons*
M. 7.	2P	140 tons
T. 9.	3P	140 tons
BR. Std. 3 (2-6-2T)	3P	
BR. Std. 3	3P	165 tons
BR. Std. 4	4P	
U.	4P	
N.	4P	200 tons
Z.	6F	200 tons
W.C.	7P	200 tons
B.O.B.	7P	
W.R. 43xx	4 MT	
53xx	4 MT	200 tons
63xx	4 MT	
73xx	4 MT	

* When used for banking purposes the combined load can be increased by 30 tons.

Table 3: Instructions for the 'Assistance of Up trains' extracted from the SR Western Sectional Appendix of October 1960.

require two engines at the rear with a third piloting the train loco on the front. Unlike operations on some inclines, the engines at the rear could be coupled to the train, as all trains were scheduled to stop in Central station where the bankers were detached.

When a banker had coupled up, its driver would sound the whistle, and if the train driver responded similarly the banker would immediately start to push; however, it was only allowed to apply gentle pressure until the train had passed clear of the track connections at the foot of the incline. If there were two engines at the front, the first loco was required to take up the weight of the train before the second driver applied power.

Two Adams 'G6' Class 0-6-0Ts were allocated new to Exmouth Junction shed in 1894 for yard and local goods work, and by 1901 five of the class were based there for duties that included banking. In 1929 the locos had four daily duties that involved shunting and carriage pilot work, but three had to be available for banking when necessary. A description of a Meldon train in 1936 related that it ran four or five times weekly and usually comprised ten 40-ton hopper wagons laden with ballast, together with a brake van, grossing more than 500 tons. The train engine was normally an 'N' Class 2-6-0 and trains would leave St David's at about 9.00pm piloted by one 'G6' and banked by two others.

The 'E1/R' Class of ten 0-6-2T engines were originally LBSCR 'E1' Class 0-6-0Ts that had been rebuilt in 1928-29 to meet a need for tank locos in the SR's Western Section; they had extended frames, larger coal bunkers and water tanks, and a pony truck was added for a radial trailing axle. Most were dispatched to Barnstaple, where they were mainly used over the line to Halwill Junction, but several were based at Exmouth Junction for a period where they were used for shunting, pilot duties and the Exmouth branch goods train; it is assumed that they would also be used for banking if required. By the mid-1930s all were based at Barnstaple, but on 14 June 1938 another observer reported that 'E1/R' Class Nos 2124, 2695 and 2697, and 'M7' 0-4-4T No 377, were acting as bankers and there was no sign of the 'G6s'. The 'E1/R's (together with a fourth engine, No 2135) had just been transferred from Barnstaple. They were only slightly more powerful than the 'G6s', but their larger coal and water capacity, roomier cabs and efficient sanding soon made them popular with crews. Observations in 1949 reported that two 'E1/Rs' were usually on banking duty, and that the Meldon Quarry trains were nearly always hauled by a 'Mogul', which would usually be assisted by an 'M7' as pilot with the two 'E1/Rs' on the rear.

'S15' Class 4-6-0s were sometimes used on the Meldon workings, and on 19 June 1953 the formation was noted as being 'E1/R' No 32135 and 'S15' No 30829 on the front with newly arrived BR Standard Class 3 2-6-2T No 82018 and 'E1/R' No 32124 behind. In 1955 it was reported that the 'E1/R' quartet were still going strong, with two banking, one used to shunt Central's goods yard and work transfer trips to Riverside yard, and one spare on any one day; an 'M7' or Standard Class 3 tank engine would assist if a third banker was needed. Exmouth Junction shed had received brand-new Maunsell 'Z' Class 0-8-0T No 30954 in 1929 to shunt the marshalling yard; this was the traditional work for this eight-strong class, but these duties were disappearing in the 1950s as they were replaced by diesel shunters. In 1956 Nos 30950 and

Above right: A broadside view of 'E1/R' Class 0-6-2T No 32697 when it was the last 'Radial' tank in use; it is assisting 'West Country' 4-6-2 No 34035 *Shaftesbury* away from St David's with the 2.25pm Plymouth to Waterloo train on 4 April 1959. *Peter W. Gray*

Right: On one of its last days at work, No 32697 has just emerged from St David's Tunnel while assisting the 11.00am Plymouth to Brighton service on Thursday 30 July 1959; this engine spent 83 years in traffic, including the period before it was rebuilt. *R. A. Lumber*

Below: On Saturday 31 October 1959 'Z' Class 0-8-0T No 30957 will pilot 'T9' 4-4-0 No 30313 as far as St David's on the 3.48pm Exeter Central to Okehampton train. On the up through road is No 30955, having banked a ballast train from Meldon Quarry. Central's frontage buildings are prominent on the skyline. *R. A. Lumber*

The Bank

30956 replaced No 30954 at Exmouth Junction, and on 18 April that year the former undertook clearance tests and was used to bank the 5.45am Barnstaple to Exmouth Junction goods train; however, the WR resisted their further use due to certain concerns including clearances in Riverside yard, where the bankers could work on transfer runs.

In early 1957 'E1/R' No 32695 was condemned, and the 'M7s' assumed a more regular role. On 26 February Nos 32124 ('E1/R') and 30669 ('M7') were the bankers. Other classes were also used, and on the same day an up early evening freight hauled by Class '700' 0-6-0 No 30690 had Ivatt Class 2 2-6-2T No 41306 (just off Exmouth branch duties) assisting in front, with No 30669 on the rear. A few days later both bankers were 'M7s'. Two more of the 'E1/Rs' were withdrawn early in 1959, leaving just No 32697 in service; on New Year's Day '0415' Class 4-4-2T No 30584 was an unusual banking engine. 'M7' activity increased further, and on 14 March only this type was being used, with three assisting 'N' No 31833 on the Meldon train, No 30044 as pilot and Nos 30668/69 on the rear. The WR was again approached regarding the use of the 'Zs' and, after further trials, they were cleared; by July 1959 all eight 'Zs' were at Exmouth Junction. The last 'E1/R', No 32697, saw some use during the final week of the old order, but on the last Saturday, 1 August, only 'M7' Nos 30024/44 and 30676 were on duty.

The 'Zs' took over from 4 August, with Nos 30954 and 30957 at work. They proved to be superior to their predecessors and were an immediate success; observers reporting that trains climbing the bank were visibly faster than before and that ten coaches appeared to be the limit for a 'Pacific' and one 'Z' banker. The class also took over some carriage pilot work and shunting at Central station and were later sanctioned to work goods trains to Yeoford. Although some of the 'Zs' had received general repairs in 1959, the others had not had attention for some time, and by 1962 most of the class required heavy overhauls; in particular their boilers were in a poor condition and, despite their efficacy, it was decided to withdraw the class rather than authorise such expenditure. They were condemned between October and December 1962 and replaced by 'W' Class 2-6-4Ts, a type that had lost its traditional London area inter-yard transfer work to diesels. 'W' No 31924 reached Exeter on 23 September and underwent clearance tests on 8 October; it and seven other 'Ws' were officially transferred on 14 October, but one was condemned before arrival and another was deemed surplus and quickly returned east.

As perhaps could be expected, with fewer driving wheels and a lower adhesive weight, the new arrivals proved inferior to the 'Zs' when either banking or yard shunting – as indeed were the other types then available, which included the BR Standard Class 4 2-6-4Ts that had been allocated to Exmouth

'Z' Class 0-8-0T No 30956 is standing on the up through road at Central station on 7 September 1962. It was withdrawn on 22 December of that year and cut up at Eastleigh Works less than a month afterwards.

Junction in 1962. On the very wet evening of 28 March 1963 a cement train of 21 'Presflo' wagons and a brake van stalled on the bank despite having 2-6-4T No 80064 and ex-GWR 2-8-0 No 3812 at the front and 'Ivatt' No 41320 and 'W' No 31916 at the rear; the Central pilot, No 80038, was then added to the front and the five engines were able to move the train. A rarer combination on 14 June 1963 saw 'Hymek' diesel-hydraulic No D7075 arrive on the cement train, and 'W' No 31911 was added as pilot with 'Pacific' No 34065 *Hurricane* and 'W' No 31914 on the back. However, on occasions the 'Ws' were in total command of the banking work, and observations on two Saturdays in August 1963 noted that Nos 31911/14/24 were on duty.

The WR took over the SR's South West network in January 1963 and by October that year all of the 'Ws' had either been withdrawn or transferred back to the SR after just a year in Exeter; No 31924 was the last to leave after spending two days banking on the 23rd-24th of that month. It is understood that to simplify matters the WR wanted to replace SR engines with either BR Standard or WR classes that could be repaired at Swindon Works, and from 7 October banking was largely taken over by pannier tanks with assistance from Ivatt 2-6-2Ts and the BR Standards.

During 1964 a combination of dieselisation and shorter trains eliminated much of the banking work, and on 11 June 'Hymek' No D7099 demonstrated the prowess of the new power when it tackled the incline unassisted with a 316-ton special from Wadebridge to Kensington that was carrying the Household Cavalry from the Royal Cornwall Show. Towards the end of 1964 a greatly reduced steam fleet meant that almost any loco to hand could be used; on 23 October BR Class 4 4-6-0 No 75005 worked a ballast train from Meldon with the unlikely pairing of 'Merchant Navy' 4-6-2 No 35020 *Bibby Line* and 0-6-0PT No 4692 on the back.

By the time that Exmouth Junction's steam duties

Left: 'W' Class 2-6-4T No 31924 is passing the South Devon carriage shed at St David's at 7.25pm on Tuesday 20 August 1963 while banking a transfer goods from Riverside yard to Exmouth Junction, which is being hauled by classmate No 31915. *R. A. Lumber*

Centre left: The allotment holder appears impervious to the charms of 0-6-0PT No 4694 and 2-6-2T No 41206 as they bank a transfer freight hauled by 2-6-4T No 80064 during the morning of Tuesday 13 April 1965; the use of steam locos for banking will cease just over a month later. *R. A. Lumber*

Below: The new order is seen from West box on Saturday 15 May 1965 as 'Hymek' Type 3 No D7070 banks North British Type 2 No D6341 on a transfer goods, which includes ten loaded coal wagons. *G. V. Lendon*

Opposite top and centre: On 22 February 1983 No 47248 is completing the ascent as it enters Exeter Central with 6O70, the 11.30 Meldon Quarry to Woking ballast train; in the second photo the train has stopped while the banking engine, 'Peak' No 46044, is detached. *Both C. M. Parsons*

The Bank

terminated from 24 May 1965, bankers was usually only required for the heavier freight trains; at the start of the final week of steam operation on the 17th 'Hymek' No D7043 arrived with a Meldon train and North British Type 2 No D6331 was added as pilot with 0-6-0PTs Nos 4694 and 4655 on the rear. Trains from Meldon on the 26th and 27th arrived behind Nos D6330 and D6313 respectively and, with diesels now used for banking, Nos D6331 and D7069 assisted the first train, and Nos D7069 and D6320 the second.

The Westbury cement trains needed assistance until about 1968 and thereafter, when the source switched to Plymstock, but when the Westbury plant became the main supplier again in 1976 the loaded trains were routed via Yeovil to obviate the need for a banker; in 1985 they were again sent via Taunton and banking resumed until the traffic was switched to a 'Speedlink' train in 1987. Otherwise it was only the Meldon trains that regularly required banking, but this stopped in 1985 when workings to the SR were routed via Westbury. However, they could occasionally be diverted and for the week commencing 25 January 1988 the 19.34 Meldon to Salisbury train was sent by its old route when it was noted being hauled by Nos 33050 and 33204 on the 25th and 26th, and Nos 33056 and 33013 on the 28th, with No 37159 banking on each occasion.

Other trains were occasionally banked. In May 1991 the Waterston to Heathfield Gulf Oil train derailed and caught fire at Bradford-on-Tone in Somerset, closing the main line for several days, and on the 18th the Burngullow to Irvine china clay train hauled by Nos 37417 and 37420 was diverted via Yeovil, with No 47371 providing assistance. On 15 November that year the 03.45 East Usk Junction to

Right: With the line closed beyond Taunton for engineering work, 6S55, the 09.11 Burngullow to Irvine china clay slurry train, was diverted via Yeovil and Westbury on 28 December 2005. To lift the 1,300-tonne train up the incline No 60022 was specially sent to Exeter to assist the train engine, No 66025; this was possibly the last occasion that a freight train was banked up the incline. *DHM*

The ill-fated 'Somerset and Dorset Railtour' on 23 May 2006 is struggling at walking pace as it nears the top of the bank behind BR Standard Class 4MT 2-6-0 No 76079 (masquerading as No 76009) and 'Battle of Britain' 4-6-2 No 34067 Tangmere, and will shortly stall beneath the Queen Street bridge. *DHM*

The bank does not cause the problems that it once did, as illustrated on 30 September 2007 when track was being renewed to the east of Central station and the start of the possession zone was actually on the incline. No 59101 *Village of Whatley* is waiting for authority to proceed with 6W36, the 14.10 ballast train from Westbury, and had little difficulty in moving its train when this was granted. *DHM*

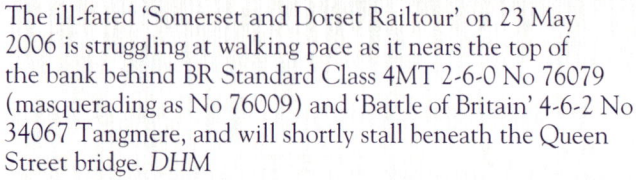

Exmouth Junction 'Network Coal' train was sufficiently heavy that No 47367 was used to bank No 37222. At other times heavy trains have been divided in Riverside yard and taken up the bank in two sections; this applied in 1998 when 'stone dust' trains ran to Exmouth Junction yard. These were either hauled by a single Class 59 loco or pairs of Class 37s, when even a portion would have weighed up to 800 tonnes, thus demonstrating the capability of the diesels. More recently, when freights have been diverted up the bank when the main line has been flooded or closed for engineering work, it has become the practice to double-head trains when additional power is deemed necessary.

A memorable day was anticipated on 23 May 2006 when the first steam double-header since 'the olden days' was scheduled to climb the bank, and it certainly proved memorable, albeit for the wrong reasons! A railtour was scheduled as a round trip from Minehead via Yeovil and Bristol with BR Class 4MT 2-6-0 No 76079 and 4-6-2 No 34067 *Tangmere* in charge. The tour had been planned and timed for 11 coaches, and with reference to Table 3 it will be noted that a 'Pacific' was permitted 200 tons (six coaches) and a Class 4MT 165 tons (five coaches), so allowing a load of 11 seems to have been in order. However, instructions also stated that assisting engines should be added to the rear when the load was more than 200 tons and that a train should not exceed 400 tons, equivalent to 12 bogies, except by special authority. In steam days the longest trains, such as the 11-coach summer Saturday Ilfracombe section of the 'Atlantic Coast Express', would have had two bankers to assist the 'Pacific' on the front. In the event the charter actually set out with 13 coaches loading to about 450 tons behind the drawbar! Although it ran non-stop through Platform 3 at St David's, its speed was limited to 15mph and by the time it emerged from the tunnel it was struggling at about 5mph; as it neared the summit the driving wheels of the 'Mogul' went into an uncontrollable slip and the train stalled. It went no further and the charter was eventually propelled back to St David's and cancelled.

'Western' Class 52 diesel-hydraulics have a high tractive effort and a reputation for getting a train moving, and in BR days were allowed to take 505 tons unassisted. This was demonstrated on 26 June 2005 when No D1015 *Western Champion* hauled the 11.33 Exeter St David's to Victoria 'Western Trident' charter train with a load of 13; it had no difficulty in mastering the bank from a standing start and was reported to have entered Central station at 30mph!

7. The GWR engine shed and locomotives

A timber engine shed and repair shop was provided at Exeter when the Bristol & Exeter Railway opened. When the company decided to have its own loco fleet, James Pearson, the former Atmospheric Superintendent on the South Devon Railway, was appointed as its Loco Superintendent in 1850; he was based in Exeter and drawings were prepared for repair workshops to be built there. The Board then decided that these should be in Bristol, and the staff and machinery were moved there, but in 1851 a new timber three-road engine shed, 150 feet by 50 feet, was provided on land between the down passenger platform and the River Exe.

The South Devon Railway had a 100 foot by 20 foot single-road engine shed at the south end of Exeter station, but when the station was rebuilt in 1862-64 the separate B&E and SDR sheds were replaced by a single building, 135 feet by 70 feet, at the north end of the B&E loco yard, and the old SDR shed was then used as a carriage shed. The shed had four roads and after 'narrow gauge' rails reached Exeter in 1876 the two roads in the west half of the shed were mixed gauge while the other two roads remained broad gauge only. While the SDR was independent through trains from the B&E changed engines at Exeter, but after amalgamation through running was introduced between Bristol and Newton Abbot using 'Singles', with SDR 4-4-0STs taking over for the heavily graded section to Plymouth.

In 1894 Exeter's engine shed was replaced by a new brick building measuring 195 feet by 70 feet; the walls had piers to

This view from the old Atmospheric Engine House in 1906 includes, from left to right, the lifting shop, engine shed, goods avoiding line and goods yard, with its large timber built shed; on the extreme right there is a glimpse of the St David's station train shed. Immediately to the right of the engine shed rakes of cattle wagons are next to the cattle dock, with some being shunted by a saddle tank, and the transhipment shed can be noted beyond the goods shed.

Sixteen engines are in the shed yard, but only one is identifiable: Dean 'Single' No 3025 *St George* is bottom left. This engine was built in 1891 as a broad gauge convertible 2-2-2 and rebuilt as a 4-2-2 in 1894. For several years this class monopolised express trains between Paddington and Exeter; this engine was re-named *Quicksilver* in 1907, but was withdrawn one year later as heavier trains required new 4-4-0s. Other older locos including saddle tanks and 0-6-0 goods engines can be seen in the yard, but there are also several modern 4-4-0s present in this transitional period; these had started to appear in 1898 when a previous practice had been reintroduced with some trains again changing engines at Exeter. As is usual in such company photographs, all the staff appear to have been briefed and are standing still while looking towards the photographer. *GWR*

carry lattice girders that spanned the four-road running shed transversely along its full length. The 'northlight'-pattern roof was in timber, with its north face glazed and the remainder slated. Offices and a 105 foot by 30 foot lifting shop were located on the west side of the main building, with a boiler house on the east side. A new turntable was located west of the lifting shop and a coal stage built in brick with a slate roof; GWR coal stages often had the depot water tank as a roof, but at Exeter the old atmospheric engine house now used as a gas works had its walls strengthened to support a 76,000-gallon water tank, which was supplied from a well fed from the River Exe.

By the time that the broad gauge was abandoned, the GWR's loco fleet was divided between seven Divisions, each centred on a major repair depot. Exeter shed was located in the Newton Abbot Division, which covered the area from Bridgwater to Penzance. As traffic increased there was a greater chance of engines going astray, and by the 1920s a loco would carry both a divisional code (NA for Newton Abbot) and a shed code (e.g. EXE for Exeter), which were painted inside the cab; as they were not readily visible they were later painted beneath the running plate immediately behind the buffer beam. To confuse matters, for traffic rather than locomotive purposes the Newton Abbot Division was known as the Exeter Division, and for a short period in the 1920s 'EXE' was noted as a divisional mark on some locos. In the 1930s each shed was given a code for clerical purposes, the last number of which represented the division concerned (e.g. '3' for Newton Abbot). Each shed in a Division was listed alphabetically and numbered in addition to this divisional number, and as Exeter was fifth in alphabetical order it was numbered 53. After nationalisation, in 1950 BR adopted the system used by the LMS, whereby the codes referred to the region ('8' for the WR), the same GWR divisional number ('3' for Newton Abbot) and a letter for each parent shed ('C' for Exeter), giving a code of 83C.

In 1902 the GWR was modernising its engine fleet with new 4-4-0s replacing the 'Singles' on express passenger trains. This transition is reflected in Exeter's allocation of 51 engines at that time, which included 17 4-4-0s from the 'Atbara' (six), 'Badminton' (one), 'Bulldog' (five) and 'Duke' (five) classes; the first-named generally worked between Exeter and Bristol or Paddington, whereas the last two classes hauled trains between Exeter and Plymouth. There were, however, still six 4-2-2s shedded there as standbys or for lighter services to the east. Goods trains were in the hands of 0-6-0s, with ten 'Dean Goods' and three of the older Armstrong 'Standard Goods' engines. There were also nine 0-6-0STs for shunting and other local work, four '517' Class 0-4-2Ts for the Exe Valley and Tiverton branches, and two 2-4-0Ts that shared duties on the Hemyock branch.

The 'City' Class was introduced in 1903 and Exeter soon received three examples, including the famous No 3440 *City*

Auto-tank No 1451 is in the shed yard on Sunday 23 February 1958. This loco was allocated new to Exeter in 1935 and, apart from a period during the Second World War, it was based there until September 1963. It is facing 0-6-0PT No 9497, which arrived brand new in December 1954 and was shedded in Exeter for all of its short life until it was withdrawn in May 1962. *G. T. Reardon*

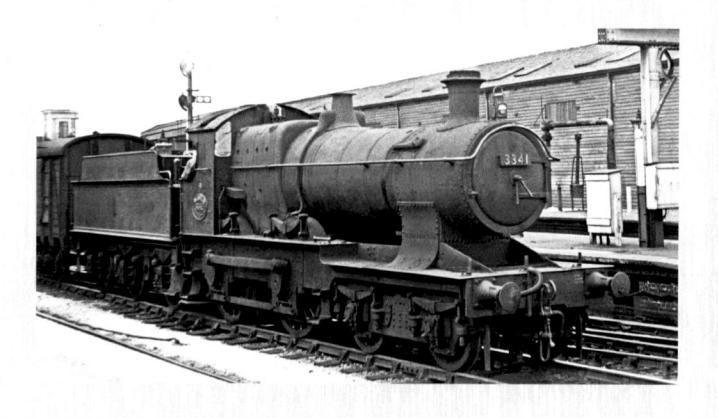

1900-vintage 'Bulldog' Class 4-4-0 No 3341 *Blasius* was based at Exeter in the 1930s, when it often worked a Saturday freight from its home city to Bristol, returning with the 4.00am freight from Bristol West yard on Mondays. After a spell at Newton Abbot it ended its days as a station pilot in Exeter from February to November 1949; it was one of only three 'Bulldogs' to acquire a smokebox number plate, and the last ex-GWR engine to carry combined name and number plates.

'Prairie' tank No 4410 is on Exeter shed in March 1952, when it was sharing City Basin branch duties with classmate No 4401, a job it continued to handle for a further year until it was allocated to Plymouth Laira shed, where it became the regular Princetown branch engine. It was withdrawn with the other two remaining members of this class in September 1955. *R. A. Lumber*

The GWR engine shed and locomotives

of Truro, as well as No 3442 *City of Exeter*. For a brief period this type monopolised services between London and Exeter, where they were usually changed, although the introduction of the 'Cornish Riviera' meant that they did then work through to Plymouth on that train. However, they were soon superseded by new 4-6-0s and were displaced elsewhere, although they did return to Exeter for short periods in later years, including No 3442 in 1907 and No 3440 in 1911.

The two-cylinder 'Saint' and four-cylinder 'Star' 4-6-0s transformed operations, and through running between Paddington and Plymouth became the usual practice, with engine changes at Exeter or Newton Abbot mostly ceasing; subsequently Exeter's importance as regards main-line work was diminished. The 'Stars' arrived from 1907 with the initial batch of ten engines shared between Old Oak Common and Plymouth Laira sheds for the main West of England services. In May 1908 Exeter received the final engine of a second batch, No 4020 *Knight Commander*, but by 1911 this loco had been replaced by No 4012 *Knight of the Thistle*, which was seen working the 11.00am Paddington to Penzance train on 3 June that year. Changes to the rosters in 1912 saw Exeter lose its example, but by August 1914, when 60 of the class were in traffic, No 4037 *Queen Philippa* was shedded there. In January 1920 the allocation was two, Nos 4052 and 4053, but a year later eight were allocated. The number continued to change and by 1923, when the number of 'Stars' had reached their final total of 73, only three were based in Exeter; these appeared on London trains and 'North & West' services from Bristol, especially on those trains where the Torbay and Plymouth portions were divided or combined at St David's.

In the early 1920s the allocation fluctuated as loco diagrams were altered. Whereas the stud of 'Stars' had shrunk by May 1922, the 'Saint' fleet had increased to seven. By then Exeter had also gained a 'Duke' Class 4-4-0, No 3279, and the railmotor allocation had increased to three, Nos 58, 72 and 86. Among the duties for an Exeter 'Saint' in the early 1920s

The '61XX' Class large 2-6-2Ts were mainly used in the London area and were rarely found in Devon, but No 6146 was at Exeter for about two years from July 1960 and is seen outside the shed on 30 May 1961. Smaller 'Prairie' tank No 5508 on the right was based there for about a year from October 1960.

were the down and up 'West of England Postal', which it could take through to Penzance.

After the 'Castle' Class 4-6-0s were introduced in 1923 they took over the main express work, and by 1926, when 30 'Castles' were in traffic, Exeter's allocation of 'Stars' had risen once again to eight, but there were now no 'Saints'. The 'Stars' handled the 'Postal' services, and a diagram in 1929 involved a 'Star' taking over the 3.30pm Paddington to Truro train at Exeter, then the next day working a Truro to Penzance local passenger service before heading the 6.45pm Penzance to Paddington TPO. On the third day it hauled a stopping train from Paddington to Didcot, then took over the 9.50pm Paddington to Penzance as far as Plymouth, and the following morning it worked back to Exeter. This meant that

Table 4: Exeter locomotive allocation on 1 January 1921			
Class	Nos	Total	Typical duties
4-6-0 'Star'	4028, 4035, 4038, 4039, 4044, 4045, 4052, 4053	8	Express passenger
4-6-0 'Saint'	2934, 2950, 2953, 2973, 2987, 2998	6	Mixed traffic
2-6-0 '4300'	4322, 4356, 4367	3	Mixed traffic
0-6-0 '2301'	2305, 2313, 2456, 2483	4	'Dean Goods'
0-6-0T '850'	863, 1223, 1932	3	Shunting, pilot, local goods
0-6-0T '1076'	1244, 1286	2	Ditto
0-6-0T '1854/1701'	1713, 1753, 1897	3	Ditto
0-4-2T '517'	559, 832, 1431, 1433, 1466, 1481	6	Branch lines
2-4-0T ex-SDR	1298, 1300	2	Hemyock branch
Railmotor	72	1	Branch lines
Total		38	

it was away from its home depot for four days and presumably the shed needed at least four engines just to fulfil this single diagram.

The '43XX' 'Moguls' were built to work the faster goods trains in place of the older 0-6-0 types, but proved very versatile and were also at home on semi-fast passenger trains or heavy mineral trains. The first 20 were introduced in 1911, and when a second batch was built in 1913 Nos 4322 and 4341 were allocated to Exeter; later other brand-new locos were received, Nos 4355 and 4356 (March 1914) and No 4367 (July 1915). For several years three were based in Exeter, but by 1926 this had risen to six with just two 'Dean Goods' 0-6-0s remaining. In May 1930 a new '2251' Class 0-6-0, No 2265, was allocated to Exeter and used on slower main-line goods turns including the 2.20am Exeter to Bristol train; however, it had gone by 1935.

Table 4 reveals that a good proportion of the allocation comprised small tank engines for the Exe Valley, Tiverton, Teign Valley and Hemyock (Culm Valley) branches, in addition to local pilot, shunting and trip work. The '517' 0-4-2Ts had been converted for auto-train operation from 1905 and were used on the first three of these branches, but the Hemyock branch required short-wheelbase coaches, and auto-coaches were never permitted. Exeter had small single-road sub-sheds at Tiverton Junction and Hemyock for the engines used on the Tiverton and Culm Valley branches, and locos would be changed on a weekly basis. Hemyock shed was, however, closed in October 1929 and the branch engine was then also kept at Tiverton Junction.

The new 'King' Class took over the premier workings in 1927, and the downgrading of the 'Castles' led to Exeter receiving its first example in September 1928; they eventually replaced its 'Star' allocation. One of the main duties for an Exeter loco was similar to the previous 'Star' turn; it alternated with an Old Oak Common 'Castle' on a diagram that included the 6.42pm Exeter to Truro, the next day's 1.35pm Truro to Penzance and 6.48pm Penzance to Paddington TPO, before finally returning home by working the 10.10pm Paddington TPO as far as Exeter. Other work for an Exeter 'Castle' included passenger services to and from Paddington such as the 1.30pm Paddington to Penzance, which was another job worked alternately with an Old Oak engine, and they also handled some of the cross-country trains via Bristol. The 'Castles' could also find themselves on freight trains, and an Exeter engine was regular deployed on an overnight perishables working to London.

In August 1928 No 4706 from the fleet of nine '47XX' 2-8-0s designed for fast vacuum-fitted goods work was transferred from Bristol to Exeter and was to remain there on and off until April 1949; there were occasional switches, however, most notably when No 4707 was shedded at Exeter for four years from March 1936. During the 1930s the type's main duty, also alternating with an Old Oak engine, was to work a circuit involving the 11.35pm Paddington to Newton Abbot fast goods and a morning 'fill-in' Newton Abbot to Exeter passenger train, then later that day it took over the 5.25pm Newton Abbot to Paddington goods at Exeter. Also that decade the Exeter '47XX' found regular employment

Table 5: Locomotive allocation on 4 May 1935			
Class	Nos	Total	Typical duties
4-6-0 'Castle'	4074, 4085, 4098, 5013, 5015, 5030	6	Express passenger
2-8-0 '4700'	4706	1	Fast fitted goods
2-8-0 'ROD'	3031	1	Heavy goods
2-6-0 '4300'	8302, 8307, 8337, 8340, 8342, 8363, 8384	7	Mixed traffic
4-4-0 'Bulldog'	3361, 3374	2	Local passenger and goods
2-6-2T '4500'	4530, 4544, 5530, 5537	4	Mixed traffic
2-6-2T '44XX'	4407, 4410	2	Basin branch
0-6-0T '850'	1992 (NB withdrawn later that month)	1	Shunting and local goods
0-6-0T '1076'	1244, 1286	2	Ditto
0-6-0T '1854'	1717, 1897	2	Ditto
0-6-0PT '2021'	2103, 2127	2	Ditto
0-6-0PT '2721'	2755	1	Ditto
0-6-0PT '5700'	5760, 7761, 9718	3	Ditto
0-4-2T '4800'	4805, 4806, 4807, 4809, 4819, 4840	6	Branch lines
0-4-2T '5800'	5812	1	Hemyock branch
0-4-2T '517'	830	1	Branch lines
Railmotors	37, 71, 80	3	Branch lines
Total		45	

on Bank Holiday Mondays on a passenger 'extra' from Exeter to Bristol.

Difficulties had been experienced with the '43XX' Class 2-6-0s on severely curved lines, where flange wear on the leading bogie became a serious problem. To overcome this, from the end of 1927 69 of the class were modified by moving the buffer beam forward by a foot and fitting a heavy casting behind it; the modified engines were given corresponding numbers in the '83XX' series, and by the mid-1930s only these were shedded west of Taunton. During the 1930s an Exeter 'Mogul' was rostered to work the 8.30pm Exeter to Cardiff freight, a train that conveyed vacuum-braked wagons for Cardiff and Newport and non-fitted wagons for the North, Taunton, Newport, Cardiff and West Wales. The load was limited to 40 wagons on leaving Exeter, many of which would have arrived from further west. Another Exeter 'Mogul' was diagrammed to work the 8.30am Exeter to Rogerstone locomotive coal empties, returning the next day with the 5.15am Rogerstone to Laira loaded coal train; by the end of the decade No 8338 was shedded at Exeter and noted as being a regular on this duty. By 1944 the withdrawal of 4-4-0s capable of running over lighter routes left a gap that resulted in restoring the surviving 'Moguls' to their original condition and numbers.

Despite many of the '45XX' Class 2-6-2Ts being used in the West from their earliest days, they were not based in Exeter until about 1922, but by January 1930 there were five there with four daily duties, two on goods trains and two on passenger workings, including local services to Newton Abbot and Kingswear. In May 1935 four were allocated, including No 4530, which arrived that month and was to stay for four years; later that year it was noted on two occasions working the 4.28pm Exeter to Trusham Teign Valley service.

The railmotor era came to an end in October 1935 when the three cars mentioned in Table 5 were withdrawn. New branch-line power had, however, appeared with the introduction of the auto-fitted '48XX' Class 0-4-2Ts in 1932; Nos 4805-09 arrived brand new in Exeter during September and October that year and others arrived later, fresh from Swindon Works, Nos 4819 and 5812 in 1933 and No 4840 in March 1935. No 4805 would be an Exeter engine for all of its life and average 34,000 miles a year until it was withdrawn in 1958; at the time of Table 5 it was outstationed at Tiverton Junction with No 5812. The latter was a non-auto-fitted variant that had shared duties with 2-4-0T No 1300 on the Hemyock branch until the latter was withdrawn in 1934; No 5812 would shortly be transferred away and thereafter two '48XX' engines were outbased at Tiverton Junction.

The 'Grange' Class 4-6-0s were introduced in 1936 and built using parts from withdrawn '43XX' class 'Moguls'; they were basically a 'Hall' with smaller coupled wheels and were primarily intended to replace the 2-6-0s on goods trains. Four were allocated new to Exeter, Nos 6813 *Eastbury Grange* and 6814 *Enborne Grange* in 1936, and Nos 6822 *Manton Grange* and 6825 *Llanvair Grange* arrived in 1937; they also worked passenger services, and Nos 6814 and 6822 were seen on the 8.00am Sheffield to Plymouth and 11.10am Paddington to Penzance passenger trains respectively on 31 July 1937. The following year, on 17 August, the former was noted on the 6.45pm Penzance to Paddington TPO. However, in December 1938 all four engines were rostered to work goods turns including the 8.40pm Exeter to Cardiff, a job shared with a 'Mogul'. A reassignment of duties in the Second World War saw all four drafted elsewhere and Exeter did not have another 'Grange' until 1956.

An interesting development early in the war saw two 'King' Class 4-6-0s, Nos 6000 *King George V* and 6002 *King William IV*, allocated to Exeter in November 1939, possibly to remove them from Plymouth when it was being subjected to heavy bombing. They were later joined by No 6004 *King George III* for a brief period, and one was regularly recorded on the 10.10pm Paddington TPO; however, all had moved back to Laira by February 1942.

After the war the 'Castle' allocation was reduced, but a diagram in the summer of 1946 saw either 'Star' No 4054 *Princess Charlotte* or one of Exeter's 'Castles' work a parcels train to Plymouth, from where it worked the 11.20am train to Penzance. The next day it hauled the 10.10am Penzance to Plymouth, where it then relieved the engine on the 10.40am Penzance to Exeter St David's – a daily tally of only just over 130 miles, illustrating that engines could be underused in the steam era. On 28 February 1947 Exeter 'Castle' No 5098 *Clifford Castle* was noted working the 5.30am from Paddington.

In May 1947 No 5026 *Criccieth Castle* was swapped for one of Laira's new 'County' Class locos. Some diagrams were more intensive and at that time No 1020 *County of Monmouth* often worked the 10.15pm Paddington to Plymouth Newspaper and Parcels train forward from Exeter at 4.47am, the 12.30am from Manchester to Penzance Mail and Passenger from Plymouth, and finally the 6.40pm Penzance to Paddington TPO as far as Exeter. On alternate days an Exeter 'Castle' then took over the last of these trains, which it worked to London. In 1948 the 'County' was regularly seen on the 11.35pm Liverpool to Penzance, but in October that year it was transferred away; no 'Counties' were then allocated to Exeter until September 1959, when the shed received two for a short period.

Exeter's smaller engines seen on main-line work in 1947 included 0-6-0PT No 9646 on Sunday 29 June, when it hauled the six-coach 7.30pm from Goodrington Sands Halt, which was the return working of the 5.00pm from Exeter; this appeared to be a job undertaken by any available engine, and on the following Sunday it was worked by 2-6-2T No 5525. The previous day Exeter 'Mogul' No 6397 replaced a failed 'King' at Taunton and brought the 13-coach 1.30pm Paddington to Penzance to Exeter unaided.

At the time of nationalisation the Exeter allocation was as shown in Table 6. The 'Hall' Class 4-6-0s were derived from the 'Saints' but with smaller coupled wheels; they were designed as a mixed traffic engine to replace 4-4-0s; hence they were allocated in the South West from the outset and were an immediate success. After a prototype, the class entered service from 1929 and almost-new Nos 4941 *Llangedwyn Hall* and 4942 *Maindy Hall* were briefly shedded to Exeter in October that year. Subsequently a series of these locos followed, but their stays were often quite short; however, No 5902 *Howick Hall* was an Exeter engine from November 1947 to July 1952. It was involved in a collision with a light engine at Uphill Junction while working an express goods train on 21 January 1951 and sustained serious damage to

Table 6: Exeter locomotive allocation on 31 December 1947			
Class	Nos	Total	Typical duties
4-6-0 'Castle'	5012, 5059, 5098	3	Express passenger
4-6-0 'Star'	4054	1	Passenger
4-6-0 'County'	1020	1	Mixed traffic
4-6-0 'Hall'	5902	1	Mixed traffic
2-8-0 '4700'	4706	1	Fast goods
2-8-0 '28XX'	2873, 3834	2	Heavy goods
2-6-0 '4300'	5321, 6301, 6397, 7316	4	Mixed traffic
4-4-0 'Bulldog'	3335, 3395, 3451	3	Local work, station pilots
2-6-2T '4500'	4530, 5525	2	Mixed traffic, including branch goods
2-6-2T '44XX'	4410	1	Basin branch
0-6-0 '2251'	2230	1	Mixed traffic
0-6-0PT '5700'	3603, 3606, 3794, 5760, 7716, 7761, 9646, 9647	8	Shunting, branch, local goods
0-6-0PT '2021'	2088	1	Shunting and pilot work
0-4-2T '1400'	1405, 1429, 1435, 1440, 1449, 1451, 1468, 1469	8	Branch lines
Total		36	

its bogie and left-side cylinder; soon afterwards ex-works No 4932 *Hatherton Hall* was moved to Exeter and on 22 April was seen working the regular 11.45am (Sundays only) freight from Exeter to Tavistock Junction via Okehampton.

When the Government instigated an ill-fated plan to introduce oil-burning, the GWR renumbered its converted engines and the '28XX' Class locos that were modified were given numbers in the '48XX' series. This meant that the running numbers of the '48XX' 0-4-2Ts were changed to the '14XX' series, which they kept after the oil-burning scheme was abandoned. In 1947, apart from the two at Tiverton Junction three were engaged on the Exe Valley line each day and another two were used on the Teign Valley route, leaving one spare. No 1469 had arrived new in March 1936 and was another that spent all of its working life at Exeter until it was withdrawn in 1958. All of the depot's '14XX' engines faced in the up direction, which meant that on Exe Valley services they were leading on the rising gradient up the main line and on the branch; it was also convenient for passengers as the auto-coaches were at the buffers in Platform 2 at St David's and also when Teign Valley services terminated in the bay platforms at either Heathfield or Newton Abbot.

By 1947 another '2251' Class 0-6-0 No 2230 was based in Exeter, but generally it was rare for one of these engines to be shedded west of Taunton, where one of their jobs was the 8.50am Taunton to Exeter pick-up goods train (due 3.30pm) and the following day's 4.00am return, which included a diversion from Tiverton Junction to Tiverton and back; it is thought that the Exeter engine may have alternated with the Taunton loco on this duty. In the late 1940s Exeter '43XX' locos were regularly used on the 'interchange' workings to Plymouth via the Southern Railway route, work that would continue throughout the 1950s.

At this time Exeter was one of the last haunts for the 'Bulldog' Class 4-4-0s, which were eking out their final years as station pilots at St David's, where they shunted carriages and parcels vans, and gas tanks to and from the gas plant. Of the three shedded there at the start of 1948, Nos 3395 *Tasmania* and 3335 were withdrawn in August and October of that year respectively, and although it continued to be erroneously shown allocated to Exeter on official lists, No 3451 *Pelican* also departed that summer. No 3400 *Winnipeg* was transferred in from Newton Abbot as a replacement and No 3341 *Blasius* also arrived February 1949, but both were withdrawn later that year.

The pilot work was then undertaken by one of the shed's 'Moguls', occasionally assisted by an 0-4-2T or 2-6-2T, or even one of the SR's banking engines. This use of a 'Mogul' meant that 'Hall' and 'County' engines worked more of the Newton Abbot and Taunton stopping trains, and a 'Hall' often worked the interchange working to Plymouth. The '94XX' Class 0-6-0PTs were introduced in 1947 to replace older pannier tanks, some of which had been built as saddle tanks in the 19th century. Exeter received No 8456 in 1950, when it was supposed to replace a 'Mogul' on pilot duties but actually spent most of its time shunting in Riverside yard; No 9439 arrived in 1951 and No 9497 in 1954. Official lists also show No 8421 as an Exeter engine, but it actually went to Truro in 1950.

A reorganisation of rosters in 1950 saw several exchanges of express engines in the Newton Abbot Division, which left just two 'Castles' at Exeter, Nos 5059 *Earl of St Aldwyn*

The GWR engine shed and locomotives

Table 7: Exeter locomotive allocation on 31 December 1955				
Class	Nos	Total	Typical duties
4-6-0 'Castle'	5003, 5021	2	Express passenger
4-6-0 'Hall'	4948, 4955, 5976, 6938	4	Mixed traffic
2-6-0 '4300'	5362, 6322, 6385, 7316	4	Mixed traffic
2-6-2T '4500'	4540	1	Branch lines
0-6-0 '2251'	2211, 2230	2	Station pilots
0-6-0PT '94XX'	8456, 9439, 9497	3	Shunting
0-6-0PT '57XX'	3603, 3606, 3677, 3794, 5760, 7711, 7716, 7761, 9629, 9765	10	Shunting, branch, local goods
0-4-2T '1400'	1405, 1429, 1435, 1440, 1449, 1451, 1468, 1469	8	Branch lines
Total		34	

and 5062 *Earl of Shaftesbury*; at the time they were regularly rostered to work a Wolverhampton to Penzance train from Bristol. Staff at this time included 95 pairs of footplatemen, 22 cleaners, 16 fitters and four boilersmiths.

In 1953 one of Exeter's 'Castles' had a complicated two-day diagram shared with a Bristol engine that involved the 9.07am Exeter to Bristol, 5.25pm Bristol to Paddington, 10.10pm Paddington to Bristol, 9.05am Bristol to Cardiff, 12.35pm Cardiff to Kingswear, and 6.25pm Kingswear to Exeter. The other Exeter 'Castle' made two return trips to Kingswear on the 8.00am and 4.19pm trains from St David's except on summer Fridays when the first of the trains from Kingswear was extended to Paddington, whence the 'Castle' ran through with Exeter men; it returned on the Saturday with the 8.50am Paddington to Paignton train.

By the mid-1950s there were still only two 'Castles' allocated, with just one booked turn shared with a Newton Abbot engine; on Mondays, Wednesdays and Fridays this involved an early morning run from Exeter to Kingswear and back, the 10.35am Penzance to Wolverhampton 'Cornishman' between Exeter and Bristol, and the 11.55am Manchester to Plymouth between Bristol and Newton Abbot. On Tuesdays and Thursdays the loco made two return trips between Newton Abbot and Plymouth before returning to its home shed with the 10.45pm train from Newton. On Saturdays the 'Castle' worked the 10.30am from Torquay to Paddington, returning the next day on the 12 noon service from London to Kingswear, from where it worked back to Exeter. The other 'Castle' was spare, but was used on a trip to Plymouth and back on Sundays.

Two duties for the '94XX' pannier tanks in 1954 included turns as No 2 Passenger Shunter at St David's and the No 2 Freight Shunter at the west end of Riverside yard. By the end of 1955 one of the '2251' Class 0-6-0s or an 0-4-2T were normally employed as the pilot at the west end of St David's, with one of the SR 'E1/R' 0-6-2T bankers used at the Taunton end. In 1955 the other 0-6-0 was diagrammed to work the Tiverton (via Tiverton Junction) goods, but it is not thought that this often happened; on 7 April No 2230 was seen working the 5.30pm Exeter to Kingswear stopper.

In 1958 a regular turn for an Exeter 'Hall' was a through working to Crewe with a freight from Marazion, but on 8 February a 'Mogul' No 7316 was seen on this train. On 26 July 1958 Nos 9474 and 9497 were observed shunting in Riverside yard, but a change was coming and in the following month a revision in Newton Abbot Division diesel shunters saw three 350hp (later Class 08) examples, Nos D3512/18/21, allocated to Exeter; they were noted on Exeter shed on 9 August. Two were rostered each day to work in Riverside yard with one spare, and they were soon joined by a fourth engine, No D3522. In March 1960 two of the smaller 204hp (later Class 03) shunters, Nos D2131/32, were allocated to take over most of the pilot work at St David's, although certain duties, including the splitting of down WR expresses, was still undertaken by the SR banker. Presumably the 03s were not a great success as they were gone by August and replaced by pannier tanks, with Nos 5412, 9480 and 9487 all observed on this work. At a time when steam duties were diminishing, it was something of a surprise when 2-8-2T No 7224 was allocated to Exeter in June 1961, the only time that one of these engines was based there. It was subsequently seen on goods work, but had moved to Aberdare by the following November.

There was quite a high turnover of engines at Exeter in the 1954-63 period, with a total of 145 different steam locos based there at one time or another, despite the average allocation being only about 35. Although dieselisation was advancing rapidly, there were still 37 steam locos there in January 1962 – one 'Castle' and 15 'Hall' Class 4-6-0s, three 'Moguls', four 'Prairie' tanks, eight pannier tanks, and six 0-4-2Ts – and there were also now five 08 diesels. Some of the remaining 4-6-0 duties were rather menial, with a 'Hall' used on the Exeter to Kingswear portion of the 'Cornish Riviera' and a 'Castle' often used as far as Newton Abbot on the 12.15pm Exeter to Paignton stopper. However, with many more diesels arriving during 1962 Exeter lost all of its 4-6-0s that year and all bar one each of the 'Moguls' and 'Prairie' tanks; the number of pannier tanks was reduced to four, but there were still six 0-4-2Ts allocated. A report from 29 December 1962 presented a forlorn scene, with only

2-6-0 No 6346 inside the shed, and withdrawn 0-4-2Ts Nos 1462 and 1470, 2-6-2T No 5190 and 2-6-0 No 7311 scattered around the yard, all minus their number plates; another 2-6-2T, No 5555, was stored. Only 12 steam engines were allocated at that time, including Nos 5555 and 6346. On that day three 0-4-2Ts, Nos 1421, 1442 and 1450, were working Exe Valley services with Laira-allocated 0-6-0PT No 6421; the latter was a rarity and spent a short period working off Exeter shed despite not featuring in the transfer lists. On 1 January 1963 it was noted on the 7.00am Riverside to Alphington Road goods trip, but was withdrawn by the end of that month when it joined the other dead engines in the shed yard.

Despite the transfer of Exmouth Junction depot to the Western Region in January 1963, the shed at St David's remained open mainly to service the engines for the Exe Valley, Tiverton and Hemyock branches. However, the shed had an air of dereliction, not least after the roof was removed when it was deemed to be unsafe. On 2 June 1963 seven condemned engines stored at Exmouth Junction arrived one by one for storage behind the coal stage – 0-6-0PT No 3679, 'M7' No 30125, '700' 0-6-0s Nos 30689, 30697 and 30700, 'Z' No 30951, and 'N' No 31409 – joining the six WR withdrawals already there, which meant that the depot now resembled a scrap yard.

The Hemyock branch closed to passengers from 9 September 1963, closely followed by the total closure of the Exe Valley line from the 7 October; this made Exeter shed largely redundant and it was closed from 14 October when only seven steam engines and five diesel shunters were still based there. Tiverton Junction sub-shed and three of the '14XX' Class 0-4-2Ts were transferred to Taunton, which assumed responsibility for the Tiverton branch during its final year of operation. The remaining staff, 0-6-0PT No 4673 and the diesel shunters were transferred to Exmouth Junction. Five of the withdrawn WR engines were hauled to Cashmore's yard in Newport for disposal on 7 and 8 October. Four more of the condemned engines were moved back to Exmouth Junction in December; on the 17th Nos 30689 and 30700 were hauled by 4-6-2 No 34078 *222 Squadron* and banked by 0-6-0PT No 4655, and on the 31st Nos 30125 and 30951 were taken away by another pannier tank, No 3759, which was banked by classmates Nos 4655 and 4694. As visiting steam engines were still reaching Exeter, the turntable remained operable for a period, and on 7 January 1964 it was used to turn 'Merchant Navy' 'Pacific' No 35022 *Holland-America Line* when Exmouth Junction's turntable was out of action.

The motive power had changed completely by 8 April 1967, with two diesel-hydraulics in the foreground, 'Hymek' No D7017 and 'Warship' No D847 *Strongbow*. Three more 'Warships', including Nos D810 *Cockade* and D839 *Relentless*, are in the background with three DMU sets. *G. V. Lendon*

The stabling point was well-filled when viewed from the old Atmospheric Engine House during the evening of Sunday 9 May 1971. Nos D6331, D6336 and 807 *Caradoc* are on the left, Nos 1663 *Sir Daniel Gooch* (later Nos 47078/47628), D6328 and 812 *The Royal Naval Reserve 1859-1959* are within the roofless shed, and Nos D4016, 6356 and D7010 are in the foreground. *DHM*

A revival started after Exmouth Junction shed closed in March 1967; a small number of staff moved to St David's and the former depot was reactivated as a stabling and fuelling point for diesel locos and multiple units. The walls of the old shed building had survived, and in 1980 facilities were improved when a single-road maintenance building was opened within the shed's footprint. In early 1986 the old repair road was shortened and new fuel tanks were installed, and a servicing shed and washing plant were provided for the new Class 142 'Skipper' DMUs. That year all BR depots were given a 'maintenance level code', which identified the type of work that could be undertaken; Exeter was given a basic Level 1 status whereby it was described as a 'Fuel point, able to supply fuel/water/oil or other daily servicing requirements'.

The GWR engine shed and locomotives

During the 'Sector' period the depot was jointly owned by the Provincial and Railfreight Sectors and, although no diesel locos were allocated, there could be a healthy number present, including those used on the Waterloo route and on freight services. It was also normal to see one or two 'departmental' locos that were employed on civil engineers work, including Meldon Quarry trains, and also the Class 08 shunters used as the Riverside pilot or on the remaining local freight trips. After Exmouth Junction shed closed the shunters came from the Newton Abbot allocation until that shed itself closed in October 1981, and subsequently from Laira; during the 'Sector' era the one remaining shunter was provided by Cardiff Canton. The number of locos on shed steadily reduced in the 1990s, particularly after the Waterloo services went over to Class 159 DMUs. For a short period after privatisation EWS continued to hire-in Exeter GW drivers for certain work but once this ended in 1999 the stabling of Class 37 locos for use on departmental work and a Class 08 for shunting ceased; thereafter any shunting needed has been undertaken by the train engine.

Exeter is now a DMU depot, but for a long time the units used on local services were maintained elsewhere, particularly Plymouth Laira. With privatisation on the horizon and Laira set to become an InterCity depot, local services became part of the Wales & West franchise and the DMUs used locally were based in Cardiff. After the franchise was divided and Exeter-based Wessex Trains became the operator in October 2001, a fleet of Class 143, 150/2 and 158 DMUs was transferred to Exeter, although heavy maintenance was still handled in Cardiff. When the operation came within the Greater Western franchise in April 2006, all the DMUs were then allocated to Bristol St Philip's Marsh depot, but from 2008 17 Class 150/2s and 12 Class 153s were transferred to Exeter. Towards the end of 2007 the depot had seen the return of the 'Pacer' type when 12 Class 142 units were sub-leased from Northern Rail; these came from storage and were not in a good condition, but Exeter staff gained some kudos in getting them into a fit state for use, and they subsequently enjoyed a reasonable degree of reliability. Five were returned to Northern Rail in December 2008 when they were replaced by eight Class 143 'Pacer' units; the remaining seven 142s returned north at the end of 2011.

During the transition period from diesel-hydraulic to diesel-electric traction, two of the former, 'Hymek' No D7044 and No D1058 *Western Nobleman*, are in company with three of the latter, Brush Type 2 No 5812 (later No 31413) and two 'Peak' Class Type 4s on 19 February 1973. *DHM*

Class 52 No D1047 *Western Lord* is stabled at the back of the old shed on 20 June 1975. *DHM*

Exeter St David's is at the centre of the 'Devon Metro' system, with frequent services to Paignton, Exmouth, Barnstaple and, from 2021, Okehampton, and the depot also services DMUs that are used on other GWR services on both the main line and on the Cornish branches. With a growing workload it was decided to enhance the facilities further, not least as it would mean a reduction in empty stock movements between Exeter and Bristol. Further developments at the depot included the installation a larger fuelling point, and heavy lifting equipment was provided in 2011.

More recently the electrification of Paddington suburban services has permitted the cascade of 'Turbo' DMUs to Bristol, and in turn additional Class 150/2 units were released to work in Devon, replacing the Class 150/1 and 153 DMUs. With a burgeoning use of local services there was a need to add further capacity by increasing both the frequency and length of trains, and to support the introduction of additional stock it was decided to enhance the facilities at Exeter. In January 2018 it was announced that £40 million was being invested in the depot, but the work was delayed due to engineering problems including the diversion of a culvert that runs under the site, as well as the Covid pandemic, but was completed in May 2021 at a final cost of £56 million. New buildings have been erected on the site of the old goods yard, including a three-storey office and staff block next to Platform 6 with a bridge constructed to link this building to the station. A new three-road maintenance shed is next to this; two of the roads can hold a five-car DMU and a shorter road is equipped with lifting jacks and a crane. The 'Pacers' were finally withdrawn in December 2020 and at the time of writing the Exeter allocation comprises 20 Class 150/2 and 11 Class 158 DMUs. Currently three of the seven daily diagrams on the Exmouth to Paignton circuit are usually worked by three-car 'Turbo' DMUs, but these are allocated to Bristol and only undergo basic servicing at Exeter.

On 28 February 1982 No 31145 is standing outside the 1980 maintenance shed, which was known locally as the 'Elephant House'. *DHM*

Network SouthEast loco No 50031 *Hood* is stabled in front of several gas oil tanks on the fuel road, and a Class 47 and another Class 50 can be glimpsed in the servicing shed behind shunter No 08849 on Sunday 28 October 1990. *Hood* was withdrawn just over three months later, but is now preserved. *DHM*

The GWR engine shed and locomotives

On 12 May 1997 a different selection of traction includes Railfreight Distribution's Nos 47313 and 47293, which are being fuelled prior to working the china clay train from Riverside to Dollands Moor, a Class 153 DMU in the servicing shed, No 37894 prior to working to Meldon Quarry, Nos 37677 and 37505, and several 'heritage' DMUs, which are stored after being the last of their type to work in Cornwall. *DHM*

Right: A similar viewpoint to the previous photo shows the new depot on 27 May 2022, with the three-storey staff block on the right. Immediately to its left, but set back and largely obscured, is the new three-road maintenance shed. The tall building in the centre is the train washing shed, with the fuel road to its left. Much of the work here is done overnight and the depot can look deserted during the day, when most of the DMU fleet is earning its keep and any units on site are likely to be behind closed doors. *DHM*

At the rear of the depot during the evening of 3 September 2021 are DMUs Nos 150202 and 166211 in the stabling sidings next to the maintenance shed; the service bridge (top left) carries fuel into the building from storage tanks located behind the camera. The old goods avoiding lines once crossed the road in the foreground. *DHM*

8. The Southern engine sheds, locomotives and other works

The LSWR had a brick three-road 170-foot-long engine shed to the east of Queen Street station for its opening, and other facilities included a water tank, a 42-foot turntable and a coal stage. As operations expanded the shed building was lengthened by 64 feet in about 1872, and a new coal stage was brought into use in August 1877. However, the depot became ever more congested, and by 1879 attention had turned to a greenfield site about a mile to the east adjacent to the junction for the Exmouth branch; a new shed was authorised in 1883 but progress was desultory and it was not opened until November 1887. This spacious building, 225 feet by 165 feet, was constructed in corrugated iron and had 11 roads that could accommodate about 40 engines; all the roads ran through the shed to a 55-foot turntable at the rear. An elevated coal stage and a shed for washing out boilers were provided to the north of the main building. Initially the Queen Street depot was kept to turn, service and stable engines, but the building was demolished around the turn of the century.

Exmouth Junction was one of the LSWR's principal sheds and was responsible for many of the turns over both the main line to Salisbury, where locos were changed on Waterloo services, and over the secondary main lines further west; engines on through services to these lines were usually changed at Queen Street. The depot also provided engines for several east Devon branch lines, and in 1920 its allocation was more than 80 engines.

A big mistake was made in the materials used to build the shed and it began falling into a state of disrepair after just 20 years of use; corrosion was apparent, with large holes in the roof and walls, and the metal frame was becoming unstable. It was decided to replace it with a ferro-concrete building, a material that was still quite innovative at the time, but substantive work did not commence until after the 1923 'Grouping' and, as with the rebuilding of Queen Street station, it was the responsibility of the newly formed Southern Railway to pay the costs of its predecessor's parsimony.

As operations had to continue during construction, the work was carried out in stages to minimise disruption and was not completed until 1928. The new shed was erected to the rear of the old one and covered the site of the turntable; a new 65-foot electrically operated model was installed in the south-east corner of the site. The 270 foot by 235 foot 12-road building was single-ended and each road had an inspection pit. A 13th road on the north side was built to a higher level and served as the repair shed with a travelling gantry crane capable of lifting loads of up to 63 tons; wheels could be removed for machining on a wheel lathe, and all but the heaviest repair work could be undertaken. Next to the lifting shop were the shed offices, stores and workshops, which included machine and smiths shops. The saw-tooth roof was supported on concrete columns; the easterly slopes of the roof over the shed section were glazed and the westerly slopes had concrete panels covered with asphalt. A concrete

'Falcon' Class 2-4-0 No 69 *Argus* with 6ft 6in driving wheels is in the shed yard at Queen Street, probably in the 1872-75 period; the loco entered service in April 1863, when it was allocated to Exeter to work trains to Salisbury. The Howell Road bridge can be noted on the right, and the shed staff standing at the higher level on the left are on the station ticket platform.

Pictured next to the brick-built LSWR engine shed at Queen Street, 'A12' Class 0-4-2 No 532 was one of the first members of a class designed for mixed-traffic work when it entered service in 1887; as this was the 50th year of Queen Victoria's reign, the class were known as the 'Jubilees'.

coaling plant with a capacity of 300 tons and capable of coaling two engines simultaneously was provided, and there was a 120-foot-high water tank that held 30,000 gallons. At its peak in BR days 400 staff were working at the shed, including 120 pairs of footplatemen. Sub-sheds were located at Bude, Exmouth, Lyme Regis, Okehampton, Seaton and Sidmouth, although the latter was closed in the 1930s; other depots at Barnstaple, Wadebridge and Plymouth Friary were independent, but their locos would visit Exmouth Junction for repair, which might mean a visit from a Wadebridge

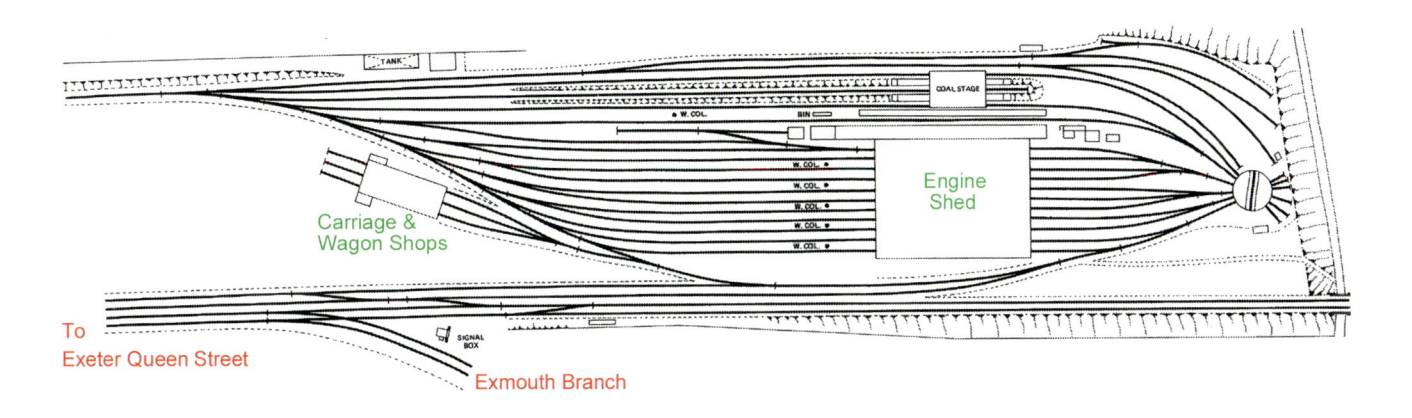

The Southern engine sheds, locomotives and other works

A plan of the first Exmouth Junction shed.

2-4-0WT or a Friary 'B4' 0-4-0T.

After the 'Grouping' all SR engines were given a prefix to differentiate the fleets of the constituent companies: locos of LSWR origin were given 'E' for Eastleigh, LBSCR engines had 'B' (Brighton) and SECR 'A' (Ashford). In 1931 it was announced that all engines were to be renumbered with the letters removed, and with certain exceptions 'E' section locos retained their existing numbers, 'A' section locos had 1000 added, and 'B' section engines had 2000 added. The 'Es' have been removed in Table 8, but the 'As' and 'Bs' are still included, apart from the 'N' Class, which was being renumbered, and to

The first Exmouth Junction shed at around the turn of the 20th century.

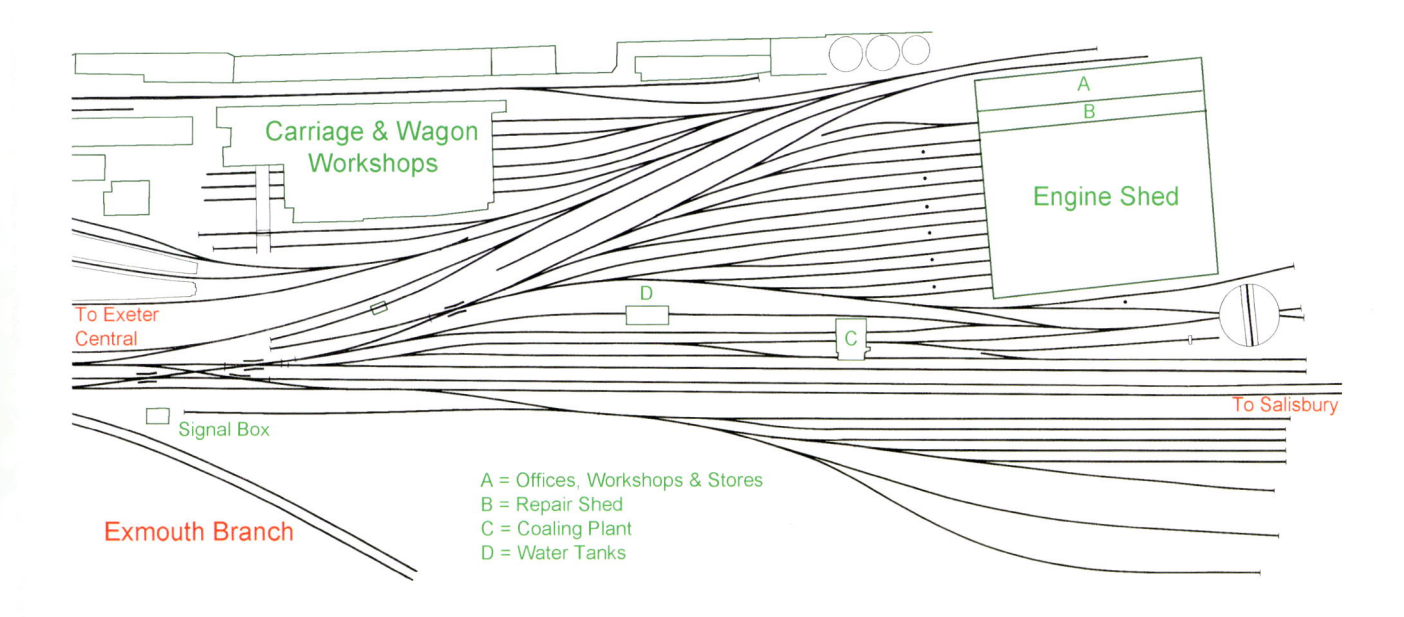

A = Offices, Workshops & Stores
B = Repair Shed
C = Coaling Plant
D = Water Tanks

A plan of the second Exmouth Junction shed.

The second Exmouth Junction shed in the 1930s.

Table 8: Exmouth Junction locomotive allocation in May 1932			
Class	Nos	Total	Typical duties
4-6-0 'N15'	448, 449, 740, 743, 744, 746, 747, 769	8	Exeter-Salisbury express passenger
4-6-0 'S15'	823-827	5	Heavy goods, semi-fast passenger
2-6-0 'N'	1826-29, 1831-33, 1835-36, 1838, 1840, 1842-44, 1846-48, 1850, 1852-56, 1858-60	26	Mixed traffic
4-4-0 'T9'	117, 283, 284, 703, 710, 711, 717, 719, 723, 732	10	Plymouth and North Cornwall line trains
4-4-0 'K10'	135, 392	2	West of Exeter, mixed traffic
4-4-0 'L11'	134, 154, 159	3	Ditto
4-4-0 'S11'	396, 399, 401, 403	4	Ditto
0-6-0 '700'	306, 326, 693	3	Local goods trains
0-6-0 '0395'	029, 083, 125, 433, 436	5	Local goods and pilot work
0-8-0T 'Z'	A954	1	Exmouth Junction marshalling yard
0-6-2T 'E1/R'	B95, B96, B695, B696	4	Shunting, pilot work, Exmouth goods
0-6-0T 'G6'	237, 259, 265, 267, 278	5	Banking, shunting, station pilot duties
4-4-2T '0415'	0125, 0520	2	Lyme Regis branch
0-4-4T 'T1'	16, 74, 364	3	Local work, including carriage heating
0-4-4T 'M7'	35, 42, 253, 320, 328, 374, 669	7	Local main-line and branch work
0-4-4T 'O2'	181-183, 185, 189, 195-199, 204, 214, 216, 221-222, 228, 231-232, 235-236	20	Branch-line trains
0-4-2 'A12'	611, 640, 643, 644	4	Local goods and passenger work, Okehampton pilot
0-4-2T 'D1'	B359, B633	2	Carriage shunting, Sidmouth branch
0-4-2T 'D1'	B214, B256, B358, B616	4	Motor-fitted for Seaton branch
Total		118	

save confusion these are listed with their new numbers.

The ten Drummond 'T9' 4-4-0s allocated in 1932 were from a class introduced in 1899 for LSWR express trains that finally totalled 66 engines. They excelled over the line between Salisbury and Exeter, where their free-running gained them the 'Greyhound' epithet. Six of the class were at Exmouth Junction by 1902, and as they were also used on the principal trains between Exeter and Plymouth another three were based at Friary shed. New 4-6-0s started to take over the express work to Salisbury before the First World War, but the 'T9s' were not entirely superseded until the 'Grouping'; thereafter further 'T9s' were transferred in to replace earlier types on secondary duties.

The most successful of the 4-6-0s were the 'N15s', which were first introduced in 1918; although they initially suffered from poor steaming, after modification they earned a good reputation for hill-climbing and further batches were produced by the SR after the 'Grouping' until the class totalled 74. The SR's publicity department gave them names associated with the Arthurian legend, and the class became known as 'King Arthurs'. This was appropriate, as SR services ran to north Cornwall, home of the legend, albeit that the class did not normally work west of Exeter. Exmouth Junction received four in 1922-23, and Table 8 shows that eight were there in 1932. An observer in 1939 noted that the 'N15s' covered all the main passenger workings to Salisbury on weekdays, and on Saturdays two Exeter engines worked trains through to Waterloo.

The 'S15s' were similar to the 'N15s', but had smaller coupled wheels (5ft 7in rather than 6ft 7in) for use on goods trains. The LSWR was mainly a passenger railway, and these were its first new freight engines since a batch of '700' Class 0-6-0s had been acquired in 1897. Twenty 'S15s' were introduced in 1920-21, and among their first duties was the 8.40pm Nine Elms yard to Exmouth Junction train; in the up direction they were diagrammed for two evening departures from Exmouth Junction that carried perishable goods to Nine Elms. These engines were mainly allocated to London sheds, but Exmouth Junction was home to No E496 from 1922 to 1928. A batch of 15 modified engines was built for the SR in 1927 and the first five, Nos E823-E827, were shedded in Exeter; they were superior to the originals and greater use was made of them on semi-fast and summer Saturday relief passenger services, when they could show a good turn of speed. Their arrival meant that the '700' Class lost its main-line goods duties, but three were still used on local work in 1932.

The largest class allocated in 1932 were the Maunsell 'N' 2-6-0s, which were only the second type of 'Mogul' in Britain when introduced by the South Eastern & Chatham Railway in 1917 for mixed-traffic duties. Their success led to the SR adopting them as its standard mixed-traffic design, and in 1924-25 a batch of 50 locos was assembled at Ashford Works using parts manufactured at the Royal Arsenal, Woolwich, in a Government scheme to maintain employment after the Armistice; this gave rise to their nickname of 'Woolworths', a nod towards both Woolwich and the cheap department stores that were opening at the time. Thirty-five of the new batch, Nos A826-860, were allocated to the Western Section, with three going to Salisbury, four to Barnstaple and the remainder to Exmouth Junction, where they gave excellent service. A contemporary comment in 1931 advised that 'engines used west of Exeter are chiefly Woolwich 2-6-0s for all classes of traffic'. By October 1933 Exmouth Junction's allocation included four brand-new 'Ns', Nos 1406-09, from an additional batch of 15 engines, and the type remained closely associated with the shed until 1964. Previously goods workings west of Exeter had been handled by 4-4-0s, '0395' and '700' Class 0-6-0s and 'A12' 0-4-2s, but these were largely superseded by the newcomers, including the Meldon Quarry ballast trains, which had been usually hauled by '700s'. In May 1932 'A12' No 640 was being employed as the Okehampton station pilot, but Exmouth Junction was soon to lose this type.

The second largest allocation in 1932 was of Class 'O2' locos, small but powerful tank engines that had been built from 1889 to 1893, when eight of the class were based in Exeter for branch and other local work. The introduction of the larger 'M7' Class 0-4-4Ts to the London area displaced some 'O2s', and by the First World War the 'Junction' allocation had risen to 16. They were used on the Lyme Regis branch for a while before joining the list of engines defeated by that light railway, but they did then provide back-up to the branch 4-4-2Ts, although they then had to work with their tanks half-full to reduce weight. Two 'O2s' were modified for Exmouth Junction's only 'push-pull' duty on the Seaton branch, but were replaced due to concerns over the efficiency of the manual equipment used. As a temporary measure in 1930 four ex-LBSCR 'D1' locos, displaced by electrification in the London area, were transferred to Exmouth Junction with a number of air-controlled motor-train coach sets; the 'D1s' were used until about September 1933, when they were replaced by 'O2s' that had been fitted with this equipment. 'D1' No B633 was kept as a spare and was later used as a stationary boiler at Exmouth Junction; by the time it was withdrawn it was the last SR engine to retain its old number.

When introduced in 1897 the 'M7s' were used on semi-fast passenger services, but after one derailed near Tavistock in 1898 on an Exeter to Plymouth train they were mainly used on London suburban services. In 1932 they were authorised over the Exmouth branch, and 16 'M7s' moved to Exeter after they were released from London due to electrification; by 1939 just five 'O2s' remained for some Exmouth branch passenger and goods work, including the Exmouth and Topsham docks branches. The 'T1s' were another class affected by the influx of 'M7s'; they had first arrived in Exeter in the 1890s, but had disappeared by 1933. The Bude branch was part of Exmouth Junction's far-flung empire, and it was quite a procedure to undertake the weekly engine change. On a Saturday the engine for the following week would pilot an Exeter to Plymouth train as far as Okehampton, then pilot the loco on the 1.00pm departure to Halwill Junction. It then worked a passenger train to Launceston before returning light to Halwill to assume its branch duties. The loco that was relieved ran light to Okehampton, then piloted a Plymouth to Exeter train.

In 1937 11 'U1' Class 2-6-0s arrived to replace some of the 'T9s', and by mid-1939 only six of the veterans were still based at Exmouth Junction, when they had three regular diagrams that covered goods trains to Eastleigh and Tavistock and passenger workings to Okehampton, Bude and Plymouth.

On 20 March 1948 'S15' 4-6-0 No 823 was recorded on the 70-foot turntable that had been installed 12 months earlier. *C. H. S. Owen*

The 'U1s' normally worked the main trains between Exeter and Plymouth and, although they also worked to Padstow, that line and the North Devon route continued to be mainly the preserve of the 'Ns'. Other 'T9s' based at Plymouth and Wadebridge shared some of the passenger work, and these were usually preferred by the crews providing the load did not exceed seven coaches, as the three-cylinder 'U1s' were reported to be heavy on coal and water. The men were no doubt pleased when, after the outbreak of war, a reduced passenger timetable led to a reshuffle of engines and the 'U1s' returned east in exchange for eight 'T9s', and the latter were soon working many of the Plymouth trains again. Heavy wartime trains brought a need to double-head mainline expresses and the 'Greyhounds' were also used as pilots between Salisbury and Exeter.

The SR began modernising its loco fleet during the war when Bulleid's 'Merchant Navy' 'Pacifics' were introduced in 1941. Although designated as 'mixed traffic' engines to overcome wartime restrictions, they were mainly intended for express passenger use and incorporated many innovative features; in a nod to the times they were described as 'air-smoothed' rather than 'streamlined', which might have been the case in peacetime. They had a numbering scheme based on continental practice to accompany their revolutionary appearance. The first of the class was No 21C1; '21' referred to the number of unpowered leading and trailing axles, 'C' the number of driving axles (three), with the final figure denoting the running number. The doyen was named *Channel Packet* and was the first to be seen in Exeter on 20 September 1941, when the engines were being tested on goods trains; these tests revealed many faults. One of the first passenger workings is thought to have been on 9 January 1942, when No 21C3 *Royal Mail* hauled a semi-fast train from Salisbury to Exeter; after receiving modifications it was then tested for several weeks in the spring of 1942 before entering regular service. The first ten locos were all at work by July that year, but were largely confined between Exeter and Salisbury while the teething problems were resolved; they were divided equally between the two cities' depots, with Nos 21C1 to 21C5 based in Exeter; extra fitters were transferred to both sheds to maintain their troublesome acquisitions. Despite their faults

'Merchant Navy' 4-6-2 No 21C8 *Orient Line* has strayed down the bank to St David's on 20 November 1948, where the driver appears to be taking a good look at something! The engine may have come down for turning if there was a problem with the Exmouth Junction turntable (the WR shed had a 65-foot turntable), but could be returning from a visit to the Weigh House at Newton Abbot's Loco Factory, where engines that had been repaired could be weighed and have their springs adjusted to even their weight distribution. Exmouth Junction was equipped with a wheel-drop but did not have any weighing facilities, so after nationalisation SR locos would go to Newton for this purpose. *J. H. Bamsey*

The Southern engine sheds, locomotives and other works

The '0415' Class of 4-4-2Ts were first introduced in 1883, and six were shedded at Exeter by March 1886; due to their suitability they worked the Axminster & Lyme Regis Light Railway from 1913 and, although the rest of the class had either been sold or scrapped by 1927, two engines survived to work that line, and a third was acquired from the East Kent Railway in 1946. No 30584 (introduced in 1885 as No 520) is at Exmouth Junction on 20 March 1954; the trio were finally withdrawn in 1961 when Ivatt 2-6-2Ts were cleared for the Lyme Regis branch. *J. H. Bamsey*

the locos did prove to be fine performers when at their best, and ten further engines were completed in 1944-45, with a final ten delivered in 1948-49.

Wartime also saw some interesting locomotives transferred to Exmouth Junction, including the return of an 'A12' 0-4-2 in 1941; No 646 was modified for use as a stationary boiler until 1944. In April 1943 six 'U' Class 2-6-0s, Nos 1621/31/34/35/38/39, arrived in exchange for 'Ns' Nos 1855-1860, which moved to Reading; the 'Ns' were slightly more powerful and had smaller driving wheels, so were better suited to hauling the heavy wartime freight traffic over the SR's Reading branch. The 'Us' did however 'do their bit' for the war effort by regularly working to a US Army depot that had been established at Newcourt on the Exmouth branch, but by December 1945 only three 'Us' remained and these soon moved on. Only six of the US Transportation Corps Class 'S160' 2-8-0 engines were allocated to the SR while working in Britain and were based at Exmouth Junction for about six months in 1943-44, when they were also used on the Newcourt trains.

After the war the SR wanted to modernise its fleet in the West and a 2-6-0 was initially proposed, a type that would have been eminently suitable. However, the economic situation meant that further electrification in the South East would be delayed and more powerful locomotives were needed there to work the continental boat trains and other expresses. Wanting to standardise on a single class, the latter need took precedence and resulted in the introduction of another 'Pacific' type, smaller but similar to the 'Merchant Navy' locomotives. Almost certainly as far as the South West was concerned this compromise resulted in the area obtaining a large fleet of over-specified engines that rarely had to work to their capacity. Initially 30 locos were ordered, with the first delivered in June 1945; all were named after western cities and towns or geographical features and were known as the 'West Country' Class. After running-in trials, Nos 21C101 *Exeter* and 21C103 *Plymouth* reached Exmouth Junction on 30 June 1945, followed the next day by No 21C102 *Salisbury*, which had been delayed while being named.

At first they only worked west of Exeter, replacing 'Ns' on the main services to north Devon, and they were working to Plymouth by October. On 19 December No 21C113 *Okehampton* was seen hauling one of the Exeter to Plymouth 'interchange' trains over the GWR route; this was possibly the first occasion on what would be a regular duty for the class for the next 13 years. They were now also appearing on main-line work to Salisbury, but an early example of 'overkill' was the regular diagramming of one in place of an 'M7' tank, when it

The 60 'O2' 0-4-4Ts were small but powerful locos built between 1889 and 1893 to replace older 2-4-0 engines, and eight were allocated to Exmouth Junction by March 1896 and sub-shedded at Sidmouth, Okehampton, Seaton, Chard and Exmouth. No 30224 was based at various sheds including Plymouth Friary and Wadebridge, but had arrived at Exmouth Junction by 1939; it was recorded on shed next to diesel No 10000 at about 3.00pm on 11 April 1953, but moved to Nine Elms in August of that year. *J. H. Bamsey*

ran tender-first on the 6.40am Exeter to Axminster stopper and returned with the 7.55am commuter working; apparently the latter was tightly timed and had suffered a poor record for time-keeping. By 1947 25 locos were based in Exeter and their range was extended to Padstow after a 65-foot turntable was installed there. Eventually 110 of these 'Light Pacifics' were constructed, and as most of the later ones were to be allocated in the South East, they were given names relating to the 1940 air battles in that area and were known as the 'Battle of Britain' Class.

Although the existing turntable at Exmouth Junction was long enough to turn the 'Pacifics', a 70-foot model was installed and ready for use by 30 March 1947; at the time there was a proposal to build larger tenders to enable through running by 'Pacifics' when hauling the new 'Devon Belle' and other expresses between London and Exeter. Also that year a 70-foot turntable was installed at Okehampton; in addition to turning the 'Pacifics', this meant that 'S15' 4-6-0s could be turned there when working ballast trains from Meldon Quarry.

After the war good-quality coal was in short supply and the Government adopted a plan to convert more than 1,200 steam locomotives to oil-burning using a heavy fuel oil generally unsuitable for other use. Exmouth Junction was one of the sheds selected for this, and oil storage tanks and pumps were installed during 1947. However, showing that little changes when it comes to Government affairs, it appears that the Treasury had not been consulted and no sooner had the scheme started than it had to be abandoned as there was insufficient foreign exchange to purchase the oil at a time when the country was almost bankrupt! 'U' Class No 1625 was the only oil-burner to work off Exmouth Junction during 1948, and on at least one occasion was observed on the Exeter to Plymouth via Newton Abbot 'interchange' working before it was re-converted to coal-firing.

When the railways were nationalised on 1 January 1948 the new British Railways announced a renumbering scheme with the broad principle that 30,000 would be added to the existing SR number; there were, however, certain exceptions, notably the abolition of the numbering system adopted by Bulleid. In 1950 a new nationwide shed code scheme was introduced, and Exmouth Junction was given the code 72A.

Exmouth Junction's 'Merchant Navy' allocation was increased from seven to eight when through engine working was introduced between Waterloo and Exeter in February 1950. Twenty-seven engine changes at Salisbury were eliminated each day and seven more at Exeter Central, although six additional changes were now made at Yeovil Junction; these alterations meant an overall reduction of 14 engines and 19 crews each day. Although time was saved by not changing locos, this was offset by having to take on water due to the absence of water troughs on the route. All ten weekday express duties between London and Exeter were now rostered for the 'Pacifics', and the 'King Arthurs' were relegated to working semi-fast and relief trains. Exmouth Junction had lost its allocation of these in 1946, but had

The Southern engine sheds, locomotives and other works

Table 9: Exmouth Junction locomotive allocation in September 1950			
Class	Nos	Total	Typical duties
4-6-2 'MN'	35001-04, 35021-24	8	Express passenger, Exeter-Waterloo
4-6-2 'WC'	34001-10, 34014-20, 34024-31, 34044-48	30	Mixed traffic
4-6-0 'N15'	30454, 30455, 30457	3	Relief passenger
4-6-0 'S15'	30823-25, 30841-47	10	Heavy goods, semi-fast passenger
2-6-0 'N'	31829-35, 31838-41, 31845/47, 31853, 31855-56, 31869, 31874-75	19	Mixed traffic
4-4-0 'T9'	30283, 30702-03, 30706-07, 30715-17, 30723	9	Plymouth and north Cornwall passenger trains
4-4-0 'L11'	30408, 30409	2	Local work west of Exeter
0-6-0 '0395'	30564, 30581	2	Snowplough duties, local goods, C&W and Okehampton pilots
0-8-0T 'Z'	30954	1	Marshalling yard shunter
0-6-2T 'E1/R'	32124, 32135, 32695, 32697	4	Banking, shunting and pilot work
4-4-2T '0415'	30582, 30583, 30584	3	Lyme Regis branch
0-4-4T 'M7'	30024, 30025, 30030/34/39, 30046/49, 30055, 30105, 30124, 30133, 30245, 30252/53/55/56, 30320/23, 30374, 30376-77, 30668-69, 30671	24	Branch lines, local passenger and goods, pilot and banking
0-4-4T 'O2'	30192/93/99, 30224/30/32	6	Exmouth branch, Topsham quay
Total		121	

received the three listed in 1950 for summer Saturday work; they were placed in store in October 1950, but reappeared for duty over Easter 1951. However, members of this class survived elsewhere until 1962 and continued to make appearances in Exeter, particularly on stopping trains from Salisbury, summer Saturday trains or when substituting for 'Pacifics'; remarkably No 30448 *Sir Tristram* was seen at Exmouth Junction on 30 September 1950 after working a cattle train through to Yeoford. On summer Saturdays in 1954 Salisbury 'Arthurs' regularly worked the Torrington portion of the up 'Atlantic Coast Express', and Nine Elms engines occasionally worked through from Waterloo and might then return with a loaded Meldon Quarry ballast train; in such cases the locos only worked east of Exeter.

The arrival of the 'Light Pacifics' led to a reduction in the fleet of 4-4-0s and 2-6-0s, and a cascade of engines meant the loss of most of the 0-6-0s, including the remaining '700' Class locos; the two surviving 'L11' Class 4-4-0s were to be withdrawn in 1951. Although 'the Junction' still had three of the 1932 allocation of 'S15s' on its books in 1950, these were now supplemented by seven engines from a final batch of ten locos that had been built in 1936 and had arrived between 1946 and 1948; the remaining three 'originals' were moved away in June 1951. Once all the smaller 'Pacifics' had been built, there was no attempt to keep the engines in the areas relevant to their names, and during April 1951 Exmouth Junction received 11 'Battle of Britain' Class engines, with a similar number of 'West Country' locomotives moving to Nine Elms.

The main change subsequent to Table 9 was the modernisation of the tank engine fleet. In June 1952 four 2-6-2Ts were allocated to Exmouth Junction, three 2MTs of an LMS Ivatt design and a new BR Standard 3MT No 82010. They had reached Exmouth Junction by July and No 41313 was sent to work the Bude branch on the 5th. Both types were tested on the Exmouth branch, with the Standards proving superior, and by September 1952 Nos 82010-13 and 82017-18 had arrived new from Swindon Works to displace 'M7s' from many of their duties. The BR tanks also worked services to Plymouth, occasionally substituting for a 'Pacific' (including the interchange workings over the WR); on 28 February 1953 No 82019 was reported working the 2.15pm Plymouth Friary to Exeter Central train when it climbed the bank to Central with five coaches unaided. At that time a regular duty for one of the Ivatt tanks included morning work on the Sidmouth branch before making an afternoon trip to Crediton to collect a milk train. A small fleet of 'M7s' was retained for station pilot duties and other local work, and motor-fitted 'M7s' were still used on the Seaton branch.

The SR route to Plymouth reached 950 feet above sea level beyond Okehampton where it skirted Dartmoor, and was prone to snowdrifts caused by strong winds blowing snow into the deep cuttings. The '0395' Class 0-6-0s had been introduced in 1881 and the three survivors in Exeter were fitted for snowplough duty in addition to undertaking local goods work. Unusually, with no 'T9' or other more suitable engine available, No 30575 worked the 3.50pm Exeter Central to Okehampton passenger train on 6 February 1953; as it was not fitted for steam heating it is to be hoped that it was not a cold day! November 1954 saw the return of a class that had not been based at 'the Junction' for several years when two '700' Class 0-6-0s, Nos 30315 and 30691, replaced two of the '0395' engines for the plough duty and also often worked the 6.30am Exmouth Junction to Barnstaple pick-up goods.

Although the SR was gradually electrifying its network, after learning about the development of diesel-electric traction in the USA it contemplated limiting future electrification to high-density traffic lines and using diesels instead on other routes such as the Exeter line. Agreement was reached with English Electric to provide three 1,750hp prototypes, but a long gestation period meant that the first, No 10201, would not be completed until November 1950; after trials it was then displayed at the Festival of Britain. In the meantime No 10202 was completed and was the first to reach Exeter in September 1951, and from 15 October it commenced a regular out-and-back working on the 1.00pm express from Waterloo and the 5.53pm passenger and mail train from Exeter. Two weeks later it began a four-leg daily diagram that included the 1.25am Waterloo and 7.30am Exeter

Diesel-electric No 10201 is taking on water for its steam heating boiler at Exeter Central after arriving with the 1.00pm train from Waterloo in April 1953; it will return to London with the 5.53pm service. Although details are sparse it is understood that this loco had 'run away' light engine down the bank from Central two months previously after arriving with the 1.25am from Waterloo, but the driver had managed to regain control before there was a serious incident. *R. A. Lumber*

departures in addition to the aforementioned trains, giving a daily revenue mileage of 687, something quite unheard of in the steam era. No 10201 finally entered full service in February 1952 on the Bournemouth line and thereafter the two engines alternated between the two routes. As might be expected, teething problems occurred in service, but they proved to be reasonably reliable and appeared to acquit themselves better than the two earlier EE diesels, Nos 10000 and 10001, on the LMR. It was decided to transfer these 1,600hp locos to the SR for comparison purposes and they arrived in March-April 1953. The third SR loco was completed in March 1954 with improvements including a new version of the engine capable of producing 2,000hp.

'0395' Class 0-6-0 No 30564 was built in 1885 as No 29, one of 70 such engines that the LSWR had for goods traffic. The last survivors were used on light goods work, and those based at Exmouth Junction were also used as Okehampton station pilots or kept for snowplough duties; No 30564 was the final one shedded there when it was seen at St David's on 10 September 1957 while waiting for the road up the bank. It was withdrawn in the following April. *R. A. Lumber*

The Southern engine sheds, locomotives and other works

On 24 May 1953 ex-LMS 1,600hp Co-Co diesel No 10000 is resting on Exmouth Junction between working the 11.00am train from Waterloo and the 4.56pm from Exeter Central, a regular Sunday diagram for the diesels. Only basic servicing was undertaken here on the five diesel locos, and planned maintenance work was carried out at Nine Elms depot; Exmouth Junction and Salisbury sheds did, however, provide many of their crews. *C. H. S. Owen*

Table 10: Exmouth Junction locomotive allocation in September 1955			
Class	Nos	Total	Typical duties
4-6-2 'MN'	35001-04, 35008, 35013, 35023-24	8	Express passenger, Exeter-Waterloo
4-6-2 'WC'	34001-04, 34013-16, 34021-34	22	Mixed traffic
4-6-2 'BB'	34056-62, 34069	8	Mixed traffic
4-6-0 'S15'	30841-46	6	Heavy goods, semi-fast passenger
4-6-0 4MT	75070-79	10	Mixed traffic on Plymouth route
2-6-0 'N'	31830-41, 31844-49	18	Mixed traffic
4-4-0 'T9'	30708-12, 30715/17	7	North Cornwall and Plymouth passenger trains
2-6-2T 3MT	82010/11/13/17-19/22-25	10	Branch and other local work
2-6-2T 2MT	41297, 41306, 41307	3	Ditto
0-6-0 '700'	30315, 30691	2	Local goods and snowplough duties
0-6-0 '0395'	30564	1	Snowplough work
0-8-0T 'Z'	30954	1	Marshalling yard shunter
0-6-2T 'E1/R'	32124, 32135, 32695, 32697	4	Banking, shunting and piloting
4-4-2T '0415'	30582-84	3	Lyme Regis branch
0-4-4T 'M7'	30021/23-25, 30044-46, 30323/74, 30667-71/76	15	Seaton branch and other local work
0-4-4T 'O2'	30193/99, 30232	3	Exmouth and Topsham quay goods
Total		121	

All five were then used on the SR until it was decided that they should be transferred to the LMR for that Region to gain operating experience prior to the arrival of Modernisation Plan diesels, and they left the SR in March-April 1955. They had proved their potential for much of the time, but apparently not enough to convince the SR to deviate from its electrification path.

Table 10 is not strictly accurate, but does reflect certain published listings by including ten brand-new BR Standard Class 4MT 4-6-0s that were being turned out at Swindon at this time. The first two were still under construction in September 1955 and were not delivered to the SR until the following month; the last ones arrived in January 1956. They were to replace 'T9' and 'N' Class engines west of Exeter, but it is understood that, as they were a tight fit on the 50-foot turntables at Barnstaple Junction, Bude and Wadebridge, they were not suited to the cyclic diagrams undertaken by the older locos; the Bulleid 'Pacifics' were not used on these rosters and their work took them through to Ilfracombe and Padstow, where there were larger turntables. The newcomers were therefore largely restricted to the Plymouth route, including the interchange duty over the WR, Meldon Quarry trains and stopping trains to Salisbury, but were otherwise underemployed and by April 1956 had started to migrate to sheds further east, and all had moved on by June.

In about March 1956 'Z' No 30954, which had been the marshalling yard shunter at Exmouth Junction for 27 years, was exchanged for No 30956, which had temporarily replaced it the previous year after it had been damaged in a collision; the new arrival was soon joined by No 30950 with the prospect of the type taking over the banking work between St David's and Central, although as advised in Chapter 6 this would not actually happen until 1959.

During the first half of the decade modifications had improved the reliability of the 'Merchant Navy' engines and had lengthened the period between general overhauls, but repair costs and a heavy coal consumption still weighed against them; consideration was even given to scrapping the class and replacing them with more economic BR Standard 'Britannia' Class engines. However, in view of the good condition of their boilers it was decided to rebuild them with Walschaerts valve gear and other conventional features, and their casing was removed to allow easier access for servicing; when modified the locos had a more traditional but still quite striking appearance. The first rebuilt engine, No 35018 *British India Line*, was completed by February 1956, then underwent trials; its first appearance at Exeter was on 26 April, when it hauled the 9.00am from Waterloo and the 4.30pm return working, with both trains augmented to 15 coaches. The second rebuild, No 35020 *Bibby Line*, underwent a series of tests between Salisbury and Exeter, and these were sufficiently successful for authorisation to be given to rebuild the class. It was then decided to do the same to the 'Light Pacifics', and the first of these, No 34005 *Barnstaple*, was completed by August 1957, with 60 eventually modified. Due to a slightly heavier axle-loading, the rebuilds were initially banned from working west of Okehampton and over the North Devon line, but from July 1959 they were permitted to operate between Okehampton and Plymouth after some strengthening work had been done to Meldon Viaduct.

In 1959 a number of WR 0-6-0PTs made redundant by dieselisation were transferred to the SR to replace some of its veteran tank engines. Former Danygraig (Swansea) resident No 4666 was seen at Exmouth Junction in early October, and both it and another Welsh expatriate, No 3633, were noted shunting at Exeter Central. Both soon moved on to

In its original condition, 'Merchant Navy' 4-6-2 No 35018 *British India Line* was not considered to be one of the better members of the class, and it was perhaps a surprise that it was chosen to participate in the 1948 Locomotive Exchanges, but it may explain why it was the first of the class selected to be rebuilt. It emerged from Eastleigh on 9 February 1956 and first appeared at Exeter in its new guise on 26 April, two weeks before this photo at Exmouth Junction on 11 May.

The Southern engine sheds, locomotives and other works

Wadebridge, but No 3679 arrived during November and stayed for several years; this was a tentative step towards the sweeping changes in the allocation during the shed's final years.

1961 saw the ousting of three ex-LSWR types that had been long-term residents, including the three 4-4-2T 'Radial' tanks, which were withdrawn after Ivatt 2-6-2Ts were cleared for the Lyme Regis branch once the track had been upgraded. Latterly the remaining 'T9' 4-4-0s had spent little time in the vicinity of their parent depot, but instead worked on diagrams based on Okehampton that took them further west. However, by 1961 four had been condemned when they needed firebox repairs; four others (supplemented by loaned preservation candidate No 30120) survived until July, when they were also withdrawn and replaced by 'Ns'. In October 1961 the last 'O2', No 30199, was transferred to Eastleigh and just five 'M7s' remained at the end of the year; the 'Zs' and 0-6-0PTs had replaced them in Exeter Central's goods yard and on carriage pilot work, but they still worked some Exmouth trains. This became rarer after a further influx of Class 2 2-6-2Ts, both of the LMS type and also temporarily the BR Standard version, and the allocation of the former had risen to 15 by September that year.

During 1962 the 'M7s' were largely confined to the Seaton branch, but in contrast it would be the depot's most modern residents that would move away that year when the ten Standard 3MT 2-6-2Ts were replaced by 12 Standard 4MT 2-6-4Ts that had been displaced on completion of the Kent Coast Electrification Scheme; this transition started towards the end of June. The sojourn of the 'Zs' as banking engines was to be relatively brief before they too were replaced by the end of that year by 'W' Class 2-6-4Ts. In 1962 the three '700' Class 0-6-0s were still at Exmouth Junction, but had no regular duties and were retained for snowplough work. Two 'Q' Class 0-6-0s, Nos 30530 and 30631, were allocated as replacements in December, but had not arrived by the 29th when '700' Nos 30697 and 30689 were dispatched back-to-back to clear the snow after blizzards had trapped 'N' No 31838 and a goods train near Lydford. One of the '700's was derailed in the

'T9' 4-4-0 No 30709 is on shed on 30 May 1961, when it was one of the last four of this class allocated to Exmouth Junction; its days are numbered and all were withdrawn just over a month later.

'M7' 0-4-4T No 30025 had a general overhaul at Eastleigh in January 1960 and is still gleaming soon afterwards while shunting in the goods yard at Exeter Central; despite working off Exmouth Junction at this time, official records show it as being a Salisbury engine and it appears to be carrying a Guildford shed plate! The building in the background is Exeter Prison, a 'facility' that has been provided in the city for many centuries, although this building dates from 1853. *Peter Doel*

deep snow and the next day No 30700 was sent to assist, and another plough was dispatched from Plymouth, but the line was not cleared until 2 January 1963. Further blizzards that month saw both the '700's and the newly arrived 'Qs' engaged in further work

Table 11: Exmouth Junction locomotive allocation on 30 December 1962

Class	Nos	Total	Typical duties
4-6-2 'MN'	35003, 35009-10, 35013, 35022, 35025-26	7	Express passenger, Exeter-Waterloo
4-6-2 'WC'	34002/11/15/20/23/30/33/35/106/107	10	Mixed traffic
4-6-2 'WC' (R)	34024/32/36/96/108	5	Ditto
4-6-2 'BB'	34063/65/66/69/70/72/74/75/76/78/79/80/81/83/84/86/110	17	Ditto
4-6-2 'BB' (R)	34056/58/60/62/109	5	Ditto
4-6-0 'S15'	30841-46	6	Goods and semi-fast passenger
2-6-0 'N'	31406, 31818/34-49/53/55-56/60/74-75	24	Mixed traffic
2-6-4T 'W'	31911-17, 31924	8	Banking, shunting and trips
2-6-4T 4MT	80035-43, 80059/64/67	12	Mixed traffic
2-6-2T 2MT	41238/70/72/84/92/99, 41306-09, 41318, 41320-23	15	Branch, banking and other local work
0-6-0 'Q'	30530, 30531	2	Snowplough duties
0-6-0PT '5700'	3679	1	Pilot and goods work
0-4-4T 'M7'	30025, 30048 (M), 30667 (M)	3	M = Motor-fitted for Seaton branch
Total		115	

NB All the 'Merchant Navy' 'Pacifics' had been rebuilt and the table indicates which of the 'Light Pacifics' were still in their original condition, and which had been rebuilt (R).

From 30 December 1962 Exmouth Junction, Yeovil Town, Barnstaple Junction and Wadebridge depots were moved to the control of the WR with the transfer of the Southern's network west of Salisbury; in total 149 locomotives were involved, including 115 based in Exeter.

The 'M7', 'N' and 'S15' classes would all have been represented when the 'new' shed was completed in 1928, but although the other classes were more recent arrivals the all-steam allocation meant that in some ways the shed had changed little since then; in contrast, 'down the hill' diesels were now hauling many WR trains. 'The Junction' was, however, seeing some visiting diesels, particularly the D63XX Type 2s that had taken over the daily Plymouth to Exeter Central interchange working in 1959.

Standard 2-6-4Ts and Ivatt 2-6-2Ts were often used on the banking work in 1963 and further pannier tanks were added to the allocation; Nos 4655 and 4694 were noted sharing duties in Exmouth Junction marshalling yard with the 'Ws'. A different form of 'Westernisation' took place on the Seaton branch from March 1963 when auto-fitted 0-6-0PTs Nos 6400 and 6430 (and later No 6412) were transferred to Exmouth Junction to replace the 'M7' tanks, although the veterans still saw some use until 2 May, when No 30048 worked the morning service for the last time; the newcomers were matched with WR auto-coaches until the branch was dieselised from 4 November. The new WR regime began making greater use of Exmouth Junction, and ex-GWR engines were sent there for servicing and repair; visitors such as Nos 4087 *Cardigan Castle* and 5014 *Goodrich Castle* were seen in April 1963, the latter receiving inside big-end attention.

The WR wanted to eliminate steam from Exmouth Junction by 1965, and from 6 May 1963 D63XX diesels took over many of the trains on the ex-SR route to Plymouth, occasionally assisted by 'Warship' Class locos; the main exception was the Brighton to Plymouth train, which continued to be hauled by a 'Pacific'. The unmodified 4-6-2s continued to work the 'ACE' to Padstow, but otherwise mainly worked over the North Devon line.

In June 1963 diesel shunters from Exeter's WR shed started working in Exmouth Junction yard. From 15 July of that year DMUs were introduced on some services over the Exeter to Exmouth branch as a prelude to almost complete dieselisation of the line in September, and the Sidmouth, Seaton and Lyme Regis branches were all dieselised in November of that year, with the sub-sheds at Exmouth, Lyme Regis and Seaton closed. However, the Lyme Regis branch reverted to steam haulage for a brief period in February 1965 when there was a shortage of DMUs; after the closure of the Torrington to Halwill Junction line at the end of that month

The Southern engine sheds, locomotives and other works

displaced single-unit 'Bubble cars' were then employed on Lyme Regis services until the branch was closed on 27 November 1965.

The DMU shortage also meant steam returning to Seaton from 8 February 1965 after Exmouth Junction received ex-GWR 0-4-2Ts, Nos 1442 and 1450, to operate there for a month. These were the final members of this class still in service and it was perhaps appropriate that they should end their careers based in Exeter, where some of the first engines had arrived new in 1932, albeit at the GWR shed. However, they were in poor mechanical condition and No 1442 failed on 13 March; this was the last scheduled day for steam operation and the final services were provided by a taxi – an inauspicious end for the very last '14XX' to work a revenue-earning train on BR.

The first of the unmodified Bulleid 'Pacifics' were withdrawn during 1963, including five of the Exmouth Junction fleet, and in November seven rebuilds were returned to the SR in exchange for six in original condition; in the event only two of the latter were kept in service and the others were either stored or withdrawn. The short-lived allocation of the 'Q' Class engines ended in July 1963 with their transfer back to the SR and replacement by WR '2251' Class 0-6-0s Nos 2214 and 2277 for snowplough duty and goods work to Barnstaple. A further shuffling of the steam fleet in 1963 saw other SR classes leave, including the 'S15s' in September and the 'Ws' in October. Five BR Standard 5MT 4-6-0s were transferred in from the London Midland and North Eastern regions to replace the former and were the first of this class allocated to Exmouth Junction; however, the type had been based at other SR sheds and had previously reached Exeter. The new arrivals soon took over most of the remaining steam work over the Plymouth line, the main exception being the Brighton train, which remained a 'Pacific' turn.

From 9 September 1963 Exmouth Junction was given a WR shed code of 83D, and after the closure of Exeter's WR shed on 14 October it took over that facility's residual work, inheriting five diesel shunters, becoming the first diesels on its allocation. The dispersal of the SR fleet saw some interesting workings from the shed at the start of 1964, with '700' No 30700 steamed on New Year's Day to haul 'S15' No 30832 to Eastleigh, both for scrap, and on the following day 'Z' No

'N' Class 2-6-0 No 31812 spent most of its life in the South East and only moved to Exmouth Junction in August 1963; it was bearing an 83D shed plate and in rather a sorry state when photographed not long before it was withdrawn on 8 August 1964. *Peter Doel*

Ex-GWR 0-6-0 No 2214 was transferred to Exmouth Junction in 1963 and was fitted with a snowplough for a test run to Okehampton on 16 October of that year, the first visit of one of this class to the former SR route. It is seen in the shed yard the following month. *C. H. S. Owen*

30951 towed '700' No 30689 for the same fate.

In February 1964 'Western' and 'Hymek' diesels had daily turns over the Plymouth route to train Exmouth Junction and Laira men, and from the start of the 1964 summer timetable there was limited steam activity on all the ex-SR routes west of Exeter, with many trains now worked by D63XX locos or DMUs, and an increasing number of 'Hymeks'. Major steam repairs ceased at Exmouth Junction at the end of May 1964 and the steam fleet became increasingly unreliable. The main line from Waterloo was still all-steam apart from the

'Battle of Britain' 4-6-2 No 34054 *Lord Beaverbrook* was another late arrival at Exmouth Junction in November 1963, and was one of the 'Light Pacifics' withdrawn on 7 September 1964 when Waterloo services were dieselised; it is pictured in front of the lifting shop, which was known locally as 'The Cathedral'. *Peter Doel*

DMUs that were appearing on some of the stopping trains, but on 10 March 1964 'Warship' No D827 *Kelly* hauled a test train between Exeter and Salisbury, and the first reported appearance of one on a scheduled service was on 1 August when No D824 *Highflyer* worked between Exeter and Salisbury and returned with the Brighton train. From the 17th 'Warships' were diagrammed for three weekday return trips between Exeter and Waterloo including the up 'ACE'; a full diesel service was introduced from Monday 7 September.

By then Exmouth Junction's 'Pacific' fleet was down to just four 'Merchant Navy' locos and 18 'Light Pacifics', and these were then either withdrawn or transferred away. At the start of 1964 there had still been 22 'Ns' based in Exeter, but this had been reduced to 12 by September when most freight facilities over the former SR routes west of Exeter were withdrawn. Official records show the remaining 'Ns' as also being withdrawn on 7 September, thus ending the type's 40-year association with Exmouth Junction; however, on that very day No 31840 was seen hauling the failed 15.50 Ilfracombe to Exeter DMU, and the next day the same engine worked a transfer goods from Riverside to Exmouth Junction. In the following weeks 'Ns' were noted on other freights, but all such 'unofficial' activity had ceased before the end of October. There were now no longer any engines of Southern origin remaining on the allocation, although diesel unavailability meant that the depot continued to receive visits from 'Pacifics' on out-and-back workings.

In Plymouth the SR shed at Friary had closed in 1963 and all the remaining steam servicing in the city was concentrated at Laira depot until it too closed to steam in 1964. As the Callington branch was still steam-worked at that time, for a short period three Exmouth Junction Ivatt 2-6-2Ts handled the work; they were stabled overnight at Callington and a changeover for servicing was effected by working each in turn a day at a time to Exeter in exchange for another loco. BR Standard tanks were also still used on the Bude branch and between Okehampton and Padstow until these services were dieselised from 4 January 1965. Otherwise the remaining steam duties were mainly freight trains, and by the end of 1964 the shed was servicing more diesel than steam locomotives each day. At the start of 1965 its steam allocation comprised 32 engines, of which 17 were BR Standard types: two 5MT 4-6-0s, four 4MT 4-6-0s, six 4MT 2-6-4Ts and five '3MT 2-6-2Ts. There were also eight Ivatt 2MT 2-6-2Ts, five pannier tanks and the two ex-GWR 0-6-0s; on 26 March one of the latter, No 3205, was seen banking pannier tank No 4694 on a transfer goods, probably as a test before it was used on a railtour the next day. Although main-line diesels were never allocated to the depot, there were seven diesel shunters; two were used as pilots at St David's, two worked in Riverside yard, and another was employed in Exmouth Junction yard. The steam fleet continued to diminish, and in the first two months of 1965 the

There is not a Southern engine in sight on 9 January 1965, with 'Hymek' Type 3 No D7097 and Type 2 No D6323 on the left and BR Standard 4-6-0s Nos 73162 and 73044 on the right; just visible behind the latter are 0-6-0PT No 9647 and Ivatt 2-6-2T No 41223. *R. A. Lumber*

two 5MT 4-6-0s, two 2-6-4Ts and a 2MT 2-6-2T had either been transferred away or withdrawn.

The work of the four BR 4MT 4-6-0s, the final tender engines in the allocation, included Meldon ballast trains, and they were also regularly employed on an 06.47 Exeter to Yeovil parcels train. Work for the remaining tank engines included the daily freights over the Exmouth and Sidmouth branches and as Central station pilots. One weekday 0-6-0PT turn commenced by hauling grain wagons from Riverside to Thorverton Mill before working a coal train to Alphington Road goods yard; another pannier tank was diagrammed to work transfer freights between Exmouth Junction and Riverside, and a third handled trips to several sidings in the Pinhoe area. Goods trains still needed banking assistance, and at least three engines still had to be available for the Meldon ballast trains and the Westbury cement trains.

A 'Prairie' tank was also rostered to work an early morning goods train to Axminster and undertake any shunting that was required both there and at the milk depot at Seaton Junction; it returned by working the 1.52pm Axminster to Exeter Central passenger train, which was the last regular steam passenger turn off Exmouth Junction. It was steam-powered for the final time on Saturday 22 May 1965 by No 82042, and the shed was officially closed to steam from the following Monday, its steam fleet being dispersed elsewhere. Despite this, the shed continued to service visiting engines that were deputising for diesels, and even on the first 'steamless' day Nos 34005 *Barnstaple* and 34051 *Winston Churchill* were in steam on the shed, and No 34052 *Lord Dowding* arrived with the 15.00 departure from Waterloo. Use of visiting 'Pacifics' on the Meldon trains diminished after May, but they were noted on two workings in June and September that year. Also at least 11 steam workings were recorded on Waterloo services between May and 26 September 1965, when the use of steam west of Salisbury was officially banned; despite this, No 34032 *Camelford* was reported to have worked the 13.00 from Waterloo on 29 November.

On summer Saturdays in 1965 a 10.00 Waterloo to Sidmouth Junction train ran with portions for Sidmouth and Exmouth, and although diagrammed for a 'Warship' on 11 September it too was hauled by *Camelford*. Also on seven peak Saturdays in July and August two additional services ran to these resorts and, although one of the trains was rostered for 'Warship' haulage, the other was steam-powered between Waterloo and Sidmouth Junction; from there the two portions were taken forward by D63XX and 'Hymek' diesels, and the steam engine ran light from Sidmouth Junction to Exmouth Junction for turning and servicing.

1965 also saw a number of steam railtours and, despite the steam ban, further excursions brought steam to Exeter in 1966. It is remarkable that the WR permitted such workings as, apart from the Somerset & Dorset line, facilities to service steam were no longer officially available on the region after 3 January 1966. Five days later a private charter promoted as 'The Last Steam Train to Exeter Central' was hauled between Waterloo and Salisbury by No 34001 *Exeter*, but unfortunately an opportunity for the engine to make a last visit to its 'home city' was missed and No 34015 *Exmouth* worked the train between Salisbury and Exeter. Although not all were actually promoted as such, during that year there were a further five 'last steam trains' to Exeter, including the LCGB's 'A4 Commemorative Rail Tour' on 27 March, which was worked from Waterloo to St David's and back by 4-6-2 No 60024 *Kingfisher*; 'Hymek' No D7048 was provided to bank the nine-coach train from St David's on the return. On 2 April another private charter was hauled by No 34006 *Bude* to Sidmouth Junction, where No D7069 took the train on a return trip to Exmouth; during this time the 'Pacific' ran to Exmouth

'Pacific' No 34015 *Exmouth* was one of the last engines to be coaled at Exmouth Junction after it arrived with a railtour on a dismal 8 January 1966; the wagon hoist can be noted on the left-hand side of the coaling plant, and there seem to be plenty of 'shed bashers' observing proceedings. *R. A. Lumber*

Junction for servicing and was probably the last engine to use the turntable before it was taken out of use.

Another tour promoted as the 'Last Steam Train to Exeter' was the SCTS 'The Devonshire Rambler' on 26 June, but the engine, No 35023 *Holland-America Line*, did not need to be turned as, after arriving at St David's, it continued its journey via the WR main line to Westbury. On 14 August Exmouth Junction had an unscheduled visit from LNER 'A2' 4-6-2 No 60532 *Blue Peter*; the LCGB managed to have it brought all the way from Aberdeen to work another tour from Waterloo to Exeter that returned via Westbury, but unfortunately it stalled on Honiton bank, reputedly due to poor-quality coal. Eventually the crew were able to raise sufficient steam to reach Exeter Central and the engine then retreated to Exmouth Junction, where the fire was rebuilt, and the tour eventually departed from St David's 160 minutes late.

During a 'bash' of Exmouth Junction shed to see *Blue Peter*, which was its final visiting steam engine, the other locos present were recorded and, being a Sunday, there were a good number, with 'Western' Class No D1010, 'Warships' Nos D801/11/16/18/20/26/48/68, 'Hymek' No D7027, Type 2s Nos D6317-19, D6322/24/25, D6330/33/36/39, shunters Nos D3519 and D4162, and a few DMU sets all seen. Two further steam tours passed the shed that year; ironically the final one, hauled by No 34019 *Bideford* on 13 November, was not actually promoted as the last steam train, but was indeed to be the last such excursion to visit the city until the 'GW150' celebrations in 1985.

The Sidmouth and Budleigh Salterton branches closed from Monday 6 March 1967, which meant that all the east Devon branches had closed bar the Exeter to Exmouth line. Other proposals at that time including the closure of the lines to Plymouth and north Devon, and work was scheduled to start on singling much of the line between Exeter and Salisbury; Exmouth Junction marshalling yard had already closed and through freight traffic over the ex-SR main line had ceased. With a greatly diminished workload, it was no surprise that 'the Junction' was closed on 5 March and all diesel servicing and carriage cleaning work was transferred to Newton Abbot. The stock used on the Waterloo and Brighton trains was now berthed there or at Goodrington, and worked between Newton Abbot and Exeter on local stopping services. Locos seen at Exmouth Junction on the last day were Nos D810/37/59/68, D6317 and D4130/62. About 90 staff were made redundant with around a dozen transferring to the WR shed at St David's, which was reactivated as a basic servicing and fuelling point. For a short period 'the Junction' repair shed was used by the nearby Carriage & Wagon department, but afterwards the shed buildings at this former 'Steam Cathedral' became increasingly derelict and were demolished, together with the coal hopper, in 1970; later the site was redeveloped for a supermarket.

Exmouth Junction Carriage & Wagon Repair Works

When the LSWR first developed the site at Exmouth Junction it established small workshops for engineering and signal work and for carriage and wagon repairs. When the first engine shed was built, its repair road was also used for the maintenance and repair of wagons, but around the turn of the century a separate three-road carriage and wagon repair shed was erected opposite the junction signal box.

When the engine shed was rebuilt, the opportunity was taken to increase the capacity of the other departments making use of the 28 acres available. In addition to the new locomotive running depot and repair shops, further improvements included a new Carriage & Wagon Repair Works, engineering shops, including a signal and telegraph section, a larger depot for the manufacture of concrete items, a stores department, and a freight marshalling yard.

The new C&W Works was opened in 1928 to the north of the original on land between the engine shed and the concrete works. The 51½-foot-wide building had two bays, each covering three roads; one bay was 300 feet long and the other 350 feet. One road had a pit to access the

On 11 July 1983 No 08954 has worked the weekday trip from Riverside yard to the Carriage & Wagon Works and is propelling HTV coal hoppers into the building for attention. *DHM*

The Southern engine sheds, locomotives and other works   105

undersides of vehicles. All routine maintenance for the SR's Western Division was carried out here, but vehicles requiring a full overhaul or repaint were sent to Eastleigh Works. At its peak the Exeter C&W Department employed about 170 men, which included some who were out-stationed at various places in the Exeter Division.

Carriage work ceased in 1967, but about 60 men were still employed on wagon repairs and a weekday trip from Riverside yard would ferry stock that required attention. By 1982 a reduction in freight traffic and the introduction of modern wagons, many of which were privately owned, meant a diminishing workload and the works was officially closed in June of that year, although a small workforce of about ten men continued there for a year or so longer. Subsequently the building was refurbished and some of the track was remodelled for use as a Civil Engineers' workshop to service and maintain track machines and other plant. This activity ceased in about 2004 and the site was cleared in 2012; afterwards some of the land was integrated into the supermarket site to provide a petrol station and larger car park.

In about 1990 the Wagon Works was refurbished when it was being used to maintain on-track plant. No 37092 has arrived on 10 June 1992 with an 'as required' working from Riverside to convey on-track plant. DHM

Raw materials for the works were imported by rail, particularly sand, which was dredged from the River Taw estuary and loaded on to the railway at Fremington Quay, and stone chippings came from Meldon Quarry. After nationalisation some work was undertaken for other regions, but the site was closed from 1 February 1965 when some of the men transferred to the WR concrete depot at Taunton.

Exmouth Junction Concrete Works

A concrete works was first established by the LSWR in 1913 for the manufacture of a range of standard pre-cast products including fence and lamp posts and station nameboards; such items had previously been made of wood. After the 'Grouping' in 1923 the Southern Railway expanded production to include other items, and that year the wooden footbridge at Pinhoe station was replaced by a concrete one that arrived as a kit of parts from Exmouth Junction; the components were delivered by rail and erected using the depot's steam crane. Reputedly this was the first such bridge to be erected, and was to prove the first of many installed throughout the SR system. When Polsloe Bridge Halt on the Exmouth branch was rebuilt in 1928, the platforms were constructed of concrete slabs supported on concrete brackets; the combined waiting shelter and booking office, flights of steps from the adjacent roads, nameboards and posts were also entirely Exmouth Junction products.

Although concrete was extensively used in the new engine shed and other structures at Exmouth Junction, the scale of that work was beyond the capabilities of the works, which was geared to producing a range of smaller standard items. Concrete sleepers were also made, but were generally considered to be a speciality during the lifetime of the works.

Various products including fencing, gates and a gradient sign are displayed in a publicity picture for the Concrete Works; as there is also an Exmouth platform sign, the photo may date from 1924, when that station was rebuilt.

9. Off the beaten track

In early years a loco would usually work within a restricted area where it could be entrusted to one driver who would not only drive it, but also maintain it and ensure that it was properly cleaned every day. This may explain why engines always seem to be so clean in early photographs with immaculate paintwork and sparkling brasswork, all possible in an era of long working days and no paid overtime. For many years the locos on GWR main-line services may have been changed at Exeter or Newton Abbot, particularly due to the different line profile west of the latter. For all of the LSWR's and Southern Railway's existence it was the usual practice to change engines at Salisbury on trains to and from Waterloo, and it was rare for an engine allocated to a shed east of Exmouth Junction to be seen west of Exeter.

Reduced working hours contributed towards a 'common user' policy, whereby locos could move from depot to depot until required at their home shed for maintenance such as a boiler washout. Even then engine changes were still frequent and it was unusual for locos to stray too far away from home, so the visit of an engine from a far-flung shed was a notable event; even the appearance of a Cornish loco east of Newton Abbot was fairly unusual. A train leaving Penzance for the north in the mid-1920s might have started behind a Cornish 4-4-0, but the addition of extra coaches and a dining car at Plymouth would require a larger engine, perhaps one of Laira's 'Star' Class 4-6-0s. At that time the engine was almost invariably changed at Bristol, where it might have been replaced by a Bristol 'Saint' Class 4-6-0 or perhaps a 'County' Class 4-4-0 that was working back to its home shed at Shrewsbury; there the GWR loco would be replaced by an LMS engine.

Hence the sight of a Great Central Railway engine in 1904 was truly remarkable. At that time the GWR and GCR were building the joint railway between Northolt (London) and Ashendon Junction (north-west of Aylesbury), and relations between the two companies were particularly cordial. Agreement was reached for GCR engines to work through to GWR metals with excursions to various destinations, and on 28 October 1904 a train left Manchester (London Road) at 11.30pm bound for Plymouth Millbay, where it arrived at 9.50am on the 29th. A Gorton crew was in charge of Class '8B' 'Atlantic' No 267 for the full 374 miles, and at the time it was thought to be the longest excursion journey ever made in the country. The return trip departed at 12.03am on the 30th and arrived back in Manchester at 9.50am the same morning.

Three similar trips were arranged in 1905. The first was on 20 April when it left Manchester at 10.15am with seven coaches including a buffet car. The loco was replaced by another 4-4-2 No 265 at Leicester, but it is understood that the same Gorton crew worked throughout to Plymouth with a GWR inspector joining them at Banbury. The train ran non-stop for 173 miles from Banbury (by which time 157 passengers were on board) via the Badminton line to avoid Bristol, and arrived in Exeter in 3hr 38min; it was booked over the 300 miles from Sheffield to Newton Abbot, with six intermediate stops, in 7hr 2min. After just a few hours'

Great Central Railway Class '8B' 4-4-2 No 267 has a gathering of admirers as it pauses at Exeter St David's with the ground-breaking Manchester to Plymouth excursion on the morning of 29 October 1904. The train consisted of five Great Central corridor bogie coaches as far as Exeter, where two GWR carriages were added.

rest, the same crew worked the train as empty stock back to Gorton on the following day. Two more excursions from Manchester to Plymouth in June 1905 were both hauled by No 267. Further trips ran in 1906 and 1907, but the GCR engines only worked as far as Bristol, where GWR locos took over.

In 1910 it appears that some of the GWR's directors had become uneasy at what they regarded as the high cost of their new express 4-6-0s compared with those being built by the LNWR; reputedly three of the latter were being built for the cost of two of Swindon's products. The LNWR had already tested its locos against engines of other companies and agreed to exchange trials in August 1910 between Euston and Crewe and over the GWR's West of England line at a time of year when expresses would have peak loadings. On the GWR No 4003 *Lode Star* was tested against the LNWR's 'Experiment' Class engine No 1471 *Worcestershire* and proved to be superior to the visitor; on 24 August *Worcestershire* worked the 11.50am Paddington to Exeter train with a dynamometer car and arrived 13½ minutes late. It later transpired that the claims as to the respective building costs were inaccurate, and the 'Stars' were only slightly more expensive than their rivals.

In 1924 the GWR's first 'Castle' Class 4-6-0, No 4073 *Caerphilly Castle* was exhibited with the LNER's new 'A1' 'Pacific' No 4472 *Flying Scotsman* at the Empire Exhibition at Wembley; the 'A1' was larger than the 'Castle' but a board displayed in front of the GWR engine proclaimed it to be the most powerful passenger loco in Britain. It was suggested that an exchange trial be arranged with a 'Castle' working for a

Off the beaten track

week on the East Coast Main Line and a Gresley 'Pacific' on the GWR. The exchange was held between 27 April and 2 May 1925, when No 4474 *Victor Wild* worked the 'Cornish Riviera Express' between Paddington and Plymouth. The 'Castle' emerged triumphant from these trials, but lessons learned led to modifications being made to the 'A1s' and the introduction of the 'A3' Class in 1928.

After the Dunkirk evacuation in 1940 it was believed that Germany would soon attempt an invasion, and 12 armoured trains were formed to patrol some of the more vulnerable sections of coastline. Each train was formed around an armour-plated LNER Class 'F4' 2-4-2T painted in camouflage colours with wagons fore and aft carrying six-pounder Hotchkiss guns and Bren machine guns. They were operated by Royal Engineers crews and manned by Royal Armoured Corps soldiers; Polish troops took over in April 1941. At first they were employed on the east coast, but three trains were sent to the South West in late July 1940 when the area's bays were regarded as potential landing places. One train was based at Newton Abbot from where it patrolled the line between Exeter and Kingswear; an Exeter enthusiast, the late John Bamsey, observed 'F4' No 7172 at Newton Abbot with this train on 17 August 1940. A year later it was moved to Cornwall, but with an improvement in the war situation the trains were stood down in 1942.

The amount of freight traffic on the GWR rose substantially during the war, particularly after the fall of France, when increased use was made of the Bristol Channel ports. To alleviate a power shortage 25 LMS Class 8F 2-8-0s were allocated to South Wales sheds in the autumn of 1940, primarily to haul freight to the London area. The locos had been built to Government order for use in France before its defeat, and were only loaned to the GWR for about nine months before they were dispatched to the Middle East, but are thought to have reached Devon during that time. From November 1940 until February 1943 the GWR's fleet was augmented by the loan of 30 LNER Class 'O4' 2-8-0s, but this type were not strangers as a batch that had been constructed for the Railway Operating Division of the Royal Engineers for use in the First World War had been purchased by the GWR after the war, and most remained in service until beyond nationalisation. Some were allocated to Devon sheds, but the number diminished in the 1930s and No 3031 was the last one allocated west of Bristol when it left Exeter in 1936; they would, however, continue to visit the county. John Bamsey noted a number of the LNER engines working goods trains in the Exeter area in 1941, including Nos 6209, 6232, 6321 and 6594.

More unusual was the loan of several Southern Railway 4-6-0s, including four 'S15s' and six 'Remembrance' Class 'N15X' engines, Nos 2327 to 2332, to the GWR from November 1941 until July 1943; these mainly worked on goods or van trains in the London area, but during 1942 Nos 2329 *Stephenson* and 2331 *Beattie* were shedded at Newton Abbot and Exeter respectively. Early that year the former frequently worked from Newton Abbot to Exeter with an early morning passenger train, and was later used on Kingswear branch goods trains, not obvious work for a loco with 6ft 9in driving wheels. By January 1943 *Stephenson* was shedded at Exeter where it regularly worked a goods train to Swindon, but apparently it was ill-suited to the task and local crews said that they were called the 'Remembrance' Class because they were unforgettably useless! The 'S15s' were, however, more appropriate and two, Nos 30496 and 30498, were allocated to Exeter in February 1942; all the SR 4-6-0s were returned in the summer of 1943 when other engines became available.

These were 80 of the LMS-designed 8Fs, which were constructed at Swindon at the rate of just under one a week from June 1943. By the end of that year 26 were at work, with 13 based in the West: seven were at Bristol St Philip's Marsh, Nos 8420, 8425 and later 8434 were shedded at Exeter, three were allocated to Newton Abbot, and another was based at Plymouth Laira. By the end of 1944 they were a very common sight in the area, with further examples allocated to Taunton and Penzance sheds. At the end of the war five were allocated to Exeter, but they were widely used and an Exeter loco could just as easily be seen working in South Wales as in the South West. The 8Fs were replaced by WD 'Austerity' 2-8-0s in 1947, but when the WR found itself short of power in the following decade a batch of these 8Fs was transferred back from July 1954 and regularly worked as far as Plymouth on heavy goods trains until as late as 1963.

Between 1942 and 1945 the three main American locomotive builders constructed a total of 2,120 Class 'S160' 2-8-0 engines for the US Transportation Corps, mainly for service in Europe after the Allied invasion. The locos were built to fit the British loading gauge, as it was envisaged that at first they would

Displaying a very different profile to British eyes, Alco-built and Old Oak Common-allocated USA 'S160' 2-8-0 No 2151 heads an up goods train at Stafford's Bridge, east of Exeter, on 11 November 1943. These locos were painted light grey but, despite being less than a year old, this engine appears to be heavily work-stained; after crossing the Channel it worked in Hungary. There were restrictions on photography during the war and this is the only photo of one of these locos working in Devon that the author is aware of. *Author's collection*

support the war effort in Britain by helping to haul the massive increase in freight in the build-up to D-Day. About 400 saw service in Britain and by the autumn of 1943 174 were allocated to the GWR; none were shedded west of Bristol, but they regularly appeared in Devon for about a year. On a single journey from Plymouth to Bristol early in 1944 an observer reported seeing five USA 2-8-0s and eight LMS 8Fs on goods trains. For a period Nos 1771, 1916, 1920, 2356, 2378 and 2590 were based at Exmouth Junction; two were observed by John Bamsey on trains to the US Army depot at Newcourt and he also saw the other four in the Exeter area between November 1943 and April 1944, either on Exmouth Junction shed or working freights; all were shipped across the English Channel from late 1944.

John also recorded a number of interesting 0-6-0 types during the war, including SR 'Q' Class engines Nos 539 and 548 at Exeter Central in June 1940, ex-Midland Railway 2F No 3039 on a down goods south of Exeter on 3 April 1941 (some of these were loaned to Bristol St Philip's Marsh shed during the war), and two pairs of WD (ex-GWR 'Dean Goods') engines in May 1944.

The 'Austerity' 2-8-0s were designed in 1942 as a simpler and cheaper alternative to the LMS 8Fs for what was hoped would be short-term use in support of Allied forces in Europe. In 1943 450 were loaned to the LNER, LMS and SR, and 80 of these were then transferred to the GWR in early September 1944 to fill the gap left by the departing 'S160s'. They were often seen in Devon, but all had crossed the Channel by the end of February 1945. After the war most were repatriated and again loaned to British railway companies; 94 went to the GWR to replace the 80 8Fs that had moved to the LMS in 1947. BR purchased these loaned locos and they continued to work into Devon until well into the 1950s.

After D-Day ambulance trains carried American wounded to a military hospital that had been established near Heathfield. The trains were routed over the Teign Valley line from Exeter and unloaded at Chudleigh rather than Heathfield, as there was better road access there for the many ambulances that were needed; after unloading, the trains continued down the branch and returned via Newton Abbot. Initially they comprised Westinghouse air-braked US Army coaches that were to go to the continent, and were hauled by LNER Class 'B12/3' 4-6-0s; these were built for the Great Eastern Railway, which was one of the few British companies to use the Westinghouse system, and they could be used on the branch due to their light axle-loading. The trains mainly ran overnight, when they had full occupation of the line, but Nos 8516, 8530 and 8549 were noted by observers; the first of these was seen climbing to Exeter Central double-headed with pilot 'T9' No 730 on an up empty ambulance train during the evening of 12 June 1944. Within a few months the US trains were sent abroad, but ambulance trains of vacuum-braked stock continued to run for a period hauled by pairs of '43XX' Class 2-6-0s.

In the Second World War it was thought quite likely that at some point either the GWR's main line from Exeter to Plymouth or the Southern's route via Okehampton would be damaged or blocked by enemy action. In this event traffic over both routes, including vital war materials, would have to be diverted over whichever line was still open, and it was essential to have a pool of crews who 'knew' both routes; it was therefore arranged for SR crews and locos to work several trains over the GWR's line each day, with GWR crews and engines working over the Southern route.

By May 1942 Laira's 2-6-0 No 7321 was regularly noted working the 2.35pm Plymouth Friary to Exeter Central train

Built by North British in Glasgow in January 1944 and still bearing War Department number 77421, an 'Austerity' 2-8-0 is rumbling over the goods avoiding line at Exeter St David's with a down freight from Riverside yard at 11.05am on 2 October 1948. It was allocated to Plymouth Laira shed from 9 August 1947 to 18 June 1949, and was given its BR number of 90292 in April 1949. *J. H. Bamsey*

Off the beaten track

Not long after leaving Exminster station, Exmouth Junction's 'West Country' 4-6-2 No 34021 *Dartmoor* is about to pass under the Exeter bypass in 1956 with the 2.15pm Plymouth North Road to Exeter St David's interchange working; the use of 'Pacifics' on these workings ended in 1959. *John Stredwick*

and, after turning and servicing at Exmouth Junction, it then returned from Central with the Plymouth portion of the 2.50pm from Waterloo. At this time another 'Mogul', No 6385, was noted arriving with the 4.40pm from Friary, although on this occasion the loco ran tender-first for servicing at the GWR shed. On 19 June 1942 'N' Class 2-6-0 No 1408 worked the 11.25am GWR stopper from St David's to Plymouth North Road. To provide flexibility on other routes a GWR working between St David's and Yeovil via Taunton and return was diagrammed for an Exmouth Junction 'T9' on load three. Similarly a return trip on SR metals from Exeter Central to Ilfracombe was handled by an Exeter-based GWR 'Mogul'.

The interchange workings between Exeter and Plymouth continued after the war, but were reduced to two turns daily except on Mondays, when the trains originating in Plymouth were worked by engines belonging to the parent line; otherwise an Exmouth Junction engine worked the 11.35 St David's to North Road service, returning with the 4.30pm train from Plymouth, and a Plymouth Friary engine hauled the 2.30pm from North Road, returning with a parcels train from St David's. Initially these trains were usually worked by 'N' Class 'Moguls', but by January 1946 they were diagrammed for a 'West Country' 'Pacific'. On the SR route an Exeter-based GWR 'Mogul' would run tender-first from its shed to collect a train from the carriage shed at Central, and haul it as the 11.46am departure to Friary; it returned from there with the 4.40pm train, and during 1945 Nos 5321, 6323 and 6397 were all regulars on this duty. Meanwhile a Laira GWR 'Mogul' worked the 2.35pm Friary to Exeter Central train and, after servicing at Exmouth Junction, it returned with the 7.05pm train from Exeter; during 1946 No 5361 was almost continuously employed on this duty, but notably 'Bulldog' 4-4-0 No 3401 *Vancouver* covered the job on 8 August. Additionally on Sundays an Exeter 'Mogul' worked a GWR goods train from Riverside to Tavistock Junction yard, Plymouth, over the SR and returned the same way with another freight.

Although the GWR work over the SR was rostered for 'Moguls', 'Hall' and 'Saint' Class engines were also permitted, but due to tight clearances a speed restriction was imposed through certain stations; on 24 December 1948 No 6913

Levens Hall was observed on the 2.35pm service from Friary. For about five years from the spring of 1949 the Laira duty was often handled by a 'Manor' 4-6-0, whereas Exeter regularly used a 'Hall', particularly during the peak period for Tamar Valley horticultural traffic, when the 4.40pm from Plymouth could have up to 10 vans added to the train at Bere Alston. In July 1951 'Star' Class 4-6-0s were authorised over the SR subject to certain speed restrictions, and Laira's No 4054 *Princess Charlotte* was seen on that depot's turn, although on one occasion it caused minor damage to the platform at Bow. By then this loco was 'on its last legs' and apparently struggled on the climb to Exeter Central with just three coaches. From 1954 BR Standard 4MT 4-6-0s were often employed on the Laira turn, and new locos from this class and Class 3MT 2-6-2Ts allocated to Exmouth Junction were used over the WR route.

Five stations on the WR route were closed between Brent and Plymouth from 2 March 1959 and the trains used to keep SR crews acquainted with the WR route were cut from the timetable. The SR also reduced the WR working over its route to just a single job each way by a Laira '63XX' engine, and with the end of the Exeter turn Nos 5339 and 6385 lost their regular work and were put into store. From 22 June 1959 the Laira duty was rostered for a D63XX Type 2 diesel; the interchange workings as such appear to have ended by the time the SR territory in the West had transferred to the WR at the end of 1962.

In 1948 the newly nationalised British Railways planned a programme of exchanges to compare the performances of engines from the 'Big Four' companies on which to base future standardisation plans. Three separate trials were used to compare express passenger, mixed-traffic and freight engines, but only the first two took place in Devon. Normal service trains were used, and they were manned by their usual crews; there were two round trips each week, with pre-test runs for crew familiarisation purposes in the first week from Mondays to Thursdays and the actual test runs in the second week from Tuesdays to Fridays. The GWR's dynamometer car was added on the latter runs.

The trains used on the WR for express engines were the 1.30pm Paddington to Plymouth and the 8.30am from Plymouth. Preliminary runs started on 19 April when 'Merchant Navy' 4-6-2 No 35019 *French Line CGT* worked the down train, and the tests began on the 20th with 4-6-0 No 6018 *King Henry VI*. In subsequent weeks the locos scheduled were ex-LNER 'A4' 4-6-2 No E22 *Mallard* (it had yet to be given its BR number) and two ex-LMS types, 'Coronation' 4-6-2 No 46236 *City of Bradford* and 'Royal

During the 1948 Locomotive Exchanges, ex-LNER 'A4' 4-6-2 No 22 *Mallard* is leaving Exeter St David's with the 8.30am Plymouth to Paddington service on 27 April 1948; this was a 'pre-test' run for crew familiarisation purposes, but the loco later disgraced itself by failing at Savernake. *Author's collection*

Off the beaten track

The LMR's 'Royal Scot' 4-6-0 No 46162 *Queen's Westminster Rifleman* is approaching Cowley Bridge Junction with the 8.30am Plymouth to Paddington 'pre-test' working on either 18 or 20 May 1948. *Author's collection*

'A4' 'Pacific' No 60033 *Seagull* was recorded in Platform 2 at Exeter Central on 11 June 1948 prior to heading the 12.40pm Exeter to Waterloo 'Atlantic Coast Express'; the 1901-vintage GWR dynamometer car is behind the engine. *Author's collection*

A little more of the dynamometer coach can be seen on either 23 or 25 June 1948, with 'Coronation' Class 'Pacific' No 46236 *City of Bradford* about to haul the same working. As there were no water troughs on the Southern Region the former LMS engines that ran over the SR were paired with borrowed eight-wheeled tenders from 'Austerity' 2-8-0s, which had larger water tanks. *Author's collection*

Scot' 4-6-0 No 46162 *Queen's Westminster Rifleman*. All apparently went well apart from on 27 April when *Mallard* sustained an overheated middle big-end bearing at Savernake while returning on its first preliminary outing, and was replaced by No 60033 *Seagull* on its subsequent trips.

On the SR the express engines were tested on the down and up 'Atlantic Coast Express' between Waterloo and Exeter Central, but a 'King' was not used due to clearance issues. The 'A4' *Seagull* started the trial by working the first preliminary run on 31 May, but it too failed at Andover with an overheated bearing on the middle cylinder connecting rod. Perhaps unwisely *Mallard* was dispatched overnight to Exmouth Junction to work the return run and, although it completed this and the following 'pre-test' round trip, it failed again at Salisbury with the same fault while working the first up test run! After its failure *Seagull* was just back from repair at Doncaster Works and was dispatched to cover the final round trip. The other engines performed without any problems; *City of Bradford* was used again, but Nos 35018 *British India Line* and 46154 *The Hussar* replaced the engines used on the WR.

The SR did not feature in the mixed-traffic trial, which used the 1.45pm Bristol Temple Meads to Plymouth train and 1.35pm return. Preliminary runs started on 28 June when ER 'B1' 4-6-0 No 61251 *Oliver Bury* worked the down train, and the tests began on the 29th with 4-6-0 No 6990 *Witherslack Hall*; other engines used were LMR Class 5 4-6-0 No 45253 and 'West Country' 4-6-2 No 34006 *Bude*, and all these runs were completed without incident.

The LMS Fairburn 2-6-4Ts were a 1945 development of a Stanier design with a shorter wheelbase, and in an early post-nationalisation 'standardisation' 41 were constructed at

Brighton Works in 1950 and 1951 for service on the Eastern Section of the Southern Region. However, four engines were temporarily allocated to Exmouth Junction in 1951 while the inspection pits at Bude were being reconstructed, as the Fairburn tanks were equipped with self-cleaning smokeboxes. No 42103 arrived on 5 September and was sent light to Bude two days later; No 42105 then reached Exeter and went to Bude on the 22nd, soon after being replaced by No 42099. The pit work was completed in October, but the locos remained at Exmouth Junction and a fourth engine, No 42102, was transferred there during November. They

A very rare view of one of the Fairburn Class 4 2-6-4Ts during their brief spell in the South West. No 42103 is at Exeter St David's at 4.50pm on a dull 22 September 1951 while working light from Halwill Junction to Exmouth Junction after completing a stint on the Bude branch. *G. T. Reardon*

Off the beaten track

were used regularly on Meldon Quarry ballast trains and for a period covered two passenger diagrams between Exeter and Plymouth, but they all returned east in January 1952.

On 24 April 1953 'Merchant Navy' No 35020 *Bibby Line* suffered a fractured driving axle while travelling at speed near Crewkerne with the 4.30pm Exeter Central to Waterloo train; fortunately the loco remained upright and the actions of the crew averted a disaster. The entire class was withdrawn from traffic on 12 May so that their axles could be ultrasonically inspected, and on examination other faults were discovered. By the next day five 'Britannia' Class 4-6-2s had been loaned by the WR for use on the SR's Western Section, and the LMR loaned two 'Britannias' for Eastern Section duties; on the first day No 70024 *Vulcan* was seen on the 9.00pm Nine Elms to Exmouth Junction freight. Additionally the ER sent six 'V2' 2-6-2s, and once these arrived the 'Britannia's were mainly confined to the Exeter road and the 'V2's largely used on the Bournemouth line. Most of the visitors were based at Nine Elms, but three 'Britannias' were temporarily allocated to Exmouth Junction, Nos 70024 *Vulcan*, 70028 *Royal Star* and 70029 *Shooting Star*.

The axles on four of the SR 'Pacifics' were found to be

Strange bedfellows at Exmouth Junction shed on 24 May 1953: Doncaster-allocated ex-LNER Gresley 'V2' 2-6-2 No 60896 sits next to Salisbury's 'King Arthur' Class 4-6-0 No 30450 *Sir Kay*. Adding to the variety, ex-LMS diesel-electric Co-Co No 10000 can be glimpsed beyond the tender of the 'V2', and the bunker of an 'E1/R' 0-6-2T is in view on the right. *C. H. S. Owen*

On loan from the Western Region's Old Oak Common shed, 'Britannia' Class 7P6F 4-6-2 No 70023 *Venus* is arriving at Exeter Central with the 3.00pm departure from Waterloo on 25 May 1953. Apparently during this period the 'Britannias' showed themselves to be fully capable of handling the 'Merchant Navy' turns, but some drivers were not overly impressed, considering them to be rough riders.
J. H. Bamsey

Crewe North shed's 'Black 5' 4-6-0 No 45350 is leaving Exeter Central with the 10.17am departure to Waterloo on 26 May 1953. It is understood that these engines were well received by crews, but during the loan period they were often rostered for 'secondary' duties including Waterloo to Salisbury semi-fast workings and Bournemouth relief trains, and it is not thought that they often reached Exeter. *J. H. Bamsey*

faulty and those on two further locos were replaced as a precaution. They began returning to traffic on 16 May, with 13 available by the next day, and all but three were in service by the beginning of June. Examinations started on the 'Light Pacifics' on 18 May, but only a small number were taken out of service at any one time. However, additional engines were temporarily transferred to Nine Elms, including seven LMR 'Black 5' and three BR Standard Class 5 4-6-0s, and a shuffling of SR resources included temporarily moving three Bath and three Battersea 'Pacifics' to Exmouth Junction. Generally the 'V2s' and 'Black 5s' performed well on the SR with less maintenance and a reduction in coal consumption when compared with the Bulleid 'Pacifics'. Only two defective axles were traced on the latter, with a further six failing to fully satisfy the examiners, and by the end of June all the borrowed engines had returned home.

During January 1956 all 30 WR 'King' Class engines were temporarily withdrawn from service for examination after the discovery of bogie fractures. 'Castles' and 'Halls' were promoted to cover some of their work and a number of Standard Class 5 4-6-0s were loaned by the LMR and SR, mainly to work in the London and Bristol areas. The LMR also loaned four 'Pacifics', 'Princess' Class Nos 46207 *Princess Arthur of Connaught* and 46210 *Lady Patricia*, and 'Coronation' Class Nos 46254 *City of Stoke-on-Trent* and 46257 *City of Salford*, and these regularly worked the 'Cornish Riviera Express' and other turns to the west. 'King' No 6012 was recorded back in

service on 9 February and the others followed quite quickly afterwards.

Although at different times six of the BR Standard loco classes regularly worked in Devon, others were never seen and two types only appeared fleetingly. The 20 Standard Class 3 2-6-0s Nos 77000-19 were built at Swindon in 1954 for use in the North Eastern and Scottish regions, and after completion spent time running in on local duties, including stopping services to Bristol. Some ranged further afield and on 16 April 1954 No 77006 was seen in Exeter while working the 10.50pm Marston Sidings (Swindon) to Plymouth Millbay fish train; it returned light two days later coupled to No 7907 *Hart Hall*. Soon afterwards No 77006 was reported to have reached Plymouth for a second time with the fish train and it was seen at Exeter again on 28 May; it has been suggested that other members of the class also worked this duty, but this has not been confirmed.

Although a number of the Standard Class 4MT 2-6-0s were allocated to SR sheds as close as Salisbury and Yeovil, they were never officially based at Exmouth Junction and

'Princess' Class 'Pacific' No 46210 *Lady Patricia* has a good head of steam as it approaches Aller Junction at the foot of Dainton bank with the down 'Cornish Riviera Express' on Friday 10 February 1956. *C. H. S. Owen*

Off the beaten track

were only occasional visitors to Exeter. However, No 76005 was a guest at 'the Junction' in April 1956 while undergoing repairs, then remained for a period when it was joined by No 76027. It was thought locally that these two were replacements for a stud of 75XXX 4-6-0 engines that had recently departed, but their stay was brief, although both engines are known to have reached Plymouth during this period.

The 30 Standard Class 2 2-6-2Ts were derived from the LMS Ivatt 'Prairie' tanks; 130 of the latter had been constructed between 1946 and 1952 and a good number worked on the SR. The BR version was built in two batches, and Nos 84020-29 were delivered new to the SR in 1957 for service in Kent; however, with the introduction of electric and diesel services they became redundant. In May 1961 Nos 84020-23 were allocated to Exmouth Junction. No 84021 had arrived by 15 June when it was seen working on the Exmouth branch, and this line appears to have been a regular haunt as on 28 June Nos 84020, 84022 and 84023 were all employed there. The LMS version had assumed duties on the Lyme Regis branch that year and it is understood that No 84022 also worked on the branch that summer. The type's stay at Exmouth Junction was to be very short and they were reallocated to the LMR around the middle of September 1961, with Ivatt 2-6-2Ts Nos 41320-23 received in exchange; apparently the SR felt that it had insufficient of the BR version to justify maintaining spares for them.

After nationalisation visits from 'foreign' engines remained notable events, and throughout steam days there continued to be a huge divide between the WR and LMR in Bristol, with through services changing engines there; this even continued into the early diesel period with the WR's diesel-hydraulics giving way to the LMR's diesel-electrics. This is reputed to have dated from the early years when the Midland Railway purchased the Gloucester to Bristol line from under the nose of the GWR and the latter made sure that its rivals were unable to penetrate any further west. This also meant that historically most regular through services from the WR to the north ran via the Severn Tunnel and the 'North & West' route to Crewe; the sole exception for many years was the 'Devonian', which ran via Birmingham to Bradford.

Although the LMS 'Jubilee' Class 5XP 4-6-0s regularly worked Midland services to Bristol, it is not thought that

On Saturday 5 May 1956 Standard Class 4MT 2-6-0 No 76005 is piloted by 'E1/R' No 32135 as it pulls away from St David's with the 8.20am Plymouth Friary to Exmouth Junction freight. The 'Mogul' worked off Exmouth Junction shed for a short period and this is one of two known workings by the type west of Exeter. *G. T. Reardon*

During its very short sojourn in Devon, BR Standard Class 2 2-6-2T No 84021 is standing outside the small sub-shed at Exmouth on 12 August 1961. *C. H. S. Owen*

one reached Devon before 15 September 1962, when No 45660 *Rooke* got as far as Exeter St David's with the 3.32pm Bristol to Penzance parcels train. Its arrival caused some consternation and it was hurriedly removed to be turned and watered before being promptly returned light from whence it came! A subsequent report indicates that a second 'Jubilee' reached Exeter, but no further details have been ascertained. However, exactly one year after the first visit on 15 September 1963, Bristol's No 45690 *Leander* worked a freight to Hackney Yard, and as the Newton Abbot turntable had been dismantled it had to go to Goodrington to be turned before working light back to Bristol.

10. Passenger services on 'Western' lines

When the Bristol & Exeter Railway reached Exeter in 1844 a first-day special train carrying the company's directors returned from the city to London after the celebrations in a fast time of 4hr 40min, but thereafter the fastest service train was the 'Night Mail', which had passenger accommodation and was scheduled to travel the 193½ miles from London to Exeter in 7hr 10min. Although this was comparable with other railways, this did not maximise the potential of the broad gauge or take advantage of a largely straight and level route, and the speed of GWR trains led the Board of Trade to oppose plans for the company to extend its broad gauge network further. This spurred the GWR into introducing its 'Exeter expresses' from 10 March 1845, which achieved fame as they were easily the fastest trains in the world at that time. Despite stopping at five intermediate stations, both the 9.30am from Paddington to Exeter and the 11.45am train from Devon completed their journeys in just 5 hours. By 12 May 1845 the schedules had reduced further to 4½ hours at an average speed of 43mph, which was quite remarkable for the period, and the down train earned the 'Flying Dutchman' nickname after a famous racehorse. Further services leaving Paddington at 5.50pm and Exeter at 6.30am were introduced to these timings in April 1846, but the schedules were extended slightly after an additional stop was made in Bridgwater, and once the B&E had taken over operations in 1849 it added stops at Weston and Tiverton Junction. Probably to economise on coal, the schedules were further slackened in 1853 and the fastest train now reached Exeter in 5¼ hours.

The overnight mail trains were heavy with frequent stops and were bad timekeepers, leading to complaints from the Post Office about the service. To rectify this the GWR introduced the 'Special Mail' in February 1855, the first dedicated postal train in the world; it usually comprised just three vehicles and left Paddington at 8.46pm with a 12.30am arrival in Bristol. From there it was combined with a passenger train to Plymouth that was due in Exeter at 3.20am; in the opposite direction the 7.10pm from Plymouth (9.45pm off Exeter) had its mail vehicles detached at Bristol. From 1858 apparatus for picking up and delivering mail bags without stopping was gradually introduced at some stations; the 'Special Mail' lost its dedicated status in 1869 when a 1st Class carriage was added to the formation. In 1895 it was renamed the 'Great Western Travelling Post Office' (TPO) and in the next year the first letter-sorting carriage was included between Paddington and Penzance.

Although the speed of GWR/B&E services during the 1850s was generally higher than elsewhere, there appears to have been an air of complacency that was shaken in 1862 when the LSWR increased the speed of its noon express from Waterloo to complete the 171½ miles to Exeter in 4¾ hours, 25 minutes faster than the quickest train from Paddington. In response the broad gauge companies reinstated the 4½-hour schedule for their 11.45am Paddington and 10.30am Exeter departures. In 1871 an LSWR train reached Exeter in 4½ hours, but improvements to the 'Flying Dutchman' schedule meant that its time to Exeter was now 4¼ hours; with a top speed of more than 53mph it was once again the fastest train in the world and this schedule was maintained until the abolition of the broad gauge. After the LSWR reached Plymouth in 1876 it was successful in capturing a good share of traffic, especially with a train that left Waterloo at 2.10pm and arrived in Plymouth at 9.05pm. After pressure from local officials, the GWR introduced afternoon expresses in each direction to meet this competition; these were as fast as the 'Dutchman' between London and Exeter and faster still to Plymouth. However, within a couple of years the LSWR had accelerated its afternoon express further to start at 2.30pm and reach Exeter in 4 hours.

The final broad gauge engines built by the GWR were the 24-strong 8-foot 'Single' 'Rover' Class 4-2-2s that were direct descendants of Daniel Gooch's successful 1847 'Iron Duke' Class. These elegant locos were used on the main express trains between Paddington and Newton Abbot. *Emperor* was the 19th member of the class when it emerged from Swindon Works in September 1880; it is waiting to leave Exeter St David's with an up train in the last decade of the broad gauge.

Table 12: Passenger services between Bristol and Exeter from October 1886 (weekdays)

Down trains at Exeter St David's

Gauge		Arr	Dep	Notes
BG	9.00pm Paddington to Penzance; fast mail and passenger	2.30am	2.40am	1
NG	6.45am Taunton to Exeter; ordinary passenger	8.05am	–	
BG	6.15am Bristol to Penzance; fast mail and passenger	8.32am	8.40am	1
BG	9.23am Tiverton Junction to Exeter; ordinary passenger	10.05am	–	2
NG/BG	7.10am Bristol to Plymouth; ordinary passenger	10.45am	11.00am	3
BG	5.30am Paddington to Penzance; passenger	11.50am	11.58am	
BG	12.55pm Tiverton Junction to Exeter; passenger	1.32pm	–	
BG	9.00am Paddington to Penzance; fast passenger	2.08pm	2.18pm	1
NG	12.35pm Bristol to Exeter; ordinary passenger	4.55pm	–	
BG	11.45pm Paddington to Penzance; express passenger	4.00pm	4.10pm	
NG/BG	10.30am Paddington to Plymouth; ordinary passenger	6.35pm	7.30pm	3
NG	6.20pm Tiverton Junction to Exeter; ordinary passenger	7.00pm	–	
BG	3.00pm Paddington to Plymouth; express passenger	7.14pm	7.18pm	
NG	1.45pm Paddington to Exeter; ordinary passenger	10.00pm	–	
BG	5.00pm Paddington to Plymouth; fast passenger	10.20pm	10.25pm	1

Up trains at Exeter St David's

Gauge		Arr	Dep	Notes
NG	6.00am Exeter to Paddington; ordinary passenger	–	6.00am	
NG	7.35am Tu/FO Exeter to Tiverton Junction; passenger	–	7.35am	
NG	8.50am Exeter to Bristol; ordinary passenger	–	8.50am	
BG	6.45am Plymouth to Paddington; ordinary passenger	9.22am	9.30am	
BG	8.35am Plymouth to Paddington; express passenger	10.25am	10.30am	
BG	10.45am Exeter to Tiverton Junction; passenger	–	10.45am	
BG/NG	9.05am Plymouth to Paddington; ordinary passenger	11.33am	11.43am	3
BG	6.25am Penzance to Paddington; express passenger	12.40am	12.50am	
BG/NG	12 noon Plymouth to Bristol; ordinary passenger	2.32pm	2.47pm	3
BG	11.15am Penzance to Paddington; express passenger	3.50pm	3.55pm	
BG	10.00am Penzance to Paddington; fast passenger	4.47pm	4.55pm	1
NG	5.10pm Exeter to Tiverton Junction; passenger	–	5.10pm	
BG	3.50pm Plymouth to Bristol Ordinary; passenger	6.24pm	6.34pm	
NG	8.25pm Exeter to Taunton; ordinary passenger	–	8.25pm	
BG	5.00pm Penzance to Paddington; fast mail and passenger	10.20pm	10.30pm	

Notes:

1 Apparatus for exchanging mail bags was in operation at a number of stations including those local to Exeter at Tiverton Junction and Cullompton; train speeds had to be reduced to 35mph when passing these stations.

2 Train runs on Tuesdays and Fridays only, presumably in connection with cattle market days.

3 Down trains narrow gauge to Exeter, broad gauge beyond, up trains vice versa

Thereafter neither company appeared interested in reducing journey times; possibly they had decided between them that it was too expensive to maintain the competition. At the time there was a crisis in the railway industry, particularly with the failure of banks that had been financing new schemes, and even established companies were getting into difficulties and economies were being made. Table 12 shows the GWR timetable in 1886, six years before the end of the broad gauge.

The through passenger service comprised eight trains running daily in both directions between Paddington and Exeter. At stations 'local' to Exeter, the two down and three up 'express' services all ran non-stop between Taunton and St David's, and between Exeter and Newton Abbot. These still had the 4¼-hour schedule between London and Exeter, apart from the 6.25am from Penzance, which was allowed an extra hour. Both up 'fast' trains called at St Thomas before running non-stop between St David's and Taunton, and of the three down 'fast' trains one stopped at Tiverton Junction and another at St Thomas; all these trains had around 5½-hour journey times between London and St David's.

Many trains carried 1st and 2nd Class passengers only, and those travelling 3rd Class had a limited number of services that they could use, and none between early morning and late in the afternoon. The 5.30am departure from Paddington was an institution known as 'The Parliamentary' after the 1844 Act of Parliament that decreed that each railway company should run at least one passenger train each day that carried 3rd Class passengers in covered vehicles. In 1886 this train was also referred to as the 'Newspaper Express'; apparently the London papers arrived rather late in the day during the broad gauge era. From 1882 the LSWR conveyed 3rd Class passengers on all of its trains and carried a larger share of the business between London and Exeter. In July 1887 the GWR introduced a new broad gauge service known as 'The Jubilee', which left Paddington at 1.00pm and Plymouth at noon, and these finally carried 3rd Class passengers during the middle of the day.

After a period of stagnation the last decade of the Victorian era saw the GWR move forward as new management brought a fresh impetus. In June 1890 a new broad gauge train known unofficially as the 'Cornishman' improved on the existing schedules by 10 minutes, arriving in Exeter in 4hr 5min from Paddington with stops at Swindon and Bristol. By 1890 3rd Class passengers could travel on all GWR trains. The opening of the Severn Tunnel in 1886 and the abolition of the broad gauge provided new possibilities, and an express to Torbay was introduced soon afterwards that included through coaches from Manchester, Liverpool and Leeds; attempts were now made to encourage holiday business from the north. In July 1896 a peak-season-only first portion (to Newquay) of the 'Cornishman' (now 10.30am ex-Paddington) was scheduled to reach Exeter non-stop in 3¾ hours; this used a relief line to bypass Bristol Temple Meads and was the longest regular non-stop run in the world. The up working became an all-year-round train in 1899 and the down train became permanent in 1902. By the Edwardian period corridor coaches were used on all long-distance trains and the 'Cornishman' had a restaurant car for 1st Class passengers; soon other trains had restaurant cars that could be used by all. Additional expresses were added to the timetable and in 1902 a train for just postal traffic was introduced between Paddington and Penzance; in a general improvement to the schedules that year even the 5.30am from Paddington now reached Penzance 3 hours earlier than previously.

In 1904 the non-stop run of the GWR's premier train was extended from Exeter to Plymouth. Named trains were catching the public's interest and in a competition launched in association with *The Railway Magazine* this flagship service was officially named the 'Cornish Riviera Limited' in 1905, at the same time being provided with new 'Dreadnought' stock. In 1906 the Great Western opened its 'Berks & Hants' deviation via Westbury, which cut more than 20 miles from the journey to the South West, and all the expresses that had previously passed through Bristol non-stop were diverted to this route with savings of up to 22 minutes. Despite the 'Limited' now being a heavier train that included slip coaches for Westbury and Exeter, the introduction of new 'Star' Class 4-6-0 locos meant that its time to Plymouth was reduced by 15 minutes to 4hr 10min. After the slip coach arrived in Exeter it then went forward to Newton Abbot on a stopping service, which meant that places like Dawlish and Teignmouth were now nearly an hour closer to London. In 1907 there were 11 trains in each direction between Paddington and Exeter and the fastest four down and two up expresses now completed the journey in around 3 hours.

By 1923 the GWR had recovered from the effects of the First World War and introduced new 70-foot coaches on the 'Cornish Riviera' that were painted in the traditional 'chocolate and cream' livery rather than the 'lake' (maroon) livery that had been introduced in the 1900s; the first of the new 'Castle' Class engines also appeared that year. Table 13 shows the regular weekday GWR passenger and mail services that could be seen at Exeter St David's in the summer of 1924.

At this time the down 'Cornish Riviera' was scheduled to run non-stop to Plymouth in a time of 4hr 7min and continued to serve Exeter with a slip coach; the up train did, however, stop in Exeter before running non-stop to Paddington in 2hr 59min. A Paddington to Kingswear service passed through St David's in both directions on a non-stop run between London and Torquay; it also served other Torbay resorts with stops at Paignton and Churston before reaching its destination. For a number of years this train had departed from Paddington at 11.45am, but this was changed to 12 noon just before the First World War and was given the 'Torbay Express' name in 1923.

Additionally there were ten down and seven up regular passenger services between Paddington and the South West that did call at Exeter; of these the only non-stop trains to Exeter were the 11.05am and 3.30pm departures, which were allowed around 3 hours from London. The other three 'daytime' trains stopped at Taunton and were timed around 3½ hours. The five overnight and evening trains all ran via Bristol and stopped at several stations; of these the two later evening trains took about 4 hours to reach Exeter, while the three overnight services were around the 5-hour mark.

The 10.00pm departure from Paddington carried the Penzance sleeping cars and also conveyed an Aberdeen to Penzance through coach that had been introduced in 1921; a Glasgow coach was added at Edinburgh and these carriages were routed via the East Coast Main Line and Great Central to reach the GWR at Banbury. From there they travelled via

Passenger services on 'Western' lines

Table 13: GWR passenger and mail services at Exeter St David's from 14 July 1924 (weekdays)		
Down trains at Exeter St David's	Arr	Dep
9.10pm Cardiff to Plymouth; parcels	1.35am	1.50am
9.05pm Paddington to Penzance; GWR Travelling Post Office	2.32am	2.38am
10.00pm Paddington to Penzance; passenger	2.41am	2.49am
6.25pm MX York to Penzance; passenger	2.56am	3.03am
10.25pm Paddington to Penzance; parcels	4.03pm	4.25pm
12.0am MX Paddington to Penzance; passenger	5.15am	5.24am
2.30am Paddington to Plymouth; newspaper	6.12am	6.16am
6.45am St David's to Newton Abbot passenger	–	6.45am
7.00am St David's to Heathfield; railmotor (Teign Valley)	–	7.00am
8.00am St David's to Newton Abbot passenger	–	8.00am
7.05am Taunton to St David's; passenger	8.22am	–
2.40am MX Shrewsbury to Penzance; mail and passenger	8.36am	8.42am
1.25am MO Crewe to Penzance; mail and passenger	8.36am	8.42am
9.00am St David's to Kingswear; passenger	–	9.00am
8.35am Tiverton Junction to St David's; motor	9.13am	–
9.20am St David's to Kingswear; passenger	–	9.20am
9.28am St David's to Heathfield; motor (Teign Valley)	–	9.28am
8.25am Dulverton to Teignmouth; auto-train (Exe Valley)	9.37am	9.45am
6.50am Bristol to St David's; passenger	10.21am	–
5.30am Paddington to Penzance; passenger	10.37am	10.45am
9.40am Dulverton to St David's; auto-train (Exe Valley)	10.52am	–
11.10am St David's to Kingswear; passenger	–	11.10am
11.25am St David's to Heathfield; auto-train (Teign Valley)	–	11.25am
10.05am Bath to Plymouth; passenger	12.10pm	12.17pm
9.00am Paddington to Kingswear; passenger	12.35pm	12.40pm
12.48pm St David's to Kingswear; passenger	–	12.48pm
11.51am Dulverton to St David's; motor (Exe Valley)	12.55pm	–
12.05pm Taunton to St David's; passenger	1.15pm	–
10.30am Paddington to Penzance; 'Cornish Riviera Limited'	pass	1/29pm
9.45am FSO Birmingham to Paignton; passenger	pass	1/39pm
11.05am Paddington to Penzance; passenger	2.7pm	2.14pm
2.20pm WSO St David's to Heathfield; motor (Teign Valley)	–	2.20pm
10.25am Birmingham to Plymouth; passenger	2.23pm	2.33pm
12 noon Paddington to Kingswear; 'Torbay Express'	pass	3/0pm
10.35am Wolverhampton to Penzance; passenger	3.19pm	3.26pm
12.05pm Paddington to Plymouth; passenger	3.37pm	3.44pm
2.10pm Dulverton to St David's; auto-train (Exe Valley)	3.45pm	–
3.50pm St David's to Newton Abbot; passenger	–	3.50pm
3.30pm Tiverton Junction to St David's; auto-train	4.04pm	–

Table 13: GWR passenger and mail services at Exeter St David's from 14 July 1924 (weekdays)

Down trains at Exeter St David's	Arr	Dep
8.15am Neyland to Paignton; passenger	4.21pm	4.47pm
10.32am Crewe to Truro; passenger	4.30pm	4.37pm
1.30pm Paddington to Penzance; passenger	4.58pm	5.03pm
5.15pm St David's to Newton Abbot; passenger	–	5.15pm
4.50pm Tiverton Junction to St David's; passenger	5.28pm	–
5.40pm St David's to Heathfield; auto-train (Teign Valley)	–	5.40pm
11.42am Crewe to Plymouth; passenger	5.48pm	5.55pm
5.45pm Tiverton Junction to St David's; passenger	6.19pm	–
3.30pm Paddington to Paignton; passenger	6.30pm	6.37pm
5.30pm Dulverton to St David's; motor (Exe Valley)	6.38pm	–
6.46pm St David's to Plymouth; passenger	–	6.46pm
6.15pm Taunton to Plymouth; passenger	7.27pm	7.45pm
4.30pm Paddington to Plymouth; passenger	8.29pm	8.36pm
7.45pm Dulverton to St David's; auto (Exe Valley)	8.53pm	–
1.10pm Crewe to Newton Abbot; passenger	9.30pm	9.45pm
6.30pm Paddington to Plymouth; passenger	10.35pm	10.40pm
9.20pm ThSO Dulverton to St David's; auto-train (via Tiverton Junction)	11.00pm	–

Up trains at Exeter St David's	Arr	Dep
9.00pm Penzance to Paddington; passenger	1.50am	1.57am
7.05am St David's to Dulverton; auto-train (Exe Valley)	–	7.05am
7.30am St David's to Tiverton Junction; motor	–	7.30am
8.05am St David's to Birmingham; passenger	–	8.05am
8.15am St David's to Dulverton; auto-train (Exe Valley)	–	8.15am
6.35am Kingswear to St David's; passenger	8.30am	–
7.10am Plymouth to Crewe; passenger	8.50am	8.58am
9.05am St David's to Taunton; passenger	–	9.05am
8.23am Heathfield to St David's; motor (Teign Valley)	9.19am	–
8.15am Paignton to St David's; passenger	9.35am	–
8.15am Plymouth to Paddington; passenger	9.54am	10.0am
10.12am St David's to Dulverton; motor (Exe Valley)	–	10.12am
8.40am Plymouth to Crewe; passenger	10.27am	10.33am
9.00am Kingswear to Bradford; passenger	10.39am	10.45am
10.50am St David's to Taunton; passenger	–	10.50am
10.33am Teignmouth to St David's; auto-train	11.13am	–
10.33am Heathfield to St David's; motor (Teign Valley)	11.29am	–
9.05am Plymouth to St David's; passenger	11.35am	–
10.05am Plymouth to Crewe; passenger	11.49am	11.56am
10.30am Plymouth to Birmingham; passenger	12.10pm	12.17pm

Table 13: GWR passenger and mail services at Exeter St David's from 14 July 1924 (weekdays)		
Up trains at Exeter St David's	Arr	Dep
11.20am Kingswear to Paddington; 'Torbay Express'	pass	12/35pm
12.40pm St David's to Dulverton; auto-train (Exe Valley)	–	12.40pm
12.45pm St David's to Taunton; passenger	–	12.45pm
9.15am Falmouth to Paddington; passenger	1.21pm	1.29pm
10.00am Penzance to Paddington; 'Cornish Riviera Limited'	1.39pm	1.46pm
12.53pm Heathfield to Tiverton; auto-train (Teign and Exe Valleys)	1.55pm	2.00pm
1.20pm Newton Abbot to St David's; passenger	2.02pm	–
1.25am FSO Paignton to Birmingham; passenger	2.13pm	2.18pm
10.10am Penzance to Crewe; passenger	2.21pm	2.28pm
1.15pm Kingswear to Cardiff; passenger	2.44pm	2.50pm
10.30am Penzance to Wolverhampton; passenger	2.52pm	3.02pm
11.0am Penzance to Paddington; passenger	3.21pm	3.27pm
12.25pm Truro to Aberdeen; passenger	3.33pm	3.39pm
3.43pm SX St David's to Taunton; passenger (4.00pm dep on SO)	–	3.43pm
3.50 pm St David's to Dulverton; motor (Exe Valley)	–	3.50 pm
2.20pm SX Kingswear to St David's; passenger	4.9pm	–
3.35pm SO Newton Abbot to St David's; passenger	4.26pm	–
3.35pm WSO Heathfield to St David's; motor (Teign Valley)	4.34pm	–
4.40pm SX St David's to Tiverton Junction; passenger	–	4.40pm
2.40pm Plymouth to St David's; passenger	5.02pm	–
12 noon Penzance to Crewe; passenger, and mail to Bristol	5.17pm	5.26pm
1.30pm Penzance to Paddington; passenger	5.35pm	5.42pm
5.50pm St David's to Taunton; passenger	–	5.50pm
6.0pm St David's to Dulverton; auto-train (Exe Valley)	–	6.00pm
4.35pm Churston to St David's; passenger	6.10pm	–
4.15pm Plymouth to Paddington; passenger	6.44pm	6.55pm
5.48pm Heathfield to St David's; motor (Teign Valley)	6.50pm	–
5.35pm Kingswear to St David's; passenger	7.28pm	–
7.35pm ThSO St David's to Dulverton; motor (Exe Valley)	–	7.35pm
6.20pm Plymouth to Paddington; passenger	7.47pm	7.52pm
6.58pm Newton Abbot to St David's; passenger	8.09pm	–
7.01pm Paignton to St David's; passenger	8.25pm	–
7.40pm Heathfield to St David's; auto-train (Teign Valley)	8.36pm	–
7.30pm Kingswear to St David's; passenger	9.23pm	–
4.30pm Penzance to Crewe; passenger	9.34pm	9.42pm
10.00pm St David's to Taunton; passenger (10.45 dep on ThO)	–	10.00pm
6.00pm Penzance to Paddington; GWR Travelling Post Office	10.28pm	10.35pm
10.15pm SO Trusham to St David's; auto-train (Teign Valley)	10.54pm	–
9.45pm Paignton to St David's; passenger	11.03pm	–

'Saint' Class 4-6-0 No 2911 *Saint Agatha* is entering Exeter St David's station in the early 1930s with a mixed rake of stock forming the 1.30am Paddington to Penzance train.

Oxford and were added to the Penzance train at Swindon. With a departure time of 9.45am from the Granite City and an arrival in Penzance at 7.25am the next day, this was the longest through working in the country at the time and any passenger completing the whole journey would have been on the rails for 21hr 40min. In the opposite direction the coaches returned via a 12.25pm Truro to Aberdeen train, which went via Westbury rather than Bristol, before following the route of the down journey.

In the up direction the 9.15am Falmouth to Paddington was the only non-stop train from Exeter; it conveyed a slip coach from Exeter to Reading and was scheduled to take 3hr 1min to reach the capital. Four other trains all stopped at Taunton and were allowed around 3¼ hours, while two more ran via Bristol. In addition to the London trains, the tables reveal that daily trains were scheduled from the extremities of the GWR system with departures from Crewe, to where the GWR had running powers, and Shrewsbury; these trains ran over the 'North & West' route via Hereford and included through coaches from Liverpool and Manchester. Other services ran from Birmingham Snow Hill and Wolverhampton via Stratford-upon-Avon and Cheltenham and from Neyland and Cardiff in Wales; the only down train from 'off-region' was one from York. There were a number of additional summer services in 1924 that mainly ran on Saturdays; these included relief trains that ran as required, while others were described as 'Excursions'. Several were from Paddington, but other originating places included Manchester, Shrewsbury, Bradford, Sheffield, Birmingham, Wolverhampton and Swansea; additionally there were several paths for 'Excursions' from unspecified (presumably varying) stations on the LMS and LNER.

Within Devon, the down TPO only stopped at Exeter, Newton Abbot and Plymouth, but mail bags were exchanged using apparatus at other stations. The mail and passenger train from Shrewsbury had portions from Manchester and Liverpool and stopped additionally at Tiverton Junction; bags on this train were exchanged 'on the fly' at Wellington and Cullompton. Newspaper and parcels trains were vacuum-braked and ran at speeds comparable with the faster passenger services; the newspapers now left London much earlier than they had in the 19th century and arrived in Exeter at 6.12am for a morning delivery.

The six intermediate stations between St David's and Newton Abbot were served by 12 down and 16 up local trains during each weekday, although not all called at some stations. St Thomas station was now only served by local services apart from the 4.15pm from Plymouth to Paddington, which was a long-distance stopping train that was not scheduled to arrive in London (via Bristol) until 2.40am, almost 10½ hours after leaving Plymouth. Local trains between Taunton and Exeter called at up to eight intermediate stations, but the service was limited with only five down and seven up trains covering the full distance between the two county towns; they were not very fast either, taking between 70 and 83 minutes to complete the 30-mile journey. There were some additional services that covered parts of the route, including several trains that just ran between Tiverton Junction and Exeter.

Subsequent timetables in the steam era saw relatively little change in the service. The July 1939 one has the 'Cornish Riviera' running non-stop through St David's in both directions; a slip coach had not been offered to Exeter passengers since new stock had been provided for this train

Passenger services on 'Western' lines

in 1929. Although the 'King' Class engines had worked this service since 1927, trains were now longer and heavier and the 'Limited' could load to 13 coaches of 1935-built 'Centenary' stock; the GWR celebrated its centenary by introducing two new sets of stock for this train, which broke with the previous practice of having a door for each compartment and instead had end doors only and a picture window for each compartment. Although the 'Torbay Express' also ran through Exeter on Saturdays, by 1939 the weekday trains now stopped at St David's and the down train was scheduled to reach the city in just 2hr 49min. Of the other fast services mentioned in 1924, the 11.05am from Paddington now departed at 11.00am and, as it was now scheduled to stop at Taunton, the time to Exeter had slipped by 2 minutes; the 3.30pm now ran to Penzance rather than Paignton and also stopped at Taunton, with 5 minutes added to the schedule to Exeter. The 12.05pm from Paddington to Plymouth no longer ran in 1939, but there were still eight other weekday departures from London that ran on similar schedules to those in 1924.

Cross-country services in 1939 included a Crewe mail and passenger train in place of the previous Shrewsbury departure. In 1924 through coaches from Bradford to Paignton were combined with other carriages from Manchester and Liverpool for the journey west, but in 1939 there was a separate train from Bradford that had been named 'The Devonian' by the LMS in 1927, although the title was not acknowledged by the GWR at this time despite half the train being composed of GWR stock. The newspaper business was important, and in 1934 the GWR introduced a 12.50am Paddington to Penzance newspaper and parcels train, which ran non-stop to Plymouth in just 4 hours, which would not have been a problem for the rostered 'King' as the load was just six vans. Exeter's papers were now arriving earlier on an additional 1.35am from Paddington to Penzance newspaper train, which reached the city at 4.40am.

Sampford Peverell station had opened in July 1928 and there was a much improved service for the now nine stations between Taunton and Exeter, with eight down and ten up trains serving the whole route. Despite the extra stop most of these trains were now marginally faster than in 1924, completing the journey in around 65-70 minutes. However, the additional Exeter to Tiverton Junction service had ceased, apart from one out-and-back morning run by an auto-train to Sampford Peverell, and the last down train of the day, which was an auto from Tiverton to Exeter and was routed via Tiverton Junction. In 1924 the 4.25pm Plymouth to Paddington overnight slow train had been the last up train of the day to serve these stations, but a Taunton train now ran in its path, and there were also two later services. In 1939 there were 14 regular down and 20 up weekday stopping services serving the six stations between St David's and Newton Abbot.

When the railways were nationalised they were

With new 'British Railways' branding on its tender, 'King' Class 4-6-0 No 6025 *King Henry III* passes Cowley Bridge Junction with the down 'Torbay Express' in July 1948.

Blue-liveried 'King' No 6012 *King Edward VI* receives attention from its driver while waiting at St David's with the down 'Cornish Riviera' on a Sunday in April 1951. *R. A. Lumber*

recovering from the after-effects of war with worn-out assets, and good steam coal was hard to obtain; although the main-line timetable was not dissimilar to the one offered by the GWR, generally the service was slower than before the war. On weekdays in 1953 there were still 10 services from Paddington serving Exeter, but the flagship trains were slower; the 'Cornish Riviera' still passed through Exeter and, although the 'Torbay Express' ran non-stop to the city during the week, it was 13 minutes slower than in 1939; on Saturdays it did not stop between London and Torquay. One of the other fast services in 1939, the 11.00am from Paddington, now took 31 minutes longer to reach Exeter despite having no extra stops. A 6.25am Bristol to Plymouth train ran that was effectively a relief to the overnight 12.35am Manchester to Penzance 'North Mail' and included a red TPO vehicle that arrived in Bristol on the 7.10pm train from Newcastle and a parcels van that ran between Leeds and Penzance; although this train had passenger accommodation, as with most overnight services at the time it was mainly concerned with mail and parcels business and had long station stops for this traffic.

By 1953 the Taunton to Exeter local service had been trimmed with only six down trains serving the intermediate stations, and only four of these stopped at Stoke Canon. Eight up weekday trains ran with an additional late evening train on Saturdays; the 9.07am Exeter to Paddington was a slow long-distance stopping train that was scheduled to take 5hr 23min to reach London. There was also a reduction in the service to the intermediate stations between Exeter and Newton Abbot in 1953. A number of up and down through trains continued to call at Dawlish and Teignmouth, and there were also three 'fast' local down weekday trains that only called at these stations on their way to Torbay; similarly there were two up 'fast' workings that stopped additionally at St Thomas. Otherwise there were 13 down and 16 up stopping trains that called at the other stations, although some omitted certain stops, particularly Exminster.

Although by the 1950s the motor-car and road coach were beginning to have an impact on the passenger business, the majority of workers were benefitting from the 1938 Holidays with Pay Act and much of the population migrated to Britain's coastal resorts by rail for their annual holidays, resulting in a rising tide of weekend travellers throughout the decade. The main rush commenced at the end of July when the start of the Midlands industrial holiday fortnight coincided with the first weekend of the school summer holidays. Many extra trains were organised to cope and it reached a point where the train planners were unable to find sufficient paths during the hours that most people wished to travel.

On Saturdays during July and August during the 1950s the railway between Taunton and Newton Abbot was almost certainly the busiest double-track main line in the country and could be stretched to breaking point, with any semblance of punctuality going by the board. To haul the trains the

Passenger services on 'Western' lines

The 12 noon departure from Penzance initially ran to Crewe and later to Manchester London Road, with through coaches to Glasgow. It could be easily identified by the TPO van behind the engine, which was added in Plymouth and would be transferred to a Newcastle train at Bristol Temple Meads. Old Oak Common's 'Britannia' 4-6-2 No 70018 *Flying Dutchman* is speeding towards the Exeter bypass at Matford in about 1953. Although well received elsewhere, drivers in the South West viewed the 'Britannias' with suspicion for reasons that included their left-hand drive, a regulator that was not as sensitive as the GWR pattern, and a typical 'Pacific' tendency to slip when starting. By early 1957 the class had moved from local sheds to Cardiff where they were better appreciated. *John Stredwick*

operators would resort to whatever was available, including freight engines, and the need for carriages would mean using antiquated stock for perhaps just six weekends in the year, which for the rest of the year would lurk in whatever siding space was available. The railway through Exeter was one of the pinch points, as both WR and SR trains had to share the line between Cowley Bridge and St David's. On peak Saturdays the usual weekday local service was virtually non-existent until early evening, as the paths were needed for long-distance extras.

Anyone witnessing this activity would perhaps have imagined that the railway was still in a good place, but to maintain stock that was used on a handful of occasions during the year was typical of the financial challenges being faced by BR, which sustained ever-increasing losses from 1956. Apart from the growth in road transport that was in part licensed by the 1953 Transport Act, and the 1955 ASLEF strike, which helped to drive more traffic away, increased wages and coal costs were not being matched by the necessary increases in ticket prices and freight charges. The WR was probably the worst-performing region and by 1961 it is thought that it was failing to cover its costs by about £30 million, more than a third of the total BR working deficit.

In an attempt to stem these losses the WR introduced a number of 'emergency cuts' to services in June 1958, which typically meant the removal of some off-peak trains during the middle of the day and evening. In the Exeter area the intermediate stations to Taunton lost three of their seven southbound services, though still retaining the northbound ones. From 13 June 1960 Stoke Canon, the closest station to Exeter on the line east, was closed; it was about half a mile from its village, which had a good bus service on the Exeter to Tiverton road. The station had been little used for years and not all of the trains in the already meagre timetable stopped there. This was a prelude to the closure of all of the remaining stations between Exeter and Taunton in October 1964, apart from Tiverton Junction; at the end the service only comprised four down and five up trains each weekday. In March 1964 Exminster, the nearest station on the main line to the west of Exeter, was also closed. This was another station about half a mile from its village, which had also had a bus service since the 1920s; the villagers had long since given up on the railway, and BR reciprocated with a service in its final year of just two down and three up trains. Devon General was providing a half-hourly service to Exeter and apparently there were no objections to the station's closure; fortunately the other stations between Exeter and Newton Abbot survived and are still open today.

After publication of the 1955 'Modernisation Plan', the WR was selected as the first region to be completely dieselised due to its poor operating ratio; this was to be done an area at a time, and the lines west of Newton Abbot were chosen as a pilot for the early elimination of steam, including all through workings to and from London and Bristol. The locomotive

On a wet 12 July 1958 steam rebounding from the signal gantry masks 4-6-0 No 1011 *County of Chester* as it leaves St David's at 4.31pm with the 8.40am Liverpool Lime Street to Paignton and Penzance service. On the left 'T9' 4-4-0 No 30717 is waiting for the road with the 2.22pm Plymouth Friary to Waterloo train. *Peter W. Gray*

A busy scene at St David's at 1.50pm on Saturday 9 August 1958 includes Exmouth Junction's 'Battle of Britain' 4-6-2 No 34061 *73 Squadron* on the 12 noon Ilfracombe to Waterloo train in Platform 3, 4-6-0 No 6012 *King Edward VI* passing through non-stop with the down 'Cornish Riviera', and Exeter-based 2-6-2T No 4117, which has arrived with the 12.10pm stopper from Taunton. *Peter W. Gray*

Passenger services on 'Western' lines

The congested section between St David's and Cowley Bridge Junction could cause delays for the SR, as seen on Saturday 21 August 1954. Just visible on the far left, 'Pacific' No 34013 *Okehampton* was held for 36 minutes with the 11.00am Plymouth Friary to Brighton train while a series of up WR workings were delayed by a train that had a coach with a hot axle box. Although by this time the errant train was now moving, there was a build-up behind, with each service held for several minutes at a signal just beyond the junction; one of these, the 8.35am Falmouth to Paddington hauled by No 6028 *King George VI*, has its tail to the camera. This meant that the Cowley Bridge signalman was unable to release the 'Brighton' as the interlocking would not permit it. Meanwhile the train on the right is moving, and 4-6-0 No 6835 *Eastham Grange* is only 7 minutes late with the 6.40am Leicester to Paignton train. *Peter W. Gray*

'Large Prairie' tank No 4165 was allocated to Exeter from February 1961 to June 1962, during which time it is seen leaving St David's with a down stopping service. *T. W. Nicholls*

works at Newton Abbot was adapted as the WR's first diesel maintenance depot, but in a change of mind the region then decided that the main diesel base would be at Plymouth Laira, and a custom-built facility was completed there in 1961. Based on favourable evidence from Germany, the region was a keen advocate of diesel-hydraulic locomotives and these began to appear on South West services in 1958, soon taking over much of the main-line passenger work. Most of the Exeter to Kingswear local services were turned over to DMUs in 1960.

Dieselisation did not stem the losses, and with a decline in long-distance travel the 1961 winter timetable was recast with services departing on a more frequent regular-interval basis to improve the utilisation of both the new traction and train-sets, and more stops were scheduled at intermediate stations such as Taunton to improve loadings. Several overnight trains to the West, including the sleepers, continued to run via Bristol, but during the day there were now six 'Warship'-hauled trains scheduled to leave Paddington at 2-hourly intervals between 8.30am and 6.30pm, which were routed via Westbury, rather than the seven that had previously departed on a more irregular basis; each train had portions for the Torbay branch and Plymouth, and five of the latter continued into Cornwall. All restaurant cars were positioned in the Plymouth sections, with none venturing further west. The 'Cornish Riviera' now stopped at Taunton and Exeter, where it arrived 2hr 52min after leaving London, and 8 minutes were then allowed to detach the Kingswear portion; the other five trains had their Torbay portions removed at Newton Abbot.

Dr Beeching's *The Reshaping of British Railways* report in 1963 revealed that more than half of the BR network only carried 4% of the passenger miles and was responsible for much of the financial loss that was being accrued; on the other hand, the other half of the system was earning enough to cover costs by more than six times. Beeching recommended that more attention be paid to the speed, reliability and comfort of inter-city services at the expense of local stopping trains, and it was during this period that the foundations were laid for the InterCity business. WR management was keen to dispel anxiety regarding the future of railways in the West, and in June 1964 a fast up early morning weekday service from Plymouth, named the 'Golden Hind', was introduced that was particularly aimed at businessmen. The train had a limited load of seven coaches hauled by a 'Western' Class loco and departed at 07.05; after stopping only at Newton Abbot, Exeter (departure 08.18) and Taunton, it had a 10.55 arrival at Paddington. The return left at 17.20 and arrived at Exeter at 20.02 and Plymouth at 21.15.

'Hymek' diesel-hydraulic No D7041 enters St David's with the 08.45 Liverpool to Kingswear service on Saturday 27 July 1963; no doubt the train is full of holidaymakers hoping that the glorious weather will last for the next fortnight. On the left a 'W' 2-6-4T awaits its next banking job, and beyond that is the tail of a disappearing down SR train. G. V. Lendon

The May 1968 timetable saw what was claimed to be the biggest ever speed-up in services between London and the West, with times cut on all the express trains; the 'Golden Hind' and 'Cornish Riviera' trains were given 3¾-hour schedules from Paddington to Plymouth with stops at Taunton and Exeter, and both reached the latter in around 2½ hours. New trains included an 09.30 service from Paddington to Torbay and a new evening service in the opposite direction, and a new 07.30 departure from Plymouth was also provided, together with a 17.30 up departure that was an hour later than the previous last departure.

In 1969 the timetable was completely revised and departures from London to the South West were now hourly from 08.30 to 19.30 each weekday; services for Plymouth or Penzance no longer conveyed Torbay portions and instead there were four separate Paignton trains each way. The latter

The first day of an accelerated timetable on 5 May 1969 sees 'Warships' Nos D819 Goliath and D808 Centaur powering away from St David's with the 10.30 Paddington to Penzance 'Cornish Riviera'. R. A. Lumber

Passenger services on 'Western' lines

also stopped at Dawlish and Teignmouth and these towns were served by extra workings using Waterloo-Exeter train sets that were now stabled at Newton Abbot, and also by three cross-country trains. These seaside towns were now served by 17 down and 12 up trains each weekday, many of which were through services; however, DMU stopping services were largely eliminated and only five trains in each direction called at St Thomas, Starcross and Dawlish Warren stations. Also in 1969 the first ever 3½-hour schedule between Paddington and Plymouth was introduced for the 'Cornish Riviera', the only intermediate stop on weekdays being Exeter, 2hr 19min from London. The 'Golden Hind' still had a Taunton stop and was allowed an additional 12 minutes to Exeter; both named trains were now for reserved seat passengers only. At this time there were seven cross-country services from the North each weekday, including an overnight train from Manchester with sleeper accommodation and trains from Liverpool and Newcastle, all running to Plymouth. There were also services from Sheffield to Paignton and Plymouth, and from Bradford to Paignton and Penzance.

Further tinkering with the timetable in 1970 gave an hourly service from Exeter to London; in addition to earlier morning and later evening departures, trains now left the city at 50 minutes past each hour from 08.50 to 17.50 except at 13.50, when the 'Cornish Riviera' maintained its 14.08 departure time. Additionally a new express, the 07.30 from Paddington to Plymouth, returning at 16.30, was given the 'Mayflower' name to mark the 350th anniversary of the sailing of the Pilgrim Fathers to America. In 1971 the 'Golden Hind' schedules were trimmed by 5 minutes in each direction and a new through service to Scotland was provided by extending the 07.10 Paignton to Newcastle train to Edinburgh; the previous Newcastle departure now left Edinburgh at 09.40. In the following year Birmingham was established as the hub for all services between the North and the South West and a wider choice of connecting services was provided. The Edinburgh train now ran to Plymouth and the schedules were slashed by up to 50 minutes through a combination of track improvements and fewer station stops. In 1972 the 'Golden Hind' was extended to Penzance.

The unreliability of steam heating boilers was an Achilles heel in early diesel operations, but the one fitted to No D165 (later 46028) is working on 19 April 1971 as the loco awaits departure from St David's with the 06.28 Leeds to Paignton train. The 'Peak' diesel-electrics first started to appear in Devon in the early 1960s, but with the withdrawal of diesel-hydraulics they handled most trains from the North from 1970 with assistance from Brush Type 4 locos. *DHM*

Class 52 No D1041 *Western Prince* is about to leave St David's on 3 May 1975 with the 07.40 Penzance to Liverpool service. *DHM*

In October 1976 High Speed Trains (HSTs) were introduced on the London to Bristol/South Wales route, and this enabled a cascade of air-conditioned stock on to South West services from Paddington, hauled by the Class 47 and 50 diesel-electric locos that had replaced the diesel-hydraulics. However, a drawback to this change was a slowing of passenger schedules, partly due to the locos having to use some of their power for the air-conditioning equipment. The HSTs were arguably the most successful train ever built for Britain's railways; they captured the imagination of the public and it has been suggested that their arrival 'saved' BR at a time when its very future was in doubt. Although HSTs were unable to reach their top speed of 125mph after Reading on the line to the South West, their superior acceleration and braking characteristics could bring time savings, and an additional 14 sets were authorised. They were first introduced between Paddington and Penzance on the 'Golden Hind' and 'Cornish Riviera' trains from 6 August 1979, and were then gradually deployed on other services, becoming the mainstay of InterCity operations for almost 40 years. The full HST timetable was introduced in May 1980 and the new schedules for both named trains reduced the schedules between Penzance and Paddington by around 30 minutes; the down 'Golden Hind' now reached Exeter in 2hr 22min with a stop at Taunton, and the 'Cornish Riviera' was 2 minutes faster without this stop. From 1982 additional HSTs were acquired for the cross-country services between Scotland and the South West.

Top: Also known as InterCity 125s, the HSTs revolutionised diesel passenger services on BR. On the first day of their operation in the South West, Monday 6 August 1979, set No 253008 is arriving at St David's forming the up 'Cornish Riviera' from Penzance. *DHM*

Centre: Class 50 diesel-electric No 50041 *Bulwark* approaches St David's with 09.35 Paddington to Penzance train on 10 May 1980. *DHM*

Right: The driver of No 47138 looks out for the 'right away' at St David's on 11 September 1982 while working the 11.50 Penzance to Cardiff service. *DHM*

Passenger services on 'Western' lines 131

The 16.00 Plymouth to Birmingham New Street HST service is powered by Nos 43017 and 43191 as it approaches Exwick fields between St Thomas and St David's stations on 3 June 1984. *DHM*

Two five-car InterCity Express Trains, Nos 802009 and 802004, form the 16.04 Paddington to Penzance service as it approaches Stafford's Bridge on 16 July 2021. The River Exe here marks the Exeter city boundary. *DHM*

In the 1985 summer service there were 15 regular weekday trains from and to Paddington, plus the sleeper service and certain extras including some 'Fridays only' trains. Of the regulars, the 'Cornish Riviera' now ran non-stop to Exeter in both directions in 2 hours exactly; the 'Golden Hind' had two stops on the down run to Exeter, and one on the up, and was allowed about 2¼ hours each way. The other trains, a third of which were still hauled by locomotives, had different stopping patterns, with some calling at up six stations, but most HST services were scheduled to reach Exeter in under 2½ hours. The loco-hauled trains were slower, especially the only surviving through service to Paignton; the 'Torbay Express' had fallen from grace with five stops each way between London and Exeter, and was allowed almost 3 hours each way for this part of its journey. The local service between Exeter and Newton Abbot had marginally improved from the nadir of 1969, with seven down and six up through trains calling at Dawlish and Teignmouth, and more local trains now served the other stations, with St Thomas seeing eight down and nine up trains each day.

In 1995, just prior to privatisation, the Paddington service was almost totally operated by HSTs and was broadly similar to that provided ten years earlier, but the times of the fastest trains had slipped; the 'Cornish Riviera' was now allowed 2hr 7min to Exeter on the down run, including a stop at Reading, and 2hr 19min on the up with two stops. The fastest timing was now that of the up 'Golden Hind', which was 2hr 3min with one stop. The 'Torbay Express' was now an HST, and with fewer stops the down train was allowed 2hr 17min to Exeter, the up service being 4 minutes faster. There were now 11 CrossCountry services each way, with trains from Leeds (two), Newcastle (two), York, Derby, Aberdeen, Dundee, Edinburgh, Liverpool and Manchester; most ran as far as Plymouth, but two continued to Penzance and two others terminated at Paignton and Exeter.

In 1995 there was a substantial improvement in the local service, which was now the responsibility of the Regional Railways sector, and 21 down and 17 up trains now called at St Thomas each weekday. What is perhaps surprising is that although the concept of through running by easily reversible DMUs had been introduced more than 30 years earlier, and more trains were now running through from Paignton to Exeter Central rather than passengers having to change trains at St David's, still only a handful of these workings were then continuing to Exmouth.

The railway was privatised on 1 April 1997 when GWR services were taken over in a management buyout; this meant that there was a smooth transition, with the BR InterCity team moving to the new franchise. The other InterCity sub-sector, CrossCountry, was franchised to Virgin Trains for 15 years with a commitment to replace the existing fleet of HSTs and Class 47 locos with 78 new 125mph 'Voyager' trains at a cost of £390 million. Although it was also planned to provide a more frequent service, there was controversy at this decision as it meant replacing seven-coach trains with four- or five-coach ones; also, as the same body shell was adopted for both the tilting and non-tilting versions of these trains, it reduced the amount of room within the carriages, and there was little overhead baggage space. This might be bearable for commuters or business passengers with little luggage, but it was not such a good idea for the many passengers using CrossCountry for leisure purposes; the transition to these trains was completed in 2002.

By 2005 there were 20 HST departures from Paddington between 07.06 and 20.35 each weekday, with two of the first four trains running via Bristol and the remainder going via Westbury. The fastest trains had regained their 2-hour schedules to Exeter, the 10.06 ex-Paddington 'Cornish Riviera' with no stops and the 12.06 'Royal Duchy' with one. There were 16 'Voyager' services each way, with departures from Glasgow (six), Edinburgh (three), Dundee, Newcastle (two), Lancaster, Leeds, Preston and Derby. Local services were now operated by Wessex Trains and these had expanded, with St Thomas now served by 24 down and 22 up trains daily; more than half the former and about a third of the latter were now running between Exmouth and Paignton.

The long reign of HSTs on the Paddington services ended when they were replaced by new Hitachi-built InterCity Express Trains (IETs) from July 2018. In December 2019 GWR introduced what was claimed to be the biggest timetable change on its routes since 1976, with the times of 75% of trains across its network altered. The Paddington service to the South West now comprised 26 down and 24 up trains, including the sleeper service to Penzance and two trains each way that were routed via Bristol; at least two trains an hour were scheduled for the greater part of the day. The nature of the route precludes any further great escalation in speed, and the two fastest down trains each day were allowed 2hr 3min for the run to Exeter, inclusive of one and two stops respectively. However, another seven trains were timetabled to take less than 2hr 10min, despite several making three stops en route.

After Virgin Trains had financial problems on its West Coast route, the Strategic Rail Authority decided to re-tender the CrossCountry franchise and this was secured by Arriva Trains in 2007. As part of the franchise commitment, the new operators leased five HST sets to supplement its 'Voyager' fleet and provide extra capacity on its core Scotland to Plymouth route. In the December 2019 timetable Exeter was served by 23 CrossCountry services each way, including four trains from Manchester Piccadilly that terminated at St David's before returning north.

11. Passenger services on 'Southern' lines

When the LSWR route to Exeter was opened most trains called at all stations, but an express left London Waterloo at 9.00am and arrived in Exeter at 2.05pm, 5 minutes quicker than the fastest GWR service at the time. In 1862 the LSWR hastened the schedule of its 12 noon express from Waterloo to Exeter to 4¾ hours, 25 minutes quicker than the fastest train from Paddington; the GWR responded and there was a period of rivalry between the two companies. Subsequently a 10.50am departure from Waterloo was introduced that reached Exeter at 3.32pm. By 1879 weekday trains were leaving from Waterloo to the West at 6.45am, 9.00am, 10.45am, 11.45am, 2.25pm and 5.00pm, and this pattern became time-honoured over the years, although these times did vary slightly.

By the turn of the century the 11.00am departure had expanded during the summer into three trains for Plymouth, North Devon and North Cornwall, with the fastest reaching Exeter in 3hr 35min. New corridor coaches with steam heating and electric lighting were ordered for use on the West of England route in 1901, and restaurant cars were provided on two of the daily services. Five minutes were shaved from the Exeter schedules that year and a further acceleration in 1903 meant that the summer 10.50am departure from Waterloo reached the city in 3hr 15min, and the former 3.00pm departure now left 30 minutes later but had an

A lunchtime express for Waterloo is emerging from the 262-yard-long Blackboy Tunnel and passing Mount Pleasant Road Halt in about 1923, not long before the engine, 'T9' 4-4-0 No 716, was modified and superheated. The steep paths leading to the platforms can be noted on the left and above the 'Greyhound'; the wagons on the right are standing on two sidings that are on the site of the later Exmouth Junction marshalling yard. There had been a roof fall in the tunnel in November 1865, which closed the line for more than a week. *Author's collection*

unchanged arrival time at Queen Street. After more dining cars were available, restaurant car services to the West were increased to four daily.

In 1904 the LSWR made a bid for the ocean liner business between Plymouth and London that had been monopolised by the GWR, and special trains carried mail and American Line passengers who had disembarked at Stonehouse Pool. Unfortunately the LSWR suffered the worst accident in its history in July 1906 when one of these expresses derailed when running at twice the permitted speed on the reverse curves through Salisbury station, resulting in a large loss of life; the schedules for these trains were then eased. After years of rivalry with the GWR the two companies came to an 'understanding' in 1910 to cease the costly competition between them and to pool competing traffic; one consequence of this was the LSWR's withdrawal from the Plymouth liner traffic.

Thereafter any notion that the LSWR and GWR were still locked in battle for the traffic to the West should be dispelled, and the pooling arrangements included most towns that were served from London by both companies, even indirectly, and revenues were distributed according to the mileages operated by the two companies. This cartel meant that there was no real need to reduce running times to any great extent, and these were not usually a determining factor for someone travelling from London to Exeter; more likely they would be influenced by how much easier it was for them to reach Waterloo rather than Paddington or vice versa. In the event the GWR was to handle more of the London business after its Berks & Hants 'cut-off' had been opened.

either Salisbury, Templecombe or Seaton Junction ran to Exeter and called at all the intermediate stations en route. Additionally a railmotor service had been introduced east of Exeter in 1906, and in 1914 the down stopping service was supplemented by six railmotor services starting at either Sidmouth Junction (three) or Honiton (three). In addition to the through services, 13 stopping trains headed west from Queen Street; some had portions for different routes, and these trains or portions ran to Plymouth (six), Bude and Padstow (three each), Torrington and Ilfracombe (five each), and Okehampton and Crediton (one each).

Initially the First World War made little difference to the timetable, but as wartime activity intensified it became difficult to maintain services and some reductions and decelerations were introduced in January 1917 to improve performance; the railmotor service also ended at that time. However, five of the

Table 14: Trains from Waterloo to Exeter on weekdays in July to September, 1914						
Waterloo	No of stops	Exeter	Time to Exeter	Eventual destinations	Restaurant cars
6.10am	8	10.23am	4hr 13min	Ilfracombe, Torrington	-
6.35am	36	12.50am	6hr 15min	Yeoford Junction	-
8.50am	10	1.08pm	4hr 18min	Plymouth	Breakfast & Luncheon Car to Exeter
10.50am	2	2.09pm	3hr 19min	Sidmouth, Exmouth, Plymouth	Luncheon Car to Exeter
11.00am	1	2.17pm	3hr 17min	Bude, Padstow	Luncheon Car to Padstow
11.10am	1	2.24pm	3hr 14min	Ilfracombe, Torrington	Luncheon Car to Torrington
11.15am	16	4.18pm	5hr 3min	Exeter Queen Street	-
12.00 noon	4	3.48pm	3hr 48min	Lyme Regis, Seaton, Sidmouth, Exmouth	Luncheon Car to Exeter
1.00pm	6	5.11pm	4hr 11min	Plymouth, Bude, Padstow	Luncheon Car to Exeter
3.30pm	2	6.55pm	3hr 25min	Plymouth	Tea Car to Exeter
5.50pm	9	10.05pm	4hr 15min	Plymouth	Dining Car to Exeter

The fastest of the trains shown in Table 14 only stopped at Salisbury, whereas the 6.35am departure stopped almost everywhere before terminating at Yeoford. Otherwise the only Waterloo trains to stop at the intermediate stations in east Devon were the 6.10am departure, which called at Honiton, the 10.50am and 1.00pm departures, which stopped at Sidmouth Junction, and the 12 noon train, which detached through coaches at Axminster, Seaton and Sidmouth Junctions for their respective branch lines. A service between Brighton and Plymouth had been introduced in July 1907 with the coaches added to the 1.00pm Waterloo train at Salisbury. During the summer season the 11.00am service became three trains to serve the LSWR's network beyond Exeter, which were scheduled to arrive in Queen Street during a 15-minute period.

Otherwise just six down stopping trains originating at

main expresses continued throughout the war and restaurant cars were still provided. After the war the timetable was reinstated, and in the summer of 1921 trains to the West of England were leaving Waterloo on the hour from 8.00am to 1.00pm, with further departures at 3.00pm and 5.00pm.

Table 15 lists the passenger services at Queen Street when the station was being rebuilt. At this time there were eight regular trains from Waterloo to Exeter each weekday, including the overnight newspaper train. Of the daytime departures only three were true expresses, the fastest being the 10.35am departure, which ran non-stop between Salisbury and Exeter, but it was no quicker than the fastest train in 1914; in a competition among employees it had been named the 'Atlantic Coast Express' ('ACE') in July 1926. Two slightly slower trains stopped only at Sidmouth Junction, and three other trains called at either four or five

Passenger services on 'Southern' lines

Table 15: Passenger services at Exeter Queen Street from 17 July 1932 (weekdays)

Down trains at Queen Street	Arr	Dep	Notes
1.30am Waterloo to Plymouth; newspaper and passenger	4.44am	4.50am	1
1.30am Waterloo to Ilfracombe; newspaper and passenger	4.44am	5.00am	1
7.30am Exeter to Plymouth Friary	-	7.30am	
6.25am Yeovil to Ilfracombe ('mixed' train from Barnstaple Junction)	8.13am	8.20am	
7.48am Exmouth to Plymouth Friary	8.16am	8.46am	
8.15am Honiton to Exeter	8.50am	-	
9.42am Exeter to Ilfracombe and Torrington	-	9.42am	
7.46am Yeovil to Exeter	9.35am	-	
10.17am Sidmouth to Exeter	11.14am	-	
7.58am Salisbury to Plymouth Friary	11.19am	11.37am	
11.48am Exeter to Ilfracombe	-	11.48am	
7.47am Basingstoke to Exeter	12.24pm	-	
8.40am Waterloo to Plymouth and Ilfracombe	1.03pm	1.09pm	2
12.45pm Seaton Junction to Exeter	1.44pm	-	
10.35am Waterloo to Ilfracombe and Torrington 'ACE'	1.49pm	1.56pm	1
10.35am Waterloo to Padstow & Bude ACE	1.49pm	2.06pm	1
10.45am Waterloo to Exeter; relief as required	2.05pm	-	
11.0am Waterloo to Plymouth (Friary)	2.22pm	2.30pm	
10.53am Salisbury to Exeter	2.48pm	-	
3.20pm Exeter to Plymouth (Friary)	-	3.20pm	
12.46am Salisbury to Torrington	3.24pm	4.12pm	
12 noon FO Waterloo to Ilfracombe	3.34pm	3.41pm	
3.15pm Sidmouth to Exeter	4.10pm	-	
11.30am Brighton to Plymouth Friary	4.22pm	4.28pm	
12.40pm Waterloo to Plymouth Friary	4.46pm	4.52pm	1
12.40pm Waterloo to Ilfracombe	4.46pm	5.00pm	1
4.35pm Seaton Junction to Exeter	5.26pm	-	
5.48pm Exeter to Okehampton	-	5.48pm	
5.20pm Honiton to Exeter	5.56pm	-	
2.47pm Salisbury to Exeter	6.02pm	-	
3.00pm Waterloo to Ilfracombe (and Torrington)	6.22pm	6.30pm	1
3.00pm Waterloo to Plymouth Friary	6.22pm	6.40pm	1
6.25pm Sidmouth Junction to Exeter	6.51pm	-	
4.45pm FX Salisbury to Barnstaple Junction	7.30pm	7.53pm	
3.05pm FO Waterloo to Ilfracombe	7.41pm	7.53pm	
8.07pm Exeter to Plymouth Friary	-	8.07pm	
7.30pm Axminster to Exeter	8.29pm	-	
8.25pm Sidmouth to Exeter	9.16pm	-	

Table 15: Passenger services at Exeter Queen Street from 17 July 1932 (weekdays)

Down trains at Queen Street	Arr	Dep	Notes
8.20pm Sidmouth Junction to Exeter via Exmouth	9.56pm	-	
6.00pm Waterloo to Plymouth (Friary)	10.02pm	10.10pm	
5.00pm Waterloo to Exeter	10.39pm	-	
10.30pm Honiton to Exeter	11.04pm	-	
11.30pm WSO Whimple to Exeter	11.49pm	-	

Up trains at Queen Street	Arr	Dep	Notes
5.50am Exeter to Sidmouth	-	5.50am	
6.30am Exeter to Waterloo	-	6.30am	
6.40am Exeter to Honiton	-	6.40am	
7.20am Exeter to Waterloo	-	7.20am	
7.30am Exeter to Sidmouth	-	7.30am	
8.2am Exeter to Sidmouth	-	8.02am	
5.52am Plymouth Friary to Salisbury	8.35am	8.45am	
7.10am Torrington to Exeter	9.10am	-	
9.35am MO Exeter to Waterloo	-	9.35am	
9.45am Exeter to Templecombe	-	9.45am	
7.10am Plymouth Friary to Exeter	9.52am	-	
8.10am Torrington to Waterloo	10.07am	10.30am	1
8.25am Plymouth Friary to Waterloo	10.23am	10.30am	1
10.45am Exeter to Seaton Junction	-	10.45am	
9.0am Ilfracombe to Waterloo	11.9am	11.20am	
10.30am Ilfracombe (and Torrington) to Waterloo	12.25pm	12.32pm	
12.35pm Exeter to Honiton	-	12.35pm	
9.40am Padstow to Waterloo	12.39pm	12.46pm	
11.05am Plymouth Friary to Brighton	1.07pm	1.13pm	
10.15am FO Padstow to Waterloo	1.17pm	1.22pm	
1.28pm Exeter to Yeovil	-	1.28pm	
10.30am Plymouth Friary to Exeter	1.54pm	-	
12 noon FSO Plymouth Friary to Waterloo	2.05pm	2.28pm	1
12.20pm Ilfracombe to Waterloo	2.20pm	2.28pm	1
3.25pm Exeter to Templecombe	-	3.25pm	3
2.5pm FO Ilfracombe to Waterloo	3.58pm	4.15pm	
2.10pm Plymouth Friary to Waterloo	4.09pm	4.30pm	1
2.20pm Ilfracombe (and Torrington) to Waterloo	4.20pm	4.30pm	1
4.35pm Exeter to Woking	-	4.35pm	
2.35pm Plymouth Friary to Exeter	5.3pm	-	
5.35pm Exeter to Sidmouth Junction	-	5.35pm	

Passenger services on 'Southern' lines

Table 15: Passenger services at Exeter Queen Street from 17 July 1932 (weekdays)			
Up trains at Queen Street	Arr	Dep	Notes
2.55pm Ilfracombe to Waterloo	5.22pm	5.55pm	1
3.50pm Plymouth Friary to Waterloo	5.45pm	5.55pm	1
6.15pm Exeter to Axminster	-	6.15pm	
4.45pm Ilfracombe (and Torrington) to Eastleigh; passenger and mail	7.01pm	7.45pm	
4.40pm Plymouth Friary to Exeter	7.14pm	-	
7.55pm WO Exeter to Exmouth	-	7.55pm	
9.15pm Exeter to Honiton	-	9.15pm	
7.09pm Plymouth Friary to Exeter; passenger and mail	9.48pm	-	
7.45pm Ilfracombe to Exeter; passenger and mail	10.07pm	-	
11.02pm WSO Exeter to Whimple	-	11.02pm	

Notes:	
1	Indicates portions that were either divided or combined in Exeter Queen Street.
2	Through coaches from Portsmouth Harbour were added at Salisbury, and this train was divided at Yeoford.
3	Conveys carriages that will be added to the 4.30pm Exeter to Waterloo at Templecombe.
4	Additionally there were 20 trains from Exmouth to Exeter that departed between 6.35am and 10.20pm, and 22 departures in the opposite direction between 5.55am and 11.0pm.

of the main stations between the two cathedral cities; in this way the SR was seeking to serve as many of the intermediate stations as it could to secure business without overly slowing the journey to Exeter. The 5.00pm departure from Waterloo was a stopper that was overtaken by the 6.00pm train at Yeovil Junction. Additionally there was a daily service from Brighton to Plymouth, which was scheduled to run as a separate train on Mondays and Fridays and on any other days where there was sufficient demand. Otherwise, on Tuesdays, Wednesdays and Thursdays coaches from Brighton were added to the 12.40pm from Waterloo at Salisbury. There were also 20 stopping services to Exeter from as far away as Basingstoke and Salisbury or as near as Honiton.

Seven of the Waterloo trains ran beyond Exeter, with two solely bound for Plymouth, but the other five were divided at Exeter or, in one case, at Yeoford; this meant that many rural stations had at least one through train to and from London each day. Otherwise the local service was not frequent, with five trains running from Exeter to Plymouth with connections for North Cornwall at Okehampton, and another five between Exeter and North Devon.

In the 1938 summer weekday timetable there were six expresses that mostly left 'on the hour' at regular intervals – 9.00am, 11.00am, 1.00pm, 3.00pm and 6.00pm. The

Exmouth Junction's 'Merchant Navy' 4-6-2 No 35004 *Cunard White Star* is in its original 'air-smoothed' condition as it accelerates past Central station's 'A' signal box with the 10.30am departure for Waterloo on 27 June 1952. *J. H. Bamsey*

exception was the 'ACE', which in the summer months still ran as the 10.35am departure, but was actually a second part (although running in advance) of the 11.00am departure. The 'ACE' had portions for Ilfracombe and Padstow, whereas the second train was to Plymouth with a coach detached at Salisbury for Seaton, and a stop at Sidmouth Junction where another carriage was removed for Sidmouth; the schedule for the first train from Waterloo to Exeter was now 3hr 6min, and the second was given an extra 6 minutes. On weekdays the main line from Salisbury was not that busy, with the handful of expresses supplemented by a range of trains serving the intermediate stations. Goods traffic was also not heavy, with the most important trains running overnight with perishable traffic. Summer Saturdays were another matter, however, and like its 'rival' the SR handled large volumes of holiday traffic and each of the express services could require relief trains.

For 20 years after the Second World War the basic service changed little from the well-established pattern, but as on the WR paid leave meant that traffic on summer Saturdays boomed. However, the Southern did not really compare with the WR, as the places that it served did not match the scale of, say, the Torbay resorts, and the SR also did not carry the vast numbers that headed west from South Wales, the Midlands and the North. Nevertheless there was plenty of business, and morning departures from Waterloo could rise from the usual three to perhaps 15 trains. In June 1947 a summer weekend Pullman train, the 'Devon Belle', was introduced, leaving Waterloo at noon and only stopping at Wilton, for an engine change, and Sidmouth Junction before Exeter. The train was divided at Central, with seven coaches and an observation saloon going to Ilfracombe and four coaches for Plymouth. Despite a fast schedule the train was not a commercial success as it was mainly aimed at the well-heeled leisure market rather than the business and commuter traffic that sustained the SR's successful Pullman trains to Brighton and Bournemouth. Subsequently changes were made to both the frequency and timings, and the Plymouth portion ceased from 1950, but after patronage continued to decline it was abandoned at the end of the 1954 season.

Historically locos had nearly always been changed at Salisbury, but through working between Waterloo and Exeter for most services was finally adopted in 1950. Another notable change occurred in the summer of 1954 when the Ilfracombe and Torrington section of the 1.15am newspaper

'N' Class 2-6-0 No 31830 received special attention at Exmouth Junction prior to hauling the Royal Train with classmate No 31845 between Launceston and Exeter on Wednesday 9 May 1956; two days later it is leaving St David's Platform 4 with the 5.52pm Exeter Central to Okehampton service. *C. H. S. Owen*

With one engine carrying its new BR number and the other its SR identity, 'West Country' Class 'Pacifics' Nos 34016 *Bodmin* and 21C113 *Okehampton* are on Exmouth Junction shed in the summer of 1948 before heading for Exeter Central where they will take over the two sections of the down 'Devon Belle' Pullman train. The engines are displaying their duty numbers, which indicate that they will be working to Ilfracombe (588) and Plymouth (613) respectively. *C. H. S. Owen*

and passenger train from Waterloo was scheduled to run through St David's without stopping; this was the first regular Southern passenger train to do this after 92 years!

While the WR was busy dieselising its services at the end of the 1950s, steam continued to reign supreme on the SR in the West. Much of the WR's financial problems stemmed from a decline in freight, but this was not such a problem for the Southern, which was dominated by its passenger business. However, it is understood that the SR knew as early as 1957 that its operations west of Salisbury were losing money heavily and failing to cover direct costs by as much as £800,000 annually; as both passenger and freight traffic was sparse in its westernmost territory, possibly the SR felt that what business was available did not justify the investment in new traction. It is, however, surprising that no attempt was made to reduce these losses by closing the more obvious loss-making lines, and none were closed to passengers after the Turnchapel branch in 1951. Rather than prune those lines losing the

Passenger services on 'Southern' lines

most money, it has been suggested that closure of much of its western network was in Waterloo's mind and nothing was therefore done to either modernise or rationalise in the interim.

At the end of 1962 BR implemented a number of regional boundary adjustments that included the transfer of this network to the WR. The Southern's problem was thus solved, but the matter was now largely in the hands of higher rather than regional authorities as Dr Richard Beeching, the head of the new British Railways Board, published his 'Reshaping' report in March 1963. This was mainly aimed at those lines thought to be financially beyond redemption, and among the proposals were the paring down of the former SR system west of Exeter to just two branches to Okehampton and Ilfracombe, and the closure of all the east Devon branches. It was estimated that the entire passenger service in the West Country (defined as being the area from the Somerset & Dorset Railway to Penzance) had lost more than £3 million in 1962 (£71 million at 2021 prices), with only the WR main line to Plymouth paying its way. It was claimed that the ex-SR network accounted for £2.3 million of this loss, with the Salisbury to Exeter route losing £660,000 annually.

The next rationalisation measures would consider 'duplicate' routes, where most of the traffic was end-to-end; it was thought that it would make economic sense to concentrate traffic on one modernised route and close the alternative line. A pilot exercise examined the two routes between London and the South West with particular attention paid to the sections between the capital and Exeter, which to a large extent were competing for the same business. It was decided that the WR main line was better suited to handle an express service as it had already received investment with some signalling modernised and the installation of some continuous welded rail, permitting higher speeds than on the SR line; in contrast the SR had been concentrating its resources on its electrification plans. On the WR only a few stations were still open between Westbury and Exeter, but of these Taunton was an important county town and railhead that warranted a regular express service. If the SR route was selected it would probably mean that the Westbury to Taunton line would be abandoned, with Taunton served by the roundabout route via Bristol.

The WR line was already fully dieselised and a costing

At 4.25pm on Saturday 9 August 1958 'T9' 4-4-0 No 30717 is 5 minutes late as it passes over Red Cow level crossing on the approach to Platform 3 at St David's with the 2.22pm train from Plymouth Friary. 'E1/R' 0-6-2T No 32697 is in the spur and will bank the train to Central, where it will be combined with the Ilfracombe and Torrington portion that should be waiting with a restaurant car attached; the train will then form the 4.30pm departure to Waterloo. *Peter W. Gray*

Salisbury's 'King Arthur' Class 4-6-0 No 30799 *Sir Ironside* is bound for its home city as it leaves Exeter Central with the 3.20pm stopping train on 18 October 1959. *R. A. Lumber*

and traffic survey conducted by both regions found that it carried five times more traffic to Exeter and beyond than the SR line; one drawback, however, was the location of St David's station, which was inconveniently distant from the city centre. Also, west of Exeter a much larger population was served by the WR route, and if the SR line was chosen, through trains to places like Torbay and Plymouth would have to reverse at St David's, with a detrimental effect on timings. Furthermore the Waterloo route still had stations open in a number of quite well-populated towns such as Yeovil, Axminster and Honiton, which had previously been neglected in the SR's desire to offer an express service to Exeter.

Operations at Exeter Central's main up platform (No 3) were performed like a well-oiled machine. At 10.20am on Saturday 13 July 1963 'West Country' 4-6-2 No 34036 *Westward Ho!* has run light from Exmouth Junction shed prior to hauling the 10.30am departure to Waterloo. Behind it another 'Pacific', No 34106 *Lydford*, has been uncoupled after arriving with the first portion of this train, the 8.10am from Ilfracombe, which was due at 10.11am; *Lydford* is signalled over the 'scissors' crossover before heading to the shed. No 34036 will then drop on to the coaches and pull them forward clear of the 'scissors'; once this is done St David's will dispatch the Plymouth portion, which is due at 10.25am. A third 'West Country', No 34003 *Plymouth*, is in the bay platform (No 1) with the 10.37am stopper to Templecombe. *Peter W. Gray*

Initial thinking at the highest level was to close the Salisbury to Exeter line, but both regional managements felt otherwise, and when the 'Beeching Part 2' plan was released the report merely stated that the route was 'not for development'. The regions were also against another idea to close the Salisbury to Yeovil Junction section and serve the line between Yeovil and Exeter Central from Paddington via Castle Cary. In the event the SR route was retained, but with the objectives of reducing its losses by replacing steam, making a more economical use of coaches through tighter diagramming, and fostering traffic in the country towns. The new service would terminate at St David's, which was to become the focal point of a connectional network of passenger services linking the rest of the country with all points in Devon and Cornwall; passengers for the ex-SR system further west would now have to transfer to connecting DMUs. This new Waterloo service was turned over to 'Warship' diesels based at the existing underused WR depot at Newton Abbot, and this meant that new maintenance facilities would not be needed on the ex-SR route.

The last all-steam British main line had six weekday departures from Waterloo in the 1964 summer timetable at the 'usual' times of 9.00am, 11.00am ('ACE'), 1.00pm, 3.00pm, 6.00pm and 7.00pm. The 'ACE' had been accelerated in the 1950s and now reached Exeter in a fraction under 3 hours with one stop west of Salisbury at Sidmouth Junction. The other five trains were scheduled to take between 3hr 17min and 4hr 8min, with the number of stops beyond Salisbury ranging from two for the fastest to up to six for the other services. The new semi-fast timetable was introduced on 7 September 1964 with five weekday departures from Waterloo at similar times; the exception was the former 'ACE' path, which was now a train to Salisbury; there it connected with the Brighton to Plymouth service, which was now the only through train to run beyond Exeter, although the 1.10am newspaper train from Waterloo did continue for a while with through coaches for Plymouth.. Four of the down trains were scheduled to take between 3hr 30min and 3hr 51min to reach Exeter Central, but they now made between five and seven stops west of Salisbury at stations acting as railheads for their surrounding areas; the 5.00pm departure took 4hr 26min but had 14 stops. Apart from the 'ACE' average times from Waterloo to Exeter were now marginally faster than before despite the increase in the number of stops.

In the reverse direction Waterloo trains now left Central at 6.20am, 7.25am, 10.35am, 2.25pm and 5.25pm, although all but the first of these actually started at St David's, and there was also a limited stopping service provided by DMUs. Nine stations west of Salisbury were closed, including Pinhoe and Broad Clyst near Exeter, but rather surprisingly Whimple was retained as a 'secondary railhead' to break the section between Honiton and Exeter. After the closure programme

Passenger services on 'Southern' lines

was completed the local service was withdrawn, with just the Waterloo trains serving the remaining stations.

With local trains and through freight services removed, the next rationalisation stage was implemented between April and June 1967 when the line was singled between Wilton South and Pinhoe apart from a 6-mile stretch of double track that was retained between Templecombe and Sherborne where trains could pass at speed. Short crossing loops were also kept at Honiton, Chard Junction and Gillingham; it was thought that the singling would save costs from the maintenance of less track and fewer signal boxes. With the benefit of hindsight this has proved a mistake; even at the outset a misjudgement of the operating capacity of the new layout meant that 4½ miles of double track had to be reinstated between Sherborne and Yeovil Junction. Unfortunately the 'Warship' diesels did not prove particularly reliable, and any failures meant that with the long sections of single track the lateness or failure of just one train could badly affect the service in both directions, a situation that remains today.

There were improvements in the 1967 timetable with some accelerations, particularly in the up direction, and BR claimed that, other than the 'ACE', on average it now provided the fastest ever service between London and any of the intermediate stations, or between any pair of these stations. At this time the final through service to Plymouth, the longstanding Brighton train, was truncated at Exeter as a prelude to the closure of the 'duplicate' route beyond Okehampton in May 1968; this meant that the only parts of the 'Withered Arm' network west of Exeter were now the branches to Ilfracombe and Okehampton. Under the Transport Act of 1968 provision was made for the Government to subsidise lines that were unremunerative but deemed socially necessary; despite the economies the line between Exeter and Salisbury was still losing money; in 1969 £573,000 was authorised to maintain the service, and in 1970 a grant of £409,000 for three years was given.

BR now wanted to rationalise the large number of diesel types that it had acquired, and this included dispensing with the diesel-hydraulic

In the last summer of scheduled steam services over the London route, 'Merchant Navy' 'Pacific' No 35025 *Brocklebank Line* is approaching Exeter Central with the 3.00pm train from Waterloo on Saturday 20 June 1964; the WR auto-coach on the right of the carriage shed had recently been used on the Seaton branch. The train was due at 6.31pm and on arrival the station pilot would couple on to the rear and pull the sections apart, including the buffet car that was in the middle of the train. *Brocklebank Line* would be uncoupled, then back through the station on the down through road to Exmouth Junction and a 'Light Pacific' would back out of the carriage sidings and couple to the front coaches, departing at 6.37pm for Plymouth. Another pilot, perhaps one of the bankers, would then run up the platform road to collect the buffet car and reverse it into the up through road to await its next journey. A second 'Light Pacific' would then back on to the rear portion and leave for Ilfracombe at 6.52pm. *Peter W. Gray*

At the start of the last scheduled week of steam operation of Waterloo services, Monday 31 August 1964, 'Merchant Navy' 4-6-2 No 35029 *Ellerman Lines* is passing the Pinhoe grain silo with the 9.00am express from Waterloo, which has through coaches for Plymouth and Barnstaple Junction; an Exmouth Junction concrete prefabricated platelayers' hut can be seen on the left, and the Pye Storage Ltd siding is on the right. *Rail Online*

Class 42 'Warship' No D820 *Grenville* is nearing St David's Tunnel as it storms up the bank with the 12.30 Exeter St David's to Waterloo train on 13 February 1971. The South Devon Railway carriage shed at St David's can be glimpsed to the right of the engine. *John Medley*

fleet. In October 1971 the Waterloo to Exeter service was taken over by SR Class 33 diesel-electrics, which had already covered some work on the line including substituting for failures; however, as these locos were less powerful than their predecessors it meant that the schedules had to be eased. There were now seven trains each way throughout, with the fastest down working now scheduled to cover the journey in 3hr 38min, although the majority of services were just shy of 4 hours. The weekday Brighton to Exeter train ended at this time, but a Saturdays-only service operated from 1972 using 'Hastings' DEMUs, and from 1977 Class 33s were also diagrammed on this working.

The Waterloo to Exeter line had reached its nadir, but since 1980 there has been a gradual revival in its fortunes. The 'Cromptons' were the main motive power until May 1980, when the service was revitalised using Class 50 locos and Mark 2 coaches that had been superseded by HSTs on the WR. This meant that it was possible to reduce journey times, although the '50s' also had reliability issues that were not helped by the stop-start nature of the service; this, coupled with sections of high-speed running, mean that the line is demanding for any diesel loco. Any failures were magnified by the single-line sections, but this was helped by opening a passing loop at Tisbury in 1986. When a '50' failed, other types such as Class 33 and 47 were employed, but the use of the former meant that it was impossible to maintain the schedules. Towards the end of the locomotive era Class 47/7 diesels were drafted in to replace the '50s', but using these ageing locos on such arduous work did not solve the reliability issue.

During BR's sectorisation era in the 1980s the 'West of England' line was part of Network SouthEast and route modernisation was considered. Alternatives such as extending the existing electrification to Exeter, or perhaps introducing mixed-mode operation from Salisbury, were considered too expensive and in the event a cheaper option became available when Regional Railways reduced its requirement for Class 158 DMUs and a three-car version (Class 159) was chosen, with a new dedicated maintenance depot at Salisbury. These were gradually introduced into service when available and the last locomotive-hauled trains ran in July 1993. The route was privatised in February 1996 when the franchise was secured by Stagecoach trading under the name of South West Trains (SWT).

After the 1967 singling Axminster was in the middle of a 15-mile section of single track, but in 2009 £20 million was spent to provide a 3-mile-long 'dynamic loop' there, which enabled the introduction of an hourly service over the route. SWT had previously operated a number of services beyond Exeter to Paignton, Plymouth and Penzance, but these ceased, releasing stock for the enhanced service. After the DfT failed to negotiate an extension with SWT in 2015, a new seven-year franchise was awarded to South Western Railway, which took over operations in August 2017. In its December 2019 timetable there were 15 departures from Waterloo to St David's between 07.10 and 21.20 each weekday; most were timed to complete the journey in about 3hr 23min, and many called at all the stations, although at some of the smaller ones only alternate trains stop to help maintain the schedules. There were also four earlier trains to Exeter from places such

Passenger services on 'Southern' lines

'Crompton' No 33013 is approaching the then closed Pinhoe station with the 10.10 St David's to Waterloo train on Sunday 16 July 1978; the grain silo is prominent in the background, and the buildings on the right once formed part of a Ministry of Food cold store. *DHM*

as Salisbury that catered for commuters and school children; in the up direction there were 17 departures to Waterloo between 05.10 and 20.25, and five shorter runs including three later trains that enabled passengers to spend the evening in Exeter.

Today conspiracy theorists still consider that the measures taken in the 1960s were due to the WR wanting to exact revenge on its longstanding rival, but economies had to be made to keep the route open, and it can be argued that WR management in fact helped to save it. Complaints are still voiced about the line's downgrading, often from those fondly remembering the 'ACE'; however, one express does not constitute a service, and the line is now much more useful to most living near it than at any time in the past. The 1960s desire to provide a better service to the intermediate stations has been more than fulfilled, and additional stations have been opened.

The first, in May 1971, was Feniton (the former Sidmouth Junction), where the village was expanding with new developments. Pinhoe and Templecombe were reopened in 1983, and a station was provided at Cranbrook in 2015 to serve a new town just outside Exeter. In this way the line has benefitted from its 'secondary' status; by comparison, the larger town of Cullompton on the Great Western main line has so far been unable to have its station reopened, mainly due to being on a line that is almost exclusively served by express trains. However, all is not perfect: the stretches of single line are still a problem, and there are various proposals to improve this. For example, it has long been an aspiration of Devon County Council to see a half-hourly 'Devon Metro' service between Exeter and Axminster, and it has lobbied for a loop to be installed between Whimple and Cranbrook to achieve this. Also the Class 159 DMUs are now 30 years old and currently there is no firm indication as to when or how they will be replaced.

After the 1960s closures two sections of the SR network west of Exeter remained as branches, to Ilfracombe and Okehampton; grant aid of £174,000 was provided for the Exeter to Barnstaple line in 1968, but not for the section to Ilfracombe, which was closed in 1970. Today Barnstaple is the terminus of a 40-mile-long branch and the railhead for all of north Devon. In 1972 a weekday service of nine trains was provided each way from St David's (one from Exeter Central) with just three trains on Sundays. By 1980 there were only seven weekday trains with some large gaps in the timetable; just one train left Exeter between the 08.50 and 14.14 departures each day. However, when Regional Railways was privatised in October 1996 there were 11 weekday trains, although the new operator, Prism Rail, quickly cut these to seven after realising that it had overbid for the franchise and was losing money; the County Council had to pay to reinstate two services. Since then there have been steady improvements, and for a period most trains ran through from Barnstaple to Exmouth using mainly two-car DMUs. In December 2019 the service between Exmouth and Paignton was doubled and a discrete timetable of 17 weekday trains (with an additional late train on Fridays), and 13 on Sundays, was introduced between St James Park and Barnstaple using

On Saturday 17 August 1991 Class 50 No 50030 *Repulse* speeds towards the overbridge seen in the background of the previous photo with the Network SouthEast 11.14 Southampton to Plymouth service. *DHM*

No 47705 accelerates up the 1 in 100 gradient from Exeter Central with the 09.25 Plymouth to Waterloo train on Saturday 24 August 1991; the much rationalised trackwork is apparent in this view. At this time the closed 'A' signal box was being used by the permanent way department but was later demolished after suffering damage caused by burst water pipes. *DHM*

On 18 November 2021, after Nos 159103 and 159005 had arrived at Pinhoe forming the 07.10 Waterloo to St David's service and cleared the single-line section from Honiton, No 159106 is now leaving as the 10.25 Exeter St David's to Waterloo service. *DHM*

Passenger services on 'Southern' lines

three-car Class 158 DMUs; in May 2021 the starting point was revised and most services now commence at Exeter Central.

Under the 'Reshaping' report a service to Okehampton was retained, whereby the station became the railhead for a large swathe of rural west Devon and north Cornwall. Partly due to the replacement buses carrying fewer passengers than expected, patronage was poor and after an application for grant aid of £150,000 under the 1968 Transport Act was refused, the branch was closed in June 1972. Fortunately the line survived to serve Meldon Quarry, and in 1994 the quarry and railway from just beyond Coleford Junction were sold to Camas Aggregates. Subsequently a heritage operation was based at Okehampton, and from 1997 to 2019 Devon County Council sponsored a summer Sunday service from Exeter that provided access to Dartmoor National Park. In 2020 the DfT launched a 'Restoring Your Railway Fund' to reinstate services that had closed during the years of retrenchment, and with its formation intact the Okehampton branch was a prime candidate; it was acquired by Network Rail and after several months of work and £40 million of investment it was reopened on 20 November 2021. The original service was eight trains a day at 2-hourly intervals, but after further work an hourly service was introduced in May 2022.

Top right: Crediton station is largely intact and has been repainted in LSWR colours. On 6 December 2020 Nos 150238 and 143621 are waiting to depart as the 11.34 Barnstaple to St James Park service, while on the left No 166220 is leaving as the 12.20 St David's to Barnstaple service. In 2022 the station probably had its best ever service, with hourly services to both Barnstaple and Okehampton crossing there for much of the day. *DHM*

Centre right: On the last day of BR services to Okehampton, 3 June 1972, Class 119 DMU set No P587 is about to leave forming the 16.17 departure to Exeter St David's. *DHM*

Below: On the first day of services over the revived branch, Nos 150233 and 150221 have just arrived at Okehampton as the 08.41 service from St David's on 20 November 2021. *DHM*

12. Goods traffic in steam days

Great Western Railway

Apart from those early railways built to handle mineral traffic, passenger business was usually foremost in the minds of the proponents of railways such as the Bristol & Exeter, and the development of goods traffic could be a slow process, with the revenue earned much less than that derived from passengers and mail. It was not until 1867 that the GWR's Goods Department was producing the larger part of its revenue, and once it was participating in the South Wales coal trade its importance grew further; during the 20th century freight provided about two-thirds of the company's revenue.

When the B&E opened, a goods yard was established on the west side of the Exeter terminus. Although the city was the administrative and financial centre for Devon, it had no great industrial importance, although there were paper mills, foundries, tanneries and breweries within the city and in the immediate district. It was, however, a distribution centre for a large area and a focal point for business activity, particularly in agriculture and related trades; these provided the staple goods traffic for the railway throughout the steam era. The GWR established a goods district at Exeter, which eventually extended beyond Taunton to the east and Newton Abbot to the west.

At one time everything that travelled any distance on land was carried by rail, and this could include some unusual items. This 2 September 1905 view includes a new bronze statue of General Sir Redvers Buller VC that has been loaded in Brentford goods yard before being dispatched to Exeter. Buller was born in Crediton in 1839 and won the Victoria Cross during the Anglo-Zulu War of 1879; he later served as Commander-in-Chief of British Forces in South Africa during the Second Boer War. The statue was funded by public subscription and erected in Exeter on the road from Crediton, about half-way between St David's and Central stations. *GWR*

Table 16: Down goods trains on weekdays in October 1886			
Gauge	Train	Exeter St David's times	Notes and instructions
NG	2.30pm Swindon to Exeter; ordinary goods	Arr 1.45am	
BG	9.45pm Bristol Pylle Hill to Plymouth; fast goods	2.00am to 2.50am	
BG	10.25pm Paddington to Plymouth; express goods	4.52am to 5.05am	Important traffic, maximum 23 loaded wagons from Reading
NG	10.40pm Paddington and Smithfield to Exeter; express goods	Arr 6.10am	Important traffic, maximum 25 wagons and van from Bristol
BG	1.00am Bristol Pylle Hill to Penzance; fast goods	6.28am to 7.30am	
BG	7.15am Crediton to Exeter	Arr 7.30am	GWR goods
NG	4.35am Bristol Pylle Hill to Exeter; ordinary goods	Arr 11.35am	
NG	10.30am Dulverton to Exeter	Arr 12.55pm	Exe Valley goods
BG	4.55am MO Paddington to Penzance; empty fish plant	12.50pm to 1.00pm	
NG	St David's to Queen Street	3.35pm to 3.36pm	LSWR transfer train
BG	1.00pm Dunball to Exeter; coal and ordinary goods	Arr 5.55pm	
BG	5.55am Paddington to Penzance; fast goods and fish empties	6.15pm to 8.10pm	
BG	6.10pm Crediton to Exeter	Arr 6.27pm	GWR goods
NG	Manchester to Exeter; ordinary goods	Arr 8.57pm	

Goods traffic in steam days

The main-line goods trains in the 1886 'Service Time Table' indicate that freight was carried on both broad and narrow gauge trains (the GWR preferred that name to 'Working Time Table', as was used by most other railways and later by BR). At this time 'ordinary' goods trains would run at about 20mph between their many stops, and even those trains termed 'expresses' would not go much faster, perhaps at no more than 25-30mph; however, these usually made a limited number of stops and hauled restricted loads to more distant destinations. The 10.25pm broad gauge train from London to Plymouth was one of these and was given the unusual name by staff of the 'Tip'; it had been accelerated in 1878 to run to Exeter at up to 35mph with a limited payload and was reputed to be the fastest goods train in the country. An engine change was made at Bristol and there were strict instructions that the new loco would be in position with any Bristol traffic attached for a swift changeover. Its progress was telegraphed ahead and 'Station Agents' were responsible for keeping 'ordinary' trains out of its way. It was only timetabled to stop at Reading (to add two wagons), Swindon (for water), Bristol and Taunton before reaching Exeter, and was scheduled to complete this 194-mile leg of its journey in less than 6½ hours.

Most freight was handled on 'ordinary' services throughout the steam era and their timekeeping was often unreliable, their operation coming second to passenger services and the limited number of express goods trains. After the B&E reached Exeter, for many years a train carried coal to the city from a wharf at Dunball on the River Parrett. The train was also a 'pick-up' goods that was scheduled to stop at nine places on its journey to either shunt traffic, collect 'overload' wagons left off preceding goods trains, or allow other trains to overtake; thus the 45-mile journey took almost 5 hours to complete. Even in the 1950s this sort of schedule would not be unusual.

Although the 2.00pm Exeter to Swindon train was described as a fast train, it was anything but, with stops scheduled for either traffic or refuge purposes at Hele & Bradninch, Kensham Siding, Cullompton, Tiverton Junction, Burlescombe, Wellington and Norton Fitzwarren. After taking 4¼ hours to travel the 30 miles from Exeter, it stopped at Taunton from 6.15pm until 7.20pm, and thereafter 'as required' stops were made at Durston if there was any 'cattle or other important traffic' to be left, and Bridgwater during the apple season to take on apples. Further stops were then timetabled at Weston-super-Mare and Bristol before arrival at Swindon, 10½ hours after leaving Exeter. The adoption of the vacuum brake for express services gave drivers more control, and by the turn of the century faster speeds were permitted for the most important trains; thanks to the installation of water troughs, the 'Tip' was now running non-stop from London to Bristol at an average speed of 37mph. It was the practice for railway staff to give nicknames to the main passenger and express goods trains for easy identification; some reflected the type of traffic carried, and a longstanding train that left Exeter at about 4.00pm for Old Oak Common was named 'The Flying Pig' in reference to its meat traffic, which included pork, bacon and ham! It handled traffic to the GWR's depot at Smithfield Market, where wagons were scheduled to arrive after midnight via the tunnels of the Circle Line; in the 1930s the train usually

Table 17: Up goods trains on weekdays in October 1886

Gauge	Train	Exeter St David's times	Notes and instructions
BG	9.30pm Plymouth to Bristol; fast goods	2.20am to 2.45am	
NG	4.30am Exeter to Manchester; ordinary goods	4.30am	Including traffic from local stations that will be added to 1.00pm Exeter
BG	6.25am Exeter to Crediton	6.25am	GWR goods
BG	7.00am Exeter to Dunball; goods and coal empties	7.00am	Including local traffic to Bridgwater
NG	1.00pm Exeter to Manchester; fast goods	1.00pm	
NG	1.40pm Exeter to Dulverton	1.40pm	Exe Valley branch goods
NG	2.00pm Exeter to Swindon; fast goods	2.00pm	
NG	Queen Street to St David's	3.08pm	LSWR transfer train
BG	5.00pm Exeter to Crediton	5.00pm	GWR goods
NG	5.30pm Exeter to Paddington and Smithfield; express goods	5.30pm	Perishable and important traffic only
BG	4.05pm Plymouth to Paddington; fast goods	6.55pm to 7.15pm	Important traffic including horses and cattle; maximum 30 trucks from Exeter
BG	12.30pm Penzance to Paddington; express goods	8.45pm to 8.55pm	Fish, meat and perishables
BG	12.45pm Penzance to Bristol; fast goods	11.05pm to 11.25pm	South Devon and Exeter traffic added

Ex-WD 'Austerity' 2-8-0 No 90624 is about to pass over Red Cow level crossing as it trundles over the goods avoiding line after leaving Riverside yard with a down freight on 16 June 1949. This engine was shedded at Llanelly at the time, but would soon move to Wakefield, then several other Yorkshire sheds until it was withdrawn in 1963. *J. H. Bamsey*

comprised about 20 'Conflats' hauled by a 'Castle' Class engine. Less imaginatively, another long-running express freight from Exeter that left at around 11.00am for Pontypool Road was named 'The Ponty'.

These 'express' services were not representative, and in 1924 the GWR reported that the standard of freight trains had been maintained in the previous 12 months with an average speed of between 6 and 7mph. No doubt this would have been partly due to the many coal trains in South Wales, but in general freight operations were much the same as they had been since Victorian times. Many stations had goods yards served by 'pick-up' trains that ambled along exchanging wagons en route. These wagons would then be added to longer-distance trains and eventually they might be delivered to their final destination by another local trip working; this repeated marshalling increased the risk of damage to or theft of the goods being carried. Although this system seems to be almost quaint today, for a century it was the only viable way of getting an item to its end destination, but it became an anachronism once road transport improved.

Exeter's goods yard was hemmed in between St David's passenger station and the engine shed. When the station was rebuilt in the 1860s goods avoiding lines were provided next to the yard to keep freight trains clear of the station, and passenger trains were not authorised to run over them other than in an emergency. The yard had a large two-road timber shed that had several cranes of different capacity to load and unload wagons with local merchandise; cattle pens were provided on the west side of the avoiding lines. A short distance to the north a brick-built transhipment shed was constructed in about 1876 to transfer goods between narrow gauge wagons that had either arrived from the east or via the LSWR, and broad gauge wagons that were still being used on all services further west. The limited siding space was also used to marshal main line trains that either originated in Exeter or called there. The yard was also the focal point for local trip workings to places both within and outside the city, including the local branch lines, and it also handled transfer trips from the LSWR. On the other side of the main line and north of the goods depot, New Yard dealt with 'full' loads such as containers and had a Cadbury's depot and a miller's warehouse adjacent to it.

After nationalisation the volume of goods handled at St David's increased, with much of the traffic previously handled at Central station's goods yard moved there; only the 'smalls' business for the city centre remained at Central. By then the traffic concentrated at St David's was handled by the 'zonal' scheme, which switched traffic for small outlying stations to road vehicles; at peak times the number of lorries could cause congestion in the vicinity of Red Cow level crossing. Each day in 1953 the goods depot handled about 200 tons of inward merchandise, and about 70-80 tons outwards.

An enlarged Exeter Ship Canal was opened in 1827 and a canal basin was in use from 1830. Initially there was an upsurge in canal trade, but the opening of the B&E had a disastrous effect and the canal clerk reported that all of the trade from Bristol and Wales had ceased and the amount from Liverpool and Gloucester had substantially diminished. Later the South Devon Railway laid sidings at Teignmouth Quay in 1851, which enabled the port to compete with the canal's coal

Goods traffic in steam days

trade, and the opening of the branch off the Exmouth line to Topsham Quay further undermined canal traffic.

Initial proposals for a rail connection to the canal were unsuccessful; although the railway had affected the canal badly, the Corporation felt that a rail link would help as it would allow seaborne imports to be railed direct to other towns rather than having to be first carted by road to St David's. Eventually on 17 June 1867 the SDR opened a 750-yard branch from its main line south of St Thomas station to the canal basin. The City Basin branch terminated in a timber yard beside the River Exe, and a siding led to two wagon turntables located at the corners of the canal basin, which provided access to both of its sides; locos were not allowed over these sidings and horses (and later either a lorry or tractor) were used to shunt them. The branch was broad gauge only despite an agreement that a third rail would be laid for traffic to and from the LSWR; however, the SDR was not in any hurry to help its rival and a third rail was not added until 1871. Even then, despite being theoretically open to 'narrow gauge' trucks, further obfuscation meant that the first such wagon did not arrive in the basin until October 1876, more than nine years after the branch had opened! This was the only section of mixed gauge track on the SDR while it was a separate company.

The most important customer on the branch was the Exeter Gaslight & Coke Co, which had been established next to the basin in 1836; incoming coal was transferred from seagoing ships to lighters in the Exe estuary. However, high canal charges and the new branch line meant that it was often cheaper to bring the coal by rail from ports such as Teignmouth. The gas company had its own siding by 1875 and further sidings were added after the works was completely rebuilt in 1878; some coal still arrived via the canal, and in 1903 the company built a tramway to transport coal offloaded in the basin. Other than coal the main freight handled by the branch in the early years was timber and grain, but there was never a great volume of goods transhipped between the canal and the railway.

At first the branch had no connection with the up main line and all trains had to use the down line only, whether they were main-line trains that had to reverse on to the branch, or more likely trip workings from St David's, which would travel both to and from the branch over the down line. However, such was the limited train frequency on the main line at that time that this would not have been a great issue. After 'narrow gauge' traffic started to be handled in 1876 a daily mixed gauge train ran from St David's and back with a match truck separating the broad and standard gauge wagons. A crossover was installed at St Thomas station in the 1880s but, as the up line was broad gauge only until the 1892 conversion, it would not have been of any use for the branch train unless it was only conveying broad gauge wagons.

When the Exeter Railway was constructed from Christow to Exeter to complete the Teign Valley route from Heathfield, the company also built the 'Canal Branch', later known as the 'Low Level Loop', a spur that ran from its line and beneath the GWR main line to a connection with the City Basin branch. It was envisaged that mineral traffic would be carried from the Teign Valley quarries to ships in the basin, but this largely failed to materialise and the spur was rarely used until an asphalt depot was established on it in 1929.

Although nowhere near the scale of larger cities, the basin area can be said to have been the industrial heart of Exeter. At the dawn of the new century an established company, Willey's Foundry, expanded and moved to a location on Water Lane next to the branch; it was the largest employer in the city at that time, with more than 1,000 workers, and was a major manufacturer of gas meters. These and other products, including gas stoves, were conveyed by rail and the company also produced munitions and equipment during both world wars. A little later a generating station was built on Haven Road near the head of the basin to supply power for Exeter's new electric tram system, and its coal supply also arrived by both rail and ship. The growth in road transport brought an increasing demand for petrol, and several companies had established depots near the basin by the end of the 1920s that were supplied by ships specially designed to fit the canal's restricted dimensions. It is understood that initially some of the petrol was transferred to rail for distribution inland, but such traffic soon transferred to road.

There were restrictions on the locos that could work

Viewed from the head of the canal basin around the turn of the 20th century, a solitary wagon is standing on the siding on the east side of the basin; a wagon turntable located at the north-east corner of the basin is just out of view to the left.
The Isca Collection

'5700' Class 0-6-0PT No 3629 is on the ungated Haven Road level crossing while shunting at the basin on 1 October 1958; the coal wagons in the left distance are in the gas works sidings and the building on the right is part of the electricity generating station. *R. A. Lumber*

the branch, but the weight of the daily train and the steep grade on the final climb to the junction meant that a suitably proficient engine was needed. The 11 '44XX' Class 2-6-2Ts had smaller driving wheels than their more numerous '45XX' Class cousins and earned a good reputation for their performance on hilly branch lines; from 1934 Exeter shed usually had at least one of these locos to work the daily City Basin goods train, which was nicknamed 'The Bucket' for some reason, and other local freight work. With the class in its final days, No 4410 was transferred away in March 1953 and thereafter pannier tanks handled the branch traffic for the rest of the steam era.

In 1947 the country's independent electricity companies were nationalised and the small generating stations were eventually replaced by larger power stations; that in Exeter closed in 1955, and probably as a result of this coal deliveries via the canal ceased in June of that year. Other traffic on the branch gradually petered out and the sidings at the basin were officially abandoned in 1965, although they had probably seen no use for several years. The gas works was modernised in the 1950s and continued to receive coal by rail; it was the last such works in the South West still producing coal gas when it closed in 1971 with the arrival of North Sea gas. Thereafter a part of the branch continued to be used for a further 20 years as a headshunt to access oil and bitumen depots, and details of this traffic are provided in the next chapter.

The Alphington Road goods yard was opened by the Exeter Railway in 1903 to serve an area quite remote from the St David's goods yard; at first it had three sidings, a wooden shed and cattle dock, and later two more sidings were added As mentioned in Chapter 4, relations between the Exeter Railway and the GWR were not always good, and this

On Saturday 21 November 1964 0-6-0PT No 4655 has just crossed the River Exe as it heads away from St David's with 9D27, the 11.00am Exeter Riverside to City Basin Junction trip, carrying coal for the gas works. This turn was actually diagrammed for a 'D63XX' diesel-hydraulic at that time. Exeter West signal box can be glimpsed on the right. *R. A. Lumber*

Goods traffic in steam days

particularly applied to the local GWR management, which was against the idea of having to work another goods station in the city. Although the GWR was obliged to do so under the terms of the agreement between the companies, a local interpretation meant that initially the GWR only handled traffic in the yard for stations that were on the Exeter Railway (ER), and any freight for places on the original Teign Valley line still had to be sent via Newton Abbot! The ER filed a case in the Railway & Canal Commission Court, which was unsuccessful, but the GWR granted some concessions prior to the hearing and goods traffic for the whole Teign Valley route was then handled via the ER. The depot mainly handled coal traffic, but other business increased after the 'Grouping' when the yard was now owned by the GWR and the company no longer felt the need to discourage its use. In 1922 a separate daily train was introduced to transfer goods between St David's and the depot; this left St David's at 4.50pm and returned from Alphington Road at 7.10pm.

Exeter has long been a centre for livestock sales; historically this would have taken place on the city's streets, but during the 19th century a site adjacent to the River Exe was used. Poor access to the railway meant that herds of cattle would clog up the streets while being driven on foot between the market and one of the city's goods yards. Sites for a new cattle market were considered, but it was not until 1939 that the market was moved to land off Alphington Road, which provided greatly improved facilities where up to 5,500 animals could be penned on market days. Two sidings and loading platforms long enough to permit the simultaneous loading of 28 wagons were provided within the market and accessed via a trailing siding off the Alphington Road branch. Due to the increased use of the branch the existing ground frame for the Alphington Road goods yard spur was abolished and the points were then worked from the City Basin Junction signal box. The volume of livestock traffic was considerable at first, but there was a downward trend after the war; animals were often handled in small numbers to widely dispersed destinations and economics favoured road transport, which could provide a door-to-door service for farms. After BR realised that it was probably losing money from the movement of live animals, the facility was withdrawn from most stations from 1 January 1963, although traffic from Exeter's market continued for a while longer. Also, until about 1965 Exeter St David's was one of a limited number of railheads still able to receive trainloads of livestock imported from Ireland.

Goods services over the Exeter end of the Teign Valley line ended in 1947, but thereafter the Alphington Road goods yard continued to be served by two daily trips from Riverside yard. Three of the sidings in the depot were removed in December 1960 to make way for a new biscuit distribution warehouse, but any rail traffic resulting from this must have been short-lived as by 1967 only the coal traffic remained, and the yard was closed when this was transferred to a new coal concentration depot at Exmouth Junction.

During the Second World War there was a massive increase in the amount of rail freight, particularly in the two years leading up to D-Day, which required a logistical effort of

Alphington Road goods yard in January 1958. Peter W. Gray

The facility to carry livestock on BR was largely withdrawn from 1 January 1963, but a service to the Exeter cattle market continued for a while longer on Friday market days. On 5 July 1963 0-6-0PT No 4673 is hauling the 5.58pm Alphington Road to Riverside trip that includes six loaded cattle wagons and four coal empties. *D. J. Frost*

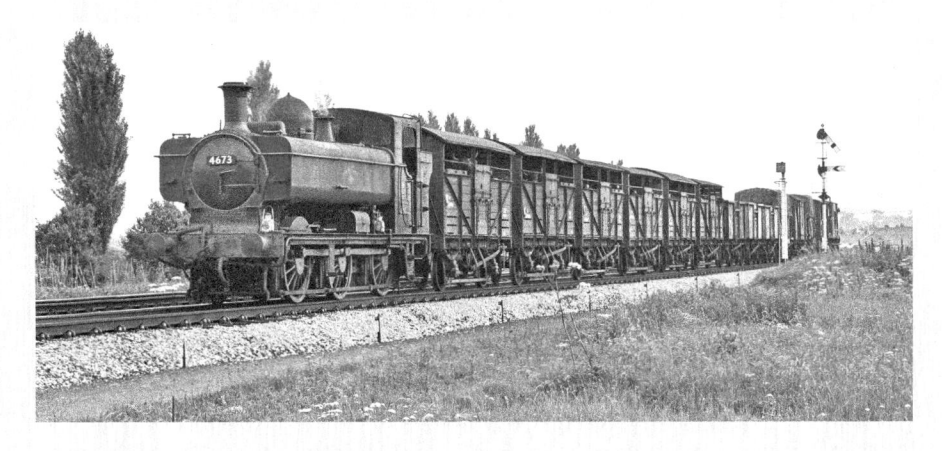

'Prairie' tank No 5560 is leaving Riverside yard on 9 December 1961 with an up pick-up goods train. The two loaded wagons are bound for Silverton station and probably contain esparto grass; a mill there produced high-quality paper using this grass, which was imported from southern Spain or North Africa and landed at Watchet harbour on the Minehead branch, from where it was taken by rail to Silverton. The economics of this short journey must have been suspect and the railway shed the traffic in 1964.
Peter W. Gray

'W' Class 2-6-4T No 31916 is entering Riverside yard during a snowstorm on 5 January 1963 with a transfer goods from the SR; this was during the 'Big Freeze' when the South West was struck by several blizzards for about two months from the end of December 1962.
C. M. Parsons

Brand-new BR Standard Class 4 4-6-0 No 75079 is beside the Teign estuary as it approaches Newton Abbot with the daily Grimsby to Plymouth fish train on Sunday 29 January 1956; trains ran from both Grimsby and Hull to Marston Sidings, Swindon, where they were re-marshalled. Wagons would then be detached en route and the train could be quite short by the time it reached Plymouth. It would have Eastern Region power as far as Marston, where the train was re-engined, a convenient way of returning locos that had received attention in Swindon Works, or as in this case delivering a new engine to its first depot. That shed is Exmouth Junction and the loco probably reached there by working an SR train from Plymouth via Okehampton.
Peter W. Gray

Goods traffic in steam days

unprecedented magnitude, one that US General Eisenhower described as having turned the UK into 'one gigantic air base, workshop, storage depot and mobilization camp'. More than a million US troops crossed the Atlantic and supplies were needed to support them prior to the invasion; afterwards the Allies had up to 36 divisions on the continent, and 20,000 tons of food, fuel, ammunition and equipment were needed to supply them each day.

A new marshalling yard named 'Riverside' was opened on 27 September 1943 on land to the north of St David's between the up main line and the Exe to support this activity. At about the same time a massive supply depot was established for US forces at Newcourt on the Exmouth branch, and it seems quite likely that there was some correlation between these developments. The goods avoiding lines now ran from Riverside, and all freight train marshalling was transferred there from the St David's goods depot; it also became the base for local trip work. However, merchandise was not normally loaded or unloaded there, and this continued to be handled at St David's. After the war Riverside continued to perform a key role in the area's goods traffic, as shown in the accompanying tables, which show the scale of activity in the summer of 1953.

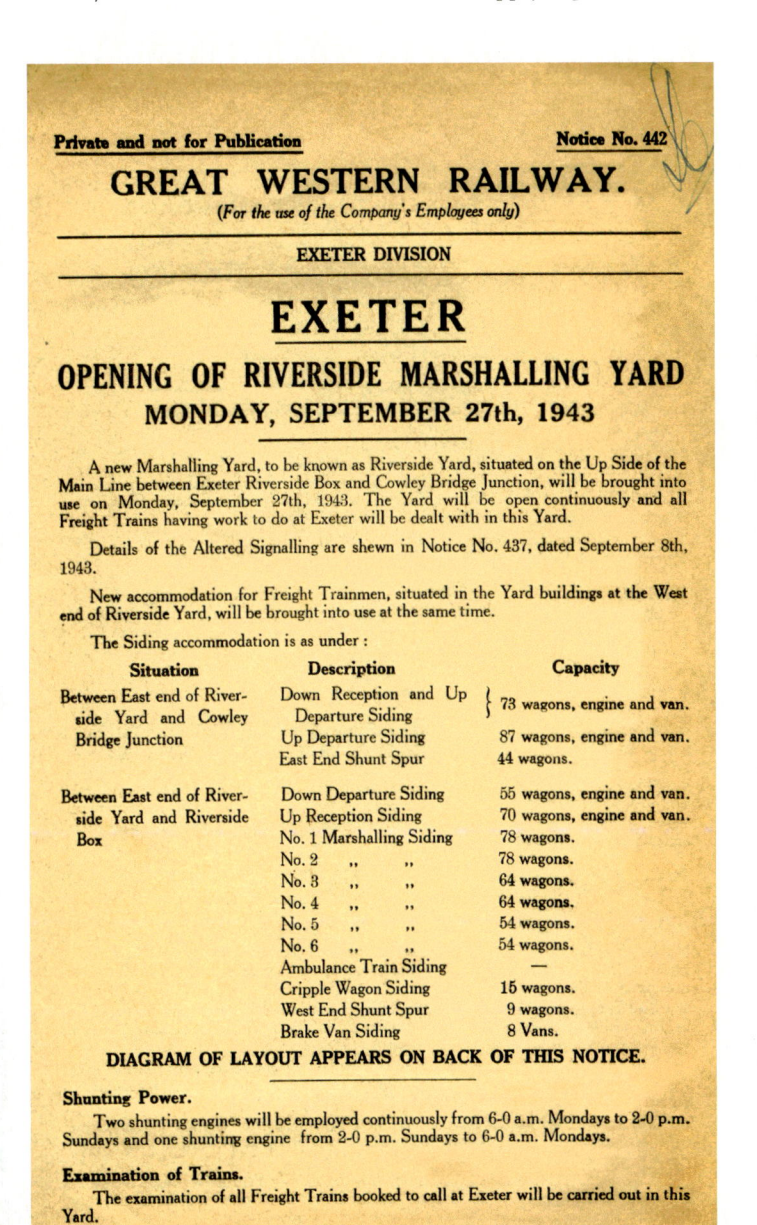

The opening of the GWR's Riverside yard.

Coal was one of the few commodities seen daily in block loads in the steam era, and the GWR imported large quantities of steam coal from South Wales solely to fuel its loco fleet; hence this traffic did not earn revenue for the railway. Swindon-built and Bristol St Philip's Marsh-allocated ex-LMS 8F 2-8-0 No 48436 is easing out of Riverside yard in 1956 with loco coal empties returning to Rogerstone yard in Newport's Western Valleys. *John Stredwick*

Table 18: Exeter Riverside (Riv) or St David's (ESD) down freight trains on weekdays			
(From the WR Exeter District Service Time Tables, 8 June to 20 September 1953)			
Train		Arr	Dep
9.45pm FX Bristol to Penzance, Class 'D' freight	ESD	Pass 12/1am	
7.55pm FO Kensington to Penzance, Class 'C' parcels and milk empties	ESD	Pass 12/14am	
7.55pm FSX Kensington to Penzance, Class 'C' parcels and milk empties	ESD	Pass 12/40am	
4.22pm SO Wadebridge to Salisbury, SR freight	ESD	12.18am	12.23am
4.50pm SX Wadebridge to Exmouth Junction	ESD	12.18am	12.23am
3.30pm FX Scours Lane (Reading) to Hackney Yard (Newton Abbot), Class 'F' freight	Riv	12.32am	12.52am
11.55pm FSX Meldon Quarry to Exmouth Junction, SR stone	ESD	12.59am	1.05am
10.55 pm FSX Bristol to Hackney Yard, Class 'D' freight	Riv	1.6am	1.35am
8.55pm FSX Paddington to Penzance, Class 'C' freight	Riv	Pass 1/22am	
7.00pm SO Frome to Hackney, Class 'H' freight	Riv	1.30am	1.50am
7.20pm Pontypool Road to Tavistock Junction, Class 'E' freight	Riv	1.52am	2.13am
3.40pm FSX Swindon to Hackney, Class 'H' freight	Riv	1.56am	2.16am
10.0pm Friary to Salisbury, SR freight	ESD	2.10am	2.16am
10.50pm FSX Marston Sidings (Swindon) to Plymouth Millbay, Class 'C' Fish	ESD	2.16am	2.48am
2.25am MO Riverside to Exmouth Junction SR transfer freight	ESD	2.28am	2.32am
5.30pm (Sun) Acton to Tavistock Junction, Class 'F' freight	Riv	2.30am	3.10am
9.32pm FSX Old Oak Common to Penzance, Class 'D' freight	Riv	3.14am	3.40am
9.20pm (Sun) Severn Tunnel Junction to Tavistock Junction, Class 'H' freight	Riv	4.4am	4.40am
10.00pm FSX Paddington to Plymouth, Class 'D' freight	ESD	Pass 4/07am	
9.00pm FSX Oxley Sidings to Hackney, Class 'D' freight	Riv	4.39am	5.00am
12.50am MSX (Q) Marston Sidings to Newton Abbot, Class 'C' Fish	ESD	4.50am	5.13am
9.00pm FSX Avonmouth to Tavistock Junction, Class 'E' freight	Riv	5.03am	5.53am
8.25pm FSX Bristol to Hackney, Class 'H' freight	Riv	5.40am	6.00am
2.00am Friary to Exmouth Junction, SR freight	Riv	6.01am	6.30am
11.20pm FSX Paddington to Hackney, Class 'D' freight	Riv	6.04am	6.24am
2.25am MO Bristol to Tavistock Junction, Class 'H' freight	Riv	6.12am	6.50am
9.15pm FSX Cardiff (Pengam) to Hackney, Class 'E' freight	Riv	6.25am	6.50am
9.15pm FSX Oxley Sidings to Plymouth, Class 'D' freight	Riv	7.00am	7.28am
7.00am Riverside to Alphington Road, Class 'K' freight	Riv	-	7.00am
2.25am MSX Bristol to Tavistock Junction, Class 'E' freight	Riv	7.28am	7.50am
12.30am MSX Avonmouth to Hackney, Class 'F' freight	Riv	8.17am	8.40am
9.13am Riverside to Hackney, Class 'K' freight	Riv	-	9.13am
4.00am SX Stoke Gifford to Hackney, Class 'H' freight	Riv	9.25am	9.51am
4.50am SX Barnstaple Junction to Exeter Central, SR freight	Riv	9.27am	10.22am
5.5am SO (Q) Marston Sidings to Newton Abbot, Class 'C' Fish	ESD	9.32am	9.49am
8.18am Tiverton Junction to Riverside, Class 'K' freight	Riv	9.45am	-
10.0pm MSX Banbury to Hackney, Class 'H' freight	Riv	10.00am	11.00am
7.40am MSX Bristol to Plymouth, Class 'C' Fish	ESD	10.09am	10.25am

Goods traffic in steam days

Table 18: Exeter Riverside (Riv) or St David's (ESD) down freight trains on weekdays (From the WR Exeter District Service Time Tables, 8 June to 20 September 1953)			
10.30am Riverside to City Basin Junction, Class 'K' freight	Riv	-	10.30am
1.20am MSX Scours Lane (Reading) to Plymouth, Class 'F' freight	Riv	11.07am	11.40am
10.16 SX (Q) Meldon Quarry to Woking, SR stone	ESD	11.28am	11.37am
3.00am SX Severn Tunnel Junction to Tavistock Junction, Class 'H' freight	Riv	11.47am	12.10pm
3.35am MSX Acton to Hackney, Class 'F' freight	Riv	12.10pm	12.40pm
1.10pm SX Riverside to Newton Abbot via Teign Valley, Class 'K' freight	Riv	-	1.10pm
1.30pm FO Riverside to Alphington Road, Class 'K' freight	Riv	-	1.30pm
4.30am MSX Bassaleg to Tavistock Junction, Class 'H' freight	Riv	12.40pm	1.30pm
1.45pm SX Riverside to Exeter Central, SR transfer freight	ESD	1.48pm	1.53pm
6.15am MSX Pontypool Road to Hackney, Class 'E' freight	ESD	2.21pm	2.52pm
1.55pm SX (Q) Meldon Quarry to Exmouth Junction, SR stone	ESD	3.08pm	3.13pm
4.10pm SX Riverside to Alphington Road, Class 'K' freight	Riv	-	4.10pm
8.20am SX Friary to Exmouth Junction, SR freight	Riv	3.38pm	4.22pm
7.10am SX Rogerstone to Tavistock Junction, Class 'H' locomotive coal	Riv	3.45pm	4.20pm
8.50am SX Taunton to Riverside, Class 'K' freight	Riv	4.20pm	-
10.30am SX Stoke Gifford to Tavistock Junction, Class 'H' freight	Riv	4.48pm	5.35pm
5.36pm (Q) Crediton to Exeter Central, SR milk	ESD	5.52pm	6.00pm
2.30pm SX Bristol to Hackney (FO) or Tavistock Junction (FX), Class 'E' freight	Riv	5.54pm	6.30pm
11.05am SX Plymouth to Exmouth Junction, SR freight	ESD	6.14pm	6.17pm
2.55pm SX Padstow to Templecombe, SR perishables (and passenger to Exeter Central)	ESD	6.29pm	6.35pm
12.45pm SX Torrington to Nine Elms, SR freight	ESD	6.47pm	6.52pm
9.25am SX Severn Tunnel Junction to Hackney, Class 'H' freight	Riv	6.55pm	7.36pm
1.20pm Bude to Exmouth Junction, SR freight	ESD	7.45pm	7.48pm
5.21pm Plymouth Friary to Feltham, SR freight	ESD	7.52pm	7.58pm
1.15pm SX Dulverton to Riverside, Class 'K' Exe Valley freight	Riv	8.2pm	-
8.00pm Riverside to Exeter Central, SR transfer freight	ESD	8.05pm	8.10pm
7.52pm SX Crediton to Riverside, SR freight	Riv	8.11pm	-
12.44pm SO Plymouth Friary to Exmouth Junction, SR freight	ESD	8.14pm	8.19pm
4.05pm SO Torrington to Nine Elms, SR freight	ESD	8.55pm	8.59pm
8.15am Banbury to Hackney (FO) or Tavistock Junction (FSX), Class 'H' freight	Riv	9.05pm	9.35pm
5.00pm SX Torrington to Nine Elms, SR freight	ESD	9.15pm	9.18pm
2.55pm SO or 3.00pm SX Wood Lane to Plymouth milk empties	ESD	10.07pm	10.20pm
3.55pm FX Severn Tunnel Junction to Tavistock Junction, Class 'H' freight	ESD	Pass 10/34pm	
9.25pm SX (Q) Okehampton to Salisbury, stone ex-Meldon Quarry	ESD	10.35pm	10.38pm
10.45pm (Q) Riverside to Hackney, Class 'H' freight	Riv	-	10.45pm
10.11pm Yeoford to Exmouth Junction, SR freight	Riv	10.50pm	11.15pm
9.02pm Barnstaple Junction to Exmouth Junction, SR freight	Riv	11.15pm	11.26pm
2.25pm FX (Q) Worcester to Plymouth, Class 'D' freight	Riv	11.36pm	11.50pm

Table 19: Exeter Riverside (Riv) or St David's (ESD) up freight trains on weekdays
(From the WR Exeter District Service Time Tables, 8 June to 20 September 1953)

Train		Arr	Dep
11.45pm Hackney to Avonmouth, Class 'D' freight	ESD	Pass 12/16am	
12.01am MX Exmouth Junction to Launceston, SR freight	Riv	12.24am	12.54am
5.05pm SX Marazion to Oxley Sidings, Class 'D' freight	ESD	Pass 12/59am	
1.45am MO Riverside to Rogerstone, Class 'F' freight	Riv	-	1.45am
7.18pm SX Drump Lane (Redruth) to Bristol, Class 'D' freight	Riv	1.15am	1.55am
1.38am Exmouth Junction to Tavistock, SR freight and mail	ESD	2.00am	2.05am
11.00pm MO Tavistock Junction to Oxley Sidings (stop for crew change only)	Riv	2.06am	2.11am
12.05am MO Tavistock Junction to Avonmouth, Class 'D' freight	Riv	2.25am	3.05am
12.05am MSX Tavistock Junction to Cardiff, Class 'D' freight	Riv	2.25am	3.05am
2.06am Exeter Central to Torrington, SR freight and mail	ESD	2.10am	3.00am
9.10pm Nine Elms to Plymouth Friary, SR freight	ESD	3.30am	3.35am
2.50am Hackney to Rogerstone, Class 'F' pools	ESD	Pass 3/35am	
3.50am Riverside to Tiverton via Tiverton Junction, Class 'K' freight	Riv	-	3.50am
1.30am SX Tavistock Junction to Crewe, Class 'D' freight	ESD	Pass 3/51am	
3.30am Exmouth Junction to Bude, SR freight	Riv	3.47am	4.12am
12.20am MSX Plymouth Laira to Bristol, Class 'H' freight	Riv	4.14am	4.45am
4.00am MX Exeter Central to Riverside, SR transfer freight	Riv	4.15am	-
4.20am Riverside to Tiverton Junction, Class 'K' freight	Riv	-	4.20am
2.25am SX Tavistock Junction to Banbury, Class 'H' freight	ESD	Pass 5/38am	
7.04pm Basingstoke to Plymouth, SR freight	ESD	5.51am	5.55am
6.10am SX Riverside to Newport ADJ (Q) or Rogerstone Class 'F' freight	Riv	-	6.10am
12.15am MX or 12.35am MO Salisbury to Torrington, SR freight	ESD	6.14am	6.15am
3.20am FSX Tavistock Junction to Acton, Class 'E' freight	Riv	6.18am	6.40am
6.35am Exmouth Junction to Barnstaple Junction, SR freight	Riv	6.56am	7.16am
7.50am City Basin Junction to Riverside, Class 'K' freight	Riv	7.55am	-
7.32am SX Exmouth Junction to Meldon Quarry, SR stone empties	ESD	7.54am	7.57am
5.45am Hackney to Riverside, Class 'K' freight	Riv	8.27am	-
9.00am SX Riverside to Dulverton, Class 'K' freight via Exe Valley	Riv	-	9.00am
4.20am SX Laira to Riverside, Class 'H' freight	Riv	9.04am	-
5.20am SX Tavistock Junction to Rogerstone, Class 'F' freight	ESD	Pass 9/30am	
9.15am SX Exmouth Junction to Eggesford, SR freight	Riv	9.33am	9.54am
9.55am or 10.28am SX (Q) Exmouth Junction to Meldon Quarry, SR stone empties	ESD	10.10am	10.15am
7.45am SX Tavistock Junction to Avonmouth, Class 'D' freight	ESD	10.45am	10.55am
10.25am SX Hackney to Avonmouth, Class 'E' freight	ESD	Pass 11/05am	
11.50am Exmouth Junction to Friary SR freight	ESD	12.04pm	12.09pm
9.30am Newton Abbot to Riverside, Class 'K' freight via Teign Valley	Riv	12.18pm	-
12.25pm Riverside to Tiverton Junction, Class 'K' freight	Riv	-	12.25pm
12.10pm SX Exmouth Junction to Riverside, SR transfer freight	Riv	12.34pm	-

Goods traffic in steam days

Table 19: Exeter Riverside (Riv) or St David's (ESD) up freight trains on weekdays				
(From the WR Exeter District Service Time Tables, 8 June to 20 September 1953)			
4.56am MSX (Q) Basingstoke to Yeoford, SR freight	ESD	1.00pm	1.02pm
2.50pm City Basin Junction to Riverside, Class 'K' freight	Riv	3.00pm	-
9.55am SX Tavistock Junction to Rogerstone, Class 'F' freight	Riv	Pass 3/7pm	
3.45pm FO Alphington Road to Riverside, Class 'K' freight	Riv	3.53pm	-
4.05pm Riverside to Swindon, Class 'E' freight	Riv	-	4.05pm
3.20pm FSX Hackney to Penarth Curve pools, Class 'F' freight	Riv	4.03pm	4.45pm
10.35am FSX Tavistock Junction to Swindon, Class 'H' freight			
5.44pm SX Alphington Road to Riverside, Class 'K' freight	Riv	5.52pm	-
12.20pm Penzance to Kensington, Class 'C' Milk	ESD	6.21pm	6.35pm
6.25pm Exeter Central to Riverside, SR transfer freight	Riv	6.40pm	-
7.20pm FSO Riverside to Paddington, Class 'D' freight	Riv	-	7.20pm
7.00pm SO Exmouth Junction to Yeoford, SR freight	ESD	7.20pm	7.21pm
7.00pm FSX Newton Abbot to Paddington, Class 'D' freight	Riv	7.40pm	8.40pm
8.45pm SX Riverside to Yeoford, SR freight	ESD	-	8.45pm
8.00pm Hackney to Rogerstone, Class 'F' freight		8.43pm	9.30pm
3.45pm Penzance to Paddington, Class 'C' perishable	ESD	Pass 9/20pm	
9.00pm FO Riverside to Cardiff, Class 'D' freight	Riv	-	9.00pm
9.00pm FSX Riverside to Oxley, Class 'D' freight	Riv	-	9.00pm
6.00pm SX Templecombe to Friary, SR freight	Riv	9.28pm	9.50pm
5.15pm FSX Tavistock Junction to Bristol, Class 'F' freight	Riv	10.05pm	10.50pm
2.50pm SX Penzance to Paddington, Class 'C' freight	ESD	Pass 11/28pm	
6.20pm Penzance to Kensington, Class 'C' Milk	ESD	11.48pm	11.58pm

LSWR and SR

When the LSWR opened, a five-siding goods yard with a single-road goods shed was provided on the north side of Queen Street station. By the 1880s two sidings ran into an enlarged shed, and at the end of the century there were 12 sidings in the yard, one of which served a long loading dock and another ran beside cattle pens. Two further yards were provided at the west end of the station on level ground on either side of the main line as it descended towards St David's; three wagon turntables on the south side and four on the north served traders, including timber distributors. The goods station also served as a marshalling yard, and the sidings in the main goods yard led to five loops where arriving trains were received and departures could be made up. However, these facilities were cramped and from 1877 a yard was developed at Yeoford near the junction of the Plymouth and North Devon lines where the re-marshalling of down trains in particular could be undertaken with wagons placed into station order.

In 1927 an 11-road marshalling yard was opened at Exmouth Junction, and an eight-siding down yard was also provided on the south side of the main line opposite the engine shed, which was used as a holding yard; henceforth almost all goods trains would either start, terminate or call at the marshalling yard, which became the focal point for the SR's freight traffic in the South West. The yard was solely used for wagon sorting and there were regular trips to Queen Street where local freight was loaded or unloaded, and transfer runs were made to the GWR goods depot at St David's.

The LSWR was mainly a passenger railway and freight traffic was not as important as on most other lines; it only derived about a third of its revenue from freight, and after the 'Grouping' in 1933 goods receipts only accounted for 24% of the SR's earnings. The merchandise that it carried in the West was similar to that handled by the GWR, with much associated with agriculture and horticulture, the most important of which was meat and other perishable traffic for the London market. In 1932 this traffic was conveyed on the 12.45pm Torrington to Nine Elms train; its initial progress was leisurely, but east of Exeter it offered an express service whereby on arrival the meat would be transferred by road to Smithfield Market. This was one of several fast overnight services that ran in both directions between Exeter and London, arriving in time for early morning deliveries. Other services from the West carried Tamar Valley fruit and flowers, and an as-required fish train was scheduled from Padstow. Special trains could be organised to carry cattle, particularly between September and December, when up to three specials a night could run to London; stocks of cattle wagons were maintained in the yards at Lydford and Yeoford for such workings.

Milk was also an important traffic that was conveyed in 17-gallon churns, carried in vans attached to the rear of passenger trains. In 1913 there were five workings each day to London; Vauxhall was the main centre in the capital, and 1,500 churns were handled daily. In the 1930s, when tank wagons were being introduced, west of Exeter they were loaded at creameries and depots at Torrington, Lapford and Crediton before being hauled to bottling plants in the London area.

\multicolumn{4}{c	}{Table 20: Exmouth Junction down goods trains on weekdays in July 1932}
Arr	Dep	Train	Notes
12.13am	-	6.25pm Templecombe to Exmouth Junction	
12.45am	7.30am	8.30pm Salisbury to Meldon Quarry	Stone empties, as required
1.43am	-	5.00pm Basingstoke to Exmouth Junction	
-	1.38am	1.38am Exmouth Junction to Tavistock	
-	-	2.10am Exeter Queen Street to Torrington	Freight and mail
2.55am	3.15am	9.32pm Nine Elms to Plymouth Friary	Starts at Exmouth Junction on Mondays
-	3.26am	3.26am Exmouth Junction to Bude	
-	3.48am	3.26am MO Exmouth Junction to Plymouth Friary	
-	-	4.15am MX Exeter Queen St to Padstow	Fish empties, as required
Pass	4/41am	1.30am Waterloo to Plymouth and Ilfracombe	Newspapers and passenger
4.01am	5.01am	1.50am Templecombe to Plymouth Friary	1.20am on Mondays only
4.33am	5.30am	10.10pm SX Nine Elms to Torrington	
8.31am	-	10.47pm SX Nine Elms to Exmouth Junction	
-	5.58am	5.58am Exmouth Junction to Exeter Queen Street	Transfer
-	6.10am	6.10am Exmouth Junction to Exmouth	
-	6.18am	6.18am Exmouth Junction to Barnstaple Junction	
-	8.53am	8.53am Exmouth Junction to Eggesford	
9.12am	-	4.30am MX Salisbury to Exmouth Junction	
-	9.18am	9.18am Exmouth Junction to Exmouth	
9.55am	-	11.53pm Feltham to Exmouth Junction	
-	11.27am	11.27am Exmouth Junction to Exeter Queen Street	Transfer
11.49am	-	12.10pm MO Nine Elms to Exmouth Junction	
-	12.08pm	12.08pm Exmouth Junction to Exeter St David's yard	Transfer
-	3.35pm	3.35pm Exmouth Junction to Exeter Queen Street	Transfer
4.27pm	-	3.12am Feltham to Exmouth Junction	
-	6.58pm	6.58pm Exmouth Junction to Yeoford	
7.12pm	-	5.15pm Sidmouth Junction to Exmouth Junction	
Pass	8/41pm	3.35pm Templecombe to Plymouth Friary	
10.30pm	-	4.30pm Yeovil Junction to Exmouth Junction	
-	11.50pm	11.50pm Exmouth Junction to Exeter Queen Street	Transfer
-	11.59pm	11.59pm SX Exmouth Junction to Launceston	12.38am MO, freight and mail

Goods traffic in steam days

The trip to Whimple mentioned in Table 21 served the Whiteway's Cyder factory, which had been established next to Whimple station in about 1895. Apples arrived by rail and the cider was dispatched in returnable casks, or in bottles loaded in wooden cases; traffic to the Midlands and North would be transferred to the Somerset & Dorset line at Templecombe, while that for London also went to Nine Elms, from where it was taken to a Whiteway's store on the Albert Embankment.

The 1.30am departure from Waterloo conveyed Fleet Street newspapers; from Salisbury it was also advertised as a passenger service to Plymouth and Ilfracombe, and after a non-stop run it stopped at Queen Street from 4.44am to 4.50am, when it was divided into two portions. The 12.50am from Plymouth Friary carried the South West's own daily, the

Table 21: Exmouth Junction up goods trains on weekdays in July 1932

Arr	Dep	Train	Notes
12.30am	1.00am	5.00pm MX Wadebridge to Salisbury	
2.40am	3.45am	10.15pm Plymouth Friary to Yeovil Junction	Starts at Exmouth Junction on Mondays
3.52am	-	12.50am Plymouth Friary to Exmouth Junction	Newspapers
4.04am	4.04am	Exmouth Junction to Yeovil Junction Including mail and newspapers to Sidmouth Junction and Honiton	
5.10am	-	4.50am Exeter St David's yard to Exmouth Junction	Transfer
6.50am	-	1.58am Plymouth Friary to Exmouth Junction	
7.10am	-	7.05am Exeter Queen Street to Exmouth Junction	Transfer
-	7.37am	7.37am Exmouth Junction to Sidmouth Junction	
9.00am	-	8.55am Exeter Queen Street to Exmouth Junction	Transfer
-	9.02am	9.02am Exmouth Junction to Whimple	
11.00am	-	10.55am Exeter Queen Street to Exmouth Junction	Transfer
12.10am	-	4.25am Barnstaple Junction to Exmouth Junction	FO arr 10.19am
2.05pm	-	1.30pm Exeter St David's yard to Exmouth Junction	Transfer
-	2.38pm	2.38pm Exmouth Junction to Yeovil Junction	
2.50pm	-	2.45pm Exeter Queen Street to Exmouth Junction	Transfer
3.15pm	-	2.55pm Exeter St David's yard to Exmouth Junction	Transfer
Pass	4/46pm	4.43pm Exeter Queen Street to Waterloo	Milk and parcels
5.31pm	-	2.40pm Exmouth to Exmouth Junction	Including Topsham Quay branch
5.33pm	-	6.15am Plymouth Friary to Exmouth Junction	
Pass	6/45pm	3.06pm Padstow to Templecombe	Perishables
-	6.55pm	6.55pm Exmouth Junction to Salisbury	
7.10pm	-	8.12am Plymouth Friary to Exmouth Junction	
Pass	7/33pm	7.30pm Exeter Queen Street to Nine Elms	SO, as required
7.45pm	-	7.40pm Exeter Queen Street to Exmouth Junction	Transfer
7.58pm	8.37pm	12.45pm Torrington to Nine Elms	
8.22pm	-	4.30pm Padstow to Exmouth Junction	Fish, as required
9.00pm	-	2.07pm Bude to Exmouth Junction	
9.50pm	-	7.54pm Okehampton to Salisbury	Ballast and stone, as required
10.03pm	10.54pm	4.52pm Torrington to Salisbury	
10.40pm	-	10.10pm Exmouth to Exmouth Junction	
11.40pm	-	11.35pm Exeter Queen Street to Exmouth Junction	Transfer

Milk was originally handled in 10- or 17-gallon churns that were carried in ventilated vans known as 'Syphons' on the GWR. The first glass-lined four-wheel tank wagons were introduced in 1927, able to carry up to 3,000 gallons; after a number of derailments six-wheel versions became standard. These were hauled in perishables trains, but during the Second World War a dedicated evening milk train from the South West to London was introduced, and by 1946 it had been joined by an earlier second train. In 1959 the 12.20pm from Penzance to Kensington was the first of these trains; normally they were hauled by a 4-6-0, but on 1 August it is running into St David's behind BR Standard 9F 2-10-0 No 92209. The Passenger Brake Van was for churn traffic and the guard, and the train might stop here to collect tanks brought by the SR from Crediton. The engine had only entered traffic in June that year when it was allocated to Laira; this type was perhaps the best of the BR steam classes and, although intended as a heavy freight engine, their excellent front-end design made them free-running and they were often used on passenger and other faster trains. *Peter W. Gray*

Western Morning News, to towns en route to Exeter.

Trains from London provided an overnight service to almost all of the SR's stations in the West and enabled businesses to deliver consignments to their customers for the start of the working day. These might include groceries, clothing and hardware – in fact, anything that today would be conveyed by a van or lorry. It was then common to recycle empty containers and there would be returning boxes, baskets or hampers, or casks in the case of Whiteway's. A massive nine-platform shed was located at Nine Elms for goods traffic that would arrive during the day and, after being weighed and recorded, was loaded into wagons that were positioned in station order. Larger destinations such as Exeter might have several of these wagons that would be detached on arrival; smaller towns might have had just a single wagon containing all the merchandise for that place, whereas the smallest destinations might be grouped together in one van.

The SR's freight business differed in one respect from the GWR in that it handled a lot less long-distance coal traffic. The railway itself did have a huge demand for coal for its locomotive fleet, and at one time the Exeter District was supplied with coal brought by coastal shipping from South Wales and landed at its own quay at Fremington in North Devon. In later steam days coal for Exmouth Junction was carried by rail from the Midlands via the Somerset & Dorset route to Templecombe. Otherwise, Welsh coal for domestic or industrial customers could arrive via the GWR at Yeovil Junction or in Exeter by way of the transfer runs from Riverside. Also coal could arrive at harbours such as Exmouth, and in 1959 a contemporary report advised that a coaster was discharging household coal there that was destined to be taken by rail over the short distance to the Alphington Road depot, and the station yards at Exeter Central, Lympstone, East Budleigh and Budleigh Salterton.

After nationalisation most of the merchandise for the greater Exeter area was handled at St David's and the Central depot only dealt with traffic for the city itself; much of the

'M7' 0-4-4T No 30023 is waiting in the rain on the down through road at Exeter Central with a short transfer goods for Riverside yard at 9.25am on Saturday 9 March 1957. *Peter W. Gray*

Goods traffic in steam days

On Saturday 14 April 1962 'S15' 4-6-0 No 30842 is easing out of the Exmouth Junction marshalling yard with the 2.00pm goods train for Salisbury. *C. H. S. Owen*

In 1929 the SR introduced a class of eight three-cylinder 0-8-0Ts for heavy shunting, and one of these powerful engines, No A954, was allocated new to Exmouth Junction, where it remained as yard shunter until April 1956. It normally worked from Tuesday to Saturday each week and was replaced by another engine on Mondays, when it had a boiler washout; the yard was closed on Sundays. Bearing its SR number 30954, it is busy at work on Saturday 23 February 1952; the engine was given the soubriquet 'Dolly' by local staff. *J. H. Bamsey*

large goods shed and other buildings were then let to outside firms. The yard at Exmouth Junction remained busy, however, and was reported to be handling 700 wagons daily in 1952.

Of the trains designated as 'express fitted' in Tables 22 and 23, the load on the 10.15pm from Nine Elms was limited to 49 wagons and a brake van from Salisbury and was vacuum-fitted throughout. To avoid delay it did not call at Exmouth Junction and ran non-stop between Salisbury and Exeter Central at an average speed of about 35mph; after arrival

Table 22: Exmouth Junction down goods trains on weekdays from 9 June 1958

Arr	Dep	Train	Notes
-	12.01am	12.01am MX Exmouth Junction to Launceston	12.20am MO, mail and freight
12.07am	-	9.45pm SX Yeovil Junction to Exmouth Junction	SO 10.15pm ex-Yeovil Junction
-	12.09am	12.09am MX Exmouth Junction to Exeter Central	12.30am MO, trip
12.52am	-	9.45am SX Tonbridge to Exmouth Junction	Ballast empties, as required
1.25am	-	10.45pm SX Yeovil Junction to Exmouth Junction	
-	1.45am	1.45am Exmouth Junction to Tavistock North	
1.53pm	-	8.20pm Redbridge Yard to Exmouth Junction	CCE materials
-	-	2.06am Exeter Central to Torrington	Mail vans only to Yeoford, then up to 42 loaded wagons to Barnstaple Junction
-	-	10.15pm MX Nine Elms to Plymouth Friary	Express fitted, at Exeter Central 2.50am to 3.25am
-	3.15am	3.15am MO Exmouth Junction to Plymouth Friary	
-	3.30am	3.30am Exmouth Junction to Bude	
3.25am	5.35am	6.10pm Basingstoke to Plymouth Friary	MO starts at Exmouth Junction
4.18am	6.00am	12.30am Salisbury to Torrington	12.50am MO
-	6.05am	6.05am Exmouth Junction to Exmouth	
-	6.25am	6.25am Exmouth Junction to Barnstaple Junction	
-	7.32am	7.32am Exmouth Junction to Meldon Quarry	Ballast empties, as required
7.45am	-	10.30pm Nine Elms to Exmouth Junction	Semi-fitted
8.38am	-	12.43am Woking to Exmouth Junction	Ballast empties, as required

Table 22: Exmouth Junction down goods trains on weekdays from 9 June 1958

Arr	Dep	Train	Notes
-	9.00am	9.00am Exmouth Junction to Exmouth	
-	9.15am	9.15am Exmouth Junction to Eggesford	
9.17am	-	8.50am Pinhoe to Exmouth Junction	Trip
-	9.55am	9.55am Exmouth Junction to Meldon Quarry	Ballast empties, as required
Pass	10/21am	4.40am SX Southampton Docks to Tavistock Junction (Exeter Central, 10.26am to 10.45am)	Express fitted, as required, via WR from St David's
11.27am	-	11.15am Broad Clyst to Exmouth Junction	
-	11.47am	11.47am SX Exmouth Junction to Newcourt Siding	SO-Q 10.15am Exmouth Junction
-	11.50am	11.50am Exmouth Junction to Crediton	
-	12.02pm	12.02pm Exmouth Junction to Exeter Riverside	Transfer goods
12.41pm	-	11.58pm Feltham to Exmouth Junction	MO 8.30am Yeovil Junction
1.30pm	-	10.25am (SX-Q) Yeovil Junction to Exmouth Junction	Motive power coal
2.38pm	-	2.18pm (SX-Q) Pinhoe to Exmouth Junction	Trip for Pye Storage Ltd
-	3.37pm	3.37pm Exmouth Junction to Exeter Central	Transfer
-	5.53pm	5.32pm SX Pinhoe to Exmouth Junction	Trip, including Pye Storage Ltd
-	-	6.20pm Exeter Central Goods to Riverside	Transfer
6.55pm	-	3.05pm Sidmouth to Exmouth Junction	
-	7.00pm	7.00pm Exmouth Junction to Yeoford	
-	-	(7.15pm Riverside to Plymouth Laira)	WR train via SR
-	7.18pm	7.18pm Exmouth Junction to Exeter Riverside	Transfer goods
-	8.00pm	6.55pm Budleigh Salterton to Exmouth Junction	
Pass	8/36pm	6.00pm SX Templecombe to Plymouth Friary (Exeter Central, 8.40pm to 9.20pm)	Semi-fitted
Pass	9/12pm	2.48pm SX Southampton Docks to Tavistock Junction (Exeter Central, 9.17pm to 9.50pm)	Express fitted, as required, via WR from St David's
9.25pm	-	10.45am MX Feltham to Exmouth Junction	Semi-fitted

at Central there was an engine change and the Exeter, Exmouth, Sidmouth and north Devon wagons were detached. Traffic for the latter area was then added to the 5.21am newspaper and passenger train from Central to Ilfracombe. Also at Central wagons for Devonport and Plymouth that had arrived on the 12.09am trip from Exmouth Junction were added to the remaining wagons from Nine Elms, and the formation behind the engine going forward comprised vacuum-fitted wagons for Devonport and Plymouth, all traffic that was to be removed at Okehampton, non-fitted wagons for Devonport and Plymouth, and finally a brake van.

In the opposite direction, the 4.15pm Bideford to Nine Elms 'express' included non-vacuum wagons as far as Barnstaple Junction but was fully fitted thereafter; it could not exceed 45 wagons from Exeter Central and the formation was firstly vans of fruit and flowers followed by all the other traffic, with all meat containers marshalled together. The 4.40pm Friary to Waterloo passenger train was one of the 'interchange' workings between Plymouth and Exeter and was booked for a 17-minute stop at Bere Alston where at peak times up to ten vans of fruit and flowers could be collected; the wagons were switched to the Nine Elms train in Exeter.

Two as-required 'express' paths from Southampton Docks were available for banana trains; there was a Fyffes's depot in Central's goods yard and any traffic for there would be removed by the station pilot. The train would then continue to Riverside yard where it would reverse and head for Tavistock Junction yard via the WR route to Plymouth. The trains described in the WTT as 'semi-fitted' may merely have had between four and six vacuum-fitted wagons behind the engine, although on certain services wagons with 'greased' axle boxes were also not permitted. Heavier trains, such as the 12.45pm Torrington to Feltham yard, could comprise up to 50 wagons east of Exmouth Junction, with at least ten vacuum-braked wagons behind the engine, but the similarly loaded 5.25pm Torrington to Nine Elms had to have 18

Goods traffic in steam days

Table 23: Exmouth Junction up goods trains on weekdays from 9 June 1958			
Arr	Dep	Train	Notes
12.08am	1.20am	4.50pm MX Wadebridge to Salisbury East	Semi-fitted (MO 1.20am Exmouth Junction)
Pass	2/5am	11.27pm (SX-Q) Okehampton to Salisbury	Ballast
2.45am	4.04am	10.10pm SX Plymouth Friary to Salisbury	Semi-fitted, (MO 4.4am Exmouth Junction)
-	-	11.50pm SX Plymouth Laira to Riverside	Via SR, Riverside arr 2.53am
3.00am	-	2.25pm MO Riverside to Exmouth Junction	Transfer goods (MX-Q 2.40am departure)
4.10am	-	4.05am Exeter Central to Exmouth Junction	Transfer
-	4.30am	4.30am Exmouth Junction to Seaton Junction	
7.11am	-	1.55am Plymouth Friary to Exmouth Junction	
-	8.10am	8.10am Exmouth Junction to Pinhoe	
-	9.00am	9.00am Exmouth Junction to Broad Clyst	
11.33am	-	5.45am Barnstaple Junction to Exmouth Junction	
Pass	11/55am	10.16am (SX-Q) Meldon Quarry to Woking, New Cross Gate or Tonbridge	Ballast; loco change at Exeter Central 11.42am to 11.50am
-	1.23pm	1.23pm Exmouth Junction to Salisbury	Semi-fitted
1.24pm	-	11.35am SX Meldon Quarry to Exmouth Junction	Ballast
-	1.35pm	1.35pm SX Exmouth Junction to Honiton	
1.35pm	-	1.09pm SX Newcourt Siding to Exmouth Junction	SO-Q 11.42am ex-Newcourt
-	2.00pm	2.00pm (SX-Q) Exmouth Junction to Pinhoe	Trip
-	2.40pm	2.40pm SX Exmouth Junction to Templecombe	SO 4.50pm departure
2.59pm	-	2.54pm Exeter Central to Exmouth Junction	Transfer
3.07pm	-	2.55pm Riverside to Exmouth Junction	Transfer goods
Pass	3/35pm	1.55pm (SX-Q) Meldon Quarry to Woking	Ballast
4.43pm	-	8.20am SX Plymouth Laira to Exmouth Junction	
-	5.00pm	5.00pm SX Exmouth Junction to Pinhoe	To Ministry of Food siding
5.01pm		3.42pm Exmouth to Exmouth Junction	
6.29pm	8.50pm	12.45pm SX Torrington to Feltham	Semi-fitted, SO ex-Exmouth Junction
Pass	7/42pm	4.15pm Bideford Goods to Nine Elms	Express fitted, Exeter Central goods yard 7.04pm to 7.38pm
8.02pm	-	7.40pm SX Riverside to Exmouth Junction	SO 8.00pm departure
8.27pm	9.45pm	5.21pm SX Plymouth Friary to Feltham	Semi-fitted
8.31pm	-	12.44pm SO Plymouth Friary to Exmouth Junction	
8.55pm	-	2.20pm SX Bude to Exmouth Junction	SO 2.30pm departure
9.33pm	10.45pm	5.25pm SX Torrington to Nine Elms	Semi-fitted; SO 4.05pm departure
10.35pm	-	10.30pm Exeter Central to Exmouth Junction	Transfer
Pass	11/35pm	9.25pm (SX-Q) Okehampton to Salisbury	Ballast; Exeter Central 10.43pm to 11.30pm
11.41pm	-	10.11pm Yeoford to Exmouth Junction	
11.50pm	-	9.02pm Q Barnstaple Junction to Exmouth Junction	

vacuum-fitted wagons. The 6.10pm Basingstoke to Plymouth train included traffic from the Great Central line that had arrived via Reading, and also wagons that had reached Salisbury from places such as Southampton; it was re-marshalled and re-engined during a lengthy stop at Exmouth Junction. Both the 10.30pm ex-Nine Elms and 11.59pm ex-Feltham trains collected exchange traffic from the Somerset & Dorset line at Templecombe, and from the WR at Yeovil Junction, and also dropped off traffic at stations east of Exeter.

In addition to the transfer runs between the SR and WR, some SR freights were booked to call at Riverside yard to exchange traffic. There was a limit on the loads that could be handled in both directions on the bank between Central and St David's, and the yard at Exmouth Junction could become congested; accordingly westbound SR traffic, wherever its ultimate destination, could be added to any train heading that way and any re-marshalling needed was then done at Yeoford. After nationalisation the WR ran through express freights between Riverside and its Tavistock Junction yard at Plymouth via Okehampton to relieve congestion on its own line.

Several trips are listed in 1958 that served businesses west of Pinhoe station, including a brickworks where a trailing siding off the up main line was provided in 1891. Known as Poltimore Siding after the company, a separate line from this siding served a grain silo constructed for the Ministry of Supply in 1938. A little to the east another siding was provided in about 1943 to serve a Ministry of Food frozen food store, where meat carcases arrived from slaughterhouses for distribution. A siding off the down main opposite the Poltimore Siding was provided in 1953 for Pye Storage Ltd, a company that distributed foodstuffs and household goods. The 8.10am trip from Exmouth Junction was timetabled to spend 15 minutes in the Ministry of Food siding before running round in Pinhoe station, and was then allowed 25 minutes in the Pye Storage siding. The 9.00am from Exmouth Junction to Broad Clyst was scheduled to shunt the Poltimore and Ministry of Food sidings, take coal to Pinhoe goods yard and also stop at Crannaford Crossing signal box to deliver a churn of drinking water! Its destination at Broad Clyst was the location for a civil engineer's depot where trackwork was assembled. A 2.00pm 'as required' trip also served the Pye Storage depot, while a 5.00pm departure from Exmouth Junction was scheduled to shunt the Ministry of Food depot, and on returning from Pinhoe at 5.32pm it could also call in the Pye Storage siding.

For many years a feature of Exeter's railway scene were the heavy ballast trains from Meldon Quarry. When the LSWR was building its line from Okehampton to Lydford, excavations in the Meldon area revealed the presence of hornfels, a metamorphic rock that is harder than the granite found on nearby Dartmoor and made excellent track ballast. The LSWR decided that it would become its main source of ballast, despite being remote from most of its network, and purchased a small privately owned quarry in 1897. This it extended, and by 1905 the annual output was more than

Salisbury's 'King Arthur' 4-6-0 No 30451 *Sir Lamorak* is waiting for the road at Exeter Central at 3.30pm on Friday 25 March 1960 after taking over the 1.55pm Meldon Quarry to Woking ballast train. *R. A. Lumber*

'N' Class 2-6-0 No 31844 is passing under the road at Cowley Bridge with the 12.45pm Torrington to Feltham freight on Wednesday 8 April 1964. Two milk tanks lead the consist and contribute to the four vacuum-fitted wagons that were required at the head of the train; it was scheduled to pass here at 6.10pm manned by an Exmouth Junction crew, who had replaced Barnstaple men at Yeoford. The train will be re-marshalled during a stop of more than 2 hours at Exmouth Junction yard, where the 'N' was diagrammed to be replaced by a 'Light Pacific'. In the foreground 4-6-0 No 4088 *Dartmouth Castle* has been relegated to humble goods work and is waiting on the Riverside yard departure road. *D. J. Frost*

107,000 tons, with usually two train departures each day. In 1953 production was up to 340,000 tons a year, with about 70% used as track ballast that was often dispatched to the engineer's sidings at Woking; the output also included chippings and 'dust', with much of the former used by the Exmouth Junction concrete works. After nationalisation the WR also started using ballast from Meldon and for a period on Saturdays from October 1949 an 'N' Class engine hauled a heavy stone train from Meldon to St David's, where it was handed over to the WR; the latter also took 'chippings' from the quarry for its Taunton concrete works.

During the run-up to 'Operation Overlord', massive quantities of stores and equipment from the USA were received at ports around the country and many sites were established throughout southern England to store the material needed for the D-Day landings and thereafter. A large supply depot was established for United States' forces in 1943 on a greenfield site at Newcourt next to the Exmouth branch, about 1½ miles north of Topsham. Apparently on Saturday 2 October that year the SR's Divisional Superintendent was asked to urgently meet with the US authorities to discuss installing a siding off the branch, needed as 150 wagons of stores were already on their way! The Divisional Engineer arranged for enough materials to lay 1,220 feet of track to be on site by the following Monday, and a three-siding yard was laid by US troops within 24 hours; SR engineers installed a connection to the running line and the Signal & Telegraph department undertook the necessary signalling alterations. By 5.00pm on the Wednesday the work had been completed and the sidings were in use.

Up to 200 wagons would arrive each day and initially most of the stores had to be placed in the open or under canvas. However, troops developed the site and 85 warehouses were constructed to provide 578,000 square feet of accommodation; 198 huts were also erected for administrative purposes or to house up to 1,000 personnel. Recently arrived from the US, Exmouth Junction-allocated 'USA' 'S160' Class 2-8-0 No 1771 was reported hauling a train of stores from Exeter to Southampton on 16 December, and on the following day it was seen working to Newcourt; another 'S160', No 1916, was also observed on the branch on 7 April 1944. 'U' Class 2-6-0s also hauled trains to and from the depot, and 4-6-0 types are thought to have visited the branch for the first time, with sightings of Class 'H15' and 'S15' locos. Initially inward trains had to run through to Topsham, where the locos would run round and head back towards Exeter on the up line before reversing into the depot. However, in January 1944 a crossover and small concrete signal box were provided at the entrance to the depot and trains could then run directly into the sidings. By February 1944 up to 300 road trucks a day would be loaded at the depot and sent to the many camps that had been established to house the invasion force, and supplies were also dispatched by rail and road to the embarkation ports. The SR's goods sidings in the Exeter area are said to have dealt with some 50,000 more wagons in 1944 than in 1938. The Newcourt depot was, however, soon wound down after the 6 June landings, and the site was returned to the British authorities by the end of July.

After the war Newcourt was used as a Royal Naval Stores Depot, served by a separate timetabled working from Exmouth Junction yard rather than the daily Exmouth branch goods train; these workings were often quite short, but as this part of the branch was virtually unrestricted they were hauled by whatever was available on Exmouth Junction shed. In the early 1950s 'T9' 4-4-0s were often used and later 'S15' 4-6-0s regularly appeared; even 'Light Pacifics' worked there occasionally, and as late as 15 March 1965 the appropriately named No 34051 *Winston Churchill* was seen on this duty. Activity reduced during the 1970s, and although the sidings were busy during the Falklands War in 1982 they are thought to have been last used in about 1984.

As the steam era was drawing to a close a block train working was introduced after Associated Portland Cement Manufacturers Ltd opened a works at Westbury in Wiltshire in September 1962; soon a regular trainload of 21 'Presflo' wagons was dispatched to a distribution depot in the Central goods yard. Historically it had been the practice to carry railborne cement in bags, but in 1954 BR had introduced pressurised 'Presflo' wagons to carry it in fluid form. Most were owned by BR, but APCM Ltd

acquired its own fleet, which displayed its brand name 'Blue Circle' on the wagons. A storage silo was installed at Central with two compartments, a larger one containing standard cement and a smaller one holding ferro-cement. Apparently when erected the silo was painted in the bright yellow livery of 'Blue Circle', but this fell foul of the local planners and had to be repainted grey! A store for specialist cement products was also provided in the yard. The first working was possibly on 9 November 1962 when the WR train engine was detached in Riverside yard and the wagons were powered up the bank by three of Exmouth Junction's 'Z' Class 0-8-0Ts, with Nos 30955 and 30952 on the front and No 30956 banking at the rear; subsequently the WR loco would work through from Westbury to Central.

On occasions trainloads arrived from other works and at least two such workings from the 'Blue Circle' Holborough plant at Snodland, Kent, were seen arriving via the former SR main line; on 19 February 1964 a train was hauled by 'Pacifics' Nos 34014 *Budleigh Salterton* and 34063 *229 Squadron*, and on 12 March by Nos 34098 *Templecombe* and 34089 *602 Squadron*. 'Blue Circle' purchased and modernised another works at Plymstock near Plymouth, and this also supplied the Central depot. The Westbury train usually operated on Tuesdays and Fridays in 1964, and although it was diagrammed for diesel haulage and an edict was issued barring steam locos on the WR west of Castle Cary after 19 May 1964, it was about 90% steam-worked for the rest of that year, usually by 'Hall' Class 4-6-0s or '28XX' Class 2-8-0s, but other classes were seen. A stop was made at Taunton for water as the Creech troughs had been removed, and after arrival the engine was turned at Exmouth Junction and returned light to Westbury. A few 'Hymek' diesel-hydraulic workings were recorded during 1964, and from the turn of the year this class started to appear regularly; there were still isolated examples of steam working, however, such as No 5961 *Toynbee Hall* on 12 March 1965, and on 10 June 2-8-0 No 3844 possibly provided the final steam haulage.

BR Standard 2-6-4T No 80059 and 4-6-0 No 6963 *Throwley Hall* are nearing their destination at Exeter Central with a cement train from Westbury on Saturday 28 September 1963. 'W' Class 2-6-4Ts Nos 31911 and 31924 are providing banking assistance at the rear of the train. *Peter W. Gray*

13. Railfreight in the modern era

In the early 1960s freight still provided about two-thirds of BR's revenue, but this was declining as road hauliers secured a greater share of the business by undercutting the railway and offering a more efficient service. A Ministry of Transport survey in 1962 revealed that nationally the transport of goods by road had increased by nearly 80% since 1952, with more than half of all freight now carried that way. This figure was distorted by the amount carried over short distances, but it was estimated that road transport accounted for about 40% of all long-haul traffic (i.e. over 100 miles) with rail and coastal shipping each carrying 30%. However, in the West the picture was probably even worse as nationally much of the rail traffic was dependent on the coal and steel industries and these traffics were not particularly relevant to the area. The survey revealed that road transport was carrying much of the traffic for the construction trades, food processing companies and distribution businesses, and these were very much the commodities carried locally.

Dr Beeching's 'Reshaping' report stated that the average turn-round time between loading and reloading a wagon was 11.9 days, and the average transit time for a loaded wagon was about 1.5 to 2 days for an average journey length of just 67 miles; road deliveries over comparable distances would be made on the day of dispatch. Beeching's conclusion was that much of the wagonload freight still being carried by rail was losing money heavily, and if there was to be a future for railfreight it would mean adopting trainload operation where possible and developing the use of container trains. Subsequently BR withdrew from handling certain commodities and had some success in building block trainload traffic.

Following the transfer of the SR lines west of Salisbury to the WR, a costing and traffic survey conducted jointly by both regions showed that the volume of freight moving between Westbury and Taunton was more than between Salisbury and Exeter, but the amount travelling between Bristol and Taunton was more than both these routes together; this was hardly a surprise as the SR lacked the connections with the industrial Midlands and North that contributed to the WR's traffic. It was decided that in the future most freight to and from the South West would go via Bristol, and merchandise trains on the Exeter to Salisbury line ended in 1965. It was also found that goods services over the 'Withered Arm' were losing money and most of these ceased in September 1964.

As wagonload traffic diminished, further economies were made, and the Tavistock Junction (Plymouth) and Hackney (Newton Abbot) marshalling yards were closed in 1971, with Riverside becoming the main yard for Devon and Cornwall.

Under the 'Modernisation Plan' the WR sought the early replacement of its steam locomotive fleet with diesel-hydraulics to improve its financial performance. Two variations of the 'Warship' Class can be seen on 8 April 1971 as North British-built Class 43 No 844 *Spartan* eases over the goods avoiding line at St David's with 6C33, the 13.05 Exeter Riverside to Truro wagonload freight, and passes Swindon-built Class 42 No D815 *Druid*, which is stabled on shed. Although the motive power has changed, things did not look much different behind the engine as the train comprises low-capacity short-wheelbase four-wheeled wagons. *Spartan* was withdrawn six months later and, with decreasing volumes of freight traffic, the avoiding line was closed in February 1978. *DHM*

Railfreight in the modern era

The Sundries Division of BR was transferred to National Carriers Ltd ownership in 1968 together with goods depots such as that at St David's. No 08849 is shunting a rake of 'Special Parcels Vans' there at about 19.00 on 6 May 1975; these were former 'Blue spot' insulated fish vans used by NCL for sundries traffic. This area is now covered by the new DMU depot. *DHM*

This did not lead to any great infusion of work there, and the continuing decline is apparent when comparing the 1970 and 1971 Working Time Tables; instead of an increase in the number of trains using Riverside, there was a reduction from the 31 listed in 1970 to 27. However, it appears that attempts were made to use resources more efficiently by replacing some short journeys with longer runs; in 1970 five trains were timetabled between Bristol and Exeter, but in the following year these had reduced to three, with additional through services from Carlisle and Crewe now terminating in Riverside. Previously three trains to Truro started at Riverside, but two of these were now extended to Drump Lane (Redruth) and Ponsandane (Penzance); however, now that Plymouth traffic was no longer being detached at Tavistock Junction there were three down and two up feeder workings between Riverside and Plymouth's new central goods depot at Friary. In 1970 seven through services had originated at Tavistock Junction for Bristol (two), Severn Tunnel Junction, Cardiff, Acton, Warrington and Carlisle, but in 1971 there were four departures from Friary to the first four of these places and two new services were now running from St Blazey to Bristol and Acton. There were several local trip workings from Riverside, and other timetabled trains in both years included daily workings to Newton Abbot and Barnstaple, trains from Severn Tunnel Junction and Acton, the 'Clayliner' service between St Blazey and Stoke-on-Trent, ballast trains from Meldon Quarry to Salisbury and either Westbury or Exeter, and an overnight 'sundries' service between Paddington and Friary.

By the 1960s rail-borne milk traffic was declining nationally as the Milk Marketing Board reduced long-distance movements to cut transportation costs. However, in October 1964 the MMB and WR signed a contract known as the 'Western Agreement', which guaranteed six milk trains each day, two from West Wales and the others from the South West. The Agreement stipulated that a minimum of 26,000 tank-loads would be handled annually. Previously the WR and SR had operated their own trains over their respective routes to London, but these now merged. Three trains ran to Kensington, from where the traffic was distributed to bottling plants in the London area; two of these started at St Erth in Cornwall, then added traffic at several locations, while the third train ran from Seaton Junction and collected tanks at Chard Junction. Instead of continuing up the SR to London it was then diverted via Yeovil and Castle Cary to Westbury, where it often terminated with its traffic added to a fourth train from Tiverton Junction, which carried milk from Hemyock to Morden South.

By 1970 there was just one trunk service from Cornwall, and Exeter had become the hub for all the milk collected on the lines radiating from the city. The 19.00 Kensington to Penzance empty tank train stopped at St David's just after midnight, and wagons were detached. Class 22 diesel-hydraulic locos outbased in Exeter provided the power for four 'as-required' trips to different loading points. One ran via Barnstaple to Torrington station, where road tankers would transfer milk into the rail tanks; a second went to Lapford on the Barnstaple branch, but a single train might have been sufficient for both locations. The depot at Seaton Junction closed that year, and a third train made an out-and-back run from Exeter to the creamery at Chard Junction. The fourth train went to the creamery at Hemyock on the Culm Valley branch. The loaded tanks were gathered at St David's and added to that evening's 14.50 St Erth to Kensington milk train. Gradually, however, these trips ceased as the various loading points were closed, Chard Junction being the last in about 1979; the daily train from Cornwall continued until all milk traffic ended in March 1980.

Beeching envisaged that there was a future for railfreight by adopting bulk trainload operations, and as seen in Chapter 12 such a service had started in 1962 from the 'Blue Circle' cement works at Westbury to Exeter Central. During 1968 the usual source for this traffic was switched to the works at Plymstock, and for a time a six-days-a-week evening departure of 'Presflos' was scheduled from there to either Exeter or Poole in Dorset. Special trains also supplied Exeter from elsewhere, including Westbury, and that works again became the main source in 1976 when the loaded trains were routed via Yeovil to save having to bank them to Central; the empty wagons were, however, returned via Taunton, and on occasions the loaded trains also arrived that way. From 1985 they were scheduled via Taunton again, but from May 1987 the traffic was carried via a new daily 'Speedlink' service from Westbury to Riverside, from where it was tripped to Central. This arrangement ended in 1990

Top right: Class 22 No D6333 is arriving at St David's with four loaded milk tanks from the creamery at Chard Junction in 1970. *G. V. Lendon*

Right: After regular milk services ended, the Milk Marketing Board kept a fleet of refurbished wagons for use in emergencies. They only saw limited use and the only major contract was in 1981, when a rake of ten tanks operated between Chard Junction and Stowmarket for a period due to a shortage of milk in East Anglia. On 22 August No 47346 is entering St David's with the returning empties from the first train, which it took from Riverside to Chard Junction. *C. M. Parsons*

Right: On 28 August 1974 a Class 47 loco is propelling six new Polybulk wagons towards the Pinhoe grain silo; this was part of the very first train of maize from Lavaur near Toulouse, which arrived via the Zeebrugge to Harwich train ferry for use as cattle feed. Twenty-two wagons had left France and the train operated in two portions in England, with each half further reduced for the final trip to Pinhoe. Further trains were expected to arrive at a rate of one every ten days or so, and after initially returning empty to the continent the wagons were used to carry a backload of china clay to Bibirist in Switzerland. The maize traffic ended in about 1978.

Railfreight in the modern era

when the carriage of cement by rail in the South West ceased completely; the last empty wagons were removed from Exeter Central on 19 January.

After the Plymstock works closed in 1999 there was a revival in cement traffic as 'Blue Circle' needed to supply a new distribution depot at Moorswater in Cornwall, and as the cement came from its works at Hope in Derbyshire the use of rail was viable once more. The traffic was operated by the English, Welsh & Scottish Railway (EWS), the new owners of most of the privatised Railfreight business, and loaded trains were usually split into two portions in Riverside yard to overcome haulage constraints over the south Devon banks. However, in 2002 the operation was acquired by Freightliner Heavy Haul, which used Newton Abbot's Hackney sidings as the staging point.

Wagonload traffic continued to decline in the 1970s and BR opted to build an air-braked network in an attempt to keep smaller volumes of goods on rail where a full trainload was not justified, but where such business was deemed potentially profitable. This was marketed as 'Speedlink' from September 1977, when it offered an overnight service between 12 main 'Network Yards' operating to strict timetables at speeds of 60mph using higher-capacity wagons that could carry perhaps 2½ times the payload of those that they were superseding. Any stops en route would be for limited marshalling only, with any wagons collected being 'pre-blocked' so that they could be added to a train

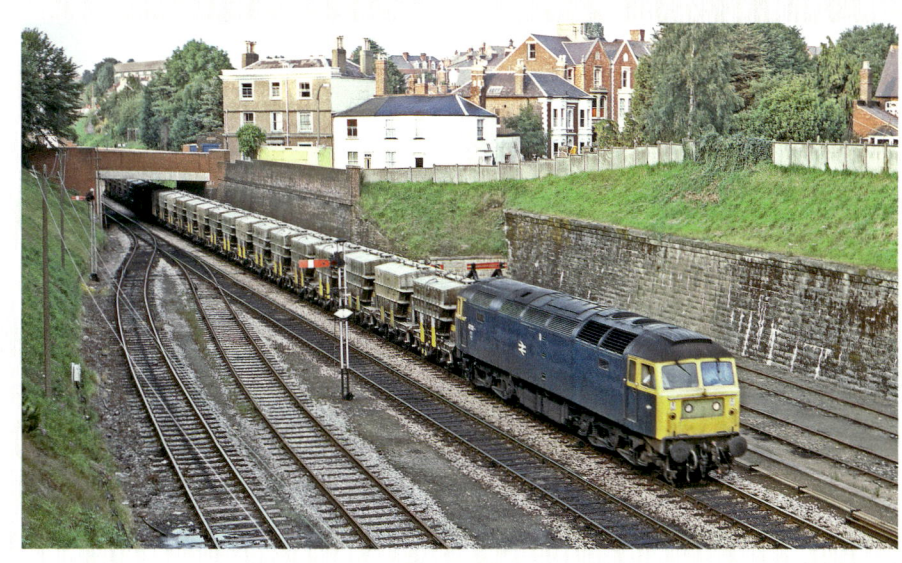

Top right: The service to the Royal Navy stores depot at Newcourt was scheduled to operate thrice-weekly as required in 1978. No 25058 is about half a mile from the depot as it works 7B70, the 11.45 MWFO trip from Newcourt to Riverside, on 14 July of that year. It has just crossed a bridge that was completed in 1975 to carry the Exmouth branch over a link road to the M5 motorway. *DHM*

Centre right: On Saturday 10 June 1972 6B65, the 18.55 Plymouth Friary to Exeter Central 'Blue Circle' cement train, is arriving at Exeter St David's behind Class 42 No 829 and 'Peak' No 151 (later No 46014); the 'Warship' then ran round the train to haul it up the incline to Central station with the 'Peak' providing banking assistance. No 829 had been withdrawn in the previous January when it lost its *Magpie* nameplates, but had been reinstated on 1 May due to a motive power shortage. *C. H. S. Owen*

Right: On 26 July 1982 No 47121 is arriving at Exeter Central with 6B22, the 16.40 MWThO train of 'Blue Circle' 'Presflo' cement wagons from Westbury Down Yard. After running round, the engine will propel the wagons into the goods yard. *C. M. Parsons*

Although 'Blue Circle' provided much of the railborne cement to Exeter, the Aberthaw and Bristol Channel Portland Cement Company had a distribution depot in New Yard near St David's station. A storage silo was not provided here and the cement was discharged from the rail wagons directly into lorries. No 47484 *Isambard Kingdom Brunel* is passing the yard with an up 'Co-op' charter train on 21 September 1981. 'Blue Circle' acquired Aberthaw Cement in 1983 and all activity was then concentrated at Exeter Central. *C. M. Parsons*

For many years Riverside yard was an important base for engineering trains. On Sunday 10 June 1984 Nos 31210 and 31180 have just arrived with a train of spoil from track renewal work on the former SR main line. After privatisation Railtrack established Westbury as a centre for infrastructure work and today such trains usually emanate from there. *DHM*

with a minimum of shunting. A key to 'Speedlink' was the use of a computerised information and control system named Total Operations Processing System (TOPS), which monitored the whereabouts of individual wagons; the South West had been chosen for a pilot scheme and trials were successfully undertaken at Exeter in 1973, covering the line to St Blazey. One of the 'Network Yards' was Severn Tunnel Junction, which was the hub for South Wales and West Country traffic, with Riverside as one of 17 'secondary yards'. However, 'Speedlink' services in the South West were slow to develop as china clay was to be the main traffic and this was still mostly carried in vacuum-braked wagons; it was not until 1982 and the introduction of air-braked wagons that 'Speedlink' was fully implemented.

During the 'Speedlink' era weekday feeder services ran from Riverside to Newton Abbot from 1981 to 1987 for ball clay traffic from the Heathfield branch, and to Barnstaple until 1987 for various commodities including cement, timber and liquid resin for a chipboard manufacturer. Additionally trips from Riverside ran to the St Thomas area for bitumen and scrap metal, to Exeter Central for a distribution company and the 'Blue Circle' traffic, Exmouth Junction (coal), Pinhoe (bricks from 1982 to 1987), Whimple (cider until 1989), Honiton (various goods including fertiliser and sugar beet), Lapford (timber), and Tiverton Junction (roof tiles from 1987 to 1990). These trips were often lightly loaded and expensive to operate, a problem that was reflected across the country. It proved difficult to retain business as road haulage prices fell in

Railfreight in the modern era

On 23 July 1985 No 50018 *Resolution* has worked a trip from Riverside and is running round at Exeter Central after collecting four empty PCA cement tanks from the 'Blue Circle' terminal and three vans from the Premier Transport depot; this was a distribution company that handled various goods, including draught Guinness from the Park Royal brewery, and used the building in the goods yard previously occupied as a Fyffes banana warehouse. *C. M. Parsons*

The Premier Transport depot was relocated to St David's in January 1986 and at about this time a new service of Ford cars began arriving from Halewood. On 15 May 1993 No 56044 *Cardiff Canton* has worked 6C46, the 07.07 SO Newport Alexandra Dock Junction to Exeter Premier Transport train, and is reversing its load of 'Cartic-4' double-deck car carriers into the Premier siding. The wagons were devised by BR engineers in 1964 in collaboration with the Ford Motor Company for the distribution of that company's vehicles; each set of four articulated wagons could carry up to 34 of the smallest cars. The '56' returned with a scrap metal train from Riverside to the Tremorfa works at Cardiff. *C. M. Parsons*

real terms, and a review of 'Speedlink' in 1990 found that it was losing money heavily; it was decided that wagonload business was not viable in an island the size of Britain and the network was abandoned in July 1992.
By then all of the aforementioned traffic in the Exeter area had either switched to road, been transferred to trainload operation or had ceased altogether.

The only traffic left at many goods yards in the 1960s was the delivery of a few coal wagons, but this was in decline as coal was replaced by other sources of power. Beeching wanted an end to this uneconomic traffic, and during the decade coal concentration depots were established throughout the country. Traditionally much of the South West's coal had arrived by coastal shipping, but after BR signed a contract with the Ministry of Power in 1964 the WR approached the National Coal Board with a plan to increase the use of rail. On 4 December 1967 a

Below: Westbrick Ltd had a works next to the grain silo at Pinhoe; it once had its own siding, but this was taken out of use in 1965, and when the company secured a contract to supply bricks for a Scottish development in 1982 it used the silo siding. The first loaded wagon was tripped to Riverside yard on 23 March 1982, where it was added to a 'Speedlink' service. On 18 April 1983 No 31231 is arriving from Riverside with two OCA wagons that will be left for loading. The SPD warehouse on the left was formerly Pye Storage Ltd, which also had its own siding from 1953 until 1968. During the implementation of the Exeter MAS scheme, the silo siding was disconnected in December 1987 prior to Pinhoe signal box closing; apparently Westbrick did not receive advance notification of this from BR, and thereafter for a period the bricks had to be taken by road to Plymouth for loading. *DHM*

Two 'Speedlink' workings are seen in Riverside yard on 14 June 1989. No 37298 is departing with 6B43, the 15.45 St Blazey to Gloucester service; this is mainly conveying clay traffic, but also has a set of empty 'Cartic-4' car carriers, and four Redland Tiles wagons loaded at Tiverton Junction have been added at Riverside. On the left No 37412 will follow with 6A28, the 20.15 Riverside to Westbury train, which comprises six empty PCA cement tanks from Exeter Central and six bitumen and eight gas oil tanks that are ultimately destined for Fawley refinery. *DHM*

concentration depot was opened on the site of the concrete works at Exmouth Junction; it was operated by Western Fuels Ltd on behalf of the NCB, and acted as a railhead for most of Devon, the main exception being Plymouth, which continued to receive coal by sea. The remaining rail-served coal yards in the county were then closed.

At first the depot received much of its supply from collieries in Yorkshire, and in early 1968 thrice-weekly trainloads from Manvers Main Colliery and a weekly train from Hickleton Colliery were scheduled in Riverside yard; additionally Welsh coal arrived in wagonload trains. However, trainload deliveries ended in 1971 and the coal then arrived on wagonload services; the last vacuum-braked coal trains ran in 1984 and thereafter the coal arrived via 'Speedlink'. Unfortunately the locations of the 'Speedlink' yards were not always compatible with the coal depots, and a dedicated 'Speedlink Coal Network' (SCN) was developed in conjunction with the NCB and the coal distribution trade; from January 1987 daily trainloads were scheduled to arrive at Exmouth Junction. Initially the service ran from Abercwmboi near Aberdare, where a large Phurnacite smokeless fuel plant was located, but during the short lifespan of the SCN the starting point changed several times in attempts to optimise efficiency. After a few months the trains ran thrice-weekly from Washwood Heath yard in Birmingham, which was an exchange hub where trains would combine wagons loaded with anthracite and patent fuels from South Wales with those carrying bituminous coal from collieries in the Midlands and Yorkshire. A new coal depot was opened at Yeovil Junction in February 1988 and thereafter loaded trains usually ran via Yeovil. These were the last regular freight movements over the former SR line to Exeter; the empties returned via Taunton, and occasionally loaded trains for just Exmouth Junction also came that way.

By 1989 the trains were starting in Radyr yard with portions exchanged at Didcot, but just a year or so later all South Wales workings were concentrated at Newport's East

Probably the last business in the South West to receive its coal directly by rail in the BR era was Wiggins Teape Ltd's Devon Valley paper mill at Hele, next to the closed Hele & Bradninch station. Latterly the coal was delivered via 'as-required' trips from Riverside; No 45045 *Coldstream Guardsman* is leaving there on 19 April 1982 not long before the traffic is thought to have ended. *DHM*

Railfreight in the modern era

No 31123 is standing at the Exmouth Junction Coal Concentration Depot on 26 March 1981 with empty coal hoppers and other vehicles that have received attention at the wagon repair works; it is about to reverse out of the yard and head for Riverside. *C. M. Parsons*

Usk yard. From October that year the trains were re-timed to run a little earlier to ensure that all shunting at Exmouth Junction was undertaken in daylight. As the demand for coal fell, regular services to Yeovil ended in July 1991 and timetabled trains to Exeter ceased in 1992. Although some specials did run for a while longer, the resident diesel shunter was sold early in 1993, which suggests that all rail traffic had ended by then.

In the financial year ending 31 March 1956 there were 296 shipments using the Exeter Ship Canal, and of these 223 brought in motor spirit; by 1958 petroleum accounted for 90% of canal trade. However, this traffic was soon threatened when both Regent Oil and National Benzole gave notice that they would cease supplying their Exeter depots by ship as their vessels were life-expired and it was uneconomic to replace them. Beeching recognised that oil was suited to movement by rail and that the business was being lost for want of the right commercial attitude and equipment. Subsequently BR was able to convince the oil companies that rail could provide a cheaper transit than either road or even pipeline, by using faster high-capacity wagons in block trains with improved techniques to reduce discharge and turn-round times. From 1963 agreements were reached with most of the major oil companies, requiring them to either lease or purchase their own wagons. Whereas nationally in 1961 less than 20% of railborne oil traffic was conveyed by trainload, by 1968 85% was carried this way and oil products were among the first types of freight converted almost entirely to block train operation. Regent Oil (a British company jointly owned by Texaco and Standard Oil) reached agreement to supply its Exeter depot entirely by rail, and new sidings adjacent to City Basin Junction were inaugurated on 9 November 1966 when the first trainload of petrol and oil arrived from Avonmouth; subsequently trains usually ran at least three times a week. In 1967 Regent became wholly owned by Texaco and its operations were rebranded accordingly. The carriage of oil by

Two generations of coal trains for Exmouth Junction CCD can be compared as they pass Exeter Central 'A' signal box. On 25 May 1972 No D7039 is working the 09.35 trip from Riverside, which comprises 12 21-ton bottom-discharge vacuum-braked HTV hoppers; 'Warship' No 814 *Dragon* has provided banking assistance and can be glimpsed beneath the New North Road bridge. In the second view on 28 April 1987, No 37200 is hauling six air-braked 32.5-ton-capacity HEA hoppers as 6C34, the 05.20 'Speedlink Coal Network' service from Abercwmboi. *J. F. Medley/J. H. Bamsey*

rail reached a peak in the early 1970s, but declined thereafter mainly due to large price increases, which caused many consumers to switch to other power; the Texaco service ceased in the summer of 1980.

A siding for King's Asphalt Ltd was opened in June 1929 on the 'Low Level Loop', the spur that connected the Teign Valley line with the City Basin branch. Traffic arrived in wagonload trains until the 1960s, but then trainloads of bitumen were conveyed from the Shell refinery at Thames Haven. Although still supplied by Shell, the traffic was sourced from Ellesmere Port from January 1981; trainloads ran to Riverside yard from where the tanks were tripped to the depot. However, this arrangement only lasted until March 1984 when Shell moved to an air-braked wagon fleet, and thereafter a daily block train ran from Ellesmere Port to Severn Tunnel Junction, with the Exeter traffic taken forward via 'Speedlink'. Soon afterwards Colas Ltd acquired King's Asphalt and in about 1985 the depot was moved to the opposite end of the loop with the wagons staged in the former Texaco sidings. This traffic ended early in 1990 after Shell moved its bitumen production to a different site that was not rail-connected.

The overnight 'Speedlink' service introduced between Westbury and Exeter in May 1987 also carried gas oil from Esso's Fawley refinery to BR's traction depots in the West, but this train was short-lived and Westbury closed as a 'Speedlink' depot in January 1990 when the cement traffic ended. Trainload Petroleum then introduced a regular service from Fawley to Tavistock Junction for the gas oil, and bitumen to Plymouth; however, only one or two tanks were delivered to Exeter each week and in 1996 supplies for there were switched to road. Services to the other depots survived into the privatisation era and EWS's initial positive approach meant that the Exeter traffic returned to rail in April 1997; however, in 2005 it was again decided that it was cheaper to serve Exeter by road, despite the train passing the depot on its journey west! The train ceased to operate altogether in October 2013 when the gas oil was sourced from elsewhere, and all First Great Western depots then received their supplies by road, reportedly with a major saving in cost.

When the Teign Valley line closed

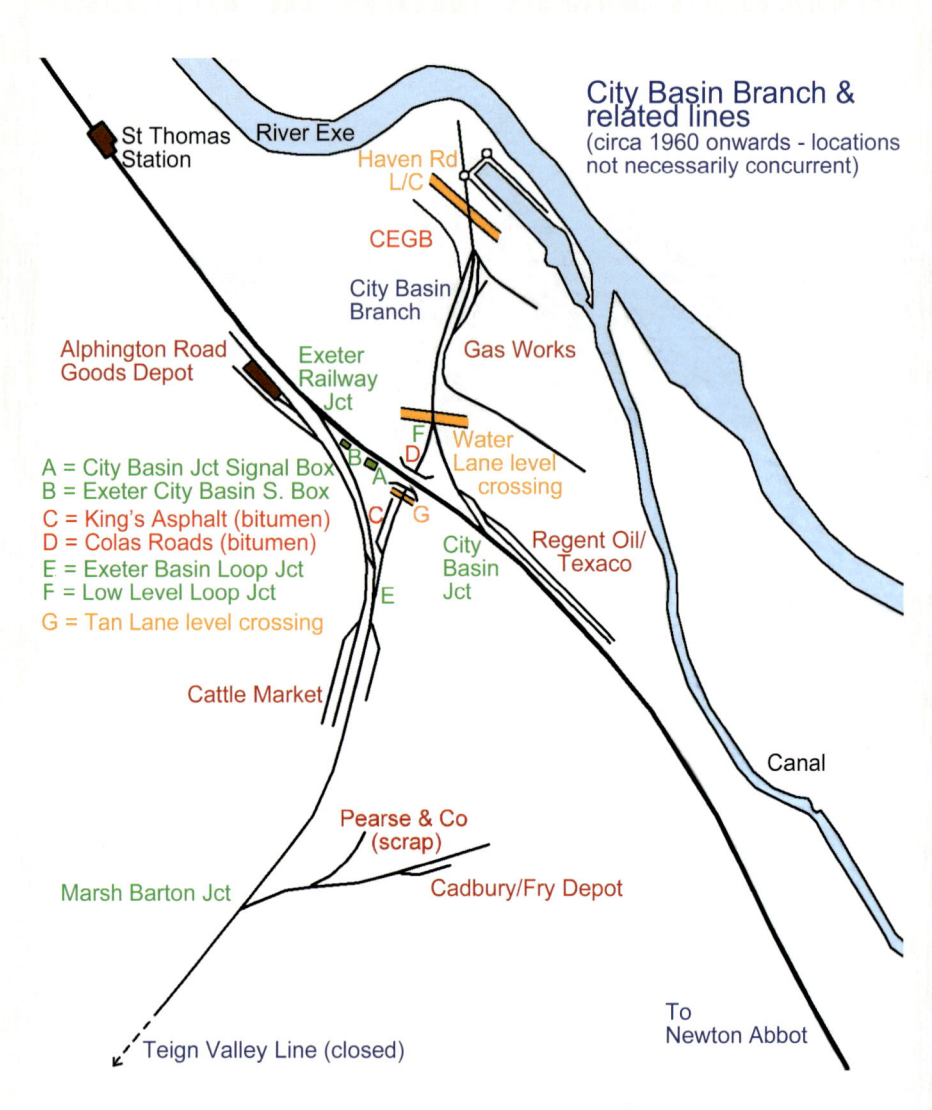

Most sources state the name of the branch as the 'City Basin' branch, but references to the 'Exeter Basin' or simply 'Basin' branch have also been recorded; similarly, the branch junction has been 'City Basin Junction' since first appearing in the Service Time Tables, but apparently the engineers often preferred 'Exeter Basin Junction'. Examination of the map reveals other confusing names, including the 1903 junction with the Teign Valley route, which was originally 'Exeter Railway Junction', a name then kept by the engineers. However, it seems that from early on the operators used 'City Basin Junction' after the signal box; this meant that until the original junction was removed in the 1990s, there were two City Basin Junctions, the second being named after a signal box that in turn had been named after the first junction! The latter name has since taken precedence over the years and is commonly used today, but the original name is shown on the map for clarity – it also makes more sense.

To further complicate matters, when the 'Low Level Loop' (originally known as the 'Canal Branch'!) was constructed beneath the main line to connect the Exeter Railway with the City Basin branch, a ground frame was provided to work both the junction at the west end of the loop and also the junction for the Alphington Road goods depot, as both were too far away to be operated from City Basin Junction signal box; this frame was known as 'City Basin Junction Ground Frame'! Thankfully after the ground frame was replaced in 1939 it was given the name 'Exeter Basin Loop Junction', as shown on the map.

Railfreight in the modern era

On Saturday 27 March 1971 Class 22 No D6315 is standing on the 'Low Level Loop' while shunting at the King's Asphalt bitumen depot. The loco had earlier hauled a coal train from Riverside yard to the gas works, possibly one of the last such trains as the works closed that year, and it then completed a busy day by working the Hemyock milk train. *John Medley*

Viewed from the Colas Roads depot, the steep grade on the first part of the City Basin branch is apparent as No 08839 descends with loaded bitumen tanks on 19 December 1989. Steam is leaking from another Shell wagon on the 'Low Level Loop' in the foreground; the bitumen needed to be kept heated above ambient temperatures while in transit to prevent it solidifying, and the wagons used for this traffic had either flame tubes or steam coils fitted as a means of heating the contents; the tank barrels were also heavily lagged. *DHM*

in June 1958 about three-quarters of a mile of track was retained from Exeter Railway Junction to near the village of Alphington, and a month later a trailing connection was opened into the new Marsh Barton Trading Estate to serve a Cadbury/Fry distribution depot that had relocated from St David's station. On 8 August of that year a spur was opened from this siding into the scrapyard of E. Pearse & Co. The Cadbury siding closed in 1971, but the spur was retained and in 1976 a Section 8 Grant was obtained to improve facilities in the yard to increase the volume of scrap metal sent by rail. The scrap was carried in vacuum-braked wagons that were tripped between Marsh Barton and Riverside yard, then taken forward in wagonload trains. After the formation of Allied Steel & Wire Ltd in Cardiff in 1982, most of the scrap went there; AS&W produced wire rodding in coil and billet form for the construction industry at its Tremorfa works, and used scrap metal as the primary raw material in an electric arc furnace. Scrap was one of the last commodities carried in vacuum-braked wagons, and when BR stopped operating this type of wagonload train a weekly trainload service was introduced between Exeter and Cardiff. From 1987 AS&W acquired its own air-braked wagons and the last vacuum train from Marsh Barton left on 24 April 1987. Thereafter the traffic was carried via 'Speedlink', but at this time BR was entering its Sectorisation period and from 23 June 1990 a weekly Trainload Metals block train was introduced. These operated until July 2002 when AS&W entered receivership; although the works was subsequently sold, the new owners no longer sourced scrap from the Exeter yard when they commenced operations.

After the scrap yard had been acquired by Sims Metal Management, rail service resumed in January 2010 with a weekly train to Sims's yard in Newport Docks operated by DB Schenker (the new owners of EWS); the train comprised 16 MBA wagons, which reportedly could carry the equivalent of 43 lorry loads. Due to having the rail connection, scrap was also brought in by road from other Sims depots in the West; the first workings conveyed scrap for export, but subsequent trains were also dispatched to Cardiff Tidal yard for Celsa Steel UK, the 'new' owner of the Tremorfa works. Apparently it is unusual for scrap merchants to commit to contracts with rail operators, and these trains were in effect run on a 'spot-hire' basis. After DBS had operated them for more than 18 months, Sims secured an alternative deal with GB Railfreight. Commencing on 6 September 2011, GBRf operated 17 trains over the following three months using leased former iron ore tippler wagons. There was a change in the way that these trains were operated; whereas DBS had split its trains in Riverside yard before running to Marsh Barton in two portions, GBRf ran through to Newton Abbot, where the loco ran round, and the whole train would subsequently reverse on to the Marsh Barton branch. For a few years the traffic was shared by the two operators, but it was erratic and finally

Shortly after running through St David's station, Class 52 No D1026 *Western Centurion* is passing Exwick fields with 6B36, the 12.25 MX Avonmouth to Exeter City Basin Texaco train, on 28 May 1975. It has the usual load of 15 45-ton tank wagons and a brake van; despite being air-braked, the van was needed as access to the Texaco depot involved reversals over the main line. *DHM*

A Class 50 loco is shunting at the Texaco terminal in May 1977 after arriving with 6B36; the main line is on the right and the diverging City Basin branch can just be glimpsed in the centre of the photograph. A part of the branch beyond the Water Lane level crossing was retained to provide a headshunt for trains accessing the terminal. *C. M. Parsons*

Since the last Class 08 shunter was transferred away, any shunting in Exeter has been undertaken by main-line engines. Before working the Riverside to Dollands Moor china clay train on 21 February 2000 No 66076 is being used to collect three empty fuel tanks from the depot and propel them to Riverside yard. *DHM*

When a weekly Trainload Metals block train was introduced for the scrap traffic, a Class 08 would shunt the wagons five at a time to the scrapyard and build the train in the Alphington Road loop adjacent to Exeter Railway Junction. Then either the shunter would take the loaded train to Riverside yard or the Class 37 train engine(s) would haul it directly from the loop; the latter is about to happen on 8 July 1990 as No 37717 waits for the road with loaded POA wagons for Cardiff Tidal yard. It is seen from the closed Alphington Road goods yard, with the 1960 warehouse on the left. The train had been made up by No 08849 and a brake van was used as the trips involved propelling movements; this has been stabled in the yard to wait for the next scrap train. *DHM*

On 24 November 2011 GBRf No 66730 *Whitemoor* is passing the site of Exeter Basin Loop Junction with the first half of a scrap metal train from the Sims Metals yard; the warehouse on the right was built on the site of the Cattle Market sidings, which had been removed in 1972. The Alphington Road loop is behind the camera and the train will be left there while the '66' propels the second half to the scrap yard; it will eventually depart as 6F30, the 16.24 Alphington Road to Cardiff Tidal yard train. *DHM*

Railfreight in the modern era

After the closure of Newton Abbot TMD in October 1981 a weekday trip operated from Riverside to the Heathfield branch, where ball clay was collected from two loading points. In possibly October 1984 No 31231 is heading 6B33, the 10.45 Riverside to Newton Abbot 'Speedlink' trip, past City Basin Junction with two empty 'Clay Tiger' hoppers for Heathfield; a Class 08 is waiting to propel an empty bitumen tank on to the main line before heading for Riverside. After freight operations had been 'sectorised', from October 1987 the Heathfield trips ran from either St Blazey or Tavistock Junction yards. *Peter Doel*

Wednesday 2 December 1998 saw the unique meeting in Riverside yard of the two longest-distance china clay trains. No 60010 is leaving on schedule with 16 tanks forming 6B68, the 09.40 Burngullow to Newport ADJ train, the first part of its journey to Irvine in Scotland. On the right Nos 47314 *Transmark* and 47360 are on 6O92, the 10.35 MO Riverside to Dollands Moor service, which has already been held for two days due to strike action by SNCF staff in France; it will eventually depart on the following day. *DHM*

On 19 May 2000 six empty timber wagons were detached in Riverside yard from 6V70, the 08.57 Cliffe Vale to St Blazey 'Enterprise' service. No 37216 had earlier arrived with a trip from St Blazey and was then used to shunt the wagons into position for loading. *DHM*

ceased in September 2015; it has been suggested that it may resume if there are sufficient volumes for a trainload operation, but this appears less likely with the passage of time.

The difficult nature of the line west of Newton Abbot has meant that Riverside yard has played a key role in staging heavy trains; this has particularly applied to china clay traffic, not least from 1989 when the noted 'Silver Bullet' trainload service began carrying clay slurry from Burngullow to a paper mill at Irvine in Ayrshire. Usually these trains would comprise up to 16 90-tonne GLW tank wagons, and although the Royal Albert Bridge over the River Tamar had been strengthened in 1968 to take 100-ton wagons, there were still restrictions on the total weight permitted over it. Additionally there were haulage constraints over the South Devon banks, so departures from Cornwall were limited to a maximum of 11 tanks, and any overload traffic was tripped in advance to Riverside where it was collected by the main train. During the 1980s Riverside was also used to build trains of china clay for export to Switzerland via the Dover to Dunkerque train ferry; after the Channel Tunnel opened this service was replaced in 1996 by a weekly train of china and ball clays to a depot at Gamalero near Sezzadio in Italy, with the wagons tripped to Riverside from various loading points. This service was discontinued in 2005 when the china clay industry was rationalised, and after it was considered more viable to import clay slurry from Brazil, the final train to Irvine ran in January 2008. Currently just one weekly china clay train operates beyond Cornwall, when up to 20 covered hoppers are hauled to Stoke-on-Trent in the Potteries. After the empties reach St Blazey, the wagons are loaded at two locations on successive days and, depending on their length, these portions are then worked separately to Riverside, from where the combined train departs early on a Friday morning.

After the end of 'Speedlink' some residual traffic remained for a while, including timber for Shotton newsprint mill that was loaded in Riverside until 1993, and Ford cars that were brought from Halewood to Exeter via a Garston to Bridgend service as far as Newport East Usk Junction, then on a connecting train to Exeter; the loaded timber wagons and empty car wagons were taken to Newport on the return working. After privatisation EWS had high hopes for wagonload business using its 'Enterprise' network, and was able to regain some business lost by BR as well as obtaining a limited amount of new traffic. Unfortunately the only regular business secured in the Exeter area was timber, which was loaded at Riverside from 1998 to 2001; otherwise the yard occasionally fulfilled its role as a staging point. Most of the business secured for 'Enterprise' in the West proved to be 'one-offs', or at best temporary in nature, and the acquisition of long-term traffic proved to be difficult. Eventually most of the traffic was either lost or shed when it was deemed to be uneconomic, and the final wagonload service departed from Riverside in 2014.

Meldon Quarry passed to the WR with the regional boundary changes in 1963, but continued to send much of its output to the SR; from 1985 these trains were routed via Westbury and all Meldon trains then called in Riverside to either terminate or for the engine to run round. From 1989 the quarry operated as a wholly owned subsidiary of BR, and was supplying up to 350,000 tons of ballast annually to Network SouthEast and the WR, with six daily departures timetabled. In May 1993 it lost the NSE work and for a period three daily departures ran as required to fulfil a WR contract for 160,000 tons per annum.

The quarry was sold in March 1994 during the privatisation process and thereafter had a chequered history, although at first traffic increased and by 1995 five weekday trains were timetabled. Railtrack then established a base for its engineering trains at Westbury and the amount of this traffic handled at Riverside reduced considerably; the establishment of a 'virtual quarry' ballast stockpile at Westbury with the stone sourced from elsewhere meant that trains from Meldon ceased in June 1998. Although Meldon did later secure some contracts, including for Network Rail, the last of these ended in July 2009 and the quarry was mothballed.

In 1997 Foster Yeoman secured a contract to provide aggregate from its Merehead limestone quarry in the Mendips for a scheme to improve the A30 road between Honiton and Exeter, which involved building a new 13-mile dual carriageway; a stone terminal was established in Riverside yard, with the first trains arriving in March of that year. The train frequency varied depending on the needs of the contract, but at peak times up to three trains arrived each day before work was completed in September 1999. The Amalgamated Roadstone Company (ARC) also had a quarry in the Mendips, and in October 1993 the two companies merged their rail operations as Mendip Rail Ltd in the quest for greater efficiencies. Trains began to run from ARC's Whatley Quarry to Devon in February 1998, when it obtained a contract to supply 30,000 tonnes of stone 'dust' each year to Flexer Construction Ltd for use as backfill in trenches being dug for ducting on behalf of Eurobell Ltd, which was laying fibre-optic cables. The first of several depots served the Exeter area and was established on the site of the Exmouth Junction coal depot. To keep prices as competitive as possible a proportion of the 'dust' was later obtained from Meldon Quarry, and most of the later trains to Exeter came from there; the operation ended suddenly in 2000 when the contractors entered receivership.

The 'A30' terminal at Riverside was revived in 2000 when Hanson PLC (previously ARC) leased the site as a distribution depot for its aggregate, with a plan to bring in 100,000 tonnes of stone a year by rail from Whatley for the local construction industry. At the time it was claimed that this would save more than half a million road miles and 5,000

Six sidings (Nos 8 to 13) were added to the west side of Riverside yard in 1966; one was later removed and outermost siding No 12 is now used for aggregate traffic. A connection with No 11 road was installed for the 'A30' contract so that locos could run round. On 24 September 1997 Foster Yeoman's No 59005 *Kenneth J. Painter* has arrived with 6Z85, the 12.45 departure from Merehead Quarry, and is about to use this crossover. When pairs of Class 37 locos were later used on these trains the headshunt had to be extended as it was not long enough for two engines. *DHM*

Railfreight in the modern era

lorry journeys between Somerset and Exeter each year. The trains do not run throughout the year but operate on what is known as a 'campaign' basis, i.e. depending on demand they will run regularly for a period while stocks are built up, then cease until the stockpiles need to be replenished. DBS operated the trains on behalf of Mendip Rail until November 2019, when Freightliner acquired the work; this service is still operating at the time of writing.

Right: On 25 February 1998 Nos 37156 and 37711 are running as 7Z95, the 10.04 Exeter Riverside to Exmouth Junction train, as they climb from Blackboy Tunnel. This was the second portion of nine wagons of a train from Whatley Quarry; the first portion is just out of sight in the yard on the right. The train was the second in a contract to carry stone 'dust' for a contract to lay fibre-optic cables in Exeter. *DHM*

In December 2011 a service commenced to carry timber from Teignbridge on the Heathfield branch to Chirk Kronospan in north Wales, where it was used in the manufacture of fibreboard. After the main line was closed in the great storm at Dawlish in 2014, trains were loaded in Riverside yard; once the line was restored both locations were served for a period, but only Riverside was used from April 2015 until the service ended. Haulage was provided by Colas Railfreight, and on 20 April 2016 that company's No 70808 is shunting its train while it is being loaded; this was the final train of the contract and it departed on the following day as 6M51, the 16.08 Riverside to Chirk Kronospan. *DHM*

14. Water, water everywhere

On several occasions in recent years the railway at Exeter has made the headlines in the national media when it was closed by flooding, particularly when on occasions these closures have lasted for quite long periods. When building a railway the route could often make use of river valleys, which helped to keep costs down by minimising the amount of engineering work, and in Devon the Bristol & Exeter Railway followed the River Culm for part of the way; it interacted with this meandering and flood-prone river at a number of places, including the village of Hele, where it crossed the Culm just south of the since closed Hele & Bradninch station. This has long been a vulnerable spot, but in steam days it was not a problem unless the flow of water was sufficient to disturb the ballast or the flood level was more than about a foot above the rails; providing speed was kept to a walking pace and the water was not deep enough to reach the fire, steam locos could plod through flooded areas without coming to harm.

At Stoke Canon the line enters the River Exe valley and crosses the river on a steel girder bridge just south of the village; beyond this bridge there is a confluence of the Exe and Culm. Rising on Exmoor, the Exe flows south for 56 miles to the sea. In the upper reaches the river and its tributaries are confined within narrow valleys that respond to rainfall and can quickly turn a gently flowing stream into a raging torrent. The river can rise rapidly at up to an inch an hour and as a rough guide heavy rainfall on Exmoor reaches Stoke Canon about 12 hours later; if the Culm is also in flood, water can rise by as much as 2 inches an hour. Between Stoke Canon and Exeter the railway runs across a flood plain for about 2 miles, and near Cowley Bridge Junction the Exe is joined by the River Creedy; the North Devon line runs along the Creedy valley, tributaries of which carry rainfall from Dartmoor.

When the B&E was being built the Exe was diverted just north of Cowley Bridge to run parallel with the railway for about half a mile, which removed the need for two bridges. Part of the old river course became a secondary channel known as the Mill Leat, which provides flood relief. About a mile east of Cowley Bridge the line crosses an Exe meander on Stafford's Bridge; after heavy rainfall excess water can overtop the river bank at this bridge and run through the fields between the railway and a road until it encounters the railway embankments at Cowley Bridge Junction; these create a bottleneck and rising floodwaters have nowhere to go except over the railway. Although a culvert was provided here, history has shown it to be inadequate in times of extreme rainfall, and by the time that water has reached here it has built up speed and washes away the ballast, as well as potentially causing damage to the embankments and other infrastructure.

There has been a long history of flooding in the low-lying St Thomas area of Exeter, but the worst event in living memory occurred in the autumn of 1960 after prolonged periods of rain. Trouble first manifested itself in the greater Exeter area on 30 September when the former SR route was inundated by a swollen Creedy and an underbridge to the east of Crediton collapsed. Further heavy rain set back repair

On 1 October 1960 there was single-line operation south of Exeter, and to the north both tracks at Hele & Bradninch station were flooded. Several services were marooned at St David's, including the 1.44pm stopping train to Taunton, which was cancelled at 3.00pm to allow No D803 *Albion* and the up 'Cornish Riviera Express' into Platform 4. Some up trains were being diverted over the Exe Valley line via Tiverton, but as the 'Warship' was not permitted over this route and no more than ten coaches were allowed, 2-6-2T No 4167 was used to remove the first five coaches and attach them to the four coaches of a special train from Plymouth to Paddington that had arrived behind No D811 *Daring*; the 'Prairie' tank is seen departing with the rest of the 'Riviera' at 4.10pm (it was scheduled to arrive at Paddington at 4.40pm!). Not long after, the flooding at Hele had subsided sufficiently to allow steam locos over the up line, and 'Mogul' No 7311 departed at 4.42pm with the special train. 4-6-0 No 1027 *County of Stafford* can be glimpsed in the photo standing at Platform 5 with the Kingswear portion of the 'Cornishman'; this finally departed more than 3 hours late at 5.35pm with the engine working through to Wolverhampton.
R. A. Lumber

work and caused damage to other sections of track, and it was not possible to reopen the line until 12 October; in the interim services from Plymouth were diverted via Newton Abbot. Also on the 30th flooding washed away ballast on the down WR main line south of Exeter and enforced single-line working between City Basin Junction and Exminster for three days. On the same day a landslip on Honiton Incline also closed the Waterloo line and, although the down line was reopened that afternoon, the up line was closed for six days. On 1 October the Culm rose and the branch line to Hemyock suffered two washouts; at one the track gave way under a train, but fortunately it managed to keep going until it reached solid ground. During the afternoon the Culm overflowed at Hele and contributed to a traffic 'pile-up' at Exeter St David's. Heavy rain continued for much of that week, but although

Water, water everywhere

Flood water is lapping the ballast on Saturday 22 October 1960 as 'Castle' Class 4-6-0 No 4037 *The South Wales Borderers* approaches what was then the A38 Exeter bypass at Matford with the 11.00am Swansea to Penzance service. The engine had been built as a 'Star' Class loco in 1910, when it was named *Queen Philippa* and was based in Exeter for a period from 1914; it was converted into a 'Castle' in 1926 and renamed in 1937. After being based at Newton Abbot for many years it returned to Exeter shed for a short period prior to its withdrawal in September 1962, having run 2,429,722 miles in its 52-year life, a record for any GWR locomotive. *Peter W. Gray*

At noon on 27 October 1960 the flood waters were starting to back up behind the plate girders of the SR bridge over the Exe at Cowley Bridge Junction, before spouting up through the deck and flowing down the line towards Riverside yard. At about 1.00pm 'Pacific' No 34011 *Tavistock*, with the 11.10am Plymouth to Brighton service, and a very late 9.27am Exe Valley train from Dulverton both reached the junction, but as the WR line appeared to be giving way the latter reversed to Stoke Canon where the passengers disembarked. However, the Brighton train was hand-signalled through and is seen slowly wading through the water; another 'Pacific', No 34065 *Hurricane*, was also allowed through with the 9.00am Waterloo to Ilfracombe train, but with water levels continuing to rise the line was then closed.

there were reports of incidents in the wider South West there do not seem to have been any further major problems in the Exeter area.

There was then a lull in the rain, but towards the end of the month it returned with a vengeance. During October Exeter had about 15 inches of rain, half the annual average, and on Wednesday the 26th a further 2½ inches fell over the Exe catchment causing the river to rise alarmingly with damage at a number of places including Hele, where the line was inundated again. The next morning the weather was largely fine and single-line working resumed at Hele, but water levels were rising around Cowley Bridge and starting to cover the track; all trains were halted at the signals, then hand-flagged through, and diesels were replaced by steam engines due to the risk of water damaging the former's traction motors. The up 'Torbay Express' hauled by No 4098 *Kidwelly Castle* was the last up WR train to get though, and after the passage of two SR trains all services stopped soon after 1.00pm. The valley between Stoke Canon and Exeter was now a huge moving lake, which was partly contained by the embankments at Cowley Bridge, where the water was banking up. Fresh rainfall from upstream added to this lake and eventually the water overwhelmed any obstacles and became a raging torrent. Property on the west bank bore the brunt as an estimated 42,000 tons of water per minute overflowed and swept through St Thomas; the flood effectively cut the city in half, with more than 2,500 properties flooded to a depth of more than 6 feet.

Up WR trains reversed at St David's and down ones initially ran only as far as Stoke Canon, but were later terminated at Cullompton after Hele was again flooded. SR trains stopped at Crediton and connecting buses were provided for both routes. St David's station was now filling up with trains and arrangements were made to send the main WR services over the Waterloo route. The up 'Cornish Riviera' departed behind No 34024 *Tamar Valley* for a journey to Paddington via Basingstoke and Reading; the up 'Royal Duchy' arrived behind No D827 *Kelly*, which was replaced by No 34104 *Bere Alston* and left 150 minutes late with banking assistance from St David's provided by No 34023 *Blackmore Vale*. A number of other diverted WR trains were hauled by 'Hall' Class locos over the SR, as larger WR engines were not permitted on the route. Meanwhile water was starting to flow south from Riverside yard and cover the track between the platforms; by 5.00pm it was up to carriage axle boxes and as the water deepened Platform 3 was deemed to be unsafe to use, thus contributing to the congestion. Eventually the water started to recede and by late evening the worst had passed.

On the following morning the down WR line and both SR lines were in operation at Cowley Bridge, with the up Western line being re-ballasted; traffic was getting back to normal fairly well, the main problem being that much of the rolling-stock was out of position. However, just a month later further incessant rain led to more flooding around Exeter, and the WR line was closed on 4-5 December with trains again diverted via the SR line to Yeovil; on this occasion the up 'Cornish Riviera' was worked by a 'County' Class engine, a type actually banned from the SR main line! The Exe Valley branch was cut in two places and a substitute bus service replaced trains until the 8th.

As a result of this devastation a flood alleviation scheme

was planned to protect Exeter, the main features of which were the construction of three flood relief channels between 1965 and 1977. The Exwick Spillway is the largest and most complex of these channels; a huge radial gate was built near St David's station to obstruct the flow of water in the Exe in times of flood and divert it into the spillway, which starts at this gate. Further south this channel runs under the railway south of the station.

At Cowley Bridge the SR route crossed the Exe on a curved multi-span wrought-iron bridge, and further west there were three bridges on the flood plain, the last of which crossed the Mill Leat, which provides the outlet from the turbines of a water works. In 1964 there was concern about the condition of all four bridges and it was considered that they were in need of renewal at an estimated cost of £327,000. At this time much of the former SR network to the West was slated for closure, with only the branches to Ilfracombe and Okehampton scheduled to be retained; the team responsible for implementing the closures felt that this expenditure could not be justified and permission was sought to close all the lines west of Exeter. However, this was not agreed and the British Railways Board gained ministerial approval to replace the four double-track bridges with two new steel and concrete single-track ones over the Exe and the Mill Leat, which were also diverted to improve their flows; the track was singled on the down alignment from the junction to just beyond the new bridges. This scheme took about a year to implement and was completed in January 1967.

There was no further major flooding in the area until October 2000, when a violent storm caused disruption across much of the country and intense rainfall comparable to that seen exactly

Above and opposite top: The railway crosses the Exwick Spillway just south of St David's station. This flood relief channel was being dug on 9 October 1971 when single-line working was in operation using the up road with a 20mph speed restriction through the work zone; No D1003 *Western Pioneer* is being flagged through while hauling 1A55, the 15.55 Paignton to Paddington train, over the new bridge.

In the second view Class 52 No D1033 *Western Trooper* is crossing this bridge with the 16.10 Penzance to Paddington service on 28 May 1975. *Both DHM*

After flooding at Cowley Bridge Junction washed away ballast in early January 1966, re-ballasting work is in progress with Class 42 No D828 *Magnificent* hauling the wagons. On the left flood water is up to the deck of the iron viaduct that carries the SR line over the Exe; this viaduct was installed when the line was doubled in 1875, but it and three other bridges nearby will be replaced later in 1966. *R. A. Lumber*

'Warship' No D825 *Intrepid* is joining the main line at Cowley Bridge Junction with the 10.40 Plymouth to Brighton train on 10 August 1966; by then this was the only daily loco-hauled passenger train operating over this route. To its left the down line is still running over the iron viaduct, but the track beyond has been removed and one of two new single-track concrete bridges can be seen; beyond these bridges a temporary connection is in use where the double track resumes. By the end of that month the new bridges were in use and the up line was then lifted. Later the Exe and Mill Leat were diverted to run under the new bridges and four old bridges were dismantled and replaced by embankments. *R. A. Lumber*

Water, water everywhere

The twin transept towers of Exeter Cathedral are prominent on the skyline on 19 July 1996 as the 16.30 Paddington to Penzance HST (power cars Nos 43145 and 43129) passes the old transhipment shed as it slows for a stop at St David's station. The radial gate on the River Exe can be seen lower right, and the start of the Exwick Spillway is further right. *DHM*

40 years previously meant that Devon faced some of its worst flooding since that time. In the ten days from 29 October there was 270mm of rain, 90mm of which fell in a 30-hour period; the usual average rainfall for the same period was about 34mm. The 30th dawned dry and sunny but the fields at Cowley Bridge were filling with the previous day's rainfall, and by 10.00 all trains were stopped as Railtrack personnel watched the flood waters approach the railway behind the inn. Not long afterwards there was a rather surreal sight as water started to bubble and then spout up through the ballast on the main line as the formation was undermined; the water continued to rise and within a couple of hours the track was largely submerged. The low-lying parts of Exeter came very close to being flooded again that day as the Exe reached its highest ever recorded level during the afternoon and nearly over-topped the defence works. Flooding in Honiton Tunnel also closed the Waterloo line, and for a period no trains were

About a mile east of Cowley Bridge Junction the main line crosses the Exe on Stafford's Bridge Viaduct, which has long been a trouble spot in times of flood. Procedures for checking bridges were tightened after the tragic October 1987 event when Glanrhyd Bridge on the Central Wales line was partially washed away by the swollen River Towy and a DMU fell into the river, resulting in four deaths. Thereafter concern over what heightened river currents may be doing to Stafford's Bridge has led to the line being closed here on many occasions, even when the railway has not actually been flooded. On 20 January 1999 the train service was continuing despite the river being in flood, but the 10.00 Cardiff to Paignton DMU was restricted to 10mph and Railtrack personnel were observing its careful progress over the bridge. *DHM*

able to run to or from the South West; however, by the next day some diversions were arranged over that route, including the overnight sleeper services and mail and freight trains. Otherwise to the east GW trains terminated at Tiverton Parkway and CrossCountry trains stopped at either Bristol or Taunton; up to 20 road coaches and buses were in use between Exeter and Tiverton Parkway at any one time, and a rail shuttle service was operated between Exeter and Penzance.

The flooding caused sections of embankment on both the main line and the Barnstaple branch to be breached and

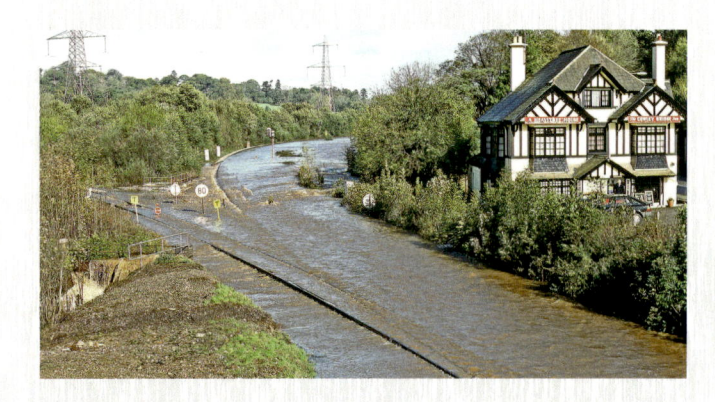

Two views of the flooding at Cowley Bridge Junction on 30 October 2000. *Both DHM*

The morning after; some of the devastation at Cowley Bridge on 31 October 2000 after the water had receded. *DHM*

The scene on 8 December 2000 after overnight flooding had undermined the track again. *DHM*

washed away. Another problem when compared with 1960 was that in the interim colour light signals had replaced the mechanical signalling and the water caused extensive damage to the signalling infrastructure, which took longer to repair than the reinstatement of the track. Another storm on 5-6 November damaged some of the remedial work, and it was not until the 8th that an engineering train was able to work over the main line east of Cowley Bridge; passenger services resumed on the 11th, but damage to sections of the Barnstaple branch meant that line did not reopen until the 20th. Then another storm on 7 December resulted in overnight flooding at Cowley Bridge, and by the morning the damage resembled that witnessed just over a month previously with sections of the repaired embankments swept away yet again. The lines were closed again until late on the 17th.

Afterwards a new culvert was built beneath the railway and there were no further major problems until 21 November 2012 when, after days of rain falling on already saturated

ground, ballast was washed away at Cowley Bridge. Repairs were undertaken, but before services could resume further rain resulted in the line being inundated on the 25th, and it was not until the 28th that the first trains were allowed through subject to a severe speed limit and hand-signalling. Less than a month later on 22 December the line was closed yet again after an Environment Agency (EA) warning that flooding was likely. In a new initiative Network Rail placed plastic booms known as 'Aqua Dams' across the tracks, which were filled with water pumped from the Exe; two were placed south of the junction with a third positioned further south to protect a signalling relay room. There was flooding, but the

Among the trains that had to be diverted when the line at Cowley Bridge was badly damaged by flooding in October 2000 were the regular Royal Mail services. On 8 November No 47798 *Prince William,* one of the two locos then used to power the Royal Train, is waiting for the 12.35 service from Waterloo to clear the single-line section before leaving Pinhoe with the 13.53 Plymouth to Bristol Parkway train. *DHM*

Water, water everywhere

booms diverted much of the water into the river; however, some damage still occurred and the main line was closed until noon on the 28th.

With global warming there was a growing concern that Exeter's flood defences needed updating and this resulted in the EA launching a £30 million scheme in 2014. Some of this work has directly benefitted the railway, including the construction of a 360-metre-long, 3-metre-high embankment downstream of Cowley Bridge, and the installation of a steel flood gate on the road leading to Red Cow level crossing. The 2012 floods also prompted NR to undertake a resilience study to consider what actions could be taken. It seems that previously it had been accepted that Cowley Bridge was a special case and that flooding events were inevitable due to its location; however, recently NR has been rather more proactive; the use of the 'Aqua Dams' proved to be reasonably effective and another simple measure taken in 2013 was to raise the signalling cabinets around the junction on to platforms. The existing culverts had proved to be inadequate and almost certainly the most important development in recent years was the installation of a new culvert; this 8-metre-wide twin-box structure of 24 precast concrete rectangular units was installed during a possession in June 2018. It proved its worth in February 2020 when there was a risk of flooding and an 'Aqua Dam' was inflated; however, in the event the excess water drained through the culverts without encroaching onto the track.

Although the 'Aqua Dams' had been fairly effective, looking forward they were not seen as the final answer. Flood modelling work undertaken by the EA highlighted that the railway adjacent to Cowley Weir on the Exe was still a weakness in its plans to protect the city, and it had input into the design of a 'demountable flood defence barrier', which was installed in May 2020. This is a multi-segmented metal gate that can be quickly assembled across the railway when there is a threat of flooding. Clearly, trains cannot run when it is deployed, but it should help to prevent damage and prolonged closure of the line; when not in use it is stored in a box next to the railway.

On 23 December 2012 at Cowley Bridge two 'Aqua Dams' have been inflated; one has been damaged but the second one managed to divert the water into the Exe. *DHM*

Colas Rail Freight's No 66849 is passing Cowley Bridge with 6C98, the 15.10 Westbury to Burngullow rail delivery train, on 7 September 2020; one of the raised signalling cabinets can be noted to the right of the engine. *DHM*

On 12 June 2018 the embankment is being excavated on the approach to Cowley Bridge Junction during the construction of a new culvert. *DHM*

Hanson-owned No 59102 *Village of Chantry* crosses the new culvert as it accelerates away with 7C28, the 13.44 Riverside yard to Whatley Quarry train of aggregate empties, on 21 March 2019. *DHM*

The newly constructed 'demountable flood defence barrier' is trialled at Cowley Bridge in May 2020. *Network Rail*

15. Men at work and at play

Looking back, it can seem that summers were always sunny, but this was not so on Saturday 23 July 1960 when it rained on and off all day, and was raining at 5.20pm when ex-GWR '4700' Class No 4705 rolled into Platform 1 at St David's with the 1.20pm Paddington to Kingswear service. The driver has climbed down from his cab and is oiling around the valve spindle and slide bars while his fireman is in the tender moving coal forward to where it will be within range of his shovel when he is back on the footplate; further down the train water and gas is probably being supplied to the restaurant car. On the left 'Battle of Britain' Class 4-6-2 No 34058 *Sir Frederick Pile* is running into Platform 3 with the 2.55pm Ilfracombe to Waterloo train. *Peter W. Gray*

On 3 August 1957 4-6-0 No 6025 *King Henry III* has the road to run non-stop through Platform 5 at Exeter St David's with the summer Saturday 12.30pm Newquay to Paddington train, but has had to make an unscheduled stop for water. Presumably the fireman had been unable to collect enough water from the troughs at Powderham to be sure of safely reaching the next set of troughs at Creech St Michael, east of Taunton. He is standing in the foreground and, having inserted the bag of the water crane into the tender, he is holding the chain that he will use to swing the bag back into place when the tank is full. The driver is largely hidden behind the crane and is waiting to turn off the water supply. In the background 'Castle' Class 4-6-0 No 5052 *Earl of Radnor* approaches Platform 1 with the 12.05pm Paddington to Plymouth train, and is passing 'E1/R' Class 0-6-2T No 32697 waiting for its next banking job. *Peter W. Gray*

'T9' 4-4-0 No 30717 has the road at St David's on 12 July 1958, but the fireman is looking for the 'right away' from the guard before it can leave with the 2.22pm train from Plymouth Friary. *Peter W. Gray*

After arriving at Exeter St David's with the LCGB's 'A4 Commemorative Rail Tour' from Waterloo on 27 March 1966, No 60024 *Kingfisher* has run to Exmouth Junction where it is being watered before being turned ready for the return trip. *C. H. S. Owen*

On 24 February 1970 Class 22 No D6339 substituted for a failed DMU on a round trip to Barnstaple; the 12.38 return working has arrived at St David's where the crew are being greeted by passenger shunter the late Chris Parsons, many of whose photos are featured in this title. *DHM*

Men at work and at play

Above: After reaching the stop board on the reception road for Riverside yard on 21 March 1997, the driver of No 37899 *County of West Glamorgan* is climbing down to use the telephone at the board to call the shunter in charge of the yard and seek his permission to continue. The train is 7C40, the 12.09 engineer's train from Newport Alexandra Dock Junction, which comprises ten 'Seacow' wagons loaded with ballast from Machen Quarry. *DHM*

Left: On 12 September 2000 the driver of No 60082 *Mam Tor* is obtaining authority to enter Riverside yard while working 6V70, the 08.57 Cliffe Vale to St Blazey 'Enterprise' train. *DHM*

Below: The Riverside yard shunter signals the driver of 'Peak' No 45029 to stop as it arrives at 18.35 on 21 June 1984 with 6C43, the 14.45 St Blazey to Severn Tunnel Junction 'Speedlink' service. *DHM*

Above: The driver of the 13.35 Penzance to Paddington HST service cleans the windscreen of power car No 43169 using a brush and bucket of water left for this purpose on Platform 5 at St David's on 14 June 2003. *DHM*

Left: Type 3 No 33103 *Swordfish*, belonging to 'spot-hire' company FM Rail, is fuelled on Exeter depot on 15 March 2006. Inspection Coach No 975025 *Caroline* (the former Southern Region General Manager's Saloon) is on the left, and the 'Crompton' will later haul it on a return trip to Barnstaple. *DHM*

Right: And a woman at work. More recent times have seen a large increase in women in front-line positions, including working as drivers, conductors or, as in this case, as an engineer. On 14 May 2014 a woman appeared to be in charge of a Network Rail track gang that was repairing a set of points at St David's, and was the only one actually working as No 31465 passed, propelling its Test Train from Riverside yard to the depot for the loco to be fuelled. *DHM*

Men at work and at play 191

Two photographers have just captured the action on Sunday 21 April 1957 as 4-6-2 No 35026 *Lamport & Holt Line* attacks the climb through St James Park Halt with the 12 noon Exeter Central to Waterloo train, which has portions from Plymouth and north Devon. The 'Merchant Navy' looks new, having been rebuilt at Eastleigh just three months earlier. *J. H. Bamsey*

Just over seven years later, on 5 September 1964, the last scheduled Saturday of steam operation on Waterloo services, enthusiasts have gathered at Exeter Central to watch the departure of the 4.30pm to London, which was also hauled by No 35026. The young lad in the foreground seems a little unsure as to what he is witnessing! *R. A. Lumber*

Above: Youthful locospotters have taken occupation of a barrow at St David's while pursuing their hobby on 3 June 1960, and at least one is jotting down the numbers of 0-6-0PT No 3679 and 'N' 2-6-0 No 31844 as they pass with the 5.52pm Exeter Central to Okehampton train. The pannier tank is presumably hitching a ride, but it is not thought to be for a banking duty as normally banking engines would be facing the other way. *G. T. Reardon*

Centre: The use of freight engines on a summer Saturday is exemplified by the appearance of Oxley shed's 2-8-0 No 3802 on 1 August 1959, which is arriving at St David's Platform 5 with the 12.42pm Newquay to Cardiff train. This visitor was no doubt appreciated by the bands of locospotters who have congregated on the platform ends. *Peter W. Gray*

Below: The appearance of rare diesel locos will also see many observers 'come out of the woodwork'. 'Deltic' No 55016 *Gordon Highlander* was only the second of the class to reach Exeter when it worked one of BR's farewell specials for the type on 28 November 1981. The 'Deltic Devonian' ran from Finsbury Park to Liverpool Street via Exeter, and has plenty of admirers during a scheduled hour-long stop at St David's. *C. M. Parsons*

Men at work and at play

Celebrations to mark the 150th Anniversary of the GWR brought steam engines back to the main line through Exeter. Two British Transport policemen are keeping the crowds at bay on 7 July 1985 as 4-6-0s Nos 5051 *Dryslwyn Castle* and 4930 *Hagley Hall* leave St David's with the 'Great Western Limited'. The special started at Paddington, with the steam engines coming on at Bristol, but they later stalled on Dainton bank and the train needed a diesel banker before it was terminated at Totnes.
C. M. Parsons

On 4 October 2003 'Pacific' No 34067 *Tangmere* worked an 'Atlantic Coast Express' charter from Waterloo to Okehampton, from where it returned tailing No 37308. It is seen leaving Exeter St David's for servicing in Riverside yard before making the return run to Paddington via the WR main line. *DHM*

16. Closely observed trains

'GWR locomotives in the Exeter District in 1897 and 1901' by 'W.B.'

I will endeavour to recall my earliest impressions of the locomotives of the GWR that were obtained in the Exeter area in 1897 after moving from Brighton. I must point out that railway literature was scarce at that time and personal observation was the only method of finding out what was happening in the locomotive world. The only line with which I was hitherto acquainted was the LB&SCR and there was the interest of seeing new classes of locomotive; although the GWR and the L&SWR both came under my notice I always felt far more interest in the larger system and I attribute this to the fact that named engines were then becoming fairly numerous on the GWR whereas on the L&SWR they had almost disappeared.

The first peculiarity to strike me as regards the GWR locomotives was the prevalence of outside coupling rods, although I afterwards discovered that there were several standard types with inside bearings. I have no written notes of the engines I saw at Exeter in the summer of 1897 but I remember the numbers and names of a good many. The bulk of the express passenger traffic was handled by two of Mr Dean's latest types, the 7ft 8in bogie singles of which 65 were in commission, and the 4-4-0 'Dukes' of which there were 40. Broadly speaking the 'Dukes' worked west of Exeter and the singles east of Newton Abbot although a few of the 'Dukes'

The first eight 'Achilles' Class 7ft 8in 'Singles' were built as broad gauge convertible 2-2-2s in 1891 and were followed by 20 standard gauge 2-2-2s in 1892, including No 3016 *Lightning*. All were rebuilt as 4-2-2s in 1894. By 1899 there were 80 locos in service and for several years this handsome class monopolised the expresses between Paddington, Bristol and Newton Abbot. At this time the GWR livery reached its most elaborate, with the basic green colour enlivened by orange and black lining, the frames were painted red, and the letters 'GWR' began to appear on the tenders in the form of a monogram with the letters closely entwined; with polished brass and copper fittings the effect must have been stunning. However, these locos had a relatively short life in the limelight as by the early 1900s they were being superseded by new 4-4-0s as trains were getting heavier with the introduction of corridor stock and restaurant and sleeping cars, and all were withdrawn between 1908 and 1915. *Lightning* is pictured in the shed yard at Exeter with the St David's train shed prominent in the background; it was allocated to Exeter during the Edwardian period and was withdrawn in March 1911.

worked as far as Taunton; about 60 of the singles and about 35 of the 'Dukes' were seen in this area in 1897.

These engines had a good deal of polished brass work and were kept very clean. The singles had the company's coat-of-arms on the driving splashers and also the arms of London and Bristol. The framing, wheels and splashers were painted dark red and the boiler, firebox and cab were green elaborately lined out in orange and black. The coupled engines were similarly painted and soon after they were built they had the plain beading on the splashers replaced by brass; the works plates were of a new type, being of cast brass with raised lettering and much larger than those used on the singles and other earlier engines. At this time the Belpaire firebox had not been introduced on the GWR; the singles had raised fireboxes (with brass coping) and the 'Dukes' had them flush with the boiler barrel. This is scarcely the place to give a history of the singles but it is of interest to recall that the first 30 were originally six-wheeled engines and also that eight of them worked for a time on the broad gauge. Bogies were added in 1894 and the engines as altered resembled the 'Achilles' Class, the first of which appeared in March 1894. The 'Dukes' first appeared in May 1895 and had 5ft 8½in coupled wheels.

A few express engines of other types put in an occasional appearance, e.g. Armstrong's 7ft singles and Dean's 2-4-0s of various classes; the Armstrong singles seen were all of the 'Sir Daniel' Class of which there were 30. I recollect that No 577 was only seen once on Bank Holiday traffic but on the other hand Nos 386, 478, 479, 582 and 586 were frequently observed. No 381 was at one time named *Morning Star* but it did not carry the name in 1897. Of Dean's 6ft 6in 2-4-0s with inside bearings I saw No 2220 daily and others occasionally, e.g. Nos 816, 824, 2206 and 2212. These belonged to two series; the first batch, Nos 806 to 825, came out of Swindon Works in 1873, while Nos 2201 to 2220 appeared between September 1881 and October 1882. The earlier ones were rebuilt in various styles according to whether they were dealt with at Swindon or Wolverhampton. All those seen at Exeter bore the Swindon stamp and I regarded them as all of the same class. Apparently No 2220 had not been rebuilt by 1897 and this may account for the fact that it was almost invariably employed as shed pilot. There was one other Dean 2-4-0 with sandwich frames, No 3210, one of a batch of 20 6ft coupled engines with inside cylinders and outside bearings. I remember that this particular engine had a rather tall dome near the chimney, much smaller than those fitted to Mr Dean's standard express engines; this engine was often in the shed yard but I never saw it on a train.

The local passenger traffic was worked by Swindon-built 2-4-0 side tank engines, Wolverhampton-built 0-4-2 side-tank engines and a few rebuilt '3521' Class 0-4-4 tank engines numbered 3537, 3544, 3551 and 3557. No 3537 was one of 20 0-4-2 side tanks with outside frames built at Swindon in 1887-88, while the other three were originally 0-4-2 broad gauge saddle tanks but so designed as to be converted for the narrow gauge. To this end these 'convertibles' had double frames and after the abolition of the broad gauge in 1892 they were all rebuilt with side tanks. Of the six-wheeled passenger tank engines the 'Wolverhamptons' outnumbered the 'Swindons' by about two to one. The former were the well-known 0-4-2T ('517' Class) of which there were ten or a dozen in the district; I cannot give the complete list but Nos 217, 529, 533 and 1476 were some of them; Nos 529 and 533 had originally been built with saddle tanks but now had side tanks. The Swindon-built 2-4-0 'Metros' that I recollect seeing at Exeter were Nos 457, 470, 624, 625, 628, 1445, 1455 and 1456.

Coming now to the goods engines, the most modern were Mr Dean's standard 0-6-0 with inside frames and 5ft wheels. I recollect the numbers of only three which I can definitely associate with Exeter, and of these 1896-built No 2489 was daily employed as station pilot; the others, Nos 2309 and 2317, were of the earliest batch built in 1883. They originally had domeless boilers but these had been replaced with boilers having a rather tall dome at the front ring. N. 2489 on the other hand had a large dome on the middle of the boiler and was a somewhat sturdier looking machine. There were also several of the older double-framed goods engines working in the district, including Nos 41, 43, 116, 300, 400, 445, 454, 504 and 712. I seem to remember that one or two of these appeared to be much more ancient-looking than the majority and I think this was mainly due to the fact that they had tall domes of small diameter and raised fireboxes with brass coping; I believe No 400 was one of these. All those I saw had short smokeboxes in 1897 but at least one of the class, No 426, had an extended smokebox that was fitted in 1894, I believe as an experiment.

The saddle tank engines were of two principal types together with sundry odd classes. I recollect three, Nos 1185, 1562 and 1569, of the standard Swindon pattern with double frames and 4ft 6in wheels that were very busy with short-distance goods traffic and shunting. The only saddle tank of the Wolverhampton pattern that I recollect seeing was No 1221 with six 4ft coupled wheels and inside frames; it had been built in 1876 and differed from the others externally in having a painted dome cover. Others of the class numbered in the 1900 series were also seen, and I believe No 1957 was one of them. As regards the miscellaneous types, Nos 1317, 1318 and 1323 were rebuilds of broad gauge engines supplied to the South Devon Railway in 1873 by the Avonside Engine Co, and a peculiarity was that they were domeless. No 1326 was another Avonside engine dated 1872 and was working as an 0-4-2, although originally an 0-6-0 tank.

By the time I left the district five years later there had been considerable developments. Fifteen more singles had been placed in service, Nos 3066 to 3080, and a large number of these put in an appearance. In December 1897 the first of the 'Badmintons' appeared and ten months later saw the advent of the 'Bulldog' engines, an enlarged 'Duke'. The 19 engines which followed had smaller boilers than *Bulldog* herself and some half-dozen of the latter ones came out new with Belpaire fireboxes; Nos 3292-3311 had names over the driving splashers with the exception of No 3310 *Waterford*, which appeared with a domeless boiler with the safety valves in the now familiar position. A combined name, number and date plate was affixed to the cab side sheets. Several of the 'Badmintons' appeared at Exeter but they were not as common as the singles and the 'Dukes'. In October 1899 another new class appeared, commonly known as the 'Camel' Class, while six months later the corresponding express type, designated the 'Atbara' Class, took the road. The singles were still fairly common in 1901 although of the newer batch a few such as Nos 3074-76 were presumably sent to the London end of the line as I never saw them in the west. The 'Dukes' were assisted by the 'Bulldogs' and the 'Camels', the newer engines gradually replacing the older ones so far as the best trains were concerned. Large numbers of the 'Atbaras' were found on the best trains between Exeter and the eastern towns but they did not go west; a down train arriving with a 6ft 8in 4-4-0 would continue its journey behind a 5ft 8in 'Camel' or 'Bulldog' engine.

The external appearance of the express locomotives in 1901 was somewhat plainer than in earlier days. The cast iron chimney introduced on No 3352 Camel became standard for new express engines, though one or two of the batch, notably No 3347 Tregothnan, had a short parallel copper-topped funnel. The lining out was rather less elaborate than before, black bands with only one orange line on each side thereof being standard. Brass firebox copings were painted green and the newer engines had less external brass work than the older types, principally on account of the abolition of the steam dome. The engines, however, still glistened with paint and polish, and most admirers will no doubt agree with me that they looked businesslike and handsome at the same time.

Most, if not all, of the Armstrong 7ft singles had disappeared and were substituted by engines of the 'Achilles' Class, which became available as the number of coupled engines gradually increased. The 7ft engines were not scrapped, however, but rebuilt as goods engines of the '388' Class; they could easily be distinguished by the raised framing over the driving axle. The fireboxes were of the round-topped pattern, for it was not until a couple of years later that the older goods engines began to have Belpaire boxes fitted. The Dean 2-4-0s were now rarely seen but there were several rebuilds of the '3521' Class, which had been rebuilt as 4-4-0 tender engines in the period 1899-1901, retaining the same boilers and wheels as previously; the one I particularly recollect was No 3535.

'A visit to the GWR sheds at Taunton and Exeter in 1920', by 'W.P.K'

While on holiday at Watchet, a very picturesque and old-fashioned village on the Bristol Channel, after a few days I could not resist the call of the locomotive and through the kindness of the Loco Superintendent at Swindon had the pleasure of a visit to Taunton and Exeter sheds. Upon my arrival at Taunton at 8.42am the following were observed in the station doing various duties: No 846 ('517' Class 0-4-2T), No 1795 (0-6-0PT), Nos 1033 and 1397 (0-6-0STs), No 461 ('Metro' 2-4-0T), No 3834 County of Somerset (4-4-0) and No 2987 Bride of Lammermoor ('Saint' Class 4-6-0). I then made my way to the shed where the following were seen: Nos 539 and 834 ('517' 0-4-2Ts), Nos 985 and 1500 ('Metro' 2-4-0Ts), No 1256 (0-6-0ST), Nos 1845, 1876 and 1954 (0-6-0PTs), Nos 2381, 2435 and 2570 (0-6-0 'Dean Goods'), No 4394 (2-6-0), No 4141 Aden ('Badminton' 4-4-0), No 3016 (ex-ROD 2-8-0), No 3342 Bonaventura (a Banbury 'Bulldog' 4-4-0), and 'Saint' 4-6-0s Nos 2916 Saint Benedict, 2949 Stanford Court and 2934 Butleigh Court. Upon my return to the station, the following were noted on goods trains, No 3025 (ex-ROD 2-8-0) and No 4380 (2-6-0).

I then boarded the 10.05am to Exeter hauled by No 2921 Saint Dunstan, arriving 5 minutes late at 10.50am. While waiting 2 hours for a friend I noted Nos 832, 1431 and 1433 ('517' 0-4-2Ts), Nos 863, 1223 and 1932 (0-6-0STs), Nos 1746, 1815 and 2776 (0-6-0PTs), No 2302 (0-6-0 'Dean Goods'), Nos 4300, 4306, 4337 and 4356 (2-6-0 mixed traffic), 'Saints' Nos 2912 Saint Ambrose, 2917 Saint Bernard, 2921 Saint Dunstan, 2922 Saint Gabriel and 2987 Bride of Lammermoor, 'Bulldog' 4-4-0 No 3324 Glastonbury, No 3834 County of Somerset (4-4-0), 'Star' 4-6-0s Nos 4006 Red Star, 4028 King John and 4060 Princess Eugenie, and '41XX' 4-4-0s Nos 4109 Monarch and 4164 Mignonette.

After my friend arrived we made our way to the shed and saw No 1298 (ex-South Devon Railway 2-4-0T), No 1481 ('517' 0-4-2T), Nos 1753 and 1897 (0-6-0PTs), No 2658 (a Laira 'Aberdare' 2-6-0), Nos 4367, 4384 and 5307 (2-6-0s),

During the 1920 visit 2-4-0T No 1300 was seen at Tiverton Junction and No 1298 at Exeter. They were two of three broad gauge 2-4-0STs that were being assembled at the Newton Abbot Factory in 1876 when the SDR was taken over by the GWR; the partly built engines were removed to Swindon and completed as standard gauge 2-4-0Ts. They were allocated to Exeter and shared duties on the Culm Valley branch from Tiverton Junction to Hemyock, which needed flexible lightweight engines to cope with its sharp curves and limited axle-loading. No 1298 was withdrawn in October 1926, but No 1300 survived until May 1934, and is seen in the shed yard at Exeter.

and Nos 2950 *Taplow Court* and 2953 *Titley Court* (both Exeter 'Saint' 4-6-0s). Returning to the station the following were noted: No 1654 (0-6-0PT), Nos 5377 and 5378 (2-6-0s), No 3823 *County of Carnarvon* (4-4-0), 'Saint' No 2998 *Ernest Cunard*, and 'Star' No 4045 *Prince John*.

Upon leaving Exeter by the 5.46pm departure these were noted on the way: No 436 (an old double-framed 'Armstrong' goods) and No 5307 (2-6-0) at Cullompton, No 1300 ('South Devon' 2-4-0T) at Tiverton Junction, and No 4109 *Monarch* ('Badminton' 4-4-0) at Wellington. At Taunton were Nos 626, 975 and 3588 ('Metro' 2-4-0Ts), No 1893 (0-6-0PT), No 511 ('Armstrong' goods) and No 4005 *Polar Star*. Thus concluded a very interesting visit with several additions to my register.

'From Torre to Exeter Central on Saturday 12 June 1943', by Peter W. Gray

In these days of the standardised railway with the minimum of equipment doing the maximum amount of work, it is interesting to look back to this day when I made a visit to Exeter to take a look at the locomotives working through the Southern Railway's Central station. One tends to think of the Great Western as a relatively standardised railway with its vast army of '57XX' Class pannier tanks and fleets of 'Castles', 'Halls' and 'Granges', so it is with some slight surprise that I note the journey from Torre to Exeter and back in 1943 involved the sighting of no fewer than 21 different classes of GWR engine and, although I did not proceed beyond Central station, a further 12 SR classes. Had I gone on to Exmouth Junction shed the class total would certainly have expanded by another five or more.

Leaving Torre behind 'Star' 4-6-0 No 4016 *The Somerset Light Infantry (Prince Albert's)*, 0-6-0PT No 9717 was noted shunting in the yard. At Aller Junction 2-6-2T No 6100 was waiting for a freight to bank and 4-6-0 No 5998 *Trevor Hall* of Laira was about to oblige as it was waiting on a down goods at the signals for us to clear the section. At Newton Abbot local 4-6-0s Nos 6808 *Beenham Grange* and 6822 *Manton Grange* were on view, as well as 2-6-2T No 4516. 2-8-0 No 3863 from Bristol passed through on an up goods before the arrival at Platform No 8 of No 5011 *Tintagel Castle* with the 8.45am from Plymouth to Liverpool. Following No 5011's exit to the shed via the scissors crossing, the Liverpool-bound coaches were propelled slowly forward by the station pilot engine to join the Paignton to Manchester section in Platform No 7. Meanwhile, our train engine had been replaced by 'Castle' No 5061 *Earl of Birkenhead* from Salop on the return half of the 'double-home' working from Shrewsbury to Newton Abbot, the longest regular locomotive working in the country during the war years. The loco was in the immaculate condition usually associated with Shrewsbury engines on this turn and had recently been repainted with 'G crest W' on the tender, replacing the previous 'shirt button' GWR emblem. 0-4-2T No 4866 (now preserved as No 1466) was working the Moretonhampstead to Paignton auto, 0-6-0PT No 7422 was carriage pilot at the east end, and open-cab pannier tank No 1736 was the New Yard pilot. The latter was a veteran '1854' Class 0-6-0T built in 1892 as a saddle tank, converted to a pannier tank in 1924 and destined to be withdrawn in April 1945. The Hackney yard shunters were hidden deep within the yard, but 2-8-0 No 3832 from PDN shed could be seen, while on the up side No 3863 and goods train were waiting in the loop for us to pass. Somewhere between Newton and Exeter we crossed 2-6-0 No 8376 (still then with its weighted front buffer beam), which was probably on the 9.38am from Exeter to Kingswear.

Arrival at Exeter St David's saw the welcome sight of 'Bulldog' Class 4-4-0 No 3335 (then unnamed, but which had been *Tregothnan* until 1930) acting as carriage pilot in Platform No 6. Visible on shed were 0-6-0PT No 3603, 2-8-0 No 4702 from PDN, which was doubtless resting after an overnight trip from London on a fast freight, 2-6-0 No 6397 and 2-6-2T No 5543, which were both based at Exeter. On the down goods avoiding line 2-6-0 No 8358 from Bristol was waiting to pull out with a westbound goods train.

The GWR shed also contained two Southern Railway locomotives, one being 'N' Class 2-6-0 No 1850, probably engaged on one of the regular 'exchange' workings between Exeter and Plymouth over the GWR route. The other was 4-6-0 No 2329 *Stephenson*, which, along with five other members of the seven-strong class, had been on loan to the GWR since late 1941, but were soon to be returned to the Southern Railway; during 1942 *Stephenson* had been a regular

Two 'Moguls' with weighted buffer beams were noted during the 1943 trip. Another of this type, No 8372, is at Platform 3 at St David's while working a down Class 'J' freight in the late 1930s.

visitor to the Kingswear branch on goods workings. Officially these were 'N15X' Class 4-6-0s of the 'Remembrance' Class, which were originally London, Brighton & South Coast Railway 4-6-4Ts that had been converted to 4-6-0 tender engines during the mid-1930s following the electrification of the Brighton Line.

Even in wartime, and despite the Government's best endeavours to discourage unnecessary travel, extra trains had to run on summer Saturdays. Some idea of the level of activity at Exeter Central that day can be gained from my record of 55 different locomotives working that afternoon from 11 different classes. The class which appeared most often was the ever-faithful 'N' Class 2-6-0, the backbone of the West of England services, 13 of which were noted. Exmouth Junction shed had a large allocation of these very useful 'Moguls', often referred to as 'Woolworths' because many were assembled from kits of parts produced at Woolwich Arsenal to relieve unemployment after the 1914-18 war. In those days, when Woolworths was the 3d and 6d store, higher-priced items were often broken down into several 6d parts. The 'Ns' were mainly used on the heavier trains west of Exeter including the loaded ballast hoppers from Meldon Quarry near Okehampton, which needed the combined efforts of four engines to hoist them up the 1 in 37 gradient from St David's to Central.

The next most prolific class was the 'M7' 0-4-4T, ten of which were seen around Central that afternoon. A 105-strong class constructed by the LSWR between 1897 and 1911 at its Nine Elms and Eastleigh Works, they were originally intended for semi-fast main-line work. However, following an accident near Tavistock on a fast train, most were transferred to the London area, returning west later in life to take over from the smaller 'O2' Class 0-4-4Ts on the East Devon branches. In 1943 the class was much in evidence at Exeter, working most of the Exmouth trains and using the bay platforms on either side of the station, and also on station pilot and carriage shunting duties as well as trip goods workings to Riverside yard.

The new 'Merchant Navy' Class 'Pacifics' had taken over the heaviest passenger duties from the N15 'King Arthur' Class 4-6-0s and the first three engines were seen. From the position in which they appear in my notes it is likely that No 21C2 *Union Castle* and No 21C3 *Royal Mail* were on the 9.00am and 11.00am trains from Waterloo respectively, while No 21C1 *Channel Packet* was hauling the 2.30pm departure to Waterloo. While these 'Pacifics' were perfectly capable of handling these heavy wartime trains on the road, getting them on the move was sometimes a problem, especially leaving Exeter Central against the adverse gradient. Their very high boiler pressure of 280lb per square inch made them prone to slipping, though it should be said in fairness that this is a characteristic of most 'Pacific' classes.

The relatively large number of nine 'N15' 'King Arthur' Class 4-6-0s seen indicates that most of the 'run if required' relief trains were running. The first of the improved 'N15' Class 4-6-0s to be built new at Eastleigh Works to the design of R. E. L. Maunsell in 1925 was No 453, and it was decided to name this engine *King Arthur* and No 454 *Queen Guinevere*, with the remainder of the class 'Knights of the Round Table', an apt choice to head trains making for the North Cornwall coast. The engines themselves were, however, too heavy to reach Cornwall, and rarely ventured beyond Exeter Central.

'King Arthur' 4-6-0 No 792 *Sir Hervis de Revel* was seen by the 15-year-old Peter Gray during his visit to Exeter Central in 1943; almost exactly three years later, on a very wet 11 June 1946, the same engine is waiting to leave Platform 3 at Central with the 12.50pm departure to Waterloo. It is painted in wartime black livery and was allocated to Exmouth Junction shed between July 1937 and November 1946, when it was transferred to Nine Elms.

Among the various Knights seen that day were *Sir Kay*, *Sir Galahad* and *Sir Bedivere*, also No 792 *Sir Hervis de Revel*, the latter noted as being fitted with a large multiple-jet blast pipe.

One of the youthful pastimes of the war years was aircraft spotting, occasionally necessary for self-preservation, but normally restricted to the identification of friendly aircraft, and my notebook that afternoon is not immune. Soon after arriving at Exeter Central, after recording that 'L11' Class 4-4-0 No 436 was preparing to take a train out to Barnstaple and that 'El/R' 'Radial' 0-6-2T No 2695 was about to attach some extra coaches to an up train, an Armstrong-Whitworth Whitley bomber lumbered into view towing a Horsa glider, accompanied by two Avro Ansons. The next working at ground level was the appearance of GWR 2-6-0 No 5321 on an 'exchange' working over the SR route from Plymouth. Mention of the 'L11' Class should be coupled with that of the 'K10' Class; both were small-wheeled mixed-traffic 4-4-0s introduced by Drummond in the early years of the 20th century. The 'L11' Class was a development of the 'K10', with a larger firebox and a lengthened wheelbase, and both were used mainly on the Barnstaple line prior to the advent of the Bulleid 'Lightweight' 'Pacifics' in 1945. The 'K10' Class, of which only No 392 was seen that day on a short goods train, were withdrawn between 1947 and 1951, and the last of the 'L11' Class a year later. However, in 1943 the 'L11s' were still very active, with six seen that afternoon, mainly on Barnstaple line trains, which they brought up to Central, handing over there to a 4-6-0 or 4-6-2 after the addition of the Plymouth portion. Similarly, in the down direction the arrival of an express from Waterloo would be preceded by the arrival of the two or three engines, which were to take its portions westwards after the train engine had detached to run back through the station towards Exmouth Junction depot.

The express 4-4-0s of the 'T9' Class have not yet had a mention, but they were well in evidence assisting the 'Ns' on the Plymouth and Padstow services, although between the arrival of 'M7' Class 0-4-4T No 323 and that of 'T9' Class

Closely observed trains

4-4-0 No 727 from Plymouth there must have been a long gap since my notebook then records the passing of seven different aircraft types: a Bristol 'Beaufighter', two more Whitleys, a 'Flying Fortress' Mark II, a Vickers-Armstrong 'Wellington', an American 'Thunderbolt' fighter, a 'Spitfire', and finally a 'Whirlwind'. Later, while 'N15' Class 4-6-0 No 791 *Sir Uwaine* was replacing 'N' Class 2-6-0 No 1829 on a Waterloo-bound train, a 'Swordfish' flew over followed a few minutes later by two 'Typhoons'. The only engines not mentioned thus far are two 'U' Class 2-6-0s working the stopping service to Yeovil, and a solitary 'HI5' Class 4-6-0, No 334, pressed into service on a Saturday relief train.

A formation of 13 'Spitfires' was observed on my way back down to St David's, where another 'Bulldog' Class 4-4-0 had appeared, No 3451 *Pelican*, probably down from Taunton on a stopping train. Two strange 'Manors' had also arrived, possibly on cross-country freight workings – No 7802 *Bradley Manor* from Bristol and No 7810 *Draycott Manor* from Banbury – the latter quite a rare visitor. The journey home on the down Liverpool behind 4-6-0 No 4077 *Chepstow Castle* was uneventful, observing 0-6-0ST No 1362 outside Newton Abbot Works, and continuing home to Torre behind 2-6-2T No 5157.

'Visitors on the "Southern" in 1953', by E. S. Youldon

Saturday 16 May 1953 proved to be a day of unusual interest as all 30 of the 'Merchant Navy' 'Pacifics' had been temporarily withdrawn from service during the previous week following No 35020 *Bibby Line* breaking an axle at Crewkerne on 24 April. I decided to call for a friend on my way to St David's station and he informed me that he had previously seen New England's (Peterborough) 'V2' 2-6-2 No 60908 working on a Waterloo to Exeter express, and that 'Britannia' No 70024 *Vulcan* had been transferred to Exmouth Junction from Laira. They had been seen on the 9.00am from Waterloo and the up 'ACE' respectively, with the former currently working off Nine Elms shed.

Hearing this, I decided to go first to Central station to wait for the down 'ACE' before going on to St David's. However, the 9.00am Waterloo produced No 35018 *British India Line*, which had just returned to traffic after a check-up, and the down 'ACE' had diesel No 10201; unfortunately I didn't know at the time that this train was running in two parts. While at Central I noticed that the Exmouth branch trains were largely in the hands of 'M7' 0-4-4Ts and Class 2 2-6-2Ts, and while I was there 'King Arthur' No 30454 *Queen Guinevere* worked in on the 2.03pm stopper from Salisbury.

'Britannia' 4-6-2 No 70017 *Arrow* is climbing towards Exmouth Junction with the 2.30pm Exeter Central to Waterloo service on 23 May 1953. Eric Youldon reported having an impressive run on this train to Axminster. The building beyond the marshalling yard on the right is part of the concrete works. *J. H. Bamsey*

I caught the 'ACE' to St David's and we were halted by the signals just outside the tunnel. On looking out of the carriage window while we were stopped, I saw the restaurant car section off the 'ACE' being backed out of the down platform and into the carriage sidings by a pilot; this meant that the train was running in two parts and I immediately regretted not waiting. At St David's I learnt that the second part would be arriving behind Cardiff Canton's No 70028 *Royal Star*, and also that two more 'Britannias', including No 70029 *Shooting Star*, were expected to transfer to the SR. The only item of interest seen at St David's was a Class 3 2-6-2T on the Plymouth portion of the 4.30pm to Waterloo.

Knowing that *Royal Star* would be at 'The Junction', I decided to go back to Central for the evening to see whether it would appear there for one of the up trains. However, the 5.53pm departure was diesel No 10000, the up milk was No 35006 *Peninsula & Oriental S. N. Co*, another engine that had returned to traffic after been checked, and the 7.50pm was No 34001 *Exeter*. The down 3.00pm Waterloo had another Exmouth Junction 'WC', No 34021 *Dartmoor*, the down 6.05pm stopper was 'S15' No 30827, and 'O2' No 30199 was busily shunting about, bearing a 71F (Ryde IoW) shed plate!

I decided to go to Exmouth Junction to see the elusive No 70028, and it was there with No 70023 *Venus* from Old Oak Common immediately behind it; both locos had a peg welded on to the right-hand (viewed from the front) smoke deflector strut to enable them take a Bournemouth route smokebox disc. Feltham 'S15s' Nos 30507 and 30513 were also on shed, the former under repair, and also there were Bath 'West Country' 'Pacifics' Nos 34040 *Crewkerne* and 34041 *Wilton*, and Wadebridge's 'O2' No 30203.

*

On the following Saturday, 23 May 1953, the late Eric Youldon did not write a report, but did note the following workings:

- Doncaster's 'V2' No 60896 was on the first part of the 9.00am from Waterloo, with 'Battle of Britain' No 34049 *Anti-Aircraft Command* on the second part.
- 'King Arthur' No 30448 *Sir Tristram* worked the 2.03pm stopper from Salisbury.
- A most interesting variety on the three parts of the 'ACE': Nos 35021 *New Zealand Line*, 70029 *Shooting Star* and another Doncaster 'V2' No 60928 respectively.

He caught the 2.30pm Exeter Central to Waterloo train, and had a 'glorious run' to Axminster behind No 70017 *Arrow*. Sightings included 'S15' No 30505 on an up goods train and '0415' 4-4-2T No 30584 working the Lyme Regis branch before he returned to Exeter on the Brighton to Plymouth train, which was hauled by No 34026 *Yes Tor*. The 4.30pm Exeter to Waterloo was powered by the returning 'V2' No 60896, and the two parts of the 3.00pm from Waterloo were hauled by Nos 10000 and 34020 *Seaton* respectively.

*

'Exeter St David's on Saturday 6 June 1959', by Peter W. Gray

This was the last but one Saturday of the winter timetable and was one of those damp summer days with the air full of what in other parts they call 'Scotch mist', a suitable day for taking cover under the awnings of Exeter St David's station. My journey from Newton Abbot behind 4-6-0 No 7018 *Dryslwyn Castle* with Driver Swain at the regulator was sadly typical of the period, with the 12.22pm to Swansea managing a top speed of 50mph by Teignmouth gasworks, thus cleverly avoiding the need to slow for the speed restriction then in force along the coastal section. A

During the June 1959 trip, auto-fitted 0-6-0PT No 5412 was noted on station pilot duties at St David's, and it was so employed exactly one week later on the 13th. Here it is in Hyde Park sidings while 2-6-2T No 5524 is standing at Platform 2 with the 11.45am Exe Valley train to Dulverton, and 4-6-0 No 4955 *Plaspower Hall* is waiting to leave from Platform 5. The '54XX' Class were rare in the far South West, but No 5412 was transferred from Taunton to Laira in 1942 to work the Yealmpton branch when it was reopened to passengers for wartime traffic. It later moved back to Taunton, but was based in Exeter from November 1954 for duty on the Teign Valley line. Peter Gray remembered being told that this was because its cab layout suited the disability of an Exeter driver who regularly worked on that line. It remained at Exeter until it was condemned in April 1962.
R. A. Lumber

At 1.23pm on a wet Saturday 6 June 1959 at Exeter St David's the fireman is standing on the tender of Laira's 4-6-0 No 6016 (which is missing its right-hand *King Edward V* nameplate) as he shovels coal forward. Train No 415 is the 9.30am from Paddington to Plymouth. On the left Exeter's 'large Prairie' No 4136 has attached to the front of the seven-coach 1.25pm stopper to Paignton. *Peter W. Gray*

maximum of 57mph was achieved beyond Dawlish Warren and again at Exminster, before we were checked by a long p.w. restriction for a mile past Cotfield signal box, to arrive at Exeter almost exactly 30 minutes after leaving Newton Abbot. Hardly the stuff of which records are made!

Already in the station was 4-6-0 No 4083 *Abbotsbury Castle* on the 7.30am from Paddington to Paignton, over 40 minutes late. On shed, among the usual Exeter residents were Swindon-built LMS Class 8F 2-8-0 No 48471 and another much more recent Swindon product, the brand-new BR Standard Class 9F 2-10-0 No 92207. Incidentally, a visit to Swindon on the following day found No 92209 complete in 'A' Shop and the frames set up for Nos 92210-12, while across the traverser 'Warship' Class diesel-hydraulics from D807 to D819 were in various stages of completion. Back at St David's on the Saturday afternoon an engine that had once worked regularly on the Teign Valley line, 0-6-0PT No 5412, had by 1959 been relegated to carriage pilot duties as the Teign Valley route had closed 12 months earlier.

An up Southern goods behind 'N' Class 2-6-0 No 31836 halted briefly on the through road, while 'M7' Class 0-4-4T No 30025 came up behind as banker and the two left noisily as 2-6-2T No 5150 arrived on the 12.30pm stopper from Newton Abbot. 4-6-0 No 6016 *King Edward V* was next to arrive at 1.20pm on train No 415, the 9.30am from Paddington to Plymouth. It was temporarily bereft of its right-hand nameplate, a most unusual sight at that time, but this was to become commonplace a few years later when the plates had begun to acquire 'collector' value and were removed to prevent their being stolen. After spending 4 minutes at Platform No 1 while the fireman pulled forward some decent coal from the back of the tender, the dining car was watered and the coach wheels were tapped, the 'King' left as soon as the line was cleared following the arrival of 'N' Class 2-6-0 No 31839 on the Plymouth portion of the 9.00am from Waterloo.

Meanwhile, Exeter-based 2-6-2T No 4136 had attached to the front of the seven-coach 1.25pm down stopper to Paignton, and she left immediately following the passage of North British 'Warship' Class diesel-hydraulic No D602 *Bulldog*, which powered through non-stop on the down 'Cornish Riviera Express'. On the other side of the station, 2-6-0 No 6338 had come off shed to head the five-coach 1.44pm 'all stations' (except Stoke Canon and Sampford Peverell) to Taunton, but it was to be 1.56pm and seven train movements later before she could get away. These included 4-6-0 No 6021 *King Richard II* on a down Paddington to Newquay extra, 'Battle of Britain' 4-6-2 No 34019 *141 Squadron* on the Torrington and Ilfracombe portion of the 9.00am Waterloo, Yeovil-based 'U' Class 'Mogul' No 31613 running light, 4-6-0 No 6027 *King Richard I* on a relief to the up 'Cornish Riviera', 4-6-0 No 5040 *Stokesay Castle* steaming through on the 10.15am Paddington to Kingswear, and ex-shops 'Warship' Class No D805 *Benbow*, which roared past with the up 'Cornish Riviera Express'. Somehow, between these movements, 2-6-2T No 5546 had raced down the main line from Stoke Canon to arrive 1 minute early with an Exe Valley branch train, the 1.15pm from Tiverton.

Another fifteen trains later the up and down 'Cornishman' expresses crossed in the station at 2.47pm, the former hauled by 4-6-0 No 7006 *Lydford Castle* and the latter by another 'Castle', No 5048 *Earl of Devon*, which took on 4-6-0 No 6988 *Swithland Hall* as pilot engine. An interesting movement later in the afternoon was when the up non-stop 11.30am Penzance to Marsh Ponds, Bristol, empty coaching stock train, hauled by 4-6-0 No 5092 *Tresco Abbey*, was diverted away from the station and used the up goods avoiding line. My return train to Newton Abbot, the down 'Royal Duchy' at 5.10pm, was the 60th train movement since arriving at Exeter at 12.58pm, and 'Warship' Class No D801 *Vanguard* improved on the performance of the 'Castle' by only 5 minutes, some indication of the speed restrictions in force at that time between Powderham and Shaldon Bridge.

Aller Junction 5, 114

17. A chronology of some events since nationalisation

On Sunday 12 April 1953 two 'Ian Allan Locospotters Club' excursions ran from Waterloo to Exeter Central using 'Pacifics' Nos 34010 *Sidmouth* and 35013 *Blue Funnel*, and two further trips were organised in connection with these that were scheduled to be hauled by '0415' Class 4-4-2Ts. In the event only one was available, and 'O2' 0-4-4T No 30199 hauled the first train from Central to Sidmouth Junction, then over the two Exmouth branches. '0415' No 30583 worked the second train in the opposite direction and the two trains passed at Exmouth. Usually restricted to the Lyme Regis branch, this was probably the first time in at least 30 years that an Adams 'Radial Tank' was seen on these branches. Here the former East Kent Railway No 5 is arriving back at Central while a Bulleid 'Pacific' blows off at the end of Platform 3. *J. H. Bamsey*

The third SR diesel-electric No 10203 had an improved engine rated at 2,000hp. Construction was completed in March 1954 and several test runs culminated in it working a 12-coach train from Waterloo to Exeter Central on 6 May; the return working is seen leaving Central on the following day. *J. H. Bamsey*

At 11.40pm on 4 April 1955 4-6-2 No 34050 *Royal Observer Corps* was entering Exmouth Junction yard with the 7.45pm freight from Yeovil Junction when it collided with the yard shunter, No 30954, causing damage to the frames, right-hand cylinders and valve gear of the 'Z'; the 'Pacific' and some trackwork were also damaged. Re-railing was not completed until the following day after the engines had been towed apart; both then went to Eastleigh Works for repair. About a week later 'Z' No 30956 was temporarily transferred from Brighton to cover for No 30954.
Author's collection

Due to its legendary exploits in May 1904, when it was claimed that it reached a speed of 102.3mph while descending Wellington bank (at which time it was allocated to Exeter shed), the GWR's 4-4-0 No 3440 *City of Truro* found a home in the old York Railway Museum in 1930. After it emerged from there in 1957 it was overhauled at Swindon and used on special trains, and on 23 May 1958 piloted 'Castle' No 5075 *Wellington* to Exeter on the 5.30am from Paddington to be in position for such a duty. Two days later on Whit Sunday it hauled an excursion from Exeter to Penzance and back, sponsored by *Amateur Photographer* magazine with prizes awarded for the best photos taken on the day. The six-coach train is pictured approaching the Clapperbrook Lane overbridge on the outward journey; the fields on the left are now covered by the Marsh Barton trading estate. *John Stredwick*

A chronology of some events since nationalisation

CITY of EXETER HOLIDAY EXPRESS

5 days travel - 5 different destinations

From **EXETER** (St. David's)

750 MILES for 45/0 INCLUSIVE

To
- PLYMOUTH (NAVY DAY AT PLYMOUTH) . . . MONDAY
- WESTON-SUPER-MARE . . . TUESDAY
- ILFRACOMBE . . . WEDNESDAY
- BOURNEMOUTH . . . THURSDAY
- FALMOUTH . . . FRIDAY

Monday, AUGUST 5th to Friday, AUGUST 9th, 1957, inclusive

Your seat reserved in a special Cafeteria Car train to a different resort each day

Book Early — Accommodation is Limited

BRITISH RAILWAYS

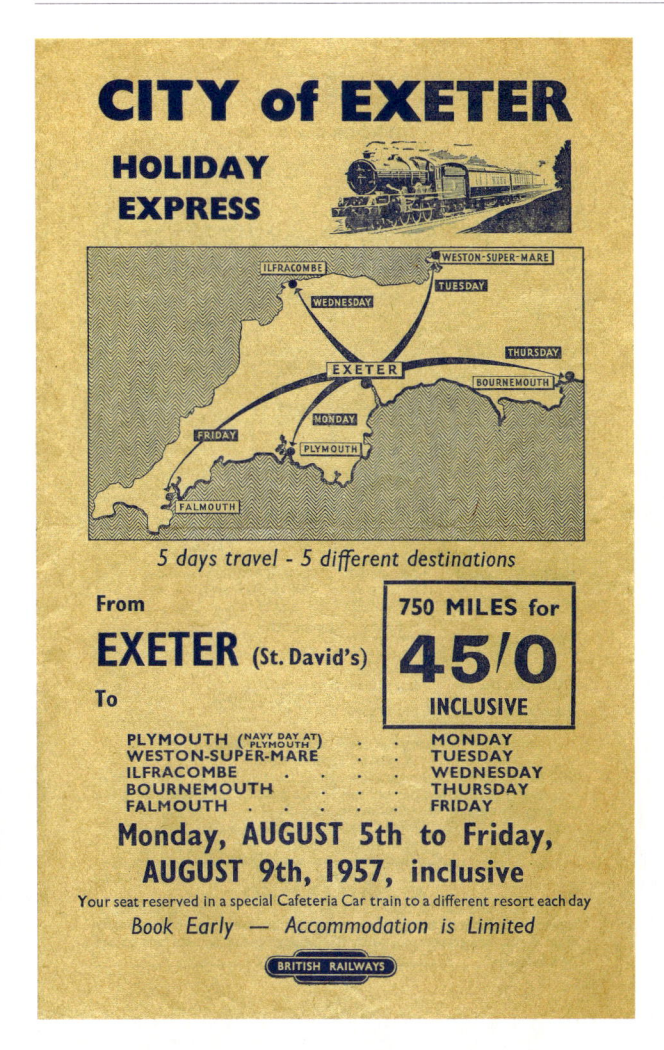

In 1956 the WR arranged programmes of excursion trains from eight cities to coincide with their industrial holiday periods; these were marketed as the 'City of … Holiday Express' and catered for stay-at-home holidaymakers by taking them to different places on five successive weekdays. Passengers were allocated the same reserved seat each day and on some trips supplementary motor coach tours were offered. The trains used otherwise under-employed carriages that normally only saw use on a few weekends each year. The scheme was a success and in 1957 it was extended to additional places, including Exeter.

In the 1958 schedule one of the 'City of Exeter Holiday Express' trains was hauled by ex-LSWR 'T9' No 30709 and ex-SR 'U' No 31790, and on 29 July took the trippers to Plymouth; it is believed that the outward run was made via Okehampton, but the excursion returned by the WR route and was recorded from the platform end at Cornwood station as it crossed Slade Viaduct. On the next day No 30709 was paired with 'N' No 31838 for a trip to Bude. *Peter W. Gray*

The first of the WR's new diesel-hydraulics, No D600 *Active*, first reached Exeter on 19 March 1958 while working a test train from Swindon to Plymouth. No D601 *Ark Royal* began appearing in June, and by early August was employed on a diagram covering the up 'Cornish Riviera Express' between Plymouth and Paddington, with which it is seen entering St David's on the 6th; it was then scheduled to work the 6.30pm Paddington to Bristol service and complete its day by hauling the 2.55pm train from Manchester between Bristol and Plymouth. *R. A. Lumber*

A celebration was held at Exeter Central on 19 July 1960 to commemorate the centenary of the Salisbury to Exeter route, and Beattie 2-4-0WT No 30587, fresh from overhaul at Eastleigh Works, was coupled to three coaches, including an ex-LSWR two-car 'gate' set normally used on the Yeovil Town shuttles, for a short trip from Exmouth Junction to Central, with passengers in period costume picked up at St James Park. The engine was then placed on exhibition in the goods yard with 4-4-2T 'Radial' No 30582 and 'Merchant Navy' 4-6-2 No 35003 *Royal Mail*. *R. A. Lumber*

A chronology of some events since nationalisation

On Saturday 26 August 1961 'Castle' 4-6-0 No 5055 *Earl of Eldon* is leaving St David's at 2.54pm with a Swansea to Penzance train. Five days earlier an embankment slip between Patney & Chirton and Lavington had affected some 200 feet of the WR main line and caused disruption for several weeks. Most trains were diverted over the single line through Devizes, or via Bristol. The SR was asked to provide paths for some trains on the final two summer Saturdays of the year, including the 26th. As reversal at St David's was ruled impractical on a busy Saturday, three trains each way were re-routed between Reading and Plymouth via Basingstoke, Exeter Central and Okehampton. On the left 'Warship' No D867 *Zenith* is waiting to climb to Central with one of these, the up 'Cornish Riviera Express'. *Peter W. Gray*

A dreary day for a celebrity sees the holder of the world speed record for steam locos, 'A4' 4-6-2 No 60022 *Mallard*, arriving at Exeter Central on 24 February 1963 with the 9.05am Waterloo to Paddington via Exeter LCGB 'West Countryman Ltd' railtour. The 'A4' will come off here and be replaced by a pair of ex-GWR 'Prairie' tanks for a trip to Tiverton Junction via Tiverton; then some of the railtourers will join a brake van tour to Hemyock hauled by 0-4-2T No 1450. In the meantime *Mallard* adjourned to Exmouth Junction for servicing before running light to Tiverton Junction to take the charter back to London.
R. A. Lumber

In the steam era the cement trains from Westbury were normally hauled throughout by an ex-GWR engine, often a 'Hall' 4-6-0 or a '2800' Class 2-8-0, although other types appeared, including 9F 2-10-0 No 92005 on 11 June 1963. There was some consternation at St David's on 2 May 1964 when 2-8-0 No 4707 arrived, as this class had never been cleared to work to Central. Eventually after a delay authority was given for it to proceed and it is seen attacking the bank with BR 2-6-4T No 80064 as pilot; pannier tanks Nos 4694 and 3759 were on the rear. After reversing its train into Central's goods yard No 4707 was hastily dispatched back to St David's light engine. Only four of the nine-strong class were still in service and all would be withdrawn within days; it has been suggested that this was the final revenue-earning duty performed by one of these engines. *John Attwood*

BR Standard 2-6-2T No 82042 is cut off its train at Exeter Central in heavy rain after arriving with the 13.52 stopper from Axminster on 22 May 1965; the conditions are appropriate for the occasion as this was the very last rostered passenger working for an Exmouth Junction-allocated engine. *R. A. Lumber*

A chronology of some events since nationalisation

On 2 October 1965 an 'Ian Allan' special train hauled by 4-6-0 No 4079 *Pendennis Castle* was the final steam departure from Paddington to the South West. At St David's the train continued to Totnes behind 2-6-2T No 4555 and 0-6-0 No 3205, which were being delivered to their new home on the nascent Dart Valley heritage railway. In a typical scene from the time, enthusiasts are using every vantage point to photograph the engines as they back on to the charter – today's Health & Safety Executive would have palpitations at seeing this! 'Warship' No D841 *Roebuck* returned the special to St David's, where in the second picture *Pendennis Castle* is seen waiting to return to Paddington. *C. M. Parsons/R. A. Lumber*

A track gang stands aside as pannier tank No 6412 hauls dead classmate No 6430 towards Blackboy Tunnel on 4 June 1966; the withdrawn engines were en route from storage at Exmouth Junction shed to Totnes for use on the Dart Valley Railway. *R. A. Lumber*

Above: On 24 August 1968 Birmingham RCW Co Type 3 No D6545 failed near the top of the bank on the 12.30 St David's to Waterloo train, with the rear coaches still in the tunnel; the resulting congestion blocked all the platforms at both St David's and Central. The guard protected the failed train at the rear with detonators, and eventually Nos D6337 and D6333 were hand-signalled up the bank by the guard, exploding the detonators on the way. After propelling the train to Central, the bankers removed No D6545 to the goods yard (as pictured), but with all roads blocked they then had to move the stranded train into Bay Platform 4 to enable the relief engine, 'Warship' No D814 *Dragon*, to run from St David's. The train eventually left 73 minutes late. *Dragon* had been scheduled to work an Ilfracombe train, but this left an hour late behind the two Type 2s. *C. H. S. Owen*

Above right: On 23 May 1970 No D846 *Steadfast* was seen to be on fire when passing Stoke Canon with the 09.30 Paddington to Paignton train; it was stopped at Cowley Bridge Junction where the ferocity of the fire prevented the loco from being uncoupled. After three fire engines attended and extinguished the flames, No 814 *Dragon* (again!) hauled the train to St David's where it removed *Steadfast* before taking the train forward. *DHM*

Just after a heavy downpour, the sun illuminates 'Warship' No 812 *The Royal Naval Reserve 1859-1959* as it is coupled to the 16.00 departure from St David's to Waterloo on Sunday 3 October 1971; this was the final day for 'Warship' operation of these services. *DHM*

A chronology of some events since nationalisation 211

In the 1979-80 football season Exeter City FC was in the old League Division Three, with Sheffield Wednesday one of its opponents; the home game with the 'Owls' was on 26 April 1980 when two 'Footex' charters were hauled by 'Peak' Class locos including No 45013, which is arriving in Central station. The 'Grecians' completed the double over their illustrious opponents that season, winning both games 1-0. *DHM*

The 09.30 Salisbury to St David's (and back) test train on 14 May 1981 was topped-and-tailed by No 33112 and, unusually, electro-diesel No 73103. The latter is leading as it passes Exeter Central on the return run with the High Speed Track Recording Coach No DB999550 and EMU set No 6103. *C. M. Parsons*

Former Exmouth Junction BR 2-6-4T No 80064 was one of the many condemned engines fortunate to be sold to the Woodham Brothers scrapyard at Barry, from where it was acquired for preservation. It was restored at Buckfastleigh on the Dart Valley Railway, but the owners decided to move it to the Bluebell Railway in 1984. It was hauled as the 07.54 Paignton (Torbay Steam Railway) to the Pinhoe grain silo siding by No 31187 on 15 March and two days later is being loaded on to a lorry for the journey to Sussex.
R. A. Lumber

Probably the most unusual working on a service train during the diesel era occurred on 1 September 1984 when Type 5 No 58002 was provided at Birmingham to assist the 12.20 Liverpool to Penzance HST after the power cars (Nos 43131 and 43149) had failed. At that time the '58s' were largely restricted to coal work in the Midlands and the driver was a Saltley-based man throughout, with guidance from conductors. The train is seen leaving St David's, but unfortunately the '58' later failed near Ivybridge with a brake pipe fault and the train only reached Plymouth after the rear power car had been coaxed back into life.
C. M. Parsons

A chronology of some events since nationalisation

Many enthusiasts today are nostalgic for BR's 'blue era', but that period could be quite drab, particularly as the locos and stock were often dirty. The appearance of Class 118 unit No P460 was quite revolutionary when it was finished in British Telecom yellow livery for advertising purposes. It was launched on a dismal day in February 1985 when it made a promotional run from Exeter to Liskeard, but is seen on a far nicer day two months later on 19 April while leaving St David's as the 18.17 departure for Honiton. *C. M. Parsons*

The motley collection of first-generation DMUs that was transferred in to replace the 'Skipper' units in 1987 showed their age and were often unreliable. To maintain services a failure might be dragged by whatever loco was available; in the Exeter area this often meant using a freight engine or a Departmental Class 50 loco that could usually be found on shed. On 3 August 1990 No 50042 *Triumph* is arriving at St David's with the 17.30 Central to Barnstaple train, comprising hybrid Class101/108 DMU No P870. Local management also unofficially procured some coaches to provide cover for failures; when not in use they were kept well out of sight so as not to be seen by higher bureaucracy and hence were known as the 'Secret Set'! *C. M. Parsons*

Steam returned to the route between Yeovil Junction and Exeter Central in 1992 when several charters were organised. As a prelude to this, 'West Country' No 34027 *Taw Valley* and BR Standard 4-6-0 No 75069 worked a 09.11 Eastleigh to Exeter Central special on 10 June 1992 to test clearances, and the locos are seen being serviced in the goods yard after arrival; most of the track in the yard had been lifted two months before. *DHM*

The last scheduled loco-hauled trains over the Waterloo to Exeter line ran on 10 July 1993. No 47716 *Duke of Edinburgh's Award* is approaching Pinhoe station with the final working from Exeter, the 13.46 St David's to Waterloo service. *DHM*

A chronology of some events since nationalisation

In May 1994 a Rail Fair was organised in Exeter to commemorate the 150th anniversary of the opening of the first railway to reach the city. Associated features over several days included railtours hauled by both steam and diesel locomotives, but the main event was an exhibition in Riverside yard on 1 and 2 May, where about 40 locos were displayed. About half were BR engines, including electric locos far from any overhead power supplies, and the rest were privately owned, including nine steam engines. About 35,000 people attended the two-day event, but on the previous day a photographer's afternoon was arranged when around 400 were able to record the exhibits that had been thoughtfully positioned for this purpose. Two steam stars on parade on 30 April were Bulleid 'Pacifics' Nos 34105 *Swanage* and 35005 *Canadian Pacific*, the latter a former Exmouth Junction engine, which contrast with more modern power in the shape of Rail Express Systems No 47744 and two heavy haul freight engines, BR's No 60033 *Anthony Ashley Cooper* and Mendip Rail's No 59102 *Village of Chantry*. An even greater contrast was provided by Peckett 0-4-0ST No 2031, which was built for Exeter Gas Works for £2,150; it arrived there in May 1942 and almost immediately suffered minor damage when the works was bombed. It was preserved in 1969 and is based on the South Devon Railway, where it was named *Ashley*. *All DHM*

The original timber bridge used to carry the down line over the River Exe south of St David's station and the later 1861 iron girder bridge for the up line were both replaced by parallel steel girder structures in 1896. By 1997 new bridges were needed and were installed over successive weekends; the down one was first and is seen on the 12 October as work was nearing completion.

On the next day power car No 43122 is leading the Virgin HST that had arrived as the 09.43 York to Exeter St David's service over the new bridge; the old up bridge is still in use, but its replacement is on the left ready to be moved into position over the following weekend.

The new up bridge is in position on 24 October as No 60036 crosses the Exe with 6C20, the 13.50 Newport ADJ to St Blazey 'Enterprise' freight, which comprises just two empty VGA vans. *All DHM*

When an HST suffered a power car failure, a loco usually assisted the train over the South Devon banks rather than rely on just one operational power car. If the failure occurred in the Exeter area help was often provided from there using any available loco; for most of the 1990s there was usually at least one Class 37 on the depot for use on engineering trains, and this would be used in such emergencies. This practice continued into the privatisation era when EWS still hired-in GW Exeter drivers for certain duties and hence both a loco and driver could be available. On Saturday 13 June 1998 former Scottish engine No 37025 *Inverness TMD* was used to assist the 08.14 Edinburgh to Newquay train after power cars Nos 43084 and 43162 had failed, and on this occasion the engine worked the train through to Newquay; it is pictured on the viaduct as it approaches St Thomas station. *DHM*

The arrangement referred to in the previous photo ended in September 1999 when EWS ceased to base engines in Exeter or hire in local men. In addition to a Class 37 being no longer available, the last Class 08 shunter outstationed in Exeter was also removed, and any shunting thereafter has been done by the train loco. No 08792 has been loaded on to a lorry during the evening of the 7th and will depart for Cardiff the next morning. *DHM*

Described by some as 'the world's most famous locomotive', 'A3' 4-6-2 No 4472 *Flying Scotsman* is illuminated by the setting sun at about 15.05 as it storms past Riverside yard on 29 December 1999 with the 'Centenarian' charter, which it hauled between Yeovil Junction and Didcot. *DHM*

No 47840 *North Star* is bearing a 'Cross Country Locomotive Farewell' headboard as it leads No 47847 *Brian Morrison/Railway World Magazine* on the 08.46 Penzance to Manchester service near the village of Rewe, about 4 miles east of Exeter, on 19 August 2002. This was the very last weekday Cross Country locomotive working and the passengers transferred to a 'Voyager' DMU in Birmingham to complete their journey. The engines were among a number given 'retro' liveries for the final months of these services. One Saturday loco diagram did continue until the end of the summer timetable. *DHM*

A chronology of some events since nationalisation

In the early hours of 18 July 2003 single unit No 153370 split the points while entering the depot at St David's, trapping four DMUs for about 8 hours and causing a number of cancellations. In the morning, standby engine No 47784 re-railed the unit by using a chain to pull it back on to the track; although somewhat primitive, the procedure proved effective! *DHM*

After running for about 150 years, the final departures for the Royal Mail Travelling Post Office trains took place on 9 January 2004. No 67007 is waiting at St David's at about 22.50 with the last up Cornish TPO, the 19.35 Penzance to Bristol Parkway, which is suitably adorned with a makeshift headboard. *DHM*

On 8 July 2007 a railtour was scheduled to run between Waterloo and Clapham Junction via Exeter St David's to mark 40 years since the end of steam on the Southern Region, although that event actually happened on the Bournemouth line. The 'Southern Sunset' was hauled by 4-6-0 No 850 *Lord Nelson* and is seen at Pinhoe; the land on the left was formerly the site of the grain silo, which had been demolished in 1989. Unfortunately the engine's brick arch later collapsed and the train was terminated at Westbury. *DHM*

A different way for a train to pass over Red Cow level crossing! After privatisation it seems that it was often both easier and cheaper to ferry stock by road, and on 29 September 2007 No 153372 is on its way to Eastleigh Works for refurbishment work. *DHM*

The track through Platform 1 at Exeter St David's was relaid on 15 March 2009 with Hanson-owned No 59104 *Village of Great Elm* used by EWS to haul a ballast train from Westbury. *DHM*

On 13 November 2011 the formation through Platform 2 at Exeter Central has been prepared for replacement rail and No 66110 is easing 'wrong line' past Platform 3 with a ballast train; grabs are waiting to unload it. *DHM*

The future arrived at St David's on 3 October 2016 when a Hitachi InterCity Express Train made its debut on a trial run from Stoke Gifford to Plymouth; it was East Coast 'Azuma' set No 800101, as none of the new GWR trains were yet in service. In the background the old order in the form of HST power par No 43132 is waiting to leave as the 20.35 Paddington to Plymouth service. *DHM*

The trackwork at Exmouth Junction was renewed during a week-long possession in October 2020, and on the 28th Nos 66148 *Maritime Intermodal Seven* and 66034 are slowly running through the worksite with a ballast train. Beyond the signal box a housing estate has been built on the site of the Down Yard. *DHM*

Index

Alphington 48-49, 175
Alphington Road Goods Depot 23, 48, 150-151, 160, 176
Ashton 46
Axminster 25, 93-94, 103, 139, 142-143

Bampton 45, 47
Barnstaple 25-26, 37, 39-40, 43, 45, 71, 73, 85, 88, 91, 96, 98, 100-101, 141, 143, 145, 162, 164, 170, 188, 190
Beeching, Dr Richard 38, 128, 139, 145, 166, 168, 171, 173
Bere Alston 110
Birmingham 131
Blackboy Tunnel 26-28, 34, 133
Bradford 123
Bridgwater 147
Brighton 100, 127, 137-138, 141-142, 182
Bristol 10, 12, 26, 64, 77, 80-81, 85-86, 106-108, 112, 114-116, 118, 124, 128, 132, 147, 167
Bristol & Exeter Railway 10-14, 44, 50, 77, 116, 146-147, 180
Broad Clyst 25, 140
Brunel, Isambard Kingdom 10
Bude branch 88, 91, 98, 102, 112, 134
Budleigh Salterton 34, 37, 104, 160

Callington branch 102
Christow 46-49, 51, 149
Chudleigh 47, 108
City Basin branch 51, 58, 78, 149-150, 173-177
Clyst St Mary & Digby Halt 34-35, 40
Clyst Viaduct 36-37, 43
Cornwood (Slade Viaduct) 205
Cotfield 52, 59
Cowley Bridge Junction 15, 17, 25, 44, 50, 64-65, 111, 123, 125, 127, 180-186
Cranbrook 143
Crediton 10, 25-26, 50, 64-67, 134, 145, 158, 180
Cullompton 122, 143, 147, 181
Dawlish 12, 33, 47, 124, 129, 132
Digby & Sowton 38, 40-42
Dulverton 28, 44-45
Dunball 147
Exeter Ship Canal 8, 10, 148-149, 173

Exeter Central 2-3, 8, 9, 17, 30-32, 35-39, 59, 62-65, 71-76, 98-100, 103-104, 108-111, 113-114, 137-145, 148, 160-162, 164-165, 169, 171, 173, 191, 198-200, 203, 206-208, 211, 214, 221
Exeter Queen Street 10, 14, 25-26, 28-30, 34-35, 59, 69, 88, 133-137, 157
Exeter Railway Junction 46, 48, 58, 174
Exeter Riverside 39, 52, 72-73, 82-83, 85, 102, 148, 150-157, 160, 164-167, 170-179, 181, 189, 215, 218
Exeter St Davids 1, 7-8, 10-19, 22, 24-26, 31, 36, 38-40, 44-47, 49-59, 64, 66-67, 69-87, 98, 102, 106-108, 110, 112, 114-133, 138-140, 142-151, 153, 157, 160, 164, 166-167, 169-171, 176, 180-183, 187-188, 190, 192-194, 200-202, 206-210, 212-213, 216-217, 219-222
Exeter St Thomas 13-15, 17, 20-23, 31, 51, 118, 124, 129, 131-132, 149, 170, 217
Exminster 14, 33, 124-125, 180
Exmouth branch 21, 26, 28-30, 32-43, 46, 71, 73, 87, 91, 103, 115, 132, 143, 149, 162, 169, 203
Exmouth Junction 26, 32, 34-38, 40, 59-61, 66-67, 70-73, 76, 84, 88-106, 108-109, 112-115, 133, 140-141, 152, 157-161, 163-165, 170, 172-173, 178-179, 188, 199-200, 204, 209-210, 222
Exton (and Woodbury Road) 33, 37-39, 43
Great Western Railway 10-14, 44, 46, 77-78, 116-123, 146-148, 150, 194-199

Hanson Group (including ARC)
Heathfield 20, 46-47, 49, 82, 108, 149, 170, 177
Hele & Bradninch 172, 180-181
Hemyock & Culm Valley branch 78, 80-81, 84, 167, 180
Honiton 25, 27-28, 104, 137, 139-141, 144, 170, 183

Ide 48
Ilfracombe 26, 102, 126, 134, 138-141, 143, 159, 182

Leeds 129
London & South Western Railway 8, 10-11, 14-15, 25-29, 33-35, 59-60, 69, 116, 149, 158
Longdown 48
Lydford 99

Lyme Regis 88, 91, 93, 99-101, 115
Lympstone 33, 37-39, 160
Lympstone Commando 37, 39, 43

Manchester 106, 132
Marsh Barton 8, 24, 174-176
Matford (Exeter By-pass) 109, 125, 181
Meldon Quarry 68-69, 71-75, 85, 91, 94, 98, 103, 105, 145, 164, 167, 178
Moretonhampstead 46-47
Mount Pleasant Road Halt 27, 29, 132

Newcastle 129, 132
Newcourt Sidings 41, 93, 153, 164-165, 169
Newcourt station 41-42
Newton Abbot 12-14, 20, 23, 47, 49, 77-78, 80-83, 85, 92, 94, 106-107, 115, 118, 123-125, 128, 132, 140, 146, 152, 166, 170, 177, 180
Nine Elms 91, 97, 113-114, 157, 159-162, 164

Okehampton 47, 69, 72, 85, 88, 91, 96, 98, 101-102, 108, 134, 137-139, 141, 143, 145, 182
Old Oak Common 113, 125, 147

Paignton 19, 21, 23, 41, 43, 48, 64, 66, 83, 118, 123, 126-127, 129, 132, 142
Pinhoe 26-27, 32, 59-60, 66-67, 105, 140-141, 143-144, 164, 168, 171, 184, 212, 214, 220
Plymouth 12-14, 26, 38, 47, 64, 78-79, 91, 93-94, 98, 101, 107-111, 114, 116-125, 128-129, 131-132, 139-141, 152, 162, 165-169, 171, 180, 182
Plymouth Friary 88-89, 91-92, 96, 102, 108-110, 126-127, 133-134, 137-139, 159, 188
Plymouth Laira 40, 79, 81, 84-85, 101, 108, 110, 128
Plymouth Millbay 106
Polsloe Bridge Halt 34-39, 42-43, 105

Rewe 218

Salisbury 25-26, 28, 75, 88, 91-94, 97, 98, 102-103, 106, 114, 133-134, 137-143, 159, 161, 166
Sampford Peverell 123
Seaton branch 38, 88, 91, 100-101, 138
Sidmouth branch 34, 38-39, 88, 100, 103-104, 162
Sidmouth Junction (Feniton) 28, 34, 39, 103, 134, 138, 143, 203
Silverton 152
South Devon Railway 11-14, 33, 77, 149
Southern Railway 29-30, 35, 59, 134-138, 158, 198-199
Staffords Bridge 131, 180, 183
Starcross 129
St Blazey 167, 172
St James Park (and Lions Holt Halt) 28-29, 33, 37, 39, 41, 43, 143, 145, 191
Stoke Canon 44, 125, 180-181

Taunton 10, 11, 12, 64, 75, 82, 84, 118, 123-126, 128, 130, 139, 146-147, 168
Teignmouth 12, 17, 33, 46, 124, 129, 132
Teign Valley line 46-49, 51, 80, 82, 149-151, 174-175
Templecombe 140-141, 143, 164
Thorverton 46
Tisbury 142
Tiverton and Exe Valley branch 15, 38, 44-46, 78, 80, 82, 84, 123
Tiverton Junction 44, 64, 80-82, 116, 123, 147, 170
Topsham 28, 33, 35-37, 39, 41, 43, 63, 66-67, 149, 164-165
Torquay 11, 124
Torrington 138-139, 157-159, 167
Totnes 12, 14, 64
Trusham 47, 49, 81

Wadebridge 88, 100
Waterloo 19, 26-29, 32, 85, 88, 91, 96, 97, 101, 109, 111, 113-114, 126, 133-144, 159, 191, 203
Westbury 64, 66, 69, 75, 104, 118, 128, 139, 165-166, 168-169, 172, 178
Whimple 140, 143, 159, 170
Whipton and Whipton Bridge Halt 26, 28
Whiteball 10
Wilton 138, 141

Yeoford 69, 73, 134, 137, 158, 164,
Yeovil 25, 94, 100, 103, 114, 137, 139-140, 172, 181